Cowboys into Gentlemen

COWBOYS INTO GENTLEMEN

Rhodes Scholars, Oxford,
and the Creation of an American Elite

Thomas J. Schaeper and Kathleen Schaeper

Berghahn Books
NEW YORK · OXFORD

First published in 1998 by
Berghahn Books

© 1998 Thomas J. Schaeper and Kathleen Schaeper

Library of Congress Cataloging-in-Publication Data

```
Schaeper, Thomas J.
   Cowboys into gentleman : Rhodes scholars, Oxford, and the creation
of an American elite / by Thomas J. Schaeper and Kathleen Schaeper.
      p.   cm.
   Includes bibliographical references (p. ) and index.
   ISBN 1-57181-116-8 (alk. paper)
   1. Rhodes scholarships--United States--History.  2. Scholars-
-United States--Biography.  3. Education--United States--History-
-Cross-cultural studies.  4. Education--Great Britain--History-
-Cross-cultural studies.   I. Schaeper, Kathleen.  II. Title.
LF503.F8S25   1998
378.3'4'0922--dc21                                          98-9831
                                                               CIP
```

British Library Cataloguing in Publication Data

A catalogue record for this book is available from the British Library.

Printed in the United States on acid-free paper.

CONTENTS

ABBREVIATIONS AND ILLUSTRATIONS

Abbreviations

NYT   *New York Times*
PPE   Philosophy, Politics, and Economics
TAO   *The American Oxonian*
Univ.   University College, Oxford

Illustrations

Cecil Rhodes, c. 1894
The Class of 1904
Frank Aydelotte
The High Street, Oxford, c. 1915
J. William Fulbright
Dean Rusk
Walt Whitman Rostow, Philip M. Kaiser, and Gordon A. Craig
Rhodes Scholar Cartoon
A Yank at Oxford
Byron "Whizzer" White
Stansfield Turner and Parents
Oxford Basketball Team, 1954
Harry S. Truman and Rhodes Scholars
Kris Kristofferson
John Edgar Wideman
Bill Bradley
The Class of 1968
Local Boy Makes Good
Rhodes Scholars Revisit Oxford, 1978
The Billingtons and the Royal Family

ACKNOWLEDGMENTS

As is true for many books, this one is the product of a collaboration between the authors and numerous other persons who gave help along the way. Without Robert Riddell and Marion Berghahn, the project would never have commenced. As editor and publisher, they had faith in what at first amounted to only a five-page proposal. John Funari was one of the first Rhodes Scholars whom we contacted. At that time he was editor of *The American Oxonian*. Up to his untimely death in 1997, John generously gave us his time and his frank opinions; he urged us to avoid doing a puff piece. Sherrill Pinney worked in the office of the American Secretary of the Rhodes Trust, housed until recently at Pomona College. Again and again she sent us copies of hard-to-find items and responded to our e-mail pleas for help in tracking down elusive details. Chris Rowley, who lives in Oxford but teaches in London, read the entire manuscript and kept us supplied with newspaper clippings and other tidbits that we might otherwise have missed. Frank Sieverts often took time off from his work in the U.S. Senate Foreign Relations Committee and the International Committee of the Red Cross to answer queries, read drafts of chapters, and send us copies of diaries, photographs, and other memorabilia from his Oxford days. As the project neared its conclusion, the manuscript benefitted enormously from the expert copyediting of Sarah Miles.

We also sent large chunks of the manuscript to several other people, and they responded with a host of insightful comments. Susan Bailey, Randy Berholtz, Christopher L. Brown, Peggy Burke, Edward K. Eckert, Sandra F. Joireman, and Bill Stephens helped to ensure that the book is as clear and accurate as possible. Of course, if our text still contains any factual errors or infelicities, we take full responsibility for them.

In a variety of ways St. Bonaventure University provided indispensable aid. Research grants enabled us to pay for travel and sundry other expenses. Theresa Shaffer, as usual, performed marvelous feats in obtaining scarce materials through interlibrary loan. Invaluable research assistance came from several undergraduate and graduate students: Carole Coveney, Donna Bunce, Christopher Heinze, Ursula Herze, Jeffrey Hice, Lisa Milbrand, and Brian Riordan.

Officers of the Rhodes Trust and the Association of American Rhodes Scholars were always generous in providing information and opinions. Thus we extend our gratitude to David Alexander, William J. Barber, Robert G. Edge, Elliot F. Gerson, Sir Anthony Kenny, James O'Toole, and the late Sir Edgar Williams.

Many others likewise have been important for our work. We have had a variety of exchanges with them – via interviews, telephone conversations, e-mail messages, and regular correspondence. They include Outi Aarnio, Mark Agrast, Carl Albert, Caroline Alexander, John Alexander, Thomas H. Allen, James Amoss, Kevin Anderson, James Atlas, Karen Avenoso, Lisa Backus, Joseph Badaracco, Charles R. Bailey, Jennifer Barber, Scott Barker, Thomas A. Bartlett, David P. Billington, Jr., James Billington, Susan Billington Harper, Baruch Blumberg, Paul Blustein, Daniel Boorstin, David Boren, John Brademas, Bill Bradley, Jennifer Bradley, Molly Brennan, Rowland Brucken, Josiah Bunting III, Melissa Burch, Ila Burdette, Benjamin Campbell, Sarah Crosby Campbell, Norman F. Cantor, Richard F. Celeste, Gail E. Christianson, Jocelyn Clapp, Nancy Coiner, Alison Richardson Cowe, Gordon Craig, James Crawford, Stephanie Dangel, Robert Darnton, Guy Davenport, Siddharth Deva, F. Remington Drury, Jr., Ronald Dworkin, Douglas S. Eakeley, James Fallows, Glenn Fine, Erwin Fleissner, Anne Ford, the late J. William Fulbright, James Griffin, Pat Haden, Robyn Hadley, Brian Harrison, Jennifer Haverkamp, Joy Hawthorne, Thomas Herman, Jeffrey T. Hilliker, David R. Howlett, Blair Hoxby, Caroline Minter Hoxby, Janice Hudgings, William Hunter, Walter Isaacson, Deborah Jacobs, Mark Janis, Jack B. Justice, Philip M. Kaiser, Nicholas Katzenbach, Shawn Kendrick, Mary Cleary Kiely, Frank H.H. King, Jonathan Kozol, Marvin Krislov, Janelle Larson, Kathy Lendech, Renee Lettow, Michael M. Lewis, William Lewis, Allan Lodge, the late Savoie Lottinville, Krzysztof Lubkiewicz, Richard G. Lugar, Timothy Lupfer, Christine Marciniak, Jason McManus, Ira C. Magaziner, Patricia Magro, Mary Norton McConnell, Ann Jorns Melvin, Hunter Monroe, Alison Muscatine, Gary Noble, Andrew Nussbaum, Joseph Nye, Lee Donne Olvey, Edward Pallesen, Raymond Paretzky,

Robert O. Paxton, Zbigniew Pelczynski, Kerry Pierce, Wayne Plasha, Michael Poliakoff, Daniel Porterfield, Lois Quam, Jeffrey Rideout, Donald Rivkin, Bernard Rogers, Andrew Rosenheim, Walt Whitman Rostow, Robert I. Rotberg, Susan Bruns Rowe, Martin Rush, Benet Salway, Gillian Salway, Peter Salway, Wesley Sand, J. Stanley Sanders, Paul Sarbanes, Richard Schaper, Kurt Schmoke, Steven L. Scully, John W. Sears, Virginia Seitz, Jeff Shesol, Sir Maurice Shock, John Simon, Neil Smelser, Howard K. Smith, Amy Staples, Elvis J. Stahr, Leonard Stark, George Stephanopoulos, Daniel Stid, Sara E. Stid, Stuart Swetland, Strobe Talbott, John Templeton, Michael Thaddeus, Lester Thurow, Janine Treves, Calvin Trillin, Stansfield Turner, Albert E. Utton, Terrance Valenzuela, Frank Verhoek, Michele Warman, Michael Warren, Sydney Webber, Jacob Weisberg, Byron White, Harrison White, Edward Wilber, Thomas Williamson, Jr., John Wofford, R. James Woolsey, Philip Zabriskie, and Jack Zoeller.

Our expressions of gratitude would not be complete without mention of the enthusiastic support received from the Schaeper and Cooney families. The person who spent the most time with "the Rhodes book" was our daughter Emily. Like us, she rejoices that it is finished at last.

PREFACE

Each year thirty-two seniors at American universities are awarded Rhodes Scholarships. These students then spend two or three years studying at the University of Oxford in Britain. The scholarships were founded by Cecil Rhodes, the British colonialist and entrepreneur, who died in 1902. This program has become the most famous academic scholarship in the world. It is the "glittering prize," and the lucky students are "golden boys" (and, since 1976, "golden girls") who reputedly have a "ticket to success" for the rest of their lives. Over the decades the winners have included scientists such as Edwin Hubble, writers such as Robert Penn Warren, jurists such as Byron White, and politicians such as J. William Fulbright and Bill Clinton. There have also been persons who later gained fame as entertainers, as did Kris Kristofferson.

The genesis of this book lay in Bill Clinton's election to the presidency in November 1992. During the election campaign and through the initial months of Clinton's first term in office, the British and American press were filled with hundreds of stories about Bill Clinton's days in Oxford and about the numerous Rhodes Scholars who served in his administration. This topic was of particular interest to us, for at that time we were serving as directors of the St. Bonaventure University summer program in Oxford. We spent most of each summer observing how our American students adapted to Oxford – and how Oxford adapted to them. We were curious to see if any detailed study had ever been done on Rhodes Scholars. Outside of the many short newspaper and magazine articles that have appeared regularly throughout the century, we found that there was no recent, thorough book on the subject. Indeed, the only books ever written on Rhodes Scholars were "in-house" products, written by British or American officials of the program. The most recent of these dated from 1955.

We therefore concluded that the time had come for an extended examination of this subject. What kinds of people have won the scholarships? What did these students do in Oxford? What did they achieve in their later careers? We believed that we were uniquely equipped to embark on such a study. Our experiences in both American and British universities and our supervision of American students in Oxford gave us first-hand knowledge of the topic. Moreover, we could bring to the project the impartiality of outsiders. Neither of us has ever received (or applied for) a Rhodes Scholarship.

If we had any doubts about the need for such a book, those worries quickly dissolved. Upon mentioning the project to a variety of friends, neighbors, and students, we received puzzled looks from many, who wondered why we were studying "roads" scholars. Other persons we met were better informed but still filled with a variety of misconceptions. One, for example, thought that the scholarships took American students to that "other" British university – Cambridge. When we began to interview Rhodes Scholars themselves we realized that many of them were also curious about the history of the program and eager to see what general conclusions we would reach.

As our research advanced, its scope widened. We could see that the finished product would be more than a volume about scholarships and the students who won them. In many ways the book has become a comparative history of British and American education and society over the past century.

We should also make clear what this book is not. It is not a guide on how to apply for and win a Rhodes Scholarship. Students who hope to do this should contact the institutional representatives appointed on every campus throughout the United States. It is likewise not a history of all Rhodes Scholars. We focus on American Rhodes Scholars, who have made up roughly 40 percent of the total. As far as we know, no one yet has done a thorough study of Rhodes Scholars from Canada, Australia, India, and the other countries participating in the program. We encourage anyone who is interested to follow our lead and produce similar books on these other nationalities. Finally, this is not a book filled with anecdotes about celebrities. Yes, we try to tell some interesting, amusing stories. And, yes, we write about the celebrities. But we also discuss the many scholars who happen to work in professions that have not made them household names.

We hope that Rhodes Scholars will forgive two small liberties that we take throughout the following pages. Among Rhodes Scholars, the sentiment is, "once a Rhodes Scholar, always a Rhodes Scholar." One is never a "former" scholar. However, in order to avoid confusion, we use "former" when we refer to those who have completed their studies in Oxford and begun their careers. Also, among Rhodes Scholars, the proper way to identify oneself is to give one's state, Oxford college, and class year. Students who try for the scholarship have the option of applying to the selection committee in either their home state or in the state where they will graduate from college. Bill Clinton, for example, had the option of applying from Arkansas or, as a student at Georgetown University, from Washington, DC. He chose the former. In Oxford he studied at University College. Therefore his proper Rhodes Scholar identification is "Arkansas and University 1968." For the sake of brevity, throughout this book we eliminate the state and college. At the first mention of a person we will give his or her class year.

One of the people who helped us most on this project was Frank Sieverts, a member of the Rhodes Scholar class of 1955. After he finished perusing the entire manuscript, he concluded, "You cover the subject, beauty marks and warts and all, as it should be." We hope that other readers will agree.

Chapter 1

RHODES, SOUTH AFRICA, AND OXFORD

> What an amazingly clever fellow Rhodes is. The only person I ever knew who combined patriotism & plunder.
>
> John Xavier Merriman, South African politician, 1895

> The man who amalgamated the diamond industry, who created the Chartered Company and dreamed of extending British influence from the Cape to Cairo ... was also the man whose guiding star was Aristotle's definition of happiness as activity in excellence, whose pocket was never without his well-thumbed Marcus Aurelius, who had the whole of the classics specially translated for himself, and whose lasting memorials are the name of a great country and an educational endowment.
>
> L.S. Amery, Senior Rhodes Trustee, 1953

The Man

When Cecil John Rhodes died on 26 March 1902 he left one final surprise for the world. In his checkered, spectacular career he had won international fame as an empire builder, colonial governor, financier, and diamond baron. Few would have guessed that he could be a philanthropist too. Yet when his will was published about two weeks after his funeral the world learned of the bequest establishing the scholarships that bear his name. The Rhodes Scholarships quickly became the most famous educational awards in the English-speaking world.

Rhodes was born in 1853 in the Hertfordshire town of Bishop's Stortford. His father was the parish vicar. The family had eleven children, nine of whom reached adulthood. Cecil was the fifth son. The family had been able to afford to send his older brothers to public school (that is, private boarding schools), but Cecil himself went to a local grammar school.

Notes for this chapter can be found on page 19.

When Cecil was seventeen his family dispatched him to South Africa. Most authorities who have written about him have stated that the reason for this move was the youth's fragile health. He was thought to have been tubercular and to have a "dickey" heart. His most recent and authoritative biographer, Robert I. Rotberg, however, sharply revises this view. Rhodes was not consumptive. Although the young man's health was often described as delicate and he occasionally suffered from what probably was arteriosclerosis, he often displayed impressive vigor and stamina. Rhodes did not suffer from constant ill health until his final years.[1]

The primary reason for sending him to Africa was economic. The family hoped that Cecil would find a career and establish himself financially. Two of his older brothers were already in South Africa. Frank was a soldier, and Herbert a cotton farmer.

The territory that today makes up the Republic of South Africa was at that time a patchwork of different lands. The British Empire controlled the colonies the Cape of Good Hope and Natal. The social and political elites there were English-speaking settlers and Afrikaners of Dutch descent. These two groups coexisted in an uneasy alliance and dominated the vast majority of blacks, coloreds (people of mixed race), and Asian immigrants. Further to the north were the Dutch republics of Transvaal and the Orange Free State, dominated by Boers (Dutch for "farmer"). There were also vast stretches of territory where native tribes such as the Bantu still dominated.

After only a year at farming, Rhodes followed his restless brother Herbert to the rough frontier town of Kimberley, where the discovery of diamonds in 1867 had created a hectic and brutal scramble similar to the 1849 gold rush in California. The young man who until that time had displayed no special talents or interests quickly found his métier. Over the next two years his hard work and clever, perhaps unscrupulous, dealings with competitors made him a fortune that would have lasted a lifetime for a person of lesser ambitions.

In 1873 Rhodes returned to England, primarily to see his ailing mother. While there he decided to seek admittance to the University of Oxford. As a budding entrepreneur who perhaps already aspired to political office, he appears to have felt the need for the polish that an Oxford education could give him. He wanted to be accepted as a gentleman and have social connections with the right sort of people. He also thought an academic degree could guarantee him a job in law or government, in the event that his business ventures failed to satisfy him economically or intellectually.

From 1873 to 1881 Rhodes alternated between terms in Oxford and trips to Kimberley, where he supervised his mining operations. The result was that he needed eight years to obtain a degree that normally would have taken three.

The story of Rhodes in Oxford is bathed in legends and anecdotes, many of these embellished to extravagant degrees by his earliest biographers. What impact did he have on Oxford? What impact did Oxford have on him? The answer to the first is close to none. The answer to the second is some, but not nearly as much as was formerly thought.

Then and now, a student seeking admission to Oxford must apply to one of the colleges that make up the University. Rhodes' first choice was University College, which turned him down. Depending on which version of the story one believes, he was rejected because he failed an entrance exam in Latin, because he had attended a local grammar school rather than a school like Eton or Harrow, or because he hoped to pursue only a pass degree. At Oxford at that time one could obtain either an honors degree or a less demanding "pass." Many sons of aristocrats and gentry who were not gifted academically or who did not have lofty career goals opted for the latter.

After his rejection, Rhodes sought admission to Oriel College. When he received Rhodes' application, Oriel's provost is reputed to have exclaimed either that, "all the colleges send me their failures" or "the Master of University sends me his leavings." Finally the provost relented and said "I think you will do."[2]

During Rhodes' periods of residence in Oxford over the next eight years, he took little part in either college or university activities. In desultory fashion he studied Latin, Greek, Politics, and Law, but, like many students, he attended few of the formal, optional lectures provided by the university. Once, when reprimanded for his lack of dedication, he supposedly responded: "I shall pass, which is all I wish to do."[3] Rather than live in college, he took digs (i.e., lived "off campus"). He joined the "smart set" in clubs like Vincent's and the Bullingdon and was admitted to a local Freemasonry lodge. One of his tutors, A.G. Butler, later eulogized Rhodes in a sonnet that goes in part:

Deep-voiced, broad-fronted, with the Caesar's brow,
A dreamer with a diamond in his hand
Musing on Empire![4]

However, on another occasion, Butler more soberly characterized his student's academic record:

His career at Oxford was uneventful. He belonged to a set of men like himself, not caring for distinction in the schools and not working for them, but of refined tastes, dining and living for the most part together, and doubtless discussing passing events in life and politics with interest and ability. Such a set is not very common at Oxford, living, as it does, a good deal apart from both games and work, but it does exist and, somehow, includes men of much intellectual power which bears fruit later.[5]

The fact that Rhodes was tall and a few years older than the average undergraduate helped to make him stand out. But what really gave him some degree of notoriety were his diamonds. Rather than rely on bankers and checkbooks, Rhodes always carried in his pockets a supply of uncut diamonds either wadded up in bits of paper or kept in a special little box. He would sell these one-by-one as he needed funds. On one of the rare occasions when he attended a lecture he evidently became bored, decided to show his gems to students sitting near him, and then accidentally spilled the collection onto the floor. When the irritated lecturer inquired about the commotion, someone called out, "It is only Rhodes and his diamonds."[6]

What did the young entrepreneur derive from his university experience? Oxford today abounds with statues, inscriptions, paintings, and buildings to remind one of Rhodes. But these are entirely the result of his later benefactions, not from any achievements of his student days. What Rhodes got was his degree and some measure of refinement – though his rough edges would always show. He appears to have made few strong friendships there, and in his later career he seldom turned to his Oxford acquaintances for help in business or politics. Oxford did, however, help to increase his appetite for reading. In his later years he had a special taste for the classics. He constantly reread the works of Aristotle and the *Meditations* of Marcus Aurelius. At great personal expense he paid for translations of many of the Latin works upon which Edward Gibbon had based his *Decline and Fall of the Roman Empire.* (This indicates his interest in history but also reveals that his knowledge of the classical languages was below that of the average Oxford student at that time.) After he returned to Africa he could often be seen sitting on a chair or rock, overseeing his mine workers, while deeply immersed in a book. Once when he was about to make a return trip to Britain he asked how long the voyage would take. When he was told twenty days, he hurried into a bookshop and purchased forty books – one for each morning and afternoon.[7]

Oxford also nurtured in Rhodes some of the ideas important in his later life. One of the most influential personages at the university in the 1870s and 1880s was John Ruskin, who used his position as Slade Professor of Fine Art to expound ideas not only on art, but politics, history, economics, and culture in general. In his celebrated Inaugural Address of 1870, Ruskin extolled the virtues and future prospects of the English:

> There is a destiny now possible to us – the highest ever set before a nation to be accepted or refused. We are still an undegenerate race; a race mingled of the best northern blood. We are not yet dissolute in temper, but still have the firmness to govern, and the grace to obey ... we are rich in an inheritance of honour, bequeathed to us through a thousand years of noble history ...
>
> And this is what she [Britain] must either do, or perish: she must found colonies as fast and as far as she is able, formed of her most energetic and worthiest men; – seizing every fruitful waste ground she can set her foot on, and there teaching these her colonists that their chief virtue is to be fidelity to their country, and that their first aim is to be to advance the power of England by land and sea ... .[8]

Some authors have claimed that Ruskin cast a spell over his eager disciple, Cecil Rhodes. The latter's connections with Ruskin, however, were probably slight or nonexistent.[9] Moreover, Rhodes did not need to pick up such ideas directly from Ruskin, for similar notions were, almost literally, in the air – especially at Oxford. The university was one of the fountainheads of the spirit of "New Imperialism" that pervaded not only England but also France, Germany, Belgium, the United States, and other western powers from the 1870s until the First World War. Although rabid imperialists made up only a minority of the dons and students in Oxford, they were extremely vocal.[10] Oxford graduates made up a disproportionate number of the men who staffed the colonial service in Africa, Asia, and elsewhere. In addition to Ruskin, one of their chief spokesmen was Benjamin Jowett, Master of Balliol College from 1870 to 1893. Jowett often preached that he wanted to "inoculate" the world with Balliol men and "govern the world through my pupils."[11]

The motives and accomplishments of western imperialists of that era look suspect, if not downright evil, to us today. When Ruskin, Jowett, the mature Rhodes and others spoke of the "superior" British race and its need to expand by taking land from "inferior" races, we might today be struck by their similarities to Hitler. He too spoke of a master race and its need for "living space." But the late nineteenth-century champions of empire never proposed the extermination of entire races of "inferior" peoples. Given the circumstances and the mentality of that period, the vast majority of the politicians, clergymen, business leaders, intellectuals, and ordinary citizens thought what they were doing was right.

Why did the British, French, Americans, and others rush to gain colonies, protectorates, and spheres of influence in all those parts of the world where they had not already gained control? There was a combination of factors. The major Western countries were the only ones that had entered into the Industrial Revolution by the late nineteenth century. This gave them the economic and military power to enforce their wills on "backward" societies. It also created a need to find additional markets around the world for their finished products and new sources of raw materials. The rapid economic growth of the major European powers and the United States likewise seemed to be a sign from God that Western civilization and Christianity were superior to all other cultures and religions. Added to this was Social Darwinism. Charles Darwin himself rejected the extension of his theories from biology to human history, but Herbert Spencer and many other philosophers and social scientists had no such misgivings. Social Darwinism permitted them to believe that the West not only had "might" but that this was "right." Europeans and Americans had no reason to apologize for their "superiority." The survival of the fittest was in the laws of nature instituted by God. Africans, Asians, and islanders in the Caribbean and Pacific would benefit from exposure to Western ideas and customs.

There were a few vehement critics of New Imperialism. Mark Twain bitterly attacked the American acquisition of the Philippines in the aftermath of the Spanish-American War. He pilloried the high-sounding motives of the United States government as mere camouflage hiding naked conquest. In his book *Imperialism,* published in 1902, British author J.A. Hobson argued that the only people to benefit from empire were big businessmen in the mother countries. Quite prophetically he said that competition for empire would also lead to war between the major powers.[12]

The overwhelming majority of Europeans and Americans were staunch imperialists at least until the First World War. In 1899 Rudyard Kipling penned his poem "White Man's Burden," written to urge the United States to acquire the Philippines. Young white men sent out to the colonies, said Kipling, were going into exile, where they served their "captives' need" rather than gaining wealth or fame for themselves. Native peoples, according to the poem, were wild, sullen, half-devil, half-child. As late as 1910, in its classic eleventh edition, the *Encyclopedia Britannica* claimed that the Vietnamese were "the worst-built and ugliest of all the Indo-Chinese who belong to the Mongolian race"; that Negroes were "easy going" and had no real hair, only wool; that "the Chinese character is inferior to the European"; that Haitians were "ignorant and lazy"; that Filipinos were "physical weaklings ... with large clumsy feet"; and that Afghans were cruel and crafty.[13]

The First World War punctured inflated Western notions of self-importance and supremacy. The so-called rational West, with its elevated sense of fair play, its Christianity, and its economic progress, very nearly blew itself to smithereens. France, Britain, Germany, and several other countries were devastated economically, socially, and psychologically by the war. As a result of the carnage, the "roaring" Twenties was more a decade of disillusionment and anxiety than of prosperity or joy. These doubts about Western supremacy lay in the future, however, well beyond the life span of Cecil Rhodes.

In 1881 young Rhodes achieved two important goals: he won election to a seat in the all-white Cape Colony parliament and obtained his Oxford degree. Over the next fourteen years his exploits brought him not only enviable wealth and political power but also international notoriety. He would retain his parliamentary seat until his death. His business affairs included the manufacture and sale of ice, ice cream, and water pumps (necessities in mining). Through the early and mid-1880s, working with two partners, he ruthlessly bought out all of his rivals in the Kimberley mines. By the end of the decade his company, De Beers Consolidated Mining, controlled more than 90 percent of the world's diamond production. (Today the company still supplies over 80 percent.) In 1889 Rhodes obtained a royal charter for his British South Africa Company, which gave him almost unlimited authority to explore and settle the vast territories that he named Rhodesia. (In 1964 Northern Rhodesia became Zambia, and in 1980 Southern Rhodesia achieved independence as Zimbabwe.) He was also instrumental in Britain's acquisition of Bechuanaland (Botswana) and Nyasaland (Malawi). He nearly succeeded in wresting Mozambique from the Portuguese and the Congo (Zaire) from King Leopold of the Belgians. Once he bragged that he would annex the planets if he could. Altogether his acquisitions for the British Empire were equal in size to Western Europe (including Britain and Ireland). He almost achieved his goal of extending British control from the Cape to Cairo.

Meanwhile Rhodes expanded both his business and his political activities. After gold was discovered in the Transvaal's Witwatersrand in 1886, Rhodes formed the Consolidated Gold Fields of South Africa Company and won a large percentage of that industry.

In 1890 he was appointed prime minister of the Cape of Good Hope Colony. Over the next five years he worked further to subdue the native tribes and to develop a *modus vivendi* with the Dutch.[14]

Until 1895 his career trajectory pointed ever upward. But then the infamous Jameson Raid brought a disgrace that would hound him until his premature death. Dr. Leander Starr Jameson was one of Rhodes' closest and most reliable associates. Rhodes entrusted him with engineering a secret raid into the Transvaal. The goal was to spark an uprising in Johannesburg that would topple the independent Dutch government of Paul Kruger. The result would be the elimination of any obstacles to Rhodes' control of the gold mines, plus the expansion of British control. The raid was a fiasco, with Jameson and many of his men being captured. Both at that time and today scholars debate the question of how much Rhodes and the British government in London knew about the raid in advance. Undoubtedly they knew its general outline, but whether they had tried to cancel or delay it remains shrouded in conflicting and vanished evidence.

At any rate, as prime minister in the Cape Rhodes was blamed for the debacle. He was forced to resign from office and to quit the board of the British South Africa Company. He retained his seat in the colonial parliament as well as his diamond and gold interests, but a cloud hung over his name thereafter.

There are deep ironies about the ignominy in which Rhodes spent his final years. He might have emerged a hero after the raid if the enterprise had succeeded. After all, successful revolutionaries usually become heroes; the unsuccessful ones are branded as rebels and traitors. Britain did want to expand its control over all of South Africa, either peacefully or by force. The Anglo-Boer War that eventually erupted in 1899 ended with British conquest of the independent Dutch states of the Transvaal and the Orange Free State. The 1895 raid thus was in harmony with general British aims. Nevertheless, the fact that it was premature and a disaster contributed to unfavorable press commentary around the world. The government in London thus repudiated both Jameson and Rhodes.

By the late 1890s Rhodes was a bloated, pasty mess. Years of smoking, drinking, and eating to excess, plus several falls from horses and a series of heart attacks dramatically altered his appearance. The news of his death, at the age of forty-eight, came as no surprise to anyone who knew him. His body was buried in the Rhodesian mountains, in a favorite spot of his called "The World's View."

Historian David Cannadine has aptly concluded that "in an age of imperial titans, Rhodes was the most titanic imperialist of all."[15] Few of Rhodes' contemporaries or later writers would disagree about the magnitude of his accomplishments. Where they do differ markedly is in their evaluations of the man and his deeds. The passages quoted at the beginning of this chapter give some indication of the extremes of opinion. Rhodes generated love or hate, never ambivalence. To his friend Jameson and his architect Herbert Baker, he was the greatest man they had ever known. In their later writings they rhapsodized over his charisma, his charm, his vision, and his generosity. Upon the death of his friend and business associate, Lord Rothschild asserted that Rhodes:

> ... was a very great man, he saw things as no one else saw them and he foresaw things which no one else dreamt of ... his great generosity bewitched those who came in contact with him ... his loss would be irreparable, were it not for the fact that he put in motion ideas which have taken root, ideas firmly established ... which will continue to grow and flourish.[16]

To others he was the devil incarnate. The great South African novelist and feminist Olive Schreiner went from liking and admiring Rhodes to despising him. She concluded that "the man's *heart* ... is corrupt."[17] Novelist and essayist G. K. Chesterton believed that:

> ... Rhodes had no principles whatever to give to the world ... . What he called his ideals were the dregs of Darwinism which had already grown not only stagnant, but poisonous ... . it was exactly because he had no ideas to spread that he invoked slaughter, violated justice, and ruined republics to spread them."[18]

Sometimes contemporaries could not even agree on his appearance and speech. The journalist Sydney Low knew Rhodes and once wrote that a belief in him "became a substitute for religion ... [He was a talker] of more compelling potency than almost anyone."[19] Rudyard Kipling, on the other hand, lauded Rhodes' imperialist deeds but thought that the man was as inarticulate as a fifteen-year-old schoolboy.[20]

Rhodes viewed himself as a dreamer, an idealist, and a loyal servant of the British Empire. He saw no conflict between his personal ambitions and what he perceived to be the general good. His earlier biographers tended to write either hagiographies or vituperative attacks. More recent authors have tended to portray him as an enigma or a bundle of contradictions. Foremost in this regard is Rotberg. His massive biography surely is definitive, despite objections to some of his interpretations.[21] Rotberg concludes that Rhodes was a man "who served both god and mammon, who was as human, fallible, gentle, charismatic, and constructive as he was shameless, vain, driven, ruthless, and destructive."[22] Even in the midst of some of the most sinister episodes of his life, he was capable of accomplishing good deeds. As prime minister of the Cape Colony, for example, he worked ceaselessly for agricultural and transportation improvements. He also fought to preserve the simple yet impressive architecture of the early Dutch settlers from rampant Victorian garishness. Throughout his career he gave money or other assistance to numerous individuals, hospitals, and charities.

Somewhat controversially, Rotberg and his collaborator, psychiatrist Miles F. Shore, also posit a psychological interpretation of Rhodes' life. They assert that his tender affection for his doting mother and his alienation from a rather distant father instilled in the boy an Oedipus complex. Through his life, they contend, Rhodes unconsciously desired to conquer rivals whom he saw as father figures.

Going yet further, Rotberg and Shore demonstrate that Rhodes was homosexual. It has long been known not only that Rhodes was a bachelor, but also that he surrounded himself with attractive young men and became petulant whenever one of his "band of brothers" chose to marry. It is also known that Rhodes frequently shattered his "manly" demeanor with fits of falsetto giggles. His contemporaries never questioned his sexuality, but rather accepted his explanation that his career kept him too busy to have a family. Although Rotberg and Shore concede that Rhodes probably never became physically active in any gay relationships, they marshal a persuasive amount of circumstantial evidence to demonstrate their point. They argue that Rhodes' sexual orientation not only contributed to his choice of assistants but also that it was a driving force in much that he accomplished in his career. His feelings of inadequacy, as he compared himself to his emotionally remote and heterosexually potent father, fueled his narcissistic, grandiose ambitions.

Several reviewers have sharply disparaged Rotberg's and Shore's reliance on clinical jargon and their speculative leaps about Rhodes' motives. At the very least, however, one can agree with Rotberg and Shore that Rhodes was, and remains, a conundrum.

By the customs of his day he was not a "bad" man. In an age of robber barons and imperialists, most of his actions were acceptable. In one important respect, however, he did fall below contemporary standards – at least the standards of the British Empire. This concerns his treatment of blacks. To be sure, the vast majority of whites in Europe and the United States in that era agreed that Africans and Asians were inferior. Some held that this inferiority was biological. Others believed the inferiority was cultural, and thus that education and religious instruction could one day lift native peoples to a higher level – though not perhaps to the level of whites.

Though nearly all British people were racist to some degree, the official policy of the British Empire was, at least nominally, color-blind. In the Cape Colony, for example, the right to vote was based on property ownership. Anyone who met the minimum require-ments was eligible to vote in colonial elections. In actual fact, few blacks and "coloreds" met these requirements. However, through the 1880s every electoral district in the Cape Colony had some blacks who could vote and some whites who could not. By the Euro-pean standards of that day, the British Empire was fairly liberal.

As a member of the Cape Parliament and as prime minister, Rhodes worked assiduously to undercut black rights. In part this resulted from his own prejudices. He did not hate the Africans, but he thought they stood in the way of British progress. In part his actions were aimed at currying favor with Afrikaner constituents in his electoral district. The Dutch settlers had always objected to the color-blind British policy. One reason for this was that the Afrikan-ers tended to be poorer than the British. The small number of whites who could not vote thus tended to be the Dutch.

Rotberg persuasively demonstrates that Rhodes sided with the Afrikaners and helped lay the groundwork for the system of apartheid that took final shape in the late 1940s. In his diamond mines Rhodes callously reduced the wages and increased the hours of his black workers. He segregated them from white workers and made them carry passes. In 1887 Rhodes supported a new law that denied the vote to all persons with communal titles to land, which in effect elim-inated all Africans. As prime minister he approved laws that distrib-uted tiny, nontransferable tracts of land to Africans. Each farm was large enough to support only one family. The result was that the eldest sons inherited the property, whereas their younger siblings were forced to seek employment at white-owned mines and plantations. Repeatedly in his speeches Rhodes said that whites "are to be lords over them ... The native is to be treated as a child." He supported a law that permitted employers to flog their non-white laborers. As a young man he wrote back to his mother about how delightful it was to possess "land of your own, horses of your own, and shooting when you like and a lot of black niggers to do what you like with."[23]

In 1895 Rhodes and Jameson were recalled to Britain for an offi-cial investigation of the failed raid. Rhodes spent a weekend at his old college in Oxford. At breakfast one day he chatted with an under-graduate. The young man hoped for a career in law. Rhodes asked him if there were any "coloured men" studying for the bar. The youth replied that yes, there were, and that he liked them. Rhodes' gruff response was "Well, I don't. I suppose it is the instinct of self-preservation. In South Africa we have perhaps a million or two whites, and many millions more of black people."[24]

In short, when Rhodes boasted on numerous occasions that he wanted "equal rights for every civilised man" he did not intend for this to apply to blacks. Rotberg argues that Rhodes "introduced a basic realignment of black-white power relations" and produced a drastic "reordering of the prevailing psychological climate."[25] To the extent that his policies foreshadowed apartheid, Rhodes contributed to the poisoned relations between blacks and whites in South Africa and neighboring countries that have lasted through this entire century.

Several politicians and writers both in the Cape and in London objected to Rhodes' racial policies. Yet the government failed to intervene. Prior to 1895 this was partly because he was so successful in expanding the empire that no one in power wanted to throw him off course. Moreover, after his disgrace, London wished to mollify Afrikaners in the Cape and Boers in the Transvaal; hence the lack of any movement to undo those racial policies favored by the Dutch.

Rhodes was not a man about whom one could be neutral. This was true in his own lifetime and remains so today. An eight-part BBC television series entitled "Rhodes," first broadcast in Britain in the fall of 1996, aroused yet new debates. Some commentators found it even-handed, but others condemned it as blatantly one-sided. It is interesting to note, however, that the "one-sidedness" depended on one's point of view. Rhodes House Warden Anthony Kenny observed that "the benefit of every doubt was given against him [i.e., Rhodes]" and dismissed the series as "poorly scripted" and filled with "atrocious acting" and a "baffling" story line.[26] One historian who reviewed the series denounced it as revisionist muck-raking of the worst sort, because it portrayed Rhodes as a sadist, a sexual pervert, and a founding father of apartheid – rather than giving Rhodes his due as a commercial statesman and innovative colonizer. Another historian, however, asserted that the series is "almost too soft" and lets Rhodes off "too lightly."[27]

The Scholarships

What prompted this man of action to establish a program of scholarships at the University of Oxford? Just as controversy and mystery continue to surround the man himself, so too there are debates about his educational bequest.

The story begins in the 1870s with what one writer has called Rhodes' long series of "weird" wills.[28] Another author has called them his "spiritual autobiography."[29] Rhodes wrote the first when he was 18 years old and the eighth and final one at age 46.[30] There is no need here to discuss the intricate twists and turns that occurred from one will to the next. All of them had in common a general vision. Rhodes believed that the English-speaking "race" was best suited to lead the world toward greater prosperity, happiness, and peace. He thus wished to promote union, or at least closer relations, among all English-speakers in order to foster this goal. The means to achieve this changed from one will to the next, but the underlying ideals remained constant.

Even while an undergraduate at Oxford Rhodes conceived himself to be a man of destiny. In 1877 he composed a revealing document called his "Confession of Faith." In it he said that his goal in life would be to render himself useful to his country. He then explained that:

> I have felt that at the present day we are actually limiting our children and perhaps bringing into the world half the human beings we might owing to the lack of country for them to inhabit, that if we had retained America there would at the present moment be many millions more of English living. I contend that we are the finest race in the world and that the more of the world we inhabit the better it is for the human race. Just fancy those parts that are at present inhabited by the most despicable specimen of human beings, what an alteration there would be in them if they were brought under Anglo-Saxon influence.[31]

This confession, which Rotberg characterizes as a "jejune effervescence," was largely incorporated into Rhodes' second will.[32] In this same will Rhodes boldly expounded on his aims in these words:

> The extension of British rule throughout the world, the perfecting of a system of emigration from the United Kingdom and of colonization by British subjects of all lands wherein the means of livelihood are attainable by energy, labour and enterprise, and especially the occupation by British settlers of the entire Continent of Africa, The Holy Land, the valley of the Euphrates, the Islands of Cyprus and Candia, the whole of South America, the islands of the Pacific not heretofore possessed by Great Britain, the whole of the Malay Archipelago, the seaboard of China and Japan, the ultimate recovery of the United States of America as an integral part of the British Empire, the consolidation of the whole Empire, the inauguration of a system of Colonial Representation in the Imperial Parliament which may tend to weld together the disjointed members of the Empire, and finally the foundation of so great a power as to hereafter render wars impossible and promote the best interests of humanity.[33]

The United States and vast stretches of the rest of the globe would not become colonies but rather independent members of a federal empire. To accomplish this task, Rhodes would leave all his wealth in the hands of a clandestine society made up of intelligent, energetic men who shared his vision. This secret club would be modeled on the Jesuits and the network of Masonic lodges. He hoped it would be "a church for the extension of the British Empire."[34]

Over the next fifteen years Rhodes continued to tinker with his plan, thereby creating new wills. The government officials or trusted friends whom he named as trustees also changed slightly from one document to the next. As his thinking evolved, the expansion of the British Empire gradually subsided in importance while the establishment of world peace grew. He came to believe that education was the best means for changing and improving the world. In 1891 he announced plans to establish a great new teaching residential university in the Cape Colony. Dutch and English students there would not only receive an education but would mix together socially; their friendships would contribute to greater harmony among the leaders of a united South Africa. In letters and speeches of the late 1880s and early 1890s he expressed doubts about the practicality of a secret society for furthering his aims. His sixth will, dated 1892, contains no mention of such a group.

The Jameson Raid and Rhodes' fall from power ended any hope for his South African university. By 1895, however, he had already concluded that such an institution would be too limited in scope – as it would affect only South Africa. Rhodes wanted to change the world. Already in his seventh will, in 1893, he had decided to establish Oxford scholarships for students from South Africa, Australia, New Zealand, Canada, and other parts of the Empire. In doing this he was in all probability greatly influenced by the writings of two contemporaries: J. Astley Cooper, editor of a London weekly magazine, and Sir Thomas Hudson Beare, a South Australian who held academic posts both in London and Edinburgh. Borrowing ideas from them he asserted:

> I consider that the education of young colonists at one of the Universities in Great Britain is of great advantage to them for giving breadth to their views, for their instruction in life and manners, and for instilling into their minds the advantages to the colonies as well as to England of the retention of the unity of the Empire.[35]

The young scholars selected were to be all-round men, studious but also fond of outdoor sports. Moreover, they were to be chosen on the basis of moral character and leadership potential. This will marked a great turning point in Rhodes' thinking. There was no mention of a secret society or of any indoctrination of the students while they were in Oxford. Rhodes still believed in the virtues of unity among English-speaking peoples, but this did not necessarily have to come through any rigid, powerful imperial framework.

In 1899 he dictated his eighth and final will. There were to be two scholars from each state in the United States and twenty "colonials," as he called them (three from Canada, six from Australia, five from South Africa, three from Rhodesia, and one each from New Zealand, Bermuda, and Jamaica.)[36] In a codicil of 1901 Rhodes added five annual scholarships for Germany. He considered the Germans to be a nordic, Anglo-Saxon race akin to the English. Rhodes also liked the Kaiser personally. Moreover, Wilhelm II had recently ordered English to be taught in all German schools. Given this token of friendship, plus the fact that Germany was nearly equal to Britain and the United States in economic and military power, Rhodes thought it best to join Germans with English-speakers in his great enterprise for world harmony. All of these students would be expected to remain in Oxford for three years, the normal span required to complete a B.A. degree.

The final will remains the basic document guiding the scholarship system. Whenever there is a question about how the program should be administered or how scholars should be chosen, everyone turns to the will to see what it says explicitly or to speculate about Rhodes' intentions.

The total value of Rhodes' estate was set at about £5 million, netting slightly under £4 million after death duties were deducted. At that time sterling was worth many times what it is today. (In 1997 the Trust's assets were worth approximately £150 million). Rhodes was wealthy, but his estate was modest compared to those of John D. Rockefeller, Andrew Carnegie, and other American "robber barons." Undoubtedly the size of his bequest would have been much larger if not for other factors. In the last dozen years of his life he devoted his attentions as much to politics as to private business affairs. He died too young to gain any returns on the vast amounts he invested in developing Rhodesia.

To oversee all the prescriptions of the will, Rhodes created what has come to be called the Rhodes Trust. The initial trustees whom he selected included distinguished elder statesmen, one of his closest business partners, his friend Jameson, his banker, and his lawyer. The Rhodes Trust continues to operate today. Over the decades it has included prominent politicians, academics, writers (including Rudyard Kipling), and persons from a variety of other professions.

Though the scholarships constitute the most famous part of the will, Rhodes also made other bequests. For example, he donated his stately residence at Groote Schuur (outside Cape Town) to the government of South Africa as an official residence for future prime ministers. He allocated £100,000 for Oriel College. That was a small part of his total estate but sufficient to raise faculty salaries and construct the formidable Rhodes Building that today still looms on Oxford's main street, "The High." Rhodes would be pleased to see it. Far above the central doorway is a large statue of Rhodes himself looking benevolently downward. Below him, to his left and right, are statues of King George V and King Edward VII.

The will gave great leeway to the trustees in the discretionary disbursement of any excess funds not needed for the scholarships. Over succeeding decades the trustees have used this discretionary power to give millions of pounds to the Oxford colleges and libraries and to the university as a whole. The Trust has also endowed several chairs and created special lectureships.

Nevertheless, the scholarships were the central feature of the will. Rhodes chose Oxford because it was his alma mater, but also because it was the oldest and still one of the best universities in the English-speaking world. He also liked its system of residential colleges. Oxford, like the "other" place (Cambridge) was not so much a university as a confederation of small, independent colleges. In his day there were twenty men's colleges in Oxford, each with between one hundred and three hundred students. In the small, enclosed atmosphere of one's college a student gained an education. Equally important, however, were the close, lasting friendships that one formed. Rhodes wanted future leaders from around the world to mix with future British leaders, thereby ensuring a united effort for peace and prosperity.

As formulated in his final will, Rhodes listed four main criteria to be used in selecting candidates:

> My desire being that the students who shall be elected to the scholarships shall not be merely bookworms I direct that in the election of a student to a Scholarship regard shall be had to
> 1. his literary and scholastic attainments
> 2. his fondness of and success in manly outdoor sports such as cricket, football and the like
> 3. his qualities of manhood, truth, courage, devotion to duty, sympathy for and protection of the weak, kindliness unselfishness and fellowship

4. his exhibition during school days of moral force of character and of instincts to lead and to take an interest in his schoolmates for those latter attributes will be likely in afterlife to guide him to esteem the performance of public duties as his highest aim.

What made these scholarships extraordinary was that they were to be based not just on academic merit but on other criteria as well. Rhodes hoped that those doing the evaluating would use good judgment and intuition in spotting candidates who had a special spark of character and greatness. To guide selectors, Rhodes provided a gauge for the importance of each of the four criteria he listed. In the final tally for every candidate, 3/10 should go for scholarship, 2/10 for manly sports, 3/10 for concern about one's fellow human beings, and 2/10 for character and leadership.

As will become clear in the chapters that follow, Rhodes' criteria and his arithmetical marking system were anything but clear to future selection committees. What, for example, did one mean by "manly outdoor sports" or "public service?" Obviously, Rhodes wanted multi-talented, energetic, forceful leaders who would somehow make the world a better place. However, the precise formula for selecting such persons would be open to discussion.

What were Rhodes' motives in establishing the scholarships? He himself claimed that he wanted to produce men who would use their Oxford education and friendships to create world harmony and progress. Some authors have scoffed at this, saying that he did it purely for public relations and for eternal fame. As early as 1891 he told a friend "I find I am human and should like to be living after my death." At another time he wrote that he wanted to "leave a monument to posterity which shall convince mankind that [I] had really lived."[37] Very probably, as with so much else in his life, he did it for a combination of altruistic and selfish reasons.

Rhodes' interest in manly vigor, sports, and energetic Anglo-Saxon leadership was something that he shared with several other world leaders of that era. The two most famous were Theodore Roosevelt and Kaiser Wilhelm II of Germany. Like Rhodes, Roosevelt was considered to be a sickly child; his adventures as a cowboy, a Rough Rider, and an African hunter may have meant for him what South African conquests signified for Rhodes. Roosevelt preached the cult of masculinity in several of his books, especially *The Strenuous Life*. Wilhelm II had a deformed left arm. Many authorities have concluded that the Kaiser's zeal to compensate for this handicap contributed to his dismissal of Bismarck, his drive to build up the German navy, and his imperialistic dreams.

Rhodes' stipulation that the scholarships were for men only was sexist, but perfectly acceptable by standards of his day. In 1900 if one spoke of well-educated leaders in government and other fields, one was speaking almost exclusively of men. In 1902 no women's groups in the United States or elsewhere protested their ineligibility for the scholarships. Not until the 1970s would there arise a strong movement to alter this part of the will.

Another interesting clause in the will is the one stating that neither "race or religious opinions" should be a factor in the selection process. Within just a few years after the publication of the will the question arose as to whether blacks were eligible. The trustees cited this clause and decided that blacks indeed could be appointed. In doing so the trustees and selection committees violated what they all probably knew were Rhodes' intentions. Like most of his contemporaries, Rhodes often used the word "race" to mean what we today would take for "culture" or "nation." When he put this clause in his will he intended to indicate that the Dutch and British "races" in South Africa and the American and German "races" could all enjoy his scholarships. He never expected that blacks would apply, much less be selected. Sir Edgar Williams, who for nearly three decades served as warden of Rhodes House in Oxford, has aptly stated that Rhodes built "better than he knew."[38] The trustees were able to follow the letter rather than the spirit of the law to make the scholarships more inclusive than their founder had anticipated.

The current warden of Rhodes House, Sir Anthony Kenny, has provided perhaps the best analysis of the seeming contradictions between Rhodes the man and the scholarships he established. In his speech at Georgetown University during a reunion of North American Rhodes Scholars in 1993, Kenny said that, apart from the stress on "manliness," the four criteria Rhodes listed for his scholars "are to this day valuable and important human qualities." Rhodes wanted evidence of high scholastic attainments, yet he himself required eight years to obtain a mere pass degree. He demanded physical vigor, as manifested in sports. Yet while at Oriel he was undistinguished in athletics. Though he showed much stamina through his career, his health was always a matter of some concern. Rhodes was one of the greatest entrepreneurs of all time, and yet there was no mention of entrepreneurship among the qualities he sought in his candidates. Instead, he wanted sympathy for, and protection of, the weak. He was an unabashed believer in the superiority of the English race, and yet he said race should play no part in the selection process. Finally, although he himself promoted more than one avoidable war, he declared his ultimate goal to be the pursuit of world peace through the international sharing of education.

In short, we might disagree about Rhodes' motives and actions. But, as Kenny concluded, we can admire that fact that "he was certainly not the man to believe that the way to make the world a better place was to make everyone else just like himself."[39]

NOTES

1. Robert I. Rotberg, *The Founder: Cecil Rhodes and the Pursuit of Power* (New York, 1988), 74, 78, 658-62, 675-77.
2. See G.N. Clark, *Cecil Rhodes and His College* (Oxford, 1953), 7; and Rotberg, *The Founder*, 86-87.
3. Rotberg, *The Founder*, 89.
4. *Oxford Magazine*, 13 (23 January 1895): 167.
5. Quoted in Clark, *Cecil Rhodes*, 5.
6. Ibid.
7. Ronald Currey, *Cecil Rhodes: A Biographical Footnote* (private printing, 1946), 11-12.
8. Quoted in Frank Aydelotte, *The American Rhodes Scholarships: A Review of the First Forty Years* (Princeton, 1946), 3.
9. Rotberg, *The Founder*, 94-95.
10. See Richard Symonds, *Oxford and Empire: The Last Lost Cause?* (Oxford, 1991), passim.
11. Ibid., 27-29.
12. J.A. Hobson, *Imperialism: A Study* (London, 1902).
13. Hans Konig, "The Eleventh Edition," *The New Yorker*, 2 March 1981, 74. For a brief introduction to this entire topic see Michael Howard, "Empire, Race & War in pre-1914 Britain," *History Today*, 31 (December 1981): 4-11.
14. For Rhodes' career in Africa, Rotberg's *The Founder* supersedes all earlier biographies. Also see Geoffrey Wheatcroft, *The Randlords: The Exploits and Exploitations of South Africa's Mining Magnates* (New York, 1986).
15. David Cannadine, review of Rotberg, *The Founder*, in *The New Republic*, 19 December 1988, 34.
16. Rotberg, *The Founder*, p. 678.
17. Ibid., 403.
18. G.K. Chesterton, *A Miscellany of Men* (London, 1912), 203-04.
19. Rotberg, *The Founder*, 5.
20. George Shepperson, "Cecil John Rhodes: Some Biographical Problems," *South African Historical Journal*, 15 (1983): 55.
21. Like Rhodes himself, Rotberg's book is a flawed colossus. See the following perceptive reviews: that of David Cannadine cited in n. 15 above; J.D.F. Jones in *Financial Times*, 6 May 1989, weekend section, xii; Geoffrey Wheatcroft, in *New*

York Times, 1 January 1989, sec. 7, 4; Conor Cruise O'Brien, in *Atlantic Monthly*, December 1988, 92-95; T.R.H. Davenport, in *South African Historical Journal*, 21 (1989): 95-100; David Alexander in *TAO*, 76 (1989): 132-43.

22. Rotberg, *The Founder*, 679.
23. Quoted in Rotberg, *The Founder*, 44. Throughout his book Rotberg deals extensively with Rhodes' racial attitudes and policies.
24. Quoted in Clark, *Cecil Rhodes*, 7.
25. Rotberg, *The Founder*, 361.
26. Warden's Christmas letter, December 1996, 10.
27. *Daily Mail*, 10 September 1996, 8; *Sunday Times*, 15 September 1996, section 10, 4; *Times Literary Supplement*, 11 October 1996, 22. Expanding on the script he wrote for the television series, Antony Thomas has published a balanced, solid book for the general public: *Rhodes: The Race for Africa* (London, 1996). Shortened to six hours, the mini-series was first aired on PBS in the United States early in 1998.
28. Christopher Hitchens, *Blood, Class, and Nostalgia: Anglo-American Ironies* (New York, 1990), 298.
29. Aydelotte, *American Rhodes Scholarships*, 1.
30. Earlier authors who studied the wills counted seven of them. For example, see Sir Francis J. Wylie in *TAO*, 31 (1944): 129-38. Rotberg shows that there were eight. Prior to the seven that can be found today in Rhodes House, there was an earlier one, dated 1871. Unfortunately, no copy of that one has survived. See *The Founder*, 74, 662-67, 700 n.39.
31. Quoted in Aydelotte, *American Rhodes Scholarships*, 4.
32. Rotberg, *The Founder*, 680.
33. For extensive discussions of the wills see Aydelotte, *American Rhodes Scholarships*, 1-19; Wylie, *TAO*, 31 (1944): 65-69, 129-38, and 32 (1945): 1-11; Rotberg, *The Founder*, 101-2, 663- 68.
34. Aydelotte, *American Rhodes Scholarships*, 8.
35. Aydelotte, *American Rhodes Scholarships*, 14.
36. Rhodes' will granted two scholarships to Canada and one to Newfoundland. The latter was still a separate British territory and did not officially become a Canadian province until 1949.
37. Quoted in Rotberg, *The Founder*, 663.
38. Williams in *TAO*, 81 (1994): 12.
39. *TAO*, 80 (1993): 245.

Chapter 2

Getting Started

Having discussed the matter with many Oxford men, I have not the least hesitation in saying that the Colonials and Americans who may benefit under Mr. Rhodes' Will may rest assured that Oxford will offer them a hearty welcome.

Letter to the editor, *Varsity*, 29 April 1902

We cannot quite agree with Mr. Rhodes' policy of encouraging the influx of transatlantic Anglo-Saxons into this country. The pushful Yank may be fond of us (if he is, he manages to conceal it fairly well), but we never knew an instance of his visiting our shores without pocketing a good pile of the less nimble Britisher's money before returning home. In view of this, it seems at first blush a trifle rash to pay others to come and continue the practice.

Article by an Oxford student, *Isis*, 3 May 1902

Reactions to the Will

The Rhodes Scholarship today is certainly the most famous and most prestigious student award in the United States – and perhaps the world. Each year's crop of new scholars is lionized in the national press and even more in each student's college and home-town news-papers. Winning one of these coveted prizes is often considered to be a ticket to success in later life.

Yet in 1902 when Cecil Rhodes' bequest became known, the reception was decidedly mixed on both sides of the Atlantic. News-papers and magazines across the United States and Britain lauded Rhodes' vision and generosity but questioned the wisdom of the scholarship plan.[1]

Most Oxford administrators and dons were flattered that their institution had been singled out in the will. They groused, however, that the money would have been better spent if Rhodes had simply

Notes for this chapter can be found on page 32.

donated it all to the university. Only £100,000 went directly to the university, and it was restricted to Rhodes' alma mater, Oriel. Even worse, several persons noted that the arrival of dozens of new foreign students each year would place a financial burden on the colleges. The scholarship would pay for each student's fees (including room and board), but the amount charged to each student was actually less then the cost of educating and housing them. To make up the difference, the colleges relied on their endowments. Several members of the university discreetly mentioned this to the Rhodes Trustees and expressed the hope that the latter would in the years to come make contributions above the ordinary expenses of each student.[2]

Many other dons and students voiced more serious misgivings. Some joked that these "perfect men" would be too good for the mere mortals of Oxford. They feared that the oldest university in the English-speaking world was about to be invaded by a horde of cowboy barbarians. Several dons complained that the scholarships would bring an end to Latin and Greek studies, which were the pride of the university. Every applicant had to pass an examination (called Responsions) in both these languages plus mathematics, before being admitted to one of the colleges. Rhodes Scholars from abroad, especially those from the vast American wilderness, would certainly be deficient in classical studies and would thus contribute to a lowering of standards. One writer expostulated that without Greek in Oxford "the human mind will decay" and feared that civilization everywhere would descend into chaos.[3]

Numerous other critics asserted that uncouth American yahoos would not only lower academic standards but also endanger the lives of serious students. Through their brute strength these frontiersmen would dominate college sports – thereby destroying the chances of ordinary British students to compete in healthful amateur athletic contests. One Oriel don consoled himself with the thought that American savages would be so busy on the sports fields that at least they would have little impact on the rest of college life.[4] The Oxford Union, the oldest student debating society in the world, discussed a motion to condemn the scholarships. The motion was defeated, but it revealed that a sizable proportion of the student body had doubts about the plan.[5]

One Oxford magazine, *Varsity*, printed cartoons depicting the American invasion. The newcomers were pictured organizing formal cheering at rugby matches (unheard of in British amateur sports), setting up lunch counters to serve buckwheat cakes, lynching the dons, and turning part of the university library into a skyscraper.[6]

Americans might have taken some comfort from the fact that these critics also expressed similar misgivings about Rhodes Scholars coming from elsewhere. *Isis*, a student publication, lampooned Australians as good-for-nothings who badly needed education. The university's Public Orator feared an outbreak of boomerang throwing in the quads. *Varsity* warned that a handful of German Rhodes Scholars would initiate a Teutonic invasion. A poem in *Oxford Magazine* feared that some of the arriving colonials would be primitive head-hunters set on decapitating the dons or "mussulmen" who would insist on bringing along their "thirty-seven moon-eyed wives."[7]

In the United States the response to the will likewise was divided, but for different reasons. Most newspapers and magazines were mildly favorable. Only a handful of writers were enthusiastic. One of these was Louis Dyer, whose article in *The Outlook* expressed the hope that the program would foster further international student exchanges and help the United States to fulfill the Renaissance dream of a "Republic of Letters."[8]

Many American academic and business leaders were dubious. Several university presidents said that students would be better off studying at American universities. This was especially true for those interested in science, an area in which even Oxford admitted it lagged far behind the better American institutions. Moreover, several university presidents noted that Oxford was still primarily an undergraduate teaching institution. Only in the 1890s had it instituted some advanced degrees, which did not as yet include a doctorate.

Harvard President Charles William Eliot suggested that Rhodes Scholars would benefit much more if they studied in German universities. Stanford President David Starr Jordan resigned himself to the existence of the program by noting that "the chief value of a scholarship at Oxford is the opportunity of studying in Germany during the vacation."[9] The universities there were reputed to be the best in Europe, especially for students pursuing doctorates. Thousands of Americans had already obtained advanced degrees in Berlin, Heidelberg, and elsewhere – compared to a much smaller number of Americans in Oxford and Cambridge. Most of the founders and early leaders of the American Historical Association in the 1880s and 1890s, for example, were products of German universities. As American universities expanded in the twentieth century, they would mostly follow German models. (It should be noted that within a few years, except for Eliot, Jordan and most other college officials surrendered their doubts and became ardent proponents of the Rhodes Scholarships.)

Other Americans raised yet additional objections. Some claimed that virile young men would be corrupted by the effete, sterile classicism of Oxford. The number of Anglophobes in the United States was higher than usual when the will was made public, owing to the Boer War. Many Americans thus objected to any scheme that would foster closer relations with Britain and perhaps even weaken the patriotism of young Americans for their native country. Andrew Carnegie stoutly proclaimed that no young Americans would even want the scholarships. Americans, he said, were interested in money and could not afford to postpone their careers by spending three years at Oxford. The zealous Anglophile Henry James also opposed the scholarships, though for a starkly different reason. He agreed with many in Britain that Oxford would be sullied by the advent of unwashed, unlettered rustics.[10]

The subsequent history of the Rhodes Scholarships would show that some of the apprehensions expressed on both sides of the Atlantic were groundless but that others were prophetic.

Selecting the "Perfect Men"

In the spring of 1902 the Rhodes Trustees held their first meetings under the leadership of Lord Rosebery, who had served as British prime minister from 1894 to 1895. The trustees took charge of disposing of Rhodes' real estate and investing the liquid capital. They quickly decided that they themselves would not be able to handle the actual management of the scholarship program. Therefore they appointed two other individuals to perform those duties. They were Dr. George Parkin and Francis Wylie. Parkin would be Organizing Secretary and Wylie the Oxford Secretary. The trustees could not have made better choices. The Rhodes Scholarships were not a sure thing in 1902. That the program survived and prospered was in no small part due to Parkin and Wylie. Each of them over the years was often called the second founder of the scholarships. Eventually their work was recognized by the government, with each man being knighted.

Parkin's selection seemed odd at first to some observers. He was a fifty-six-year old Canadian. Prior to his appointment as Organizing Secretary he was serving in Toronto as headmaster of Upper Canada College, a prep school along the lines of the best British public schools. But Parkin proved ideal for his new job. He was an Oxford graduate. In fact, he had matriculated on the same day as Cecil Rhodes in 1873, though there is no evidence that the two knew each other then or later. In his first term at Oxford Parkin had been elected secretary of the Union, and in its chambers he won fame for his debates on behalf of the British Empire. Following graduation he pursued a career in Canada, Australia, and England as a spokesman for the Church of England and for the Imperial Federation League. His interest in bringing colonials into closer relations with Britain made him ideally suited to carry out Rhodes' dream of Anglo-Saxon unity and world peace. His eloquence, good humor, and personal charm would also be important. From 1902 until his retirement in 1920, Parkin administered the program and spent much of his time traveling to the United States, Germany, and the dominions and colonies within the Empire.

When it became clear that Parkin would not be able to watch over the scholars once they had arrived at the university, early in 1903 the trustees appointed Wylie to the post of Oxford Secretary.[11] Wylie was a fellow of Brasenose College, where he tutored and lectured in philosophy. He gave up the security and perquisites of an Oxford don to take on the risky challenges of making Rhodes' plan work. The fact that he was a well-respected, academic "insider" would prove to be of immense importance for his new work. Until his retirement in 1931 it was he who labored to gain admittance for Rhodes Scholars into the various colleges – for the latter insisted that the foreigners meet the same requirements as other students. Wylie and his wife would also serve as confessors, mentors, travel advisors, and tea party hosts.

Parkin's immediate task in 1902 and 1903 was to establish a system for selecting the scholars. Germany presented no problem, for Rhodes' will stipulated that the Kaiser would choose the five annual winners. South Africa also had a fairly simple mechanism for its seven scholars. Rhodes had specified that the four scholars from Cape Colony would come from four schools that he listed. The heads of those schools could nominate one of their students each year. Natal had one scholarship and Rhodesia three. Parkin immediately appointed the Directors of Education in those two territories to select the winners. As for Canada, Jamaica, Bermuda, and the United States, Rhodes had outlined no selection procedure. For this and for most other aspects of the administration of the program Rhodes gave his trustees – and through them Parkin – great leeway.

Parkin immediately corrected what he saw as several flaws in Rhodes' scheme. Concluding that Canada had been given too few scholarships, he increased its number from three to nine.[12] Regarding the United States, the will had simply specified two per state.

Some detractors have accused Rhodes of being so ignorant about the United States that he assumed there were still only thirteen states. However, his financial calculations indicate that he anticipated supporting up to one hundred Americans. After his death the trustees and Parkin quickly decided that they could support thirty-two new Americans per year, this making ninety-six residing in Oxford at any given time.[13] One final revision Parkin and others deemed necessary concerned the age of the scholars. Rhodes clearly expected that they would come to Oxford straight from secondary school. In Oxford they would join other eighteen-year-old "freshers" for three years of study. Parkin wisely judged that most eighteen-year-old high school graduates from the United States and elsewhere would be unprepared emotionally and academically for the experience. He decided that all scholars must have completed at least two years of university study prior to going to Oxford. Their added maturity and training would better prepare them for separation from their families and for the rigors of Oxford.

Henceforth candidates in the United States and most other constituencies would have to be between the ages of nineteen and twenty-five. They also had to be unmarried. Oxford colleges were not equipped to house married students. Moreover, a married student, living in a flat somewhere in town, would miss much of the social life of his college – thereby destroying Rhodes' hope that future world leaders would mix together fully while in residence.

As to the methods of selection, Parkin decided to allot that task to committees composed of political and academic leaders in each country or dominion. He spent most of 1903 and 1904 traveling the globe. He met hundreds of officials and worked to establish committees in Canada, the United States, South Africa, Rhodesia, New Zealand, Australia, Bermuda, and Jamaica. The United States presented his greatest challenge. It had far more territory, more people, and more colleges and universities than any of the others. It would also send more scholars – more than half of the total.

Due to the difficulties of getting the mechanism up and running, Parkin concluded that in the United States and most of the dominions it would not be possible to send students to Oxford in 1903. Therefore the first American scholars did not reach England until the fall of 1904. One immediate puzzle in the United States was how to send thirty-two scholars from forty-eight states. (Actually, there were only forty-five states, but the territories of Oklahoma, New Mexico, and Arizona were allowed to participate. Oklahoma achieved statehood in 1907; the other two in 1912.)

One had to keep in mind that Rhodes wanted students from each of the states. After consulting with many university and civic leaders, Parkin concluded that the best solution would be to send one scholar from each state in 1904 and 1905, but no Americans at all in 1906. A rotation like this would produce a three-year cycle of 48, 48, and 0 – an average of 32 per year. The colleges in Oxford eventually complained that this system created housing and other problems, when in some years they had to find room for over forty Americans and in others none. Thus in 1915 Parkin devised a new scheme. Henceforth in any given year only two-thirds of the states would elect scholars, producing thirty-two traveling to Oxford each autumn.

In every state Parkin assembled a committee. It generally consisted of the presidents of the four or five most prominent universities in the state. In some states the governors also participated. This happened even though President Theodore Roosevelt had advised Parkin against it. Roosevelt warned that governors would always be looking ahead to the next election and that this might influence their choice of winners.[14] In other countries during the early years of the program government representatives played an even greater role. In Canada, for example, the committees included the lieutenant-governor, the chief justice, and the chief superintendent of education, as well as college presidents.

By the spring of 1904 the machinery was set up and the first batch of scholars was selected. The process would remain little changed until after the First World War. A candidate first had to declare the state in which he was applying. This could be the state in which he resided or the state in which he went to school. Of course, a student who was from Massachusetts and attended Harvard University had but one choice to make. However, a student from North Dakota who attended Harvard had two options. This remains true to the present day.

Following this, each student had to pass a qualifying examination in Greek, Latin, and mathematics. Then, upon recommendation by his college or university, he and other candidates met with the selection committee for an interview. After a day of interviewing the finalists, the committee notified the winner. The future Rhodes Scholar then listed several Oxford colleges, in order of preference. This list was sent to Wylie, who did his best to win admittance for the student in one of the preferred colleges. The following autumn the student traveled to Oxford, at his own expense. (Nowadays the Rhodes Trust pays for transportation.) Once in Oxford, he received a yearly stipend – set initially at £300. This sum was sufficient for college lodging and other fees plus all personal expenses, but only if the student was frugal.

A process for selecting Rhodes Scholars that looked fine on paper proved to be anything but that during the next dozen years or so. One problem resulted from the criteria mentioned in the will. Rhodes Scholarships differed from all others in that the recipients had to demonstrate more than just academic ability. They also had to show character, concern for their fellow human beings, leadership potential, and an interest in "fighting the world's fight" in some form of public service. How could one evaluate all these intangibles? Parkin and the committees agreed that each scholar must be "superior" in at least one of the areas and "good" in the others. But whereas one could assess academic performance by grades and other solid evidence, how could one gauge character and leadership ability? Addressing a conference of university and college presidents in Chicago in 1903, Parkin answered this query in straightforward fashion. All that committee members had to do was select the man whom they envisaged becoming president of the United States, chief justice of the Supreme Court, or U.S. ambassador to Great Britain![15] This advice provided a lofty ideal. It would also haunt the program in later years, as the careers of Rhodes Scholars came to be measured against it.

Despite the initial flurry of publicity the program received when Rhodes' will was made public, recruitment remained a nagging problem through the First World War. Again and again the selection committees and Parkin lamented the fact that many potential applicants were not aware of the scholarships. Indeed, most Americans quickly forgot about them or became hazy about their details. This was true even of the *New York Times.* In 1909 the newspaper misleadingly announced the appointment of a woman Rhodes Scholar.[16] Of course, having a female scholar would have violated Rhodes' will. Not until 1976 would an Act of Parliament permit amending the will in that fashion. What had happened in 1909 was that an organization called the Society of American Women established a fund to send one female student per year to study in Britain. There was no connection to the Rhodes Scholarships at all.

Besides insufficient publicity, another serious obstacle was the qualifying exam. Between 1904 and 1918 some two thousand students took it, but only about half passed.[17] Of course, many other likely candidates shied away from the examination and never applied at all. Most candidates had little problem with the mathematics or the Latin; the big hurdle for most was the Greek. Virtually all British students had studied both of the classical languages in secondary school. In the United States most applicants had studied Latin in high school or college, but few outside of classics majors had taken Greek. Some successful candidates claimed that the language exams were not too difficult and that any intelligent young man could easily pass that section of the test if he studied Greek privately for a few months beforehand.[18] Nevertheless, not too many wanted to invest so much time preparing for an examination, particularly when a passing grade in itself did not guarantee winning a scholarship. After years of complaining, Parkin was able to get the Oxford colleges and the Rhodes Trustees to agree to a compromise. After 1909 candidates could take the initial qualifying exam in mathematics and Latin and postpone the Greek part until after they were notified of their appointment to a scholarship.[19] The new Rhodes Scholars, however, were still required to take the Greek section prior to arrival in Oxford.

Even with this compromise, however, the number of applicants did not increase markedly. Through the First World War the number of qualified applicants who could be considered by the committees averaged only about one hundred per year. That was an average of two or three candidates for each scholarship. In some states, especially the less populated ones, the number of candidates might be none or one. In situations where only one or two candidates presented themselves, the committees sometimes judged that no one was worthy. This meant no scholar was appointed that year. From 1904 to 1918, when the selection system was changed, there was only one year (1916) when all of the available scholarships were distributed.[20] In 1905 ten of the available forty-eight slots went unfilled. In short, some of the recipients won their scholarships virtually by default.

To make matters worse, there were many examples of blatant abuse or laxity by the committees. In many states the appointment of Rhodes Scholars became a rather cozy, gentlemanly rotation among the handful of prominent universities. Thus in a given year the scholarship might go to the candidate from university "A," the next year to the choice of university "B," and so on until the series began again.[21] Parkin did his best to curtail this practice, but with only limited success.

Few of the committee members had any first-hand experience of Oxford, and this hampered them when they tried to pick students who would thrive in a foreign country and a different educational system. When the committees conducted their interviews and their deliberations the results sometimes were capricious. The will spoke of "moral force of character" as a criterion. In more than one instance committees who had to choose between two or more candidates used this as a basis for picking whichever young man happened not to smoke or play cards.[22] Elmer Davis later regaled people with the story of how he emerged a winner. In the fall of 1909 five Indiana candidates took the qualifying examination. Three passed it, but one of them became ill. Davis and another young man were thereupon invited to meet with the selection committee. Davis summarized his "interview" as follows:

> I presumed that they wanted to test our general knowledge, and I forti-
> fied myself with all sorts of reading. But when the educators sat down at
> table they ignored us and began to trade ideas on what a tough job
> being a college president was. I didn't know anything about that and
> kept still. But the other fellow was hell-bent and resourceful. He talked.
> I got the appointment.[23]

Thanks to this rather quixotic manner of winning his scholarship, Davis entered Oxford in 1910 and went on to become one of the most popular and distinguished American novelists, newspaper journalists, and radio commentators from the 1920s through the 1940s. He headed the Office of War Information during the Second World War and following that gained admiration as one of Joseph McCarthy's earliest and most vehement critics.

On numerous occasions Parkin let it be known that he did not think the United States was sending its best men to Oxford. In later years some of the first Rhodes Scholars themselves admitted that their quality had not been not uniformly high in the first two decades of the program. They have also acknowledged that many of the early committees tended to select "he-men," thus favoring the captains of the varsity sports teams over the superior students. Not surprisingly, no Rhodes Scholar himself later admitted that he was one of the mediocre ones. It was always some "others" who came from the bottom of the barrel! Nevertheless, it is safe to say that the average Rhodes Scholar from these early years was an above-average student at the university from which he came. Some, indeed, were outstanding intellectuals – as was demonstrated by their academic records in America and Oxford and by their professional careers. Only above-average students would have desired additional schooling in Oxford and would have been able to pass the qualifying examination. But certainly, as a whole, these pioneer Rhodes Scholars were not supermen.[24]

They were, however, a fairly representative cross section of American society. As far as can be determined, none was the scion of a extremely wealthy family – but such students did not usually apply for scholarships. They came from middle and working-class families. Some had worked their way through college. One member of the 1904 class, Lawrence Henry Gipson of Idaho, had been both a stagecoach driver and a printer's "devil" and typesetter at his father's small-town newspaper.[25] The fathers of these early Rhodes Scholars included bankers, physicians, insurance salesmen, teachers, lawyers, businessmen, and farmers. There were Jews, Catholics, Mormons, and representatives of every major Protestant denomination. The class of 1907 included one black, Alain Locke (who will be discussed further in the next chapter). There was even a set of three brothers: Christopher, Felix, and Frank Morley (1910, 1917, 1919).

The scholars represented a wide array of universities and colleges. There were forty-three Americans in the class of 1904 – no candidates passed the qualifying examination in five states. These forty-three men came from forty-three different institutions. This kind of even dispersal no longer occurs. Changes in the selection process plus other factors in later decades have helped Ivy League and a few other elite universities to claim more than half of the scholars in any given year. Early in the century there was a greater tendency for a bright Nebraska or Wyoming boy to attend a university in his home state rather than elsewhere. Moreover, the college presidents in each state generally preferred to give the scholarships to students who had remained in their home state for their education. Thus the 1904 scholar from Kentucky was a student at Kentucky State University, the Kansan came from the University of Kansas, the Georgian from the University of Georgia, and so on. Not that the elite schools were excluded. The Massachusetts representative, for example, came from Harvard, and the New York winner was a Cornell man.

One ominous question loomed ahead for this melting pot of rambunctious Americans: What would happen to Cecil Rhodes' grand scheme for producing the best men for the world's fight once the scholars reached Oxford?

NOTES

1. For example, see *NYT,* 5 April 1902, 1; 6 April 1902, 5; 7 April 1902, 1; 25 January 1903, 7; 2 February 1903, 1; 19 July 1903, 9; 9 October 1903, 8; 11 October 1903, 4; 24 March 1904, 5.

2. Lord Elton, ed., *The First Fifty Years of the Rhodes Trust and the Rhodes Scholarships* (Oxford, 1955), 11, 61; *TAO,* 51 (1964): 74-83.

3. Thomas Case, "The Influence of Mr. Rhodes' Will on Oxford," *National Review,* 39 (1902): 424. Also Elton, *First Fifty Years,* 59-60.

4. *NYT,* 9 October 1903, 8. Also see *TAO,* 2 (1915): 34-44, 21 (1934): 123-31.

5. *The Times,* 9 May 1902, 10C.

6. See *TAO,* 21 (1934): 127.

7. *TAO,* 21 (1934), 126-27; Graham Topping, "The Best Men for the World's Fight?" *Oxford Today,* Trinity Issue, 1993, 6.

8. Louis Dyer, "The Rhodes Scholarships," *The Outlook,* 13 December 1902, 885-86.

9. *TAO,* 42 (1955): 21 and 52 (1965): 87.

10. Elton, *First Fifty Years,* 4, 10, 59; *TAO,* 5 (1918): 81-83, 32 (1945): 8-9, 50 (1963): 64-66, 51 (1964): 76-78, 81 (1994): 3.

11. Initially his title was "agent," but that was soon changed to "secretary."

12. That is, eight for Canada proper and one for Newfoundland.

13. See Wylie's article in *TAO,* 31 (1944): 65-69.

14. Elton, *First Fifty Years,* 8; *TAO,* 37 (1950): 65; 54 (1967): 103.

15. Elton, *First Fifty Years,* 9.

16. *NYT,* 30 January 1909, 2. Also see 28 January 1914, sec. 4, 2.

17. Aydelotte, *American Rhodes Scholarships,* 26; *TAO,* 81 (1994): 8.

18. Elton, *First Fifty Years,* 186; Frances Margaret Blanshard, *Frank Aydelotte of Swarthmore* (Middletown, CT, 1970), 49.

19. Elton, *First Fifty Years,* 63-64.

20. Aydelotte, *American Rhodes Scholarships,* 25; *TAO,* 1 (1914): 63-83. Of course, through the entire history of the program there have also been instances where persons who received the scholarships ended up not using them. A handful of students have died sometime in the months before arriving in Oxford. Over the past ninety years there have also been several students who accepted the scholarships and then later, for personal or academic reasons, decided not to go. The program has never selected alternates or replacements, and thus these positions have gone unfilled.

21. Blanshard, *Aydelotte,* 51; *Alumni Magazine* (by the Alumni Association of American Rhodes Scholars), 3 (January 1910): 2.

22. *TAO,* 37 (1950): 65-66; 44 (1957): 55.

23. Quoted in Milton Mackaye, "What Happens to Our Rhodes Scholars?" *Scribner's Magazine,* January 1938, 9.

24. Elton, *First Fifty Years,* 21, 187; Aydelotte, *American Rhodes Scholarships,* 25-30; George Parkin, *The Rhodes Scholarships* (Boston, 1912), 216-17; *TAO,* 1 (1914): 63; 39 (1952): 114; 40 (1953): 185; 54 (1967): 39.

25. Leslie V. Brock, "Lawrence Henry Gipson: Historian. The Early Idaho Years," *Idaho Yesterdays,* 22 (1978): 9; Diane Windham Shaw, comp., *Guide to the Papers of Lawrence Henry Gipson* (Bethlehem, PA, 1984), 1.

Chapter 3

THE SETTING

Yet, O ye spires of Oxford! domes and towers!
Gardens and groves! Your presence overpowers
The Soberness of reason; till, in sooth,
Transformed, and rushing on a bold exchange,
I slight my own beloved Cam, to range
Where silver Isis leads my stripling feet;
Pace the long avenue, or glide adown
The stream-like windings of that glorious street-
An eager novice robed in fluttering gown!

William Wordsworth, 1820

Oxford trains scholars of the real type better than any other place in the world. Its methods are antiquated. It despises science. Its lectures are rotten. It has professors who never teach and students who never learn. It has no order, no arrangement, no system. Its curriculum is unintelligible. It has no president. It has no state legislature to tell how to teach. And yet – it gets there. Whether we like it or not, Oxford gives something to its students, a life and a mode of thought, which in America as yet we can emulate but not equal.

Stephen Leacock, 1922

Town and Gown

What was this university to which Rhodes wanted to send his scholars? Oxford was the oldest university in the English-speaking world. Just how old remains a matter of dispute. Some diehards still claim that the university can be traced to 872, when King Alfred the Great supposedly recognized a group of scholars in the city. Nearly all authorities today, however, agree that the real establishment of the university dates to around 1200. The first residential colleges were established in the mid-thirteenth century. Even this point, however, raises some debate. Still today three of the colleges – Merton, University, and Balliol – vie for the honor of being the oldest.[1]

Notes for this chapter can be found on page 45.

By 1900 the number of colleges had grown to twenty. In addition to the three oldest, some of the other more venerable or largest included the following: New College, which was indeed "new" when it was created in 1379; All Souls, founded in 1438, perhaps the only college in the world that has no students (its members being engaged primarily in research); Magdalen, founded in 1458, perhaps best known to tourists because of its extensive deer park and gardens; and Christ Church, founded by Henry VIII in 1546, a cathedral and bishop's residence as well as a college.

From its origins, the residential college system has given Oxford (and Cambridge) its distinctive flavor. In many ways, as several authors have said, the university is merely a holding company for the colleges. The latter have always been independent institutions, each with its own governing body, buildings, endowment, and faculty. Down to the present day it is the college, not the university, which occupies most of a student's daily life. One is admitted to the university at the start, in the matriculation ceremony. During the years to follow one might attend some lectures provided by the university or participate in one of the university athletic matches against Cambridge or other universities. Moreover, it is the university that administers final examinations and grants degrees. Yet the "university" in 1900, and still in many respects today, represented a faint abstraction compared to the concrete reality of the colleges.

Nearly all of the colleges were huddled next to one another near the urban center. The city of Oxford had been a thriving market town and administrative center since the Middle Ages. Prior to the advent of Morris Motors, the local economy was dominated by handicrafts and cottage industries. The city's location was ideal, for it was about as centrally located as one could get – both in geography and trade. About fifty miles northwest of London, Oxford borders the River Thames and is on or near many of the major roads linking southern and northern England. The coming of canals and railroads made it even easier to reach. Oxfordshire had been an area known for its beautiful, though not especially prosperous, farmlands. Immediately to the west, however, is the region known as the Cotswolds, which in the eighteenth and nineteenth centuries was world-famous for the quantity and quality of the wool it produced. That trade has dwindled in the twentieth century, but the charming Cotswold villages remain. With names like Bourton-on-the-Water, Chipping Campden, and Upper (and Lower) Slaughter, still today they are a favorite retreat for tourists. Most of their cottages are built with the famous golden limestone from the local quarries. That same

"Cotswold stone" was used for many of the Oxford colleges as well as for the Duke of Marlborough's palace at Blenheim.

Matthew Arnold called Oxford the city of "dreaming spires." Even today, despite the noxious incursions of motor traffic and modern architecture, one is overcome with the beauty of the city. When one looks at it from nearby Boar's Hill or Port Meadow, it almost seems that the entire town is composed of medieval steeples and towers. The main thoroughfare, the High Street, curves its way along the colleges, churches, and shops and remains one of the most impressive avenues in all of Britain.

Through the late nineteenth century the yearly editions of the Baedeker guide to England described Oxford as "on the whole more attractive than Cambridge to the ordinary visitor" and advised the traveler to "visit Cambridge first" or "omit it altogether if he cannot visit both."[2] In James Hilton's 1933 novel *Lost Horizon,* when one of the characters first sees Shangri-La he sighs wistfully and says it reminds him of Oxford. To be fair, one must admit that Cambridge has more than its share of admirers who prefer it to Oxford. Certainly both college towns possess enough majesty and quaintness to seduce both students and tourists.

When the first American scholars arrived in Oxford in the fall of 1904 they would have had difficulty finding the "university." Most of the buildings belonged to the separate colleges. Each college resembled a medieval castle, with high walls surrounding it on all sides and one main entrance. This entrance was the porter's lodge, staffed by a head porter, a deputy head porter, and so on down the line. Though the streets outside might be bustling with traffic, life inside the college was serene. Depending on the size of the college, there might be one or several quads, each one with a dizzying array of gardens. Most of the students lived in college during at least two of their three years of study. Most of their tutors also lived in college. Until the late 1870s all college fellows had to be unmarried, and a high proportion of them were Anglican clergymen. The teaching fellows resided in two or three-room flats that were scattered around the residence halls. In 1904 more than half of the college fellows still fitted the old mold. The other, "modern" faculty lived in apartments or houses elsewhere in the city – this was especially true for those who had families. The colleges had no accommodations for married persons.

This mingling of students and faculty was at the heart of what Cecil Rhodes wanted to impart to his scholars. An Oxford education was about more than just book learning. It provided an environment in which students and teachers lived, studied, dined, and socialized together. Most students played on one or more of their college sports teams in intramural contests against the other colleges. If everything worked well, life in such a closed community built character, stimulated discussion and reflection, and produced life-long friendships.

Oxford was thought to combine all good features of a large university and a small college. The total student body numbered about three thousand at the turn of the century. The colleges offered an intimate atmosphere and individualized instruction, whereas the university furnished a comprehensive library (the Bodleian), science laboratories, and lecture halls. The university also provided a governing apparatus through which the colleges could work in common. The titular head of the university was the chancellor, whose position was largely ceremonial. The person who actually managed the day-to-day affairs was the vice-chancellor, who generally was selected from the heads of the colleges. The vice-chancellor worked closely with the Hebdomadal Council, which functioned as a type of cabinet. Two other, larger bodies also governed university affairs. Congregation consisted of members of the administrative and academic staff who held M.A.'s from the university; this body acted as the university's parliament, voting on all major changes. Finally, there was Convocation, the name given to the body of all Oxford M.A.'s whose names were listed in the college books. By 1900 the powers of this last body had waned, being limited to the right to vote in a handful of occasional elections – for example, selecting a new chancellor or a new professor of poetry. This administrative machinery continues in effect down to the present day.

The Oxford M.A. has never been an academic degree. Rather, it gives one a kind of permanent membership in the university as a corporation. There are three requirements for obtaining this degree: one must have graduated with an earned degree (the B.A. or some higher level); one must wait until twenty-one terms after matriculation – in other words, about five years after graduation; and one must pay a nominal fee. These three criteria having been met, one can apply for and receive the M.A.

The basic teaching method in the colleges was the tutorial. There were some lectures provided by the university, but these were strictly optional – which meant that students tended to ignore them, unless the particular lecturer was an especially fine speaker. An old, standard joke in Oxford was that the invention of the printing press had made lectures unnecessary, but that respect for tradition kept anyone from abolishing them.

In the standard tutorial, a student went once each week to his tutor's rooms in college. In a one-on-one encounter the student read an essay he had written based on readings of the previous week. The tutor would stop him occasionally to ask questions or to poke holes in the student's evidence or logic. There were no grades, no quizzes, no midterm examinations. Nor was there an accumulation of credits earned by the taking of separate, semester-long courses. At the end of the first year there might be a preliminary examination. As long as a student passed that, he was authorized to continue. At the end of the third year (or in some courses of study, the fourth) there would be several days of essay examinations. The examinations were administered and graded by a panel appointed by the university. In other words, the tutor did not examine and grade his own student. This arrangement encouraged a tutor and his student to feel that they were partners rather than antagonists. This same system operates to this day.

When a student performed splendidly in his final examinations, this reflected well on him as well as on his tutor and college. Most students obtained an "honours" degree, which was divided into four classes. Only a small percentage of students managed to get a "First" in their examinations. This was equivalent, in the United States, to graduating magna or summa cum laude. Achieving a "Second" was respectable, but a "Third" was cause for dismay. The lowest passing grade was a "Fourth," which was something the recipient might try to hide for the rest of his life. Below this were the students who obtained mere pass degrees, those who failed their examinations, and those who departed before completing their studies.

The tutorial system gave great freedom to students. They were in "class" only one or two hours per week. If they wished to do well, they had to discipline themselves through hours of solitary reading and writing in their rooms. Of course, this system also posed great dangers. A carefree student might very well spend his three years sleeping, drinking, and socializing. Or a student might have the misfortune to end up with an unsuitable tutor. Usually a college had only one faculty member for each field of study. Thus, for example, the tutor in modern European history might be a renowned expert in his specialty as well as a caring mentor who worked closely with his students. On the other hand, he could also be a mediocre scholar, a heavy drinker, and an odious tyrant. In the latter case a student could very well be "stuck" for his entire three years. The English-born Canadian humorist Stephen Leacock once described the system this way:

... I gather that what an Oxford tutor does is to get a little group of students together and smoke at them. Men who have been systematically smoked at for four years turn into ripe scholars ... . A well-smoked man speaks and writes English with a grace that can be acquired in no other way.[3]

The areas of study for which one could obtain a B.A. degree at the turn of the century were largely the traditional ones that had been the heart of Oxford's greatness. The number one field, both in terms of fame and in the number of students, was Literae Humaniores, or "Greats" as it was called. This was a rigorous program of study in classical Greek and Roman literature, philosophy, and history. Greats was widely considered to be the very best course for the training of the mind. An extraordinarily high percentage of the statesmen and bureaucrats who administered the British Empire were "Greats" men.[4] Oxford's other strengths lay in the fields of philosophy, theology, law, modern history, and modern literature. Oxford still looked with skepticism at such new fields as psychology, engineering, and sociology and consequently had few offerings in these areas. In biology, chemistry, and physics Oxford was, by its own admission, far behind the better American universities.

When the forty-three American Rhodes Scholars of 1904 reached Oxford they encountered not only an educational system radically new to them but also a bewildering array of unfamiliar customs and terms. One's teacher was a "tutor." This tutor usually also was a permanent fellow of the college. These fellows or tutors might also be called "dons." The academic year was divided into three terms, each of eight weeks. The fall term (October to December) was called "Michaelmas," the winter term (January to March) was "Hilary," and the summer term (April to June) was "Trinity." One did not "major" in a field, but rather "read" it. Final examinations were "Honours Schools" or simply "schools." If one referred to the college dons as a group or to their meeting rooms, one used the term "SCR" (Senior Common Room). Student government or the main student meeting room was the "JCR" (Junior Common Room). The dons who took meals in the college hall sat at "High Table," on an elevated platform. Elaborate ceremonies often occurred as the dons entered the hall for a meal. At Queen's College, for example, there were two trumpet blasts, one to the east and one to the west. After dinner in the evening, each college's dons retired to the SCR for coffee, port, sherry, and snuff. The heads of the colleges had their own particular titles: master, warden, principal, dean, president, rector, or provost. A student's non-academic adviser was his "moral tutor." A student who was temporarily expelled was "rusticated." The fees owed to a college for room, board, and other charges were "battels." The area near the college kitchen where one could purchase food supplies for one's room was the "buttery." When an undergraduate attended evening meal in college, was outside the college after dusk, or went to tutorials, he wore either a commoner's or a scholar's gown. The special outfit worn at matriculation and when taking examinations was "subfusc." The university police who patrolled the city streets at night to ensure the good behavior of students were "bulldogs." (Until 1868 the bulldogs had authority over everyone on the streets of Oxford at night. There are stories about them arresting prostitutes and bullying them in Latin.[5]) Alumni were called "old members," and alumni reunions were "gaudies." All students, dons, and other residents of the City of Oxford were "Oxonians."

If these and other terms were not enough, there were also a myriad of abbreviations, nicknames, and odd pronunciations. St. Edmund Hall, actually a college but called a hall, was "Teddy Hall." Christ Church was a college but was never called one. Instead, it was usually referred to as "ChCh" or "House." Hertford College was pronounced "Hartford" or "Harford," but never "Hurtford." Magdalen College and the bridge adjacent to it were pronounced "Maud-lin." – though a couple of blocks away Magdalen Street and the Church of St. Mary Magdalen were "Mag-de-lin." The similarly named college in Cambridge also was "Mag-de-lin." One of the two rivers flowing through Oxford was the "Isis" – known as the Thames everywhere else. The other river was the Cherwell – pronounced "Char-well."

The rowing contests in the early spring were "Torpids," but the similar races in early summer were "Eights." All the rowing contests were "bumping races" or "bumps." (There were too many boats to fit across the narrow Isis, and so the boats were strung out in single file. The aim was to bump the boat in front of one's own, thereby advancing in the standings.) Most of the colleges owned punts, which, like Venetian gondolas, were propelled by long poles. The student in charge of his college's punts was the "admiral of the fleet." Whereas an American varsity athlete won a "letter," his counterpart in Oxford won a "blue." This entitled a student to wear a coveted blue jersey, blue blazer, blue scarf, blue necktie, or blue hat-band. (Oxford was dark blue, Cambridge light blue.) Blues were awarded only to athletes who made the university team for a match against arch-rival Cambridge. A full blue was awarded in cricket, football (i.e., soccer), rugby, rowing, and track. Half-blues were awarded for sports like tennis, golf, boxing, and fencing. A half-blue article of clothing had white stripes over a blue base.

Rhodes Scholars and other foreigners in Oxford might not understand even a word of the ceremonies that occurred at the beginning and end of their years in Oxford. Matriculation and graduation occurred in Christopher Wren's magnificent Sheldonian Theatre. Most of the words uttered by the university's chancellor and other dignitaries were in Latin. Newly arrived Americans would also discover that their class year was determined by the date when they entered Oxford not when they graduated.[6]

Tradition reigned supreme. A story regarding New College is probably apocryphal yet accurately illustrates the Oxford state of mind. Sometime in the nineteenth century it was discovered that the beams in the roof above the dining hall were full of beetles and rotten. The college council despaired at finding old oak trees that would provide replacements of a suitable caliber. One of the younger fellows ventured to suggest that the college might own forests containing the right kind of trees. (Like several of its counterparts, New College possessed vast tracts of land throughout the country.) College officials contacted their chief forester, who had not visited Oxford for many years. His response went something like, "Well, sirs, we was wonderin' when you'd be askin'." He then revealed that some years after the college was founded in the fourteenth century a grove of oaks had been planted to replace the beams in the college hall. For over five hundred years the chief foresters had tended the grove, awaiting word that new beams were needed.

Early in the twentieth century many hallowed customs were still retained in full force. At Magdalen whenever a don passed away the college slaughtered one of its deer and served it for dinner. Magdalen was the center of each year's May Morning celebrations, when at 6:00 a.m. on the first of May choristers sang from the top of the college tower, to the delight of the throngs below. Every third year the Lord Mayor of Oxford inspected the medieval city wall that ran through New College; since the fourteenth century the college had been permitted to use the wall as part of its structure in return for keeping it in good repair. On the fourteenth of January in the first year of each century there was a ceremony called "All Souls Mallard." The warden led a torch-lit procession through the grounds of All Souls, searching for a mallard which, supposedly, had been startled out of a drain when the college was being constructed. In the other ninety-nine years of each century the "Mallard Song" was sung at the college gaudy. Except for the bulldogs and the slaughter of deer, these customs and terms remain little changed today.

During its eight centuries of existence, the university had experienced its ups and downs. In the high and late Middle Ages, its philosophers, theologians, and jurists were the equal of any at the University of Paris or other renowned centers of scholarship on the continent. On the other hand, the eighteenth century marked a low point. Standards sank to abysmal depths, with many of the tutors paying more attention to the comfortable perquisites of life as an Oxford don than to maintaining high standards for themselves and their students. The future economist Adam Smith spent six years at Balliol in the 1740s. Only rarely did any tutor inquire about his activities, and so he spent most of his time reading whatever he chose. Once he was nearly expelled when someone discovered that he owned a book unfit for undergraduates: David Hume's *A Treatise on Human Nature.* His contemporary Edward Gibbon called his fourteen months at Magdalen College "the most idle and unprofitable" of his entire life.[7] The nineteenth century, however, witnessed a revival. By 1900 on the whole Oxford was again equal or superior to the best institutions in the United States and on the continent.[8]

The list of its graduates was indeed impressive. Over the centuries they included Roger Bacon, Thomas Wolsey, Sir Walter Raleigh, John Donne, Thomas Hobbes, Robert Boyle, John Locke, Jonathan Swift, John Wesley, Samuel Johnson, Percy Bysse Shelley (who was expelled from University College in 1811 after publishing "The Necessity of Atheism"), John Henry Newman, Charles Dodgson (Lewis Carroll), T.E. Lawrence, Oscar Wilde, and J.R.R. Tolkien. Sixteen of the thirty-two men who had served as prime minister in the period from the 1720s to 1900 were Oxford graduates, and traditionally Oxford represented a majority of each prime minister's cabinet. From 1604 to 1950 the university also elected its own two members of Parliament. Given Oxford's preeminence in academe, government, and other fields, it is not surprising that when one began one's studies there one "went up." An expelled student was "sent down." The person who successfully graduated "went down."

The value of an Oxford education both for the students and for the nation did not always go unquestioned. On the one hand, the statesman William Gladstone believed that "To call a man an Oxford man is to pay him the highest compliment that can be paid to a human being." On the other, the writer Max Beerbohm admitted, "When I was growing up, I was an amiable, studious, and well-mannered youth. It was only Oxford that made me insufferable."[9] Because of the university's sometimes overblown sense of importance, George

Bernard Shaw argued that Britain would be better off if both Oxford and Cambridge were razed.

Traditionally, Oxford was a sort of finishing school for the scions of noble or wealthy families. In college one would get a smattering of learning but also gain social polish and make valuable friends. The great majority of students thus were content to obtain a gentleman's "Second" or "Third." Most of the "Firsts" were won by scholarship students. These were usually the bright, ambitious sons of lower-middle or working-class families. They had won any of the dozens of open scholarships offered by the colleges.

One additional feature that could not escape the notice of any visitor to Oxford was the utter masculinity of the place. The students, the dons, and even the housekeepers were male. This idiosyncrasy would not have puzzled most of the new arrivals, for many of the American colleges and universities from which they came, especially those along the eastern seaboard, were also male-only.

There were female students in Oxford. They were, however, "in" but not quite "of" the university. Between 1878 and 1893 five women's colleges had been founded. They were Lady Margaret Hall, Somerville College, St. Hugh's College, the Society of Oxford Home Students (later renamed St. Anne's College), and St. Hilda's College. These institutions existed in a kind of academic limbo. They were farther from the city center than their male counterparts. They were also poorer. Some of the twenty men's colleges, by contrast, owned tens of thousands of acres throughout the country plus entire blocks of real estate in Oxford and London. Women were permitted to attend most of the university lectures, and they could sit for the same examinations taken by their male counterparts. During these occasions, however, they sat apart, were carefully chaperoned, and could not speak to the men. Moreover, the university did not grant degrees to the women; they had to be content with diplomas granted by their colleges.[10]

Settling In

In October 1904 the first class of American Rhodes Scholars arrived in Oxford shortly before the start of Michaelmas term.[11] Nearly all of them had sailed together from Boston in the *S. S. Ivernia*. This sailing party was the beginning of a tradition that would last nearly eighty years. In their days on board ship they would form strong bonds with each other. Many of these friendships would last not only through their Oxford years, but also through their careers.

On board the *Ivernia* the scholars found awaiting them a message sent by President Theodore Roosevelt. He offered his congratulations and also reminded them that they had an obligation to uphold the best traditions of American scholarship and culture.[12] The nervousness that many of them already had about this new scholarly experiment was thus compounded by the knowledge that their government would be looking over their shoulders.

At sea the young men were objects of curiosity to their fellow passengers, who wanted to see these perfect specimens of American youth. After the first awkward day of trying to live up to their image, most of them resorted to beer and cards. One of the poker groups acquired the name Chianti Club, and it continued its regular sessions after arrival in Oxford.[13]

In 1904 and most years thereafter, the group was met at the Southampton or Liverpool docks by the Oxford Secretary, who then escorted them by train to Oxford. For nearly thirty years the Briton who greeted them as they disembarked from the ship was the avuncular Francis Wylie. After arrival at the Oxford train station he dispatched them by cab to the porters' lodges of their respective colleges. Frank Aydelotte (1905) later recounted how he and two other scholars first entered Brasenose College. At the lodge they asked whether they should report to someone and were told that they might see the vice-principal, one Dr. Bussell. After climbing his staircase they found "a man with a red and white schoolboy complexion and a monocle, wearing a very high choker collar." Aydelotte announced "We are the new Rhodes Scholars." Glancing through his monocle Bussell exclaimed in a squeaky falsetto voice, "How quaint." Surprised and embarrassed, but also amused, they quickly retreated, realizing that they had encountered a "character." They also realized that they had committed their first of many *faux pas*. It was indeed quaint for newcomers to make an occasion of their arrival in a place where to be casual and unimpressed was the standard behavior.[14]

Just as Cecil Rhodes hoped that Americans would come from all regions of the United States, so too he expected that they would be spread throughout the colleges in Oxford. If too many ended up in one college, this would deter them from mixing thoroughly with British students. Starting in 1904 and continuing to today, newly-appointed scholars were asked to list several colleges in order of preference. Most of the young men knew little or nothing about Oxford and selected those colleges they had heard were the oldest and most prestigious. This set a tradition that has, with slight changes, carried through to the present time. The colleges that were most popular among the Americans through the first half of the century were Christ Church, Balliol, Merton, Exeter, and Lincoln.[15] Most Rhodes Scholars failed to obtain their first choice in college. Furthermore, no college was obligated to accept a Rhodes Scholar. As things developed, what happened was that most colleges accepted one or two per year. Francis Wylie also did his best to distribute the scholars as widely as possible.

With the exception of Aydelotte and his companions, Rhodes Scholars generally went straight from the lodge to their rooms. They had several surprises awaiting them. Residential halls in the older colleges were not arranged in "floors," where dozens of students had rooms extending down long hallways. Instead, the traditional Oxford arrangement was staircases. Every few yards along the outside of the building there was a doorway leading up a staircase. On each landing, extending up three or four floors, there were perhaps two or three doors, each one leading to a student's rooms. On average there were about a dozen students in each staircase.[16]

Upon reaching the correct door in the proper staircase, the student then encountered his second surprise: his "scout." This was usually an older, formally-dressed gentleman, whom they assumed to be a college administrator. To their shock they discovered that this man called them "Sir." He was, in effect, the manservant for the "gentlemen" of his staircase. Each scout was a college employee but also depended heavily on end-of-term tips from his charges. The scout awoke each man at around 7:30 a.m. on weekdays and brought breakfast, lunch, and afternoon tea to each student's room. The scout also tidied up the rooms each day and ran errands around town – e.g., taking clothes to the cleaners or purchasing food and other supplies.

Immediately after weathering the shock of having a scout, the Rhodes Scholar discovered that he would have two, or sometimes three, rooms at his disposal. The usual two-room allotment, known as a "set," included a bedroom and a sitting room. One ate, studied, and entertained in the latter.

The euphoria induced by having two rooms for oneself alone was soon tempered by disappointments. Rhodes Scholars learned that the furniture in the rooms usually belonged to the previous occupant. One had to purchase it in order to keep it. The Americans also discovered that other immediate expenditures were required, such as sending the scout out to purchase plates, cutlery, towels, and other incidentals. There was a fireplace in each room, for which the scout would need to purchase coal. The rooms might be impressively large, but students soon realized that they were cold and drafty. Worse than that, the antique residence halls also possessed antique plumbing – or, more often, no plumbing at all. In hundreds of diaries and letters home, the pioneer Rhodes Scholars bemoaned the fact that toilets and bathtubs might be located in quads at the opposite end of the college. The Americans thus discovered what English public schoolboys already knew: education and the building of character were not meant to occur in an environment of warmth and convenience.[17]

NOTES

1. The best, most detailed account is the multi-volume *History of the University of Oxford*, published by Oxford University Press, gen. ed. T. H. Aston. The early period is covered in the first two volumes: J.I. Catto, ed., *The Early Oxford Schools* (1984) and J.I. Catto and Ralph Evans, eds., *Late Medieval Oxford* (1993).
2. *Baedeker's Great Britain* (London, 1887), 30.
3. Stephen Leacock, "Oxford As I See It," *Harper's*, May 1922, 741.
4. Symonds, *Oxford and Empire*, 31, 35, 189-91.
5. Jan Morris, *Oxford* (Oxford, 1978), 56.
6. One of the best guides to the terms and customs of Oxford is Christopher Hibbert, ed., *The Encyclopedia of Oxford* (London, 1988).
7. *TAO*, 43 (1956): 7.
8. In addition to the aforementioned *History of the University of Oxford*, one should consult John Prest, ed., *The Illustrated History of Oxford University* (Oxford, 1993).
9. *TAO*, 54 (1967): 10.
10. Brian Harrison, ed., *The History of the University of Oxford*. Vol. 8: *The Twentieth Century* (Oxford, 1994), 345-49; Amery, *My Political Life*, I:45.
11. As their selection process was less complex, scholars from Germany, South Africa, and Rhodesia were the first to arrive, in the fall of 1903.
12. *TAO*, 50 (1963): 65; 52 (1965): 126.
13. *TAO*, 37 (1950): 66, 54 (1967): 103.
14. Blanshard, *Aydelotte*, 58.
15. Aydelotte, *American Rhodes Scholarships*, 133; Elton, *First Fifty Years*, 66-67.
16. Most residence halls built since the latter part of the nineteenth century are arranged by floors rather than staircases.
17. Elton, *First Fifty Years*, 80; Blanshard, *Aydelotte*, 59-60; *TAO*, 66 (1979): 123.

Chapter 4

YANKS AND BRITS

To sum up my impressions of Oxford I need only one short sentence – *I am glad to be here.* I have no doubt that my three short years at this ancient university will prove to be the most profitable years of my life. Not only shall I be better equipped intellectually, but I shall ever feel the improving influence of Oxford life, and the subtle charm of this beautiful city. I do not wonder that the sons of Oxford ever look back with fondness to their college days, and I know that I too shall look back to them with equal fondness.

Stanley Royal Ashby, class of 1906

Of course there is good cooking in Oxford, as there are crossbows and hoopskirts on sale in New York City; but in both cases you must work to find them … . [I recall] Oxford chiefly as a place where too many bells were always ringing in the rain, and the English countryside as a locale whose principal attraction lay in the fact that when you were broke you could live there for about one fifth the cost of a vac in the Continental capitals.

Elmer Davis, class of 1910

Getting Acquainted

When the first wave of Americans arrived in the fall of 1904 Oxford newspapers and magazines were filled with the same sort of warnings that had appeared after the will had first been announced. *Isis* published cartoons showing Rhodes Scholars lynching their dons and riding bucking broncos.[1] As things turned out, the early Rhodes Scholars did not hang anyone and brought no horses with them, but they did provide entertainment, puzzlement, and consternation. Even before their accents could be heard, their clothes gave them away. Almost invariably, they bedecked themselves in splotches of bright colors and wild plaids. In every class there were several who also sported huge Stetson hats. These gave rise to a new music hall ditty, which proclaimed, "If I only had a hat like a Rhodes Scholar, I'd be happy for life."[2]

Notes for this chapter can be found on page 60.

One member of the first class, William Crittenden, was a genuine California frontiersman. He carried a pistol in his trousers. One morning soon after arrival at Trinity College he became irritated when his scout was tardy in running an errand. Crittenden thereupon fired a shot out his bedroom window. That certainly roused staid, old Oxford from its slumbers. The college president immediately summoned Crittenden and requested that the gun be deposited with the college for safekeeping.[3] Crittenden's classmate Henry Hinds, from North Dakota, also brought a revolver with him. Becoming bored at a lawn party for freshers, he decided to liven up the affair by shooting at the heels of one unfortunate British student, whom he chased around the gardens.[4] Here too the college appears to have been lenient. Neither Crittenden nor Hinds was "sent down." The former eventually got a Second in law and the latter a First in geology.

Another thing that set the Americans apart was their manners. They were louder and more outgoing than the typical British student. Another member of the class of 1904, Ralph Blodgett of Missouri, discovered this in his first evening at Wadham College. He entered the hall for dinner, marched up to a group of older students and boldly introduced himself. "My name's Blodgett," he declared, to which they responded with stony silence and dropped jaws.[5]

Rhodes Scholars had to discover what the British already understood. New students were mere "freshers." Only after they passed their preliminary examinations, usually at the end of the first year, did they acquire senior status. Whether they were natives or foreigners, freshers were not expected to speak to senior students unless the latter initiated the engagements.[6]

Rhodes Scholars also had to learn that in Oxford they were "commoners," not "scholars." The term "scholar" was reserved for those students who had won scholarships offered by the colleges themselves. These students were entitled to wear to dinner and lectures gowns that were more elaborate than those of their classmates. Through the succeeding years numerous Americans would win some of these awards in competitions held while they were in Oxford. Only these Rhodes Scholars were "scholars" in British eyes.

Britain was not so much unfriendly as indifferent. Young men who had been star athletes, top students, and home-town heroes in the States arrived in Oxford to find that the Red Sea did not part for them. They were expected to accommodate themselves to Oxford, not vice versa. A university that was accustomed to educating future prime ministers, famous authors, and members of the House of

Lords was not going to become excited by the arrival of a few dozen Rhodes Scholars from the United States, Germany, and the various regions of the Empire.

In a few cases British students did go out of their way to make life uneasy for the Americans. If it was the Americans who were singled out, that was partly because there were more of them than all the other Rhodes Scholars combined. It was also because of Britain's uneasy fascination with the strapping giant of a nation that was just then emerging as a world power and possible rival. Finally, it was also because the Americans, in their personalities and their educational backgrounds, were less like the British than were most of the other Rhodes Scholars.

One American from these early years who was singled out for special treatment was the product of a big state university in the South. He was a member of Phi Beta Kappa, a football star, and a respectable baritone. As he departed for Oxford his home-town newspaper lauded him as "the Perfect Man." The Associated Press picked up this article, and it was published in newspapers in New York and elsewhere. Correspondents for the major London dailies were amused by it, and they cabled copies to their head offices. When the ship carrying Rhodes Scholars arrived in England, this young man was swarmed by reporters and photographers. Whereas freshers normally were ignored, the "perfect man" was invited to party after party by senior British students. It took a while for the American to figure out why he was so popular. The organizers of the festivities were charging guests a shilling for the privilege of seeing "the perfect man."[7]

The great majority of Rhodes Scholars, however, had a less remarkable transition to Oxford life. Upon the advice of their scouts and others, they quickly relegated their fraternity pins, Stetsons, turtleneck sweaters, and brightly colored pants and shirts to storage trunks. Using the first installment of their stipends, they rushed to the gentlemen's shops on the High to purchase gray flannel pants ("bags") and tweed jackets.

One newcomer had nearly the reverse experience of Crittenden and Hinds. Just as Hugh Moran of California was moving into his rooms at Wadham in October 1905, he was greeted at the door by a fellow of the college. The gentleman had heard that Moran was from the western states. The visitor inquired, "And I say, do tell me, did you ever know Billy the Kid?" The don was somewhat disappointed to learn that Moran did not know the famous outlaw. However, at least the American was able to say that he had been reared in cattle country.

The don introduced himself as R. B. Townshend and astonished the American by announcing, "Some years ago I had a rahnch – a horse rahnch, in Coloraydo. Glorious country that!" Townshend then related his personal background. He had always considered himself an outdoorsman, and after graduating from Cambridge he struck out for Colorado. He took up horse ranching: "not thorough-breds, you know, but mustangs and cow ponies, and all that. Those were the days ... . Cattle coming in from Texas, and plenty of holdups and cattle rustling."[8]

Upon the death of his father, the disconsolate Townshend had to return to England. There he married a lady "of some substance and excellent family." The new Mrs. Townshend refused to go to America, and so they settled in Oxford. Townshend took up the life of an Oxford don, tutored in the classics, and wrote scholarly books. On the side he published children's adventure stories about the Wild West.

Townshend invited Moran to his home for the following Sunday afternoon. The don lived just up the Banbury Road, one of the major avenues passing through the city. To his astonishment, Moran was told to expect some horseback riding and "a bit of roping." When he arrived at the "rancho," Moran was taken to the back garden, for some roping and "a bit of a shoot." In the "corral" Moran discovered that the horse was made of wood and the steer that would be roped was a log with some branches serving as horns. Moran then pro-ceeded to have a try at roping, managing to bring the "steer" to the ground on his third try. Townshend then introduced the visitor to a motley group of neighborhood boys, who formed a sort of boys' scout troop. Producing a pair of .22 caliber rifles, Townshend guided his scouts through a session of target practice.

Moran's fast friendship with this unusual rancher/don was excep-tional. Most American Rhodes Scholars experienced something between the warmth of Moran's welcome and the rude treatment of "the perfect man."

Most also adjusted to the fact that British aloofness resulted more from reserve and timidity than from any sort of anti-American ani-mus. Reminiscing decades later, one American admitted that his first two terms were torture. He got along well once he learned to tame his American "enthusiasm" and accept British indifference to his superior achievements in his pre-Oxford existence.[9] Also the Amer-icans had to break their habit of yelling to each other or to British students while out on the streets. One of the early scholars later noted that the best advice he had ever received on how to adjust to British customs and sensibilities was always to keep his fork in his left hand and his tongue in his cheek.[10] Some Americans never made the adjustment. Of the class of 1904, one young man who could not adjust to Oxford committed suicide – a second died of natural causes. Another was so overworked in his studies that he had a nervous breakdown that turned out to be permanent. Each succeeding year there was at least one American who resigned the scholarship and returned home early. Every year or so there was also someone who got married and thus had to relinquish the scholarship.[11]

Other Americans went to the opposite extreme. They donned plus-fours, carried canes, and affected British accents. What were natural habits for the British became artificial mannerisms for their American emulators. One of the most outlandish of these specimens was Edwin Hubble (1910). Soon after he moved into Queen's, he adopted a British accent that he would keep the remainder of his life. He punctuated every sentence with anglicisms like "jolly," "ripping," "splendid fellows," "chap," and "bah Jove." When he arrived back home in America, his family was shocked to see him in plus fours and a flowing cape.[12]

Perhaps with little comprehension of what the words meant, these fake Britons marched around singing "Gaudeamus Igitur" with more fervor than any native would have displayed.[13] Some of these types also outsnobbed British students in looking down at some of their fellow Rhodes Scholars – those who were not from the "good" universities back home or who refused to smooth their rough American edges while in Britain.[14]

One of the pleasures of being an Oxford student that the Americans soon came to enjoy was being regarded as a gentleman all over town. Scouts, porters, shopkeepers, and waiters called them "sir." This was part of the deference given by the working classes to their "betters." Gentlemen often did the most ungentlemanly things, but this could usually be forgiven or accepted, provided they did them with style and paid their bills – though these need not be paid immediately. Rhodes Scholars discovered that their new status enabled them to run up tabs at the tailors, in Blackwell's bookshop, in restaurants, and in virtually every other commercial establishment. Of course, they were expected to pay up by the end of the academic year. Many businesses were exceedingly patient in this matter.[15]

Another feature of Oxford life that Americans readily enjoyed was the pervasive alcoholic haze that hung over the place. Most Americans, that is. Two or three members of each class were teetotalers, especially those from prohibitionist states like Kansas. These few stuck out as curiosities both to their fellow Americans as well as to the British. Tobacco, beer, wine, sherry, and brandy were staples in the rooms of nearly every undergraduate. Replenishing these supplies was usually the job of the scouts. Rhodes Scholars together with other students usually gathered each evening in one of their rooms, to talk, sing, smoke, and drink. This was the socializing factor that had been so important in Cecil Rhodes' thinking when he established the scholarships.

The students usually drank hefty amounts of beer with their evening meals in the college halls. Anyone who committed a *faux pas* or became the butt of a joke had to drink an entire tankard of ale without taking a breath; this was called "sconcing." If a college's boat won the Eights races, becoming "Head of the River," both dons and students would enjoy a tumultuous Bump Supper in the college hall.

Students were not, however, permitted to enter any of the public houses (that is, pubs) in town. The university proctors and the colleges fined any student caught in those premises. This prohibition did not result from any desire to protect innocent youths from the demon alcohol. Rather, it derived from two other factors. One was the goal of protecting young men from women "of the wrong sort." The other stemmed from the separation of social classes in England. "Gentlemen" did not socialize with the working classes in public establishments. Instead, they drank at home or in their private clubs. Oxford students could drink in their rooms, in the JCRs, and on the college barges moored on the Isis near the boat race area. First-year students often got to know one another by partaking in "freshers' drunks." The ubiquitous parties held at the end of each term were "jolly ups."[16]

Each college had a variety of student clubs and societies. Officially these organizations were for the purpose of debates, chess, bridge, and fine dining. Unofficially, some of them were mere excuses for getting drunk. Many a Rhodes Scholar marveled at the frequency by which club meetings turned into saturnalia, with participants breaking all the glasses and furniture in sight. (The colleges added the cost of repairs to the battels each student had to pay.) There were numerous student clubs that rented rooms from private landlords in the town. The most exclusive was Vincent's Club, in which students usually dressed formally for gourmet meals. The rowdiest was the Bullingdon Club, whose exploits have been recorded in fictionalized form by Evelyn Waugh and numerous other writers. Many of these clubs survive today, though their exploits have become less raucous.

The feature of Oxford life that perhaps was most peculiar and confining for Rhodes Scholars was the myriad of rules regarding comings and goings in each college. Most Rhodes Scholars were between twenty-two and twenty-four years old when they arrived, whereas the typical British fresher was eighteen. This age difference not only created a barrier in social relations, but it meant that older men were subject to rules designed to control freshmen. Many of these regulations were no worse than those in effect on American campuses through the first half of this century, but they seemed onerous to Rhodes Scholars.

The colleges were male bastions, and academic study was meant to be a semi-monastic vocation. Thus one was not permitted to bring women into college, except on a few special occasions per year, and then only for a couple of hours in the afternoon. Most colleges required attendance at chapel each morning, though in many cases non-Anglican students could petition for exemption. Some rules had, as one bemused American stated, "the pleasant savour of antiquity."[17] These included the prohibitions on playing marbles or shooting arrows in the High Street. Others were more irksome. For example, one could be fined if caught playing billiards after 10:00 p.m. or if one were spotted walking in town after dusk without wearing one's gown. A student generally had to ask permission if he wished to be outside college after 9:00 p.m. Then there were the gates. For reasons of security, going back centuries, the colleges still locked their front gates each night, usually at midnight. Dons could ring the front bell and be admitted after that hour. But students who returned after midnight or who stayed out all night were fined heavily or "gated" – that is, forbidden to leave college for several days. No wonder that some Americans considered their new homes to be more like prisons.

Joiners or Outcasts?

Once the initial fears of a Yankee invasion had been overcome, how did the Americans get along socially with their fellow students and others whom they met? By the end of their first or second terms, the overwhelming majority did splendidly. The record through the First World War shows steady involvement in a broad range of social activities. Several were elected to the presidency or other offices in their JCRs. Many were active in their college debating societies. William Bland (1910) had the distinction of becoming the first American elected to the presidency of the Oxford Union.[18]

Lawrence Henry Gipson was a member of the Lincoln College Sunday Evening Debating Society. One week he was asked to join a debate and take the position that Great Britain, having lost the United States, should dissolve its Empire and grant independence to all its colonies. Gipson gamely took up the challenge, though he was vehemently booed by other students. A week later, news of the debate having spread, Gipson also gained the wrath of Rudyard Kipling. Despite this, however, Gipson loved his Oxford experience. That debate sparked his interest in the topic and led him, later in his career, to embark on his Pulitzer Prize winning fifteen-volume series *The British Empire before the American Revolution.*[19]

Franklin Russell (1911) rowed for Brasenose, but he achieved his greatest popularity through his championship skills in chess. He amazed fellow students by his ability to play several boards simultaneously – while blindfolded. He played "Board 1" on the Oxford chess team in matches against Cambridge and was one of the top boards in the combined Oxford-Cambridge teams that played matches against London clubs. He also participated in the all-England team in contests against Scotland.[20]

Frank Morley (1917) became active in political and social causes and was one of the founders of the Oxford Labour Club.[21] Other Rhodes Scholars succeeded in introducing some American customs to their new friends. Southerners, for example, helped to make mint juleps a popular drink among many undergraduates. Rhodes Scholar singing groups like the Oriel Quartette introduced Britons to ragtime.[22] During the course of his three years in Britain nearly every Rhodes Scholar was invited on several occasions to spend weekends or parts of the holidays in the homes of his British classmates or other Britons who wanted to offer hospitality to the Yanks.

One Rhodes Scholar ended up marrying the daughter of his scout.[23] That shows how well many of the Americans were getting along socially. Yet, ironically, it also indicated that they would never get absorbed completely into British ways. This union of the educated elite with a member of the domestic servant class was something that the typical Oxford student would never consider.

Some Americans were so active socially that it is amazing that they kept up their studies. Whitney Shepardson (1910) was on the rowing, rugby, and tennis teams for Balliol, secretary to the Arnold Society, president of the Brakenbury Society, and a member of Vincent's Club. Yet he won the prestigious Gladstone Memorial Prize for an essay he wrote and obtained a First in Modern History. The most anglophilic of the early scholars and the one who attracted the most attention was Christopher Morley. He was the oldest of the three Morley brothers to win the scholarship. Their parents had emigrated from Britain to the United States in 1887. The father, Frank Morley, Sr., was professor of mathematics at Haverford College in Pennsylvania. In 1900 the family moved to Baltimore, where Professor Morley joined the faculty at Johns Hopkins University. All three sons, however, returned to Haverford for their college education.[24] Chris (or "Kit," as his English relatives called him) was a thoroughgoing American and yet was to have a lifelong love of all things English. He was enchanted when he first entered New College in 1910. He never tired of showing visitors the magnificent gardens, the medieval tower, the cloisters, and the well-known Warden: Rev. W.A. Spooner, or "the Spoo," whose spoonerisms added luster to the already venerable institution. Even as a student Morley possessed the rotundity that would later be part of his fame, but he cheerfully tried to do his part in college sports. His chief interests, however, lay in activities like afternoon teas in country inns, debates, and discussions at the college literary society. His first book, a collection of poems entitled *The Eighth Sin*, was published by Blackwell's while he was still in Oxford.[25]

Despite the evidence for the Americans fitting in socially, there were nagging problems that refused to go away. From the beginning, the newcomers were thought to be too cliquish. The Americans hung around too much together rather than blending in with other students. They even experimented with a variety of nicknames that would set them apart: Rhodesters, Rhodesmen, Rhodents, Rhodians, Rhodensians, Rhododendrons.[26] Rhodes Scholars clustered together each week in the homes of three different ladies who came to be their "mothers" away from home. Miss Crocker, Miss Guiney, and Mrs. Thayer were Americans who lived in Oxford. They delighted in giving food and entertainment to their homesick young countrymen.[27]

Starting in 1904 and continuing for several years nearly all the American scholars pooled their funds, hired rooms at the poshest hotel in town (the Randolph), and commissioned the preparation of an American-style Thanksgiving feast. The usual meal consisted of "mock turkey," Brussels sprouts, potatoes, and "American ices" (i.e., ice cream). The Americans hoped that perhaps within a quarter of a century they might be able to train the English chef to match the standards of American culinary excellence.[28]

The thing that seemed most anti-social was that the Americans formed their own clubs. Some were short-lived, like the Hermit

Crabs, a literary club formed in 1912.[29] The one that had the most members and lasted longest was the one whose very name trumpeted its foreignness: the American Club. It survived from 1904 to 1926 and would reappear, sometimes under slightly different names, on and off until the 1980s. This club's headquarters was usually a nondescript set of rooms rented somewhere in town. There one could usually find American magazines and newspapers scattered around on tattered furniture. College pennants were tacked to the walls. The highlights of the year were the two or three times when famous Americans who were visiting Oxford might stop by and give a little speech. In the years prior to 1914 the club was visited by such persons as Mark Twain, Theodore Roosevelt, and William Jennings Bryan.[30]

Occasionally British opposition to the club became serious enough to cause major concerns for George Parkin and Francis Wylie. They had their misgivings about the organization, but they did not interfere.[31] In October 1910 *Daily Mail* declaimed:

> … the American Rhodes Scholars … do not foster that good understanding [with the British]. As one of the Oxford undergraduates he should join in their social life. He should make friends with them, should in fact become their brother during his three years at the University. He does none of these things. After the first week at Oxford the American murmurs at British insularity and retires into his shell, the American Club, where he reads American newspapers, discusses American politics, sings American songs and might just as well be back in America for all the good he does himself in Oxford.[32]

This article produced a flurry of debate both in Britain and the United States and created the biggest crisis faced by the young program. The *New York Times* ran a series of articles with titles like "Rhodes Scholars Disappoint Oxford."[33] One Rhodes Scholar voiced the opinion of all his classmates when he reacted to the *Daily Mail*: "Oh, it makes us hot!" The Americans noted that most of them participated widely in British sports and social clubs. What was wrong, they asked, if occasionally they gathered among themselves to read and talk about home?

Despite this controversy, the American Club survived. The *Daily Mail* article clearly exaggerated a criticism that only a few Britons had about only a few the Americans. Furthermore, more rational observers agreed that a small group of people from any nation might tend to band together occasionally if they found themselves living together in a foreign land.

The American Club was little different from what the British students themselves sometimes did. Those who had become friends at

Eton or other public schools often stuck together and formed their own clubs in Oxford. Here again it was the Americans on whom the spotlight shone. They were from that upstart, rambunctious world power that fascinated, and, sometimes, repelled Europeans. Rhodes Scholars from elsewhere came from less important nations and were too small in number to attract the kind of attention that Americans did. At the same time that the American Club was formed, scholars from British dominions formed a Colonial Club, and the Germans had their own club. Yet these clubs attracted virtually no attention or controversy.

The Issue of Race

One of the least happy of the early Rhodes Scholars was Alain LeRoy Locke (1907). He was black. Those who did the most to ostracize him were not the British, but his fellow American Rhodes Scholars. He had been born and raised in Philadelphia, where his father was a lawyer and his mother a public school teacher. He obtained his B.A. at Harvard, where he made Phi Beta Kappa. That in itself was remarkable, for until the 1960s no more than two or three blacks could ever be found in any of the top American universities. Locke decided to apply for a Rhodes Scholarship because he wanted to study the issue of color outside the United States.

Since 1904 the American selection committees had wondered whether blacks were eligible to apply. Whenever they asked the Rhodes Trustees, the latter always said "yes." The trustees cited Rhodes' will, which said that neither race nor religion should be an issue – though, as noted earlier, Rhodes had never envisaged this clause including blacks.

At Harvard Locke scored first in the qualifying exam, beating seven white students. He chose to apply from his home state of Pennsylvania. The selection committee there had received such laudatory reports about him from Harvard that they made up their minds in his favor even before seeing him. They were shocked to discover that he was black, but they concluded that this should not serve as an excuse to reverse their earlier decision.[34]

When the news of his election spread through the United States and Britain, the reaction was swift. Newly elected Rhodes Scholars and those already in Oxford, particularly those from southern states, protested the inclusion of a Negro in their "brotherhood." Some threatened to resign. A delegation went from Oxford to London, where they presented their case to the trustees. The latter, however, stood behind Rhodes' will and refused to invalidate Locke's award.[35]

After Locke received the scholarship, he proceeded to apply for admittance to an Oxford college. Five colleges rejected him, on the basis of his race. One wonders how they knew in advance that he was black. It must have been Francis Wylie who, for whatever reason, mentioned it. The rejection by five colleges was unusual, because every Oxford college at that time had at least a handful of blacks or persons of "color." These were students from the British Empire in Africa and Asia. At any rate, we shall never know all the details. Locke finally was accepted by Hertford College.[36]

After arriving in Oxford, Locke was denied membership in the American Club, which meant that he also was excluded from the annual Thanksgiving feast. His three years in Oxford were lonely. There is no evidence from that period or from later decades that any of his classmates ever befriended him. His name is absent from their correspondence and publications. In 1908 at Thanksgiving the guest speaker was to be a don from Balliol. Upon discovering that Locke was not invited, the don backed out and hosted a special dinner at his college to which he invited Locke and all the other Rhodes Scholars. Americans from the southern states boycotted that affair.[37]

Locke's frictions with his classmates probably also stemmed from his homosexuality, though he never "came out" in Oxford. Indeed, he was still grappling with his sexual orientation during that period of his life. Perhaps his classmates did not even realize he was gay. But obviously he was a dandy. After George Parkin first met Locke he commented that the young man had "the grace and politeness of manner of a Frenchman or an Italian."[38]

Locke's foppish manners enabled him to mix well with many British students. From the late nineteenth century at least until the 1930s Oxford students were divided into three types. In the middle were the great mass who had no strong eccentricities or distinctive lifestyles. On the two extremes, numbering perhaps ten to twenty percent each, were the "hearties" and the "aesthetes." The hearties were what we today call the jocks. They played in the rougher sports and belonged to clubs like the Bullingdon rather than to the debating societies. The aesthetes dressed well, had exaggerated mannerisms, and favored poetry, refined dining, and the gentler sports. In the last decades of the nineteenth century the most famous aesthetes were the Brasenose don Walter Pater and the Magdalen student Oscar Wilde. In later decades aestheticism was personified most famously by Harold Acton, a student in the 1920s, and by the character of

Sebastian Flyte in Evelyn Waugh's *Brideshead Revisited*. The popular assumption was that all the hearties were lustily heterosexual and the aesthetes gay – though by no means was this always the case.

Locke also formed close associations with some black and colored students from Africa and India. Much of the inspiration for his later career as a spokesman for the "New Negro" came from these acquaintances. They taught him about the magnificent cultural accomplishments of non-whites.

In addition to the antipathy Locke faced from his fellow Americans, he experienced other problems. He started out reading Greats but soon realized that his command of Latin and Greek was insufficient. He then switched to philosophy. At the end of his third year he was not ready to take his exams. Instead of completing his work at Oxford, in 1910 he enrolled at the University of Berlin. There too, he failed to get a degree, but he did complete a long paper that he submitted in Oxford as a thesis for a B.Litt. Oxford, however, deemed the thesis inadequate, and Locke returned home in 1912 with no degree to show for his five years away. He appears, however, to have had cordial relations with Parkin and Wylie and with his tutors. In 1918 he obtained a Ph.D. from Harvard, though in the 1920s he considered returning to Oxford to obtain a degree there. Academically, therefore, Locke's experience in Oxford produced no concrete results but appears to have been beneficial and not altogether unpleasant.[39]

On the other hand, Locke did encounter social problems while living in Britain. He called Oxford the "Imperial Training School." He disliked the British sense of superiority and paternalism, particularly as it applied to any foreigners whose skin color might indicate that they were from the colonies.[40]

On the whole, however, he found that few Britons exhibited the racial prejudices held by most Americans. This caused a different sort of problem for him. Within weeks of arriving in England, Locke published a magazine article entitled "Oxford: By a Negro Student." For the most part the essay was a balanced, even favorable, description of Oxford society and traditions. However, near the end he addressed the question of race. He acknowledged that in Britain there were "no race distinctions" and "no race curiosity." In short, his race was not an issue in most of his social dealings. This bothered him, because his blackness was important to him. He asserted that

One cannot be neutral toward a class or social body without the gravest danger of losing one's own humanity in denying to some one else the most human of all rights, the right to be considered either a friend or an enemy, either as helpful or harmful. So for the good of every one concerned, I infinitely prefer race prejudice to race indifference.[41]

He feared being engulfed in a homogeneous mass. Oxford thus helped to instill in him the germ of his ideas about black pride and creativity.

Should one condemn the white Rhodes Scholars for their racism? A handful of them opposed the exclusion of Locke from the American Club, but none appears to have gone out of his way to befriend him. Locke died in 1954, and the *American Oxonian* published an obituary. Generally such pieces were written by fellow classmates or by other Rhodes Scholars who had come to know the deceased well. In contrast, the person who wrote this one appears never to have known Locke personally. The obituary praises Locke for his professional accomplishments, but it has none of the intimate reminiscences typical of other obituaries printed in the magazine.[42]

Distasteful as their attitudes seem for us today, the Rhodes Scholars who shunned Locke were acting as most Americans would have done at that time. Blacks were excluded from many jobs, schools, clubs, and restaurants even in the northern states. Not long before Locke went to Oxford, President Theodore Roosevelt had brought a storm of criticism upon the White House by inviting Booker T. Washington to lunch. Thus Rhodes Scholars were no worse than most of their contemporaries, but neither were they in the vanguard of change.

In the aftermath of the controversy sparked by Locke's appointment, selection committees avoided doing anything to encourage blacks. No records were kept about the race of applicants, but few, if any, blacks applied for the scholarships over the next half century. There were relatively few blacks in American colleges, and most of them were in Negro colleges or state universities – hardly the kinds of institutions that produced most Rhodes Scholars. Not until 1963 would there be other black American Rhodes Scholars.

NOTES

1. Richard Harrity, "63 Years of Yanks at Oxford," *Look*, 4 October 1966, 82.
2. Ibid.; *TAO*, 1 (1914): 43; 38 (1951): 84.
3. *TAO*, 49 (1962): 199.
4. *TAO*, 51 (1964): 240.
5. Elton, *First Fifty Years*, 88.
6. Stanley Royal Ashby, "An American Rhodes's Scholar at Oxford," *MacMillan's Magazine*, n.s. 1 (1906): 182-83; Parkin, *Rhodes Scholarships*, 195.
7. Mackaye, "What Happens," 11. Unfortunately, Mackaye does not provide the name of the Rhodes Scholar in question.
8. *TAO*, 45 (1958): 63.
9. *TAO*, 26 (1939): 18-19.
10. *TAO*, 56 (1969): 238.
11. *TAO*, 50 (1963): 70; Mackaye, "What Happens," 11. Also see various issues of the *Alumni Magazine* and the early pages of *A Register of Rhodes Scholars, 1903-1981* (Oxford, 1981).
12. Gale E. Christianson, *Edwin Hubble: Mariner of the Nebulae* (New York, 1995), 64, 76, 84, 87; *TAO*, 66 (1979): 122.
13. *TAO*, 52 (1965): 218.
14. *Alumni Magazine*, 3 (January 1910): 24.
15. *TAO*, 68 (1981): 159; 76 (1989): 158.
16. *TAO*, 2 (1915): 21; 25 (1938): 176.
17. Ashby, "American Rhodes' Scholar," 183.
18. *Alumni Magazine*, 6 (1913): 4.
19. *TAO*, 56 (1969): 225-29.
20. *TAO*, 65 (1978): 307.
21. *TAO*, 27 (1940): 174.
22. *TAO*, 43 (1958): 143.
23. Mackaye, "What Happens," 11.
24. Frank, Jr., started at Haverford but finished at Johns Hopkins.
25. *TAO*, 54 (1967): 159-60.
26. *Alumni Magazine*, 4 (1911): 23; *NYT*, 2 October 1910, 12; *TAO*, 8 (1921): 109, 13 (1926): 16.
27. Thomas Daniel Young and George Core, eds., *Selected Letters of John Crowe Ransom* (Baton Rouge, 1985), 47, 48; *Alumni Magazine*, 6 (April 1913): 36; *TAO*, 14 (1927): 19, 37 (1950): 18-21, 65 (1978): 110.
28. *Alumni Magazine*, 1 (December 1907): 12; 2 (January 1909): 5-6.
29. Young and Core, *Selected Letters*, 47, 48.
30. *Alumni Magazine*, 3 (January 1910): 1; *TAO*, 1 (1914): 18, 2 (1915): 40; 68 (1981): 159- 62; Young and Core, *Selected Letters*, 35-36; Aydelotte, *American Rhodes Scholarships*, 61.
31. Parkin, *Rhodes Scholarships*, 201; Elton, *First Fifty Years*, 89-90.
32. Quoted in *TAO*, 68 (1981): 161.
33. *NYT*, 2 October 1910, 12; 11 October 1910, 4; 16 October 1910, sec. 5, 9.
34. Jeffrey C. Stewart, "A Biography of Alain Locke" (Ph.D. dissertation, Yale University, 1979), 105-7.
35. Elton, *First Fifty Years*, 99-100.
36. Leonard Harris, ed., *The Philosophy of Alain Locke* (Philadelphia, 1989), 294.
37. *TAO*, 66 (1979); 125; Stewart, "Biography," 111-13.

38. Stewart, "Biography," 142.
39. Stewart, "A Biography," 122.
40. Alain Locke, *Race Contacts and Interracial Relations: Lectures on the Theory and Practice of Race*, ed. Jeffrey C. Stewart (Washington, DC, 1992), xxxvii, 29, and passim.
41. Alain Locke, "Oxford: By a Negro Student," *Colored American Magazine,* 17 (1909): 190. (Reprinted from *Independent.*)
42. *TAO,* 41 (1954): 258-59.

Chapter 5

THE SCHOLAR-ATHLETES

[An American Rhodes Scholar] has been reading for honours, and I [could] never wish for a more satisfactory pupil. His essays were always thorough, thoughtful, and well expressed. His work showed a rare combination of originality and ingenuity with sound judgment and common sense. In college life he was a strong influence, and always for good. Taking him all round, we have had no better man in college since he has been with us, and few as good.

Oxford don, 1911, New York Times

As to the American Rhodes Scholars, I am much impressed by the men personally. They are above the average, I think, as regards keenness and industry. I should describe them as thoroughly good fellows, but I do not think they compare with the better average undergraduates as regards scholarship and training … they seem very deficient in scholarship in a wider sense. Some are terribly rough intellectually, with little or no literary sense and very limited command over expression. In the composition of an English essay they have, as a rule, almost everything to learn.

Oxford don, 1911, New York Times

Sports

When Rhodes' will was first made public, many Britons anticipated that the chief benefit to Oxford would be the addition of hearty Americans to its sports teams. Some Oxonians even hoped that the Americans would help to establish permanent dominance over Cambridge. The Americans would be slightly older, larger, stronger, and more experienced than the average undergraduate.

Virtually every American did join at least one of his college teams. Rhodes Scholars unanimously praised the amateur spirit of English athletics. Sports in American universities were already becoming big business, spectator affairs, with highly paid professional coaches and rigorous training programs. Rhodes Scholars echoed Teddy Roosevelt, who bemoaned the win-at-all cost attitude and the high number of injuries and deaths incurred in American football.[1]

Notes for this chapter can be found on page 76.

The key words in British university sports were amateurism and participation. The coaches were unpaid students. The ideal was that every able-bodied student play on one or more of his college's teams in matches against the other colleges. There was no desire for large numbers of spectators. One played for exercise, for fun, for camaraderie, and for the vigor to resist the cool temperatures that were the norm both indoors and outdoors. The very best athletes from all the colleges were selected for the all-university squads that faced the Cantabs (i.e., Cambridge) each year in the varsity matches.

The Americans were not expected to help much in the sports unfamiliar to them – especially cricket. However, each year they did make significant contributions in rowing, track and field, tennis, and rugby. Dozens of the early Rhodes Scholars won blues or half-blues or were captains of their college teams.[2] The most illustrious was Lawrence Hull (1907), who led the Oxford track team against Cambridge in 1909. He won the quarter-mile and the hundred-yard dash, despite pain from a recently sprained ankle. His athletic feats and friendly personality made him a hero, and one of his fellow Americans reported that the British were eating out of his hand. In 1910 he served as president of the Oxford University Athletics Club.[3]

Nevertheless, there was a down side to these successes. Though Americans as a whole never came to dominate any sports in this early period, many British students and journalists thought that the upstart newcomers had an unfair advantage. The ordinary British public schoolboy had little chance against these older, ruthless behemoths.[4] Harold Merriam (1904) was branded "daucedly ungentlemanly" for tackling an opposing player in a rugby match.[5] In response to such criticisms, the colleges banded together in 1914 to impose restrictions on Rhodes Scholars in sports. These new rules did not specifically mention Rhodes Scholars, but they were clearly the target. Thereafter no student who had attended another university prior to Oxford could participate in "freshers" sports. This would prevent eighteen-year-old Britons from having to compete against much older Rhodes Scholars. Furthermore, no student over the age of twenty-four could compete in any sport whatsoever.[6]

Lawrence Hull himself, by that time back in the United States, admitted the justice of these rules. He added, however, that the fear of Americans dominating British amateur sports was terribly overblown. "The simple fact," he said, "is that the American Rhodes Scholars have not come up to expectations in athletics."[7] Only about one American per year earned a blue. The only sport where Americans were consistently among the leaders was track.

The controversy over the 1914 regulations soon subsided, and in general the Americans' athletic contributions were heartily appreciated.

Academic Performance

For most Americans, academic studies in Oxford ranked third, trailing social life and sports. For evidence of this one can consult early issues of the two quarterly magazines that they published. After Earle Murray (1904) returned home in 1907, he thought it would be a grand idea if Rhodes Scholars maintained contact with one another throughout their careers. He immediately began publishing the *Alumni Magazine.* That venture was modest and never became the thriving enterprise he had anticipated. Losing enthusiasm for the project, Murray ceased publication in 1913. The following year, however, Frank Aydelotte determined to revive the idea and to establish a full-fledged alumni association. The new journal was *The American Oxonian,* and he mailed it to every scholar returning from Oxford. Each person also automatically became a member of the Alumni Association of American Rhodes Scholars (the word Alumni was later dropped). Thanks to Aydelotte's unflagging zeal, the journal and the association would flourish to the present day. If one looks at the *Alumni Magazine* and early issues of *The American Oxonian,* one sees that far fewer than half of the pages concern the academic side of life in Oxford.

How did the Rhodes Scholars perform as "scholars"? In view of the difficulty in the early years of recruiting large numbers of applicants and the busy social and athletic lives that they led once they arrived in Oxford, it is not surprising that their academic record was decidedly uneven.

In fact, the academic performance by American Rhodes Scholars in general was a distinct disappointment, both to British and American observers and to the Rhodes Scholars themselves. The final results for the class of 1904 were as follows: seven read in their fields but did not obtain degrees; one took a pass degree; one obtained a diploma (for a course of study not leading to a full degree); one took an advanced degree (the B.Sc.); three obtained Fourths; twelve got Thirds; eleven achieved Seconds; and six were awarded Firsts.[8]

This was distinctly below the level of performance of the top British students (those in Oxford on scholarships). It was, however, about the same level of performance as the average Oxford student. Yet one must also recall that prior to the Second World War the caliber of the average Oxford student was not stellar; providing that one came from the right sort of family or attended the right kind of public school, one could gain entry. Rhodes Scholars, who were "perfect" men, chosen through rigorous competitions, were supposed to be far above the average.

Their record remained lackluster through the 1920s. In all approximately fourteen percent obtained Firsts, compared with twenty-seven percent of British scholarship students.[9] Again and again the pages of the *Alumni Magazine* and *The American Oxonian* lamented the poor showing of Rhodes Scholars or offered excuses to explain it. The inaugural issue of the *Alumni Magazine* in 1907 admitted that much improvement was needed but pleaded that the results "are all that can be expected from the pioneers." It boldly (and inaccurately) predicted that by 1920 all Rhodes Scholars would take Firsts.[10] The first issue of the *American Oxonian* appeared in April 1914 and featured an article by an Oxford don named Sidney Ball. He was a fellow of St. John's College, and his article was entitled "Oxford's Opinion of Rhodes Scholars." Regarding their academic record, he diplomatically said that it was "goodish" rather than first-rate.[11]

A report commissioned by the Carnegie Foundation in 1911 was more blunt. The study quoted dozens of Oxford dons. In a couple of instances the tutors acknowledged that a small number of the Americans were first-rate. The other Rhodes Scholars were generally regarded as pleasant but equal only to the average Oxford student. The tutors' comments included the following: one American had "not been properly taught" in the United States; the newcomers were "typical Americans" (this was not meant as a compliment); the Americans were "restless and volatile" and could not settle down to hard work; they suffered from a "curious superficiality of training" and in some cases were "singularly uneducated" or had linguistic attainments that were "slender."[12]

George Parkin himself had to deal with the issue in public. The most that he could say on behalf of his American charges was that, although their record contained few marked successes, at least there were few who failed their exams. On several occasions he beseeched American universities to do more to advertise the program and improve the numbers and the quality of the applicants, so that Rhodes Scholars would indeed be the pick of each year's crop.[13]

To be fair, one must remember that for each American who got a Fourth or a failure there was at least one who got a First. In addition, each year one or two successfully completed a thesis and obtained an advanced degree (a B.Sc. or B.Litt). There were also a couple each year who received some of the prestigious prizes and awards distributed by the colleges.

Why, however, did most of these early scholars not meet expectations? Part of the reason was that expectations were too high. Anything less than all of them gaining Firsts was bound to provide fodder to critics. Another problem was that the Americans indeed were restless and volatile. Like a majority of Americans in that period, most of them had come from small towns, and few had traveled widely. Arriving in a foreign land for the first time, they did not want to stay cooped up in their rooms or in libraries and laboratories for the next three years. They wanted to see and do everything.

This included travel. The pioneer Rhodes Scholars, like their successors today, were encouraged by the Oxford Secretary to leave Oxford during the winter, spring, and summer vacations. Future world leaders, after all, needed a broad range of experiences. The vacation periods took up more than half of the year. Provided that one was frugal in Oxford or had a private source of income (usually one's family), a Rhodes Scholar could travel widely. Hardly any missed this opportunity, and most of them visited five or more European countries before returning to the States.

Frank Aydelotte later remarked that many a Rhodes Scholar missed getting a First in his exams because of his extensive travels. This wanderlust was a major difference between the Americans and the British. The typical British student had already traveled widely in Britain and on the continent, and he knew that throughout his life he would have ample opportunities to continue such forays. In contrast, everything was new to the Americans, and they could not be sure when, or if, they could ever return. Their wanderings gave them many precious memories and broadened their cultural horizons, but also hurt their studies. To the typical Oxford student, the eight-week terms were a period of moderate study plus heavy doses of sports and socializing. Vacations for the British were the times when those who were serious about their work did most of their reading. A British student would go home with trunks full of books; if he did travel, he took his reading with him and holed up in scenic spots where he could spend his daylight hours studying. For most – though not all – Rhodes Scholars, however, travel and holidays were just that and no more. Hence, when they returned to Oxford for the next term they had made little progress in the huge reading lists they would have to master before "schools."[14]

An additional reason for their relative lack of self-discipline was the newness of the tutorial system. Back home it was harder to slack off – one had quizzes, midterms, written assignments that received grades, and semester courses that had to be passed. But in Oxford a student was on one's own. Providing that one met his tutor each week and submitted a paper of at least minimal quality, one could coast for three years. Of course, the student who did this was unlikely to get a First or a Second in the one or two week's worth of essay examinations that came before graduation. Several Americans later admitted that they and many of their friends had not worked hard.[15]

The dons also presented problems for some students. The tutorial system was one of the glories of Oxford and Cambridge. Whereas in the American lecture system, a student could be a somnolent, passive receptacle into which a professor tried to pour knowledge, tutorials compelled a student to be responsible for his own learning. But, as noted, it could be disastrous if the mix between tutor and student was not congenial. The range of the Americans' experiences ran the entire length of the tutorial spectrum. One's tutor might be brilliant and friendly, or mediocre and antagonistic; intimidating or shy and quiet; bombastic or humble; gentle and constructive in his comments on a paper, or ruthless in his determination to destroy every thought and sentence; "normal" or eccentric in the extreme; passionately interested in the welfare of the students or supremely indifferent.

What the Americans often failed to realize was that if the dons were seemingly offensive or brutal, they were that way for the British students too. If a tutor disliked a student essay, it was expected that he say so and challenge the student to work harder or express himself more clearly. British students were already accustomed to this kind of treatment, but Americans came from a system where professors took more pains to find something positive to say about even the worst papers.

A handful of Americans formed immediate and lasting bonds with their tutors. William Fleet (1904) was mediocre as a student, receiving a Third in classics, but his tutor liked him so much that they vacationed together in Italy. One day while they were dining in an Italian restaurant another American entered – a large, loud, older man with rather rough language. Fleet felt embarrassed, got up, and asked his fellow countryman to stop bringing "discredit on our people."[16] Other Rhodes Scholars also traveled with their tutors. Most of them were also welcomed occasionally to their tutors' homes for afternoon tea. Finally, some tutors unfailingly offered the Americans tobacco and sherry during their weekly meetings.

There were many amusing incidents as the clash of competing cultures wound its way through these weekly sessions. One Rhodes

Scholar in the class of 1907 warily made his way to his tutor's rooms for their initial conference. The don offered him a drink, only to discover that the American was a teetotaler. Then the don asked if his charge would have a smoke. The youth responded, "No, thank you. I never smoke, either." "Well, what do you do?" asked the perplexed don, "You know, you must have some vice." After a moment's embarrassed silence, the don happily found a solution. "I have it," he exclaimed, "Do you chew chewing gum?" Happily, the student could admit to this bad habit. The don had no gum to offer him, for that commodity was still a novelty in England. Soon thereafter the student ordered a large supply from home and sent some to his tutor. The result was that the two became fast friends.[17]

John Crowe Ransom (1910) experienced one of the most awkward first encounters. He planned to read Literae Humaniores at Christ Church. His studies began this way:

And I was very confident, and I finally got to my philosophy tutor who was a very eminent philosopher named Blount. And he said, "Have you read any philosophy?" And I said, "Yes, I had two years of philosophy at college." "What did you take?" And I said, "We took a course in deductive logic – Aristotelian logic." And he said, "Whom did you read?" And I said, "We had a book by Noah K. Davis." And he said, "Ah, I don't know the name; but did you do anything else?" And I said, "Well. we had a course in inductive logic." And he said, "What did you read?" And I said, "We had a book by Noah K. Davis." And he said, "A most ubiquitous man." And then he said, "Did you take any other courses?" I said, "Yes, then we had a course in ethics." And he said, "Whom did you read? But please don't say Noah K. Davis." I said, "Noah K. Davis." And he said, "My education is faulty. I don't know Noah K. Davis. But did you take any other courses?" I said, "Yes, then we had a course in psychology" And he said, "I can't bear it, but I feel that you had Noah K. Davis." I said, "Yes." And it was perfectly true that we had had Noah K. Davis, and no other philosopher, living or dead. And so he said, "Come to my rooms next Thursday evening at eight, and bring me an essay entitled, "What is Thought?"[18]

This widely read Davis was an author whose textbooks were used in all the philosophy courses that Ransom had taken at Vanderbilt University.

Ransom quickly adapted to the Oxford system and enjoyed a full life of study, sports, and socializing. He and his tutor quickly got over their rough start, and Ransom just missed getting a First in schools.

Others never got on well with their tutors. Ebb Ford (1905) was a droll, proud Mississippian who was not intimidated by his law tutor at Christ Church, a man named Carter. The two sparred verbally during Ford's first term, and the American was "gated" for insulting his tutor. Ford steadfastly refused to apologize. Somehow the two reestablished a working relationship, and Ford was awarded a First in jurisprudence. It galled him, however, when he learned that the tutor was bragging that one of his protégés had won such an honor.[19]

Carter would haunt many years' worth of Rhodes Scholars. Several decades later a Rhodes Scholar wrote in an obituary of his classmate, Robertson Paul, of the class of 1913:

> He was reading Jurisprudence, and along with Valentine Havens (an equally keen youngster) met as his tutor Mr. Carter, one of the crustiest and most sardonic among the antediluvians of Christ Church. These two young bloodhounds from the backwoods set out on the trail of a savage old bear. No one could tell who had the better sport or who dealt the more sanguinary blows. But all three emerged victorious, for both pupils won first class honors.[20]

In the case of these students, a tutor's intimidating manners apparently did spur them to do great work. In many other cases, however, the opposite resulted.

Warren Ault (1907) was generalizing, but nonetheless reflecting the view of perhaps half of the Americans, when he asserted that the dons were "unwelcoming, if not downright disdainful."[21]

There were yet other reasons for the Americans' less than glittering academic performance. One was the education that they had received prior to arriving in Oxford. Many British observers, American educators, and Rhodes Scholars themselves concluded that the lackluster performance in Oxford was proof of the sorry state of American education. Rhodes Scholars who were twenty-two years old and had graduated with honors in some of America's best universities were having trouble keeping up with eighteen-year-old British freshers. A 1906 *New York Times* article on Rhodes Scholars reported that education in the U.S. was "mongrel." Americans got a smattering of knowledge in a wide variety of areas but studied nothing in depth. Thus they were not prepared for serious work in Oxford.[22]

Despite the jeremiads on both sides of the Atlantic about the condition of American schools and universities, a neutral observer can see that the problem was not that American education was inferior, but rather that it was different. American high schools and universities stressed giving students a well-rounded education. Regardless of his aptitudes, a student took courses in the natural and social sciences, the humanities, the fine arts, and even physical education. In British secondary schools students began to specialize in their last two years.

Their studies in university were even more specialized. Thus a student entering an Oxford college in 1904 intending to study modern European history would already have been concentrating in that area for the previous two years. Furthermore, during his three years in Oxford that is all he would "read." A new student planning to read French literature was expected already to be fluent in French and to have a good knowledge of the major writers. On the other hand, Rhodes Scholars arriving in Oxford with B.A.'s in hand from American universities would perhaps have spent only one-fourth of their time studying history, and that history would have included perhaps all periods and all parts of the world. Thus a twenty-two-year-old Rhodes Scholar hoping to read in modern European history would have far less background in the subject than his eighteen-year-old British rival.

This situation continues to the present day. There are advantages and disadvantages to each system. Americans are educated more widely but less deeply, whereas their British counterparts are trained more narrowly but more profoundly. Oxonians would argue, however, that their system is not as narrow as it might appear. The Oxford student in modern history can learn about other fields through the hothouse atmosphere of the college where he/she lives, eats, and socializes with students and dons from all the other disciplines. Furthermore, Oxonians would assert that the heavy stress on students training themselves to read, write, and analyze prepares them for all sorts of careers.

An additional problem that soon became apparent was that the great majority of Americans arriving in Oxford had already obtained B.A.'s in the United States. They did not "need" a second undergraduate degree – even if the Oxford undergraduate degree did oblige them to delve deeper into a subject than they had previously. A second B.A. was not going to add much to their résumés back home. Those who planned to obtain a Ph.D. or to attend law or medical school would be starting from scratch after they returned from Oxford. Their three years in Britain would not have counted toward the additional degrees needed for their careers.

Most Rhodes Scholars nevertheless chose to read for a B.A. in Oxford. Many were compelled to pursue studies in areas other than those they would have liked. George Parkin warned Rhodes Scholars that in the fields of chemistry, biology, and physics Oxford was not equal to the better American universities – though for Canadians and colonials Oxford was superior.[23] Edwin Hubble (1910), for example, chose to study jurisprudence though his real interest lay in astronomy. The situation in the social sciences was little better; sociology and psychology were still suspected of being newfangled and trendy. Engineering was just beginning as a subject for serious study, and there was no such thing as a course in business. Oxford was many things, but it would not stoop to being vocational! In addition, one could not read American history, for the dons insisted that the United States was too young to have enough history worth extended study. This dismissive attitude, however, was not the result of any cultural or nationalistic prejudices. Oxford treated recent British events in the same way – by ignoring them. In the early years of the twentieth century anyone who read "modern" history studied the seventeenth and eighteenth centuries, with Napoleon being about as recent as most tutors would permit.

The fields most popular among Americans were law (jurisprudence), modern history, and English literature. Law in Oxford was an undergraduate field of study. One who aspired to become a barrister in Britain would obtain a B.A. in law and then study at one of the Inns of Court in London. Jurisprudence in Oxford differed markedly from what one encountered in American law schools, for in Britain it included heavy doses of history and Roman law.

Over the years American law and medical schools gradually made some allowances for Rhodes Scholars returning from England. Scholars who obtained a B.A. in law and then the more advanced B.C.L. (Bachelor of Civil Law) could be granted exemption from the first year of law school. Scholars who obtained a B.A. in physiology generally were able to skip their first year of medical school.

Students who aspired to careers in academe had a more difficult problem. Oxford did not offer a doctorate.[24] It did, however, offer two advanced research degrees, the B.Litt. (for work in literature, history, philosophy, and so on) and the B.Sc (for any of the natural sciences). These degrees required two or three years of extensive research on a particular topic and the production of a thesis of approximately 30,000 to 40,000 words. These research degrees had been established in the 1890s, partly to attract British and American students who otherwise might flock to German universities. There were at least three major problems facing Americans who chose to pursue these degrees. The first had to do with their very name. Everyone in Oxford knew that a Bachelor of Literature was an advanced degree, probably equal in rigor and work to an American Ph.D. But in the United States "B.Litt." signified little more than "B.A." Thus the holder of one of these degrees still faced the prospect of returning home to find that he must still attend an American graduate program before becoming eligible for a position in an American university.

The second problem regarding the research degrees was that, even if Rhodes Scholars wanted to pursue them, few had the necessary training. As noted above, most Rhodes Scholars found that work for a B.A. was challenging enough. The typical British student working for a B.Litt. was prepared for extensive, original, independent research. He had already experienced five years of specialized training in the field: his last two years in secondary school and his three years of B.A. work. On average two or three Americans per year opted for an advanced degree.

One of the most successful was Frank Aydelotte, who obtained a B.Litt. He studied sixteenth-century English literature, and his thesis turned into his first book: *Elizabethan Rogues and Vagabonds* (1913). He was exceptional in that he thrived on the challenge, though he always insisted that his B.Litt. should have been considered the equivalent of a Ph.D. He was fortunate in not having to attend graduate school upon return to the United States. Prior to going to Oxford he had already obtained a master's degree at Harvard. The combination of M.A. and B.Litt. sufficed to get him his first teaching job, at Indiana University.

The third problem with the research degrees was that the "independent" research and writing was independent in the extreme. Rhodes Scholars working for B.A.'s had enough trouble disciplining themselves for their weekly tutorials. Those working on a B.Sc. or B.Litt. might be lucky to see their supervisors once a term. They were expected to have the necessary background and intelligence to work unsupervised for two or three years and produce an important, original thesis. Already feeling homesick and alone in a foreign culture, some Americans failed at the effort.

All of the above considerations make it easy to understand another reason for the disappointing academic performance of the Americans. In Oxford they were working for degrees that would not mean much to graduate schools or future employers back in the United States. For a British student, on the other hand, obtaining a First or a Second was important for prestige and careers. But in the States, few persons, if any, would know whether a man had received a First, a Second, a Third, a Fourth, a mere pass, or no degree at all. In short, most Rhodes Scholars came to realize that they did not need to work as hard as they had prior to coming to Oxford, or as hard as they would once they returned home. Those who obtained Firsts or advanced degrees did so from a sense of personal pride, from genuine enthusiasm for their work, or from a desire to live up to expectations.

For some Americans the most important thing was simply being able to put "Rhodes Scholar" on their résumés. Few employers or acquaintances would inquire about what one had actually done in Oxford. For most Americans, therefore, the scholarship presented an opportunity to "have it all" – some study mixed with camaraderie, sports, living in a foreign country, and travel.

Rhodes Scholars from some British dominions tended to do better than the Americans, both socially and academically. Canadians, Australians, and others came from educational systems modeled on that of Britain and thus had fewer problems adjusting. Obtaining a degree from Oxford also meant much more to Canadians and others than it did to Americans, for Oxford was far superior (in fact as well as in reputation) to any university in their homelands. From the early days to the present, Rhodes Scholars from Australia and New Zealand have tended to hold the best academic records in Oxford.[25]

Report Card for the Early Years

What kind of report card can one give the scholarship program for its first fifteen or so years? Certainly most of the Rhodes Scholars enjoyed the experience. Even if they found many of the students and dons unfriendly, or at least cool, they valued the opportunity to live abroad. They made valuable friendships among themselves, and some of them were introduced to academic studies that would have a great bearing on their careers.

Surprisingly, one aspect of their lives in Oxford that they did not complain about was the near absence of women. Most Rhodes Scholars came from male-only universities and considered higher education for women to be more a frill than a preparation for a career. To be sure, the scholars occasionally joked about or bemoaned the fact that there were few women around. The women from Lady Margaret Hall and the other women's colleges generally stayed away from the men. Also, Americans observed that the women students dressed in such bulky, heavy sweaters and skirts that one felt little attraction toward them anyway. There is no evidence of any scholar ever protesting against the ban on marriage. Those who did marry prior to the end of their three years accepted the fact that they would have to resign their scholarships.

If Americans found many Britons unreceptive to their new-world chumminess and enthusiasm, they could always count on the warm hospitality of Mr. and Mrs. Wylie. Afternoon teas with the Oxford

Secretary and his wife provided consolation for many a dispirited lad. When the first batch finished their work in 1907 and returned to their homes, Wylie began the practice of sending all former Rhodes Scholars cards and letters on their birthdays. This soon amounted to hundreds per year. He continued this practice long after he retired, until his death in 1952. He never lost touch with "his men."

The fact that most Rhodes Scholars enjoyed their Oxford experience was demonstrated clearly when most of Europe became engulfed in war in the summer of 1914. With the exception of the German scholars, the Americans and all the others rallied to the cause of Britain and its allies.

Like the Americans, the German scholars had never distinguished themselves academically in Oxford. What made the Germans unique was their selection process. They were chosen directly by the Kaiser, and nearly all of them came from the nobility or the political elite. Their aristocratic background shone through when the first five arrived in Oxford in the fall of 1903. Francis Wylie described how he first met some of them:

> I turned, to find myself facing three immaculate young Germans, complete with top hats, frock coats and patent-leather boots. They clicked their heels as one man, and bowed ... And there was I, straight from golf on the old links ... muddy and bedraggled ... I carried them off and gave them tea; and that was the last I saw of the top hats.[26]

Due to the requirements of universal military service in their country, most of the Germans were permitted to remain in Oxford for only two years. This meant that few of them could take degrees. Despite this handicap, they appear to have got along well socially.[27]

When war was declared most of the Germans in Oxford returned home. Several of them, along with Germans from earlier years, served with distinction in their country's army. It was perhaps a small mark of the success of Cecil Rhodes' plan that friendships with German scholars enabled Americans and others to avoid some of the excesses of wartime propaganda. Germany may have become the enemy, but Rhodes Scholars knew that Germans were not cannibalistic Huns. After obtaining parliamentary authorization to amend the will, the trustees abolished the German scholarships in 1916 and in their place allotted more awards for students from the British Empire.[28]

By early 1915 the student population of Oxford had dwindled from about 3,500 to 600. Besides the Rhodes Scholars, about the only men left were those unfit for military service. With the naive, gung-ho spirit that filled many bright young men in 1914, the Americans in Oxford were enthusiastic about this war to end all wars. Virtually every American there devoted his vacations to working for the Red Cross, the YMCA and other groups that provided ambulances, cared for the wounded, and distributed food. Some obtained leaves of absence from Oxford so that they could remain in France or Belgium. A handful of current and past Rhodes Scholars, impatient with their government's neutrality, joined the British Army. One of these, William Fleet, was killed in action in May 1918 while serving in the Grenadier Guards. Dozens more volunteered for the U.S. Army after the United States entered the war. Twelve American Rhodes Scholars died in the war, while doing relief work or serving in uniform. Nearly three hundred either joined the armed forces or held war-related jobs in Washington. In addition to the dozen Americans, fifty-eight Rhodes Scholars from elsewhere also died in the fighting.[29]

If the Americans, on the whole, valued their Oxford experience, the reaction of Oxford was decidedly more mixed. At one extreme there was an article that appeared in the *Oxford Magazine* late in 1904. It admitted that the Rhodes Scholars had not brought the revolutionary changes that many had feared. The article also expressed the hope that the Americans' impression of Oxford was as favorable as Oxford's view of them.[30]

Others in Oxford, however, shared the opinions of Max Beerbohm. His farcical 1911 novel *Zuleika Dobson* is an Oxford classic. It concerns the lovely Zuleika, who comes to Oxford to live with her grandfather, the head of the fictional Judas College. She is a *femme fatale* in the most literal sense. She breaks the hearts of so many young men that finally every male student in Oxford drowns himself in the Isis. At the end of the story she sets off to conquer Cambridge too. One of the secondary characters is an American Rhodes Scholar, one Abimelech V. Oover. He is so obtuse and earnest that he grates on everyone's nerves. When the snuff is passed around after dinner he enthusiastically outperforms all Englishmen in its use. One of his "friends" among the British students avers that "Americans have a perfect right to exist. But he did often find himself wishing Mr. Rhodes had not enabled them to exercise that right in Oxford."[31]

It would be most accurate, however, to state that a majority of dons and students showed little feeling about the newcomers one way or the other. To have showered attention on the Americans would have been a most un-Oxonian thing to do. For centuries the university had received visitors and students from among the most illustrious families in the world. The Rhodes Scholars were novelties, but, except for an occasional problem here or there, they were nothing to cause excitement.

Even if many in Oxford might wish to deny it, however, the Rhodes Scholars were already forcing the venerable institution to make adjustments. The university slowly realized that laboratories and faculty in the sciences and in law would have to be improved, because of the heavy demand in these areas by Americans. In addition, the desire by some Rhodes Scholars to obtain advanced degrees forced the university to give more structure and substance to its B.Litt. and B.Sc. programs. Additional changes would come in the years ahead.

NOTES

1. Frank Aydelotte, *The Oxford Stamp* (Freeport, NY, 1967; orig. ed. 1917), 22-40; Aydelotte, *American Rhodes Scholarships*, 73-74; Blanshard, *Aydelotte*, 130; *Alumni Magazine*, 3 (January 1910): 13-16; *TAO*, 2 (1915): 14; Ashby, "American Rhodes's Scholar," 183-84.
2. Robert Hale, "Oxford Again – A Rhodes Scholar Goes Back," *The Outlook*, 11 July 1923, 378; Aydelotte, *American Rhodes Scholarships*, 60; *Alumni Magazine*, 1 (December 1907): 15.
3. *NYT*, 2 October 1910, 12, and 16 October 1910, sec. 5, 9.
4. *TAO*, 1 (1914): 33, 21 (1934): 130.
5. *TAO*, 65 (1978): 112.
6. *TAO*, 1 (1914): 20-35.
7. *TAO*, 1 (1914): 25. Also see 81 (1994): 10.
8. *TAO*, 3 (1918): 107; 65 (1978): 113; *Register of Rhodes Scholars*, 4-12.
9. Aydelotte, *American Rhodes Scholarships*, 55.
10. *Alumni Magazine*, 1 (December 1907): 4.
11. *TAO* ,1 (1914): 11.
12. *NYT*, 12 March 1911, sec. 5, 5.
13. Parkin, *Rhodes Scholarships*, 228.
14. Aydelotte, *American Rhodes Scholarships*, 62; Parkin, *Rhodes Scholarships*, 159. One who did successfully combine reading and travel was John Crowe Ransom. See Young and Core, *Selected Letters*, 58.
15. *NYT*, 5 July 1907, 7; *TAO*, 57 (1970): 578.
16. Elton, *First Fifty Years*, 105-6.
17. *Alumni Magazine*, 1 (December 1907): 14-15.
18. Thomas Daniel Young, *Gentleman in a Dustcoat: A Biography of John Crowe Ransom* (Baton Rouge, 1976), 41.

19. *TAO*, 34 (1947): 214.

20. *TAO*, 58 (1971): 51.

21. *TAO,* 68 (1981): 159. Also see 65 (1978): 110.

22. *NYT,* 6 December 1906, 8.

23. Parkin, *Rhodes Scholarships,* 214-15.

24. At graduation ceremonies (called Encaenia) the university always awarded several honorary doctorates, and by 1900 about a dozen prominent Americans were among the hundreds who had received them. Oxford also granted doctoral degrees called D.Litt. (for any field in the humanities) and D.Sc. (for the natural sciences). These were slightly more substantial than honorary degrees, but far removed from the Ph.D.'s awarded in German and American universities. A D.Litt., for example, might be bestowed on a man who had received a B.A. at Oxford at least ten years earlier and who was now a don at one of the colleges. The D.Litt. would be a reward for especially noteworthy scholarly accomplishments. Most dons, however, had only a B.A. and the non-academic M.A.

25. For some discussion of Rhodes Scholars besides those of the United States, see Elton, *First Fifty Years,* and Carleton Kemp Allen, *Forty Years of the Rhodes Scholarships* (Oxford, 1944).

26. Elton, *First Fifty Years,* 78-79.

27. Elton, *First Fifty Years,* 109-10.

28. Harrison, *Twentieth Century,* 3-5.

29. *NYT,* 5 December 1914, 3; 13 December 1914, 4; 28 October 1915, 3; 24 December 1915, 2; 30 June 1918, sec. 3, 6; 3 November 1919, 8. Elton, *First Fifty Years,* 104-6, 220-21. *TAO,* 1 (1914): 92, 100; 2 (1915): 45-58, 138; 3 (1916): 35-36, 51-60, 116-18; 4 (1917): 52-53; 5 (1918): 96, 116; 7 (1920): 161.

30. Quoted in *TAO,* 21 (1934): 131.

31. *Zuleika Dobson: An Oxford Love Story* (London, 1991; orig. ed. 1911), 86.

→ Chapter 6 ←

PROGRAMMATIC CHANGES

What men get out of Oxford is like what they get from most other opportunities, pretty proportioned to what they put into it: the eye sees that it
has brought with it the power of seeing, and students learn mostly only
the answers to questions which they already have in their minds. More
than most universities is this true of Oxford. Here, it may truly be said, is
God's plenty in the way of educational opportunity; but here also the student is left in the utmost degree of freedom to take or to leave, according
to his choice. Good things are not forced upon him. He must have the
will to take, he must know what he wants, and he must be wise enough
not to try to seize too much.

Frank Aydelotte, American Rhodes Scholarships

Reforms

The War of 1914 marked a stunning turning point in world history.
It shattered the confidence that Europeans and Americans had in
their rationality and their moral and cultural superiority. The "White
Man" had shown that he could be just as savage as any other people
on the globe. A sense of disillusionment and anxiety replaced the
naive optimism of the *belle époque*, and colonial peoples around the
world began to speak of independence. By 1919 Europe could no
longer deny that the United States and Japan had achieved Great
Power status. The confusion of the war helped pave the way for
Lenin's victory in Russia in the fall of 1917. Moreover, the real or
imagined injustices of the Versailles Peace Settlement watered the
seeds of Fascism and Nazism.

Fittingly, the period from 1917 to 1920 also brought revolutionary
changes for Oxford and for Rhodes Scholars. In 1917 the university
voted to establish a full-fledged doctoral program for the D.Phil.
degree. This represented a huge step, for previously the university
had gloried in its undergraduate tutorial system. More than the

Notes for this chapter can be found on page 86.

establishment of the B.Litt. and B.Sc. degrees in the 1890s, the creation of the D.Phil. signaled Oxford's acknowledgment that a world-class university must promote research as well as teaching.

The change also resulted from the complaints of Rhodes Scholars and other Americans, who bemoaned the lack of a doctoral degree that would be meaningful for their careers back home. The approaching end of the war was a perfect time to bring an end to this criticism. Since 1914 virtually no Americans had crossed the Atlantic to study in German universities. To prevent them from going there after the return of peace, Oxford hurriedly established its D.Phil.[1]

Another major change came in 1920, with the granting of full and equal status to the five women's colleges. Henceforth, women received the same degrees as men. Of course, decisions made on paper did not automatically translate into actions and attitudes. The women's colleges were "poor sisters" in terms of their financial resources and esteem. Official equality also did not mean coeducation. Women and men still sat apart in the lecture halls. Only in the 1970s did some of the undergraduate men's and women's colleges start to admit members of the opposite gender.

For Rhodes Scholarships there were also innovations during this period. In 1918 the Rhodes Trust appointed Frank Aydelotte to serve as its secretary in the United States. By 1925 similar national secretaries were selected in all the British dominions and colonies. Henceforth, Aydelotte and the other secretaries would supervise the direction of the program in their respective constituencies. This included advertising, public relations, recruitment of applicants, supervision of the selection process, and advisement of new Rhodes Scholars.

Due to his devotion to the task plus the fact that more than half of all Rhodes Scholars were Americans, Aydelotte soon came to play a role almost as important as those of Parkin and Wylie in the administration of the program. On his own initiative, since 1914, Aydelotte had revived both the quarterly journal (renaming it *The American Oxonian*) and the alumni association. When he was appointed American Secretary in 1918 he was a professor of English at M.I.T. In 1921 he assumed the presidency of Swarthmore College. At that time he handed over the editorship of the magazine to another former scholar, Tucker Brooke (1904), but he remained American Secretary until 1952. For nearly four decades he was, in effect, "Mr. Rhodes Scholar" in the United States.[2]

One of the first things that he did as Secretary was institute a new method of selection. He was unhappy with the low number of applicants and the overall quality of those selected – though, of course, he himself had been among them. Starting in 1919 the selection committees that he appointed in each of the states consisted of former Rhodes Scholars. They replaced the college presidents and governors who had done the job since 1904. He thought former scholars would be better able to choose candidates who would enjoy the social experience and succeed academically. Also, former Rhodes Scholars would be more likely to promote the program and increase the number of applicants. To ensure that the program did not become too much like a closed society or cult, he always chose as committee chair a non-Rhodes Scholar. This was usually a prominent businessman, politician, or academic from each respective state. These changes soon produced desirable results, and national secretaries in Canada, Australia, and elsewhere soon adopted the same methods.[3]

Oxford itself was also responsible for the increase in applicants. The new D.Phil. could be used as a recruitment tool. Even more important, however, was the university's decision in 1919 to drop the qualifying examination required of all Rhodes Scholars. It had been the Greek section of the test that had scared away many potential candidates. Soon after Rhodes Scholars were freed from the "burden" of learning Greek, the university eliminated the requirement for all students.[4]

This abandonment of one of the main pillars of its classical tradition was due in part to pressure from Rhodes Scholars, but it had been an issue of debate for more than two decades. Oxford's decision was also a reaction to what Cambridge had done. That "other" university had ended its Greek requirement for all students a few months earlier, and Oxford feared looking antiquarian and losing students to its competitor. Many in Oxford resented being forced by Cambridge to make this concession to the twentieth century. Cambridge had been debating this question for nearly fifty years, and yet Oxford dons condemned the "indecently prompt action" of their rival.[5]

Yet another concession by Oxford to Rhodes Scholars was the granting of senior status. Normally freshers admitted to the colleges were considered junior members until they passed the preliminary examinations at the end of their first year. After that, usually for the next two years, they were considered seniors. Prior to the First World War, Oxford granted immediate senior status to a handful of American Rhodes Scholars – those from a select few of the most prestigious universities. The list of universities was enlarged to about 150 in 1919, and by 1922 virtually every scholar who came to Oxford with a bachelor's degree from any American university was granted senior status.[6]

This change was important both socially and academically. Socially, it meant that they escaped some of the snubbing to which freshers were subject. Academically, it meant that most scholars could now obtain a B.A. in two years instead of three. This would permit him to return sooner to the United States to enter a career or graduate school. Or, even more frequently, it permitted him to spend his third year in Oxford pursuing an advanced degree. Getting such a late start on an advanced degree meant that a scholar would complete his thesis after returning to the United States or that he would have to use his own financial resources for an additional year or two in Oxford.

This period also witnessed changes in the central administration of the program. Francis Wylie remained as Oxford Secretary until 1931, when he was succeeded by C.K. Allen. Allen had been Professor of Jurisprudence at University College and would hold his new post until 1952. Through the 1920s and 1930s the Secretary's powers and responsibilities grew. This was partly due to the retirement of George Parkin in 1920. By that time the program was firmly established, and thus there was no longer a need for an "Organizing Secretary." The Rhodes Trustees continued to maintain their headquarters in London. In 1919 they appointed one of themselves to the position of General Secretary. That person would supervise the management of the endowment funds and make decisions on broad policy issues.[7] Increasingly the Oxford Secretary handled daily affairs and corresponded with Aydelotte and the other national secretaries.

The end of the decade also witnessed some important developments. As noted above, the granting of senior status made it possible for many scholars to obtain a B.A., B.Sc., or B.Litt. – but not a D.Phil. – in two years. Nonetheless, many were dragging out their studies to three years. In many cases this was because they did not study hard enough in their first two. To encourage all scholars to work harder, Francis Wylie gradually made the scholarship into a two-year program.[8] One could apply for a third year only by demonstrating its necessity. In most cases the extension was granted. This was especially true for students who had completed a B.A. and wanted to go on for an additional degree, or for students pursuing a D.Phil. In the 1930s most scholars remained for a third year, but in later decades most chose to return home after the second.

An event of particular importance occurred in 1929. This was the gala opening of Rhodes House. About two hundred former scholars from around the world, half of them Americans, returned to Oxford to participate in the celebrations. They were joined by dignitaries like the Prince of Wales, Prime Minister Stanley Baldwin, and the Archbishop of Canterbury.[9]

Situated on South Parks Road, near the heart of the university area, this imposing edifice was designed by Herbert Baker, who had been Cecil Rhodes' friend and architect in South Africa. Aesthetically, the building was not universally admired. A quarter-century after it was built, the head of the trustees could find no warmer words of praise than "imposing Cotswold pile."[10] What it lacked in beauty, it made up for in size. It was designed to serve several functions. It became the residence of the Oxford Secretary. Up to then Francis Wylie had conducted all of his business from his home. Now he and his wife would have spacious living accommodations plus several rooms for storing all the records of the program. The Secretary now also had facilities for entertaining the current scholars. Each fall there would be a formal dinner for new scholars and each summer a grand affair for those about to go down. In addition, Rhodes House was a place where scholars could listen to guest lecturers. The building contained several impressive meeting rooms and halls, but what most impressed many visitors was the fact that the building possessed eight fully modern toilets. Part of the structure was set aside as a branch library of the Bodleian. Rhodes House Library quickly became the chief repository for most books relating to the United States and the British Commonwealth. Finally, Rhodes House was a gift to the city and the university as a whole. Many of its rooms were open to the public, and the university began to use it for various meetings and conferences. In keeping with the magnificence of his new surroundings, the Oxford Secretary now acquired a second title: Warden of Rhodes House.

One final change came in the 1920s. Despite the inclusion of former scholars on the selection committees and an increase in the applicant pool, the academic record of American Rhodes Scholars improved only marginally. Frank Aydelotte gradually came to discern what he believed to be the major flaw. It still lay in the selection process itself. Cecil Rhodes had wanted scholars to come from each state of the Union, thus guaranteeing the widest geographical distribution. This meant, however, that smallest states, in terms of population, produced just as many Rhodes Scholars as the largest states. Inevitably, the applicant pool in North Dakota, Nevada, and Idaho was much smaller than in states like New York, Pennsylvania, and California. In the 1920s there were still some instances of committees in the less populated states deciding that no candidate was worthy; thus some slots went unfilled. Worse than that, some committees, when faced with mediocre candidates, went ahead and made appointments anyway. Aydelotte reported that a few Oxford colleges had become upset with the caliber of these men and were threatening to reject all future scholars from those states.[11]

In the mid-1920s Aydelotte began to float an idea that George Parkin had first mentioned years earlier. He wanted to make sure that each appointment came from a sufficiently large applicant pool. In 1929 he finally proposed his idea to the Rhodes Trustees and to the Association of American Rhodes Scholars.[12] The result, approved by both organizations, was the district plan. This new scheme involved a departure from Rhodes' will, and thus required an Act of Parliament for authorization. Both Houses gave their assent.

Beginning in 1930, for what would be the class of 1931, the United States would be divided into eight regional districts. Each of these consisted of six states.[13] There were still some glaring differences in population between the districts. Nevertheless, even the regions in the western half of the country would now produce enough candidates to allow committees to choose men of the highest quality – or so it was hoped.

The new selection procedure was now split into two stages. An applicant first applied to his state committee. The latter selected two candidates who would progress to the district level. The district committee would then interview the twelve finalists – two from each state. After a day of interviewing, the committee would then inform four of the anxious twelve that they had been chosen. The eight districts thus combined to produce thirty-two scholars each year. All this took place within one week, usually in early December.

The district plan might seem justifiable and non-controversial to an outside observer. However, it met with howls of protest at the time and continues to meet some objections today. Though most former Rhodes Scholars who participated in the 1929 vote gave it their approval, there was a vocal core of opposition. Some argued that the novelty was objectionable because it violated Rhodes' will. Defenders of the reform, however, countered that it maintained Rhodes' desire for geographical distribution and bolstered Rhodes' aim of attracting the "best men." Other critics lambasted it because it was yet another slander against the quality of earlier appointees. Numerous scholars from the initial years were getting fed up with being told that they had not been good enough for Oxford.

Finally, some adversaries claimed that the new system would benefit larger states at the expense of smaller ones. There was some truth to this. Formerly, all states had been on an equal footing. In the district plan, however, the final committee could chose a total of four scholars from the six states represented. This meant that at least two states would not produce a scholar that year. Furthermore, if the committee chose two candidates from a single state this would eliminate yet another state.

The reform's proponents, on the other hand, pointed out that it could in some cases favor the less populous states. Two of the candidates chosen by a district might just as well be from Rhode Island or Arizona as from a demographically larger state like Florida or Ohio. The final decision would depend on the caliber of the twelve finalists each year. Indeed, as Aydelotte was able to demonstrate within a few years, the smaller states, proportionate to their population, did outperform the larger ones in producing winning candidates.[14]

Growing Popularity

The end of the war produced a veritable flood of American and other Rhodes Scholars into Oxford. The appointment of scholars had continued between 1914 and 1918, but few of them went to Oxford. Most scholars in the dominions and colonies entered the armed forces to fight for the British Empire. The situation of the Americans was different. Most of those who were already in Oxford in 1914 stayed there to finish their work. Some obtained exemptions from part of their degree requirements so that they could take their exams early and return home. Newly appointed Americans were advised not to go to Oxford, and most of them accepted that advice. Not knowing when the war would end, Parkin stopped all Americans from "coming up" in the fall of 1918.

The result was that by 1919 there were a couple of hundred American and other Rhodes Scholars who had been forced to leave Oxford early or who had never come at all. The trustees decided in 1919 to allow all of these "war" scholars to take up their scholarships if they wished, and several did so in 1919 or 1920. The German scholarships, however, remained abolished. Only in 1929 were they re-established. In 1920 one new scholarship was created – for Malta.[15] In addition, several extra Rhodes Scholars from all constituencies were appointed in the classes of 1919, 1920, and 1921.

Many of the scholars who had postponed coming up were in their mid- to late twenties by the time they reached Oxford. They were unusual in another respect too. Dozens of them had married during the war. After much soul-searching, the trustees decided to contravene Rhodes' will. These men were permitted to take up their scholarships and to bring their wives, and in numerous cases, their children, with them. Francis Wylie and his wife did their best to help these families find appropriate housing in the city. However, Wylie could never completely adjust to this novelty. He later wrote:

> It was a distracted life the married Rhodes Scholars lived, torn, as they were bound to be, between the rival claims of wife, Schools and College. They could satisfy any two of these; but not, to the full, all three. I remember meeting one of them wheeling a perambulator down one of Oxford's dreariest streets, his wife being busy with a second baby. He was a first-rate man, and did in fact get a First: but, beyond an occasional game of football, he could seldom escape from his student nursemaid existence. I felt glad that Mr. Rhodes could not see that pram.[16]

The rise in the number of applicants in the 1920s resulted partly from the changes mentioned above. The increase also reflected the favorable word-of-mouth advertising by the hundreds of former Rhodes Scholars who were now active in their careers. Nearly all Oxford veterans were reporting that the experience was enriching and broadening, if not always "fun." Dozens of these former scholars were teaching in public high schools or exclusive prep schools. By 1920 more than two hundred were professors at colleges and universities. These teachers were in a perfect position to encourage bright students to apply. Thus, from the 1920s to the present day, probably more than half of all Rhodes Scholars have taken courses from former scholars. Don Price (1932), for example, was inspired to apply because two of his English literature professors at Vanderbilt – John Crowe Ransom and Robert Penn Warren (1928) – had won the award.[17] Daniel Boorstin (1934) learned about the scholarships from one of his Yale professors, F.O. Matthiessen (1923).[18]

Whereas prior to the war the number of applicants had hovered around one hundred per year, in the 1920s it averaged about four hundred and in the 1930s approximately six hundred.[19] The popularity of the scholarships is also indicated in two other ways. Already in this period there were several cases of the awards being won by sons or younger brothers of former scholars. Obviously the new winners would not have applied if they had not heard favorable reports from their family members. Some examples include the three Morley brothers already cited, Clayton and Byron White (1935 and 1938), Don and Karl Price (1932 and 1937), and Matthew Brown (1908), father of Gerald Brown (1938). There were at least a half-dozen other similar cases prior to the Second World War. In most instances the sons and younger brothers even entered the same colleges as their predecessors, such as the Morleys at New College and the Whites at Hertford.

The popularity of the scholarships is also revealed by the fact that many college sophomores and juniors sought advice on how to prepare themselves so that by the time they were seniors they met the criteria for winning. Though no statistics are available, it is also evident that dozens of applicants who failed to win on their first try applied again a year later. They spent the intervening year in graduate school or in jobs, often working on projects that would impress the selection committees. Several of these applicants did win on their second or even their third tries.[20]

What did the scholars of the interwar period discover once they arrived in Oxford? That will be the topic of the next two chapters.

NOTES

1. Harrison, *Twentieth Century*, 6, 15; Aydelotte, *American Rhodes Scholarships*, 57. Oxford, and nowadays a handful of other British universities, uses the term "D.Phil." instead of "Ph.D." Not to be outdone by its adversary, Cambridge established a Ph.D. program in 1920.
2. Items by and about Aydelotte in *TAO* are too numerous to list. For his obituary see 44 (1957): 49-62. Blanshard, *Aydelotte*, is thorough and valuable, though too partial toward its subject.
3. *TAO*, 6 (1919): 128-29; Aydelotte, *American Rhodes Scholarships*, 27-29, 38.
4. Harrison, *Twentieth Century*, 29,37; *TAO*, 6 (1919): 38, 43, 49, 129.
5. *TAO*, 6 (1919): 51.
6. Elton, *First Fifty Years*, 112-13; *TAO*, 8 (1921): 102-6.
7. Between 1919 and 1925 several persons served as General Secretary. From 1925 to 1939 Philip Kerr (later Lord Lothian) held the post. He was succeeded by Lord Elton (1939-1959). Since 1959 the position of General Secretary has been held by the Oxford Secretary.
8. Elton, *First Fifty Years*, 23; *TAO*, 16 (1929): 120-21; 19 (1932): 164-65.
9. *TAO*, 16 (1929): 1-3, 163-91.
10. Elton, *First Fifty Years*, 26.
11. Aydelotte, *American Rhodes Scholarships*, 30.
12. In 1928 the word "alumni" was dropped from the association and the organization acquired a constitution and board of directors. See *TAO*, 15 (1928): 79-96, 179, 243.
13. Applicants from Washington, DC, had already for several years been placed with those from Maryland.

14. Aydelotte, *American Rhodes Scholarships*, 31-37; *TAO*, 15 (1928): 64-65; 16 (1929): 143- 48; 17 (1930): 52-53, 63, 69-97; 25 (1938): 87-89, 157-62.
15. At first Malta produced one scholar every three years. After 1942 it was one per year.
16. Elton, *First Fifty Years*, 108. Also see *TAO*, 6 (1919): 123-25; 7 (1920): 152-54.
17. Don K. Price, "A Yank at Oxford: Specializing for Breadth," *American Scholar, 55* (1986): 195.
18. Boorstin interview, 9 June 1994.
19. *TAO*, 10 (1923): 7-8; 11 (1924): 56; 18 (1931): 1-3; 22 (1935): 138.
20. *TAO*, 21 (1934): 187-92; 50 (1963): 135; Laurence A. Crosby and Frank Aydelotte, eds., *Oxford of Today: A Manual for Prospective Rhodes Scholars* (New York, 1922).

Chapter 7

INTERWAR YEARS

Society and Study

If only those gates would open.
If only those gates would yawn.
Down the Turl I would be lopin'
Before you even knew that I was gone.
But they're not, so what's the use?
I've got those claustrophobia blues.

If only this town had a woman
Who would sell herself at reasonable rates.
If only Oxford were human,
I could get my mind off those gates.
But she's not – a screw is loose.
I've got those claustrophobia blues.

Those walls are creepin' up upon me.
They're gettin' closer every day.
I can't see the stars for the bolts and the bars,
Oh-de, oh-de, oh-de-ay!

If only this damn monastery
Would burn to the ground or such!
If only the porter had a fairly decent daughter
Who'd be susceptible to the touch.
But he hasn't, I've hidden the booze.
I've got those claustrophobia blues.
Claustrophobia blues!

"Claustrophobia Blues," song by
Walt Whitman Rostow and Gordon Craig

Déjà Vu

The Rhodes Scholar experience of the 1920s and 1930s retained many similarities and yet was remarkably different from that of the earlier years. Like their predecessors, most of the Americans of this generation too were from small towns and had traveled little previously.

Notes for this chapter can be found on page 110.

J. William Fulbright (1925) later admitted that going from Fayet-teville, Arkansas, to Oxford was a "tremendous shock," like Alice in Wonderland.[1] At the University of Arkansas he had been an avid golfer and a star on the tennis and football teams. In later life he admitted that his Rhodes Scholarship owed more to his athletic prowess and to the campaigning of his mother with members of the selection committee than to his academic record.[2] Initially he was embarrassed by his intellectual inadequacy. He found his essays "hard as the dickens to write" and he felt like a "bonehead."[3] But he loved the friendly atmosphere at Pembroke College. He had the good fortune to study history under a brilliant young Scotsman named Ronald Buchanan McCallum; Fulbright happily reported to his fam-ily that his tutor had "not yet acquired the academic air."[4] Within a few weeks he settled into a comfortable routine of tea, rugby, lacrosse, conversation, reading, and cultural outings. He spent most vacations roaming through France, Germany, Austria, Poland, and the Balkans. He was elected president of the Teasel Club and the Johnson Literary Society. He made many close friendships, though occasionally he was taken aback by the British tendency to belittle Americans as "a bunch of rich damn fools."[5] Decades later he recalled that in Oxford he had "a hell of a good time."[6] By the time he returned to Arkansas he had become a pipe-smoking, tweedy intellectual.

Dean Rusk's introduction to Britain was equally dramatic. He was born in Cherokee County, Georgia, in 1909. His father had been a Presbyterian preacher until a voice ailment had forced him to give that up. The elder Rusk then became a farmer, a schoolteacher, and finally a mail carrier. Dean was the fourth of five children. The doc-tor who delivered him was a veterinarian, and as a small boy Dean wore underwear made out of flour sacks. Once his sixth-grade teacher sent him home because he had come to school barefoot. Defiantly his mother sent him back to school the following day – still without shoes. His grit and native intelligence made him a star high school student. He worked his way through Davidson College and won election to Phi Beta Kappa. All through college he planned to apply for a Rhodes Scholarship, for he knew that it might be the only way for a boy from a poor family to do graduate work. In order to meet the athletic part of the criteria, he taught himself basketball and made the Davidson team.[7]

Before he reached New York City in 1931 to board a ship for Britain, the farthest he had ever been from Georgia was North Car-olina. As the Cunard liner pulled out of the harbor a deck steward offered him a ham sandwich. Rusk took one bite, tasted the English mustard, and threw it over the side. "This rube from Georgia had a great deal to learn," he wrote many years later in his memoirs.[8] During the next several days at sea an Englishwoman made him the center of attention. Learning that he was from Georgia, she asked, "Oh, isn't that the place where you butcher your Negroes?" Trying to maintain his poise and offer witty repartee, he answered, "Oh, yes. And we consider them rare delicacies."[9]

Upon arrival in London he was taken aback by some of the *risqué* signs and advertisements. One large billboard displayed a stork with its beak pointed skyward. The message below it declared: "GUINNESS'S STOUT KEEPS YOUR PECKER UP!" (Actually, what Rusk interpreted as a smutty double entendre was an innocent British colloquialism, meaning "keep your chin up.") He noticed on urinal stalls, in Greek letters, the warning, "Players with short bats should stand close to the wicket." Even before he reached Oxford he could see that Britain "was a far cry from Georgia Presbyterianism."[10]

Despite these inauspicious beginnings, Rusk soon adapted to life at St. John's College. He grew a bushy red beard during a trip to the Lake District and wrote home that Oxford life was the most pleasant he had ever experienced.

Rusk made many friends although he did not share the prejudices or lifestyles of the upper-class British students who still predominated there. He was appalled by their continuing belief in the right and duty of the Anglo-Saxon race to rule the world. On a more mundane level, he found that "bath and toilet arrangements … were far too primitive for a society that had launched the Industrial Revolution." He judged British food to be "tastelessly prepared," but he acknowledged that "most Englishmen would be appalled to eat what passes for home cooking in Georgia." Yet he admired British courage and the average Oxford student's sense of obligation to enter a career in public service.[11]

He managed to discipline himself so that he studied an adequate amount and also had time for everything else:

> Academics at Oxford were leavened by another of Oxford's quaint, incongruous traditions. While we were expected to learn and do well on our final exams, we were not to be unduly bookish. During vacations – and almost half of the Oxford year was taken up by vacations – we would cram our suitcases full of books and bone up on our studies. The trick at Oxford was to arrange your affairs so as to have time to enjoy the "Oxford life": bull sessions with students; debates and sports; dropping in on professors' homes on Sundays. We even played a fair amount of bridge although not much poker, which was regarded as an American frontier game …

Oxford's relaxed pace was a welcome change. Working my way through Boys High and Davidson, I had always had to run from one commitment to another. At Oxford I first experienced some of the leisure that goes with learning. The Rhodes scholarship paid my bills, although just barely. But no one worked his way through Oxford; this just wasn't done.[12]

The ubiquitous presence of alcohol was perhaps even more important to the Americans of this period than it had been earlier, due to the passage of the eighteenth amendment to the Constitution. Throughout the pages of *The American Oxonian* in these decades former Rhodes Scholars repeatedly decried Prohibition. The open availability of beer and stronger drinks in Oxford was immensely good news for all but a handful of arriving scholars. Even a boy from the Bible Belt like Dean Rusk fell under its sway:

There was lots of drinking, and despite my Presbyterian heritage, I got caught up in it. Soon after my arrival, at a party for one of my English classmates, I was handed a glass of sherry. I had never so much as touched a drop of alcohol, excepting those times when my father administered his medicinal drops of corn whiskey. I sat there staring at that glass for a long time, finally lifted it, took a sip ... and fell from grace.[13]

Two other Americans have left an extraordinary portrait of themselves and the Oxford of that period through the songs they wrote and sang for anyone who would listen. Walt Whitman Rostow and Gordon Craig (both Balliol, 1936) composed numerous ditties, including the one that heads this chapter. Both enjoyed Oxford, but like students of any place and age, they also found fault with their surroundings. They were irked especially by the closure of the college gates at night and by the absence of women in their colleges. With clever lyrics and syncopated rhythms they entertained fellow students in their rooms at night. Rostow played the piano and Craig sang. Their song "Sherry Party Girl" bemoaned a charming female who would drink one's booze and accept a date to the theater (only in the most expensive seats), but whose love life never went beyond the platonic. Some of their other songs had titles like "Let me go, Mr. Warden, let me go," "Drink Her Down," "What the Hell Goes On?", and "How'm I Doin', Oxford? Not So Well." "Drink Her Down" goes in part as follows:

Oh wine's a mocker and strong drink
Will drive you to the fiery brink.
Yet I think these Oxford days
Are best seen through a vinous haze.

...
A drink for sailor man is rum,
It always makes my kidneys numb.
Hits me right beneath the crotch –
I guess I'd better stick to scotch.
Now cognac is a kind of brandy.
It looks and smells and tastes just dandy.
When I drink this ghastly brew
My breath turns blue. So do you.[14]

While in graduate school at Yale after leaving Oxford, Rostow continued to regale classmates with these songs.[15] Forty years later the two friends reunited in a recording session to preserve their creations for posterity. Their mature renderings can be heard on cassette at the Lyndon Baines Johnson Library in Austin.

Rhodes Scholars of this period still had some difficulty adjusting to British mannerisms and cuisine, and some Britons still looked askance at the rather noisy intruders. Generally, however, there was a less rough edge to these encounters than previously had been true. Hedley Donovan (1934) later recalled fondly the occasional forthright compliment, "But you don't *seem* like an American."[16] John Monk Saunders (1918) found the cultural differences a source of both humor and profit. In the 1920s Saunders became one of the most prolific and popular screenwriters in Hollywood and married one of its most glamorous stars, *King Kong*'s Fay Wray. His *Wings*, starring Clara Bow, Richard Arlen and Gary Cooper, was one of the last great silent films; it was voted best picture of 1927 in the first year of the new Academy Awards. Other credits included *Dawn Patrol* and *Nikki*. In 1938 MGM produced his *A Yank at Oxford*, which starred Robert Taylor, Lionel Barrymore, Maureen O'Sullivan, Edmund Gwenn, and Vivien Leigh. This film plays up the stereotypes of both nationalities. Taylor is an athletic, cocky American who wins a scholarship to effete, stuffy Oxford. His boorish manners and ignorance of Latin make him the butt of several jokes. But his prowess as a runner and oarsman wins over all of Oxford. By the end of the story the young American and Oxford have come to love one another. Saunders avoided using the term "Rhodes Scholar" in the script, but the London *Times* and other British and American papers rightly assumed that the movie was a parody of the scholars and their adventures in Oxford. (Most film critics agreed that this clash of cultures lost much of its light-hearted buoyancy when the movie was remade in 1984 as *Oxford Blues*.)

Oxford adhered to time-honored traditions in these years, but there were signs that dons and students were winking at the rules more than previously. One example of this concerns the closure of the college gates at night. Don Price (1932) had a tutor who explained to him that "Americans just don't understand." It was perfectly all right to climb over the walls after midnight; you just had to avoid getting caught.[17]

Some scouts, however, did not want to bend college traditions. When John Fischer (1933) was seen scaling the Lincoln walls late one night his scout ratted on him. Fischer was fined £20, which badly depleted his resources. Paradoxically, all turned out for the good. In desperate need of cash, he wrote an article on the British Labour Party and sent it to *Harper's*. The magazine not only paid him for it, but later offered him a job. Eventually he became the editor-in-chief.[18]

Though Americans skirted some rules, in other ways they appeared almost more British than the British. One can see this in their response to economic and social changes in Oxford. In the 1920s Oxford was transformed into an industrial town. In part this was due to William Morris, who in 1934 became Lord Nuffield. Working in his bicycle repair shop on Longwall Street (now a part of New College), he began to design automobiles in the early years of the century. By the 1920s his factory in Cowley, on the outskirts of Oxford, was among the first in the world to mass produce cheap cars. Morris vehicles provided jobs for thousands of the local citizens and also helped to clog the streets and foul the air. Added to this was a huge surge in tourists, especially in the summer. To meet the needs of the tourists and the factory workers, low-cost chain stores began to replace some of the more fashionable shops along the High, Cornmarket, and other major streets.

In short, Oxford was witnessing the same transformations as other cities in Europe and the United States. It is interesting to note that some of the people in Oxford who were most vocal in opposing this modernization were the American Rhodes Scholars. They wanted to preserve Oxford's antique charm, except for the primitive plumbing. Their litany of complaints was unending. The "petrolizing" of the city created motorists who drove much too fast, regarding no traffic rules. The rumble of lorries was loosening the stones in medieval buildings. Automobiles were now allowed to park in the scenic Broad Street. Most of all, the Rhodes Scholars hated the crass, noisy tourists who were discharged from buses each day and wandered around disrupting the beauty of the sacred quads. The irony in this is heightened by the fact that most of these visitors were Americans. Rhodes Scholars, who once were feared as the alien invaders, now themselves were girding up to protect "their" Oxford.[19]

Vacations

One feature of the Rhodes Scholar experience that remained virtually unchanged was travel. Most scholars were journeying through the continent for nearly half of any given year. They were not always like Dean Rusk in packing their luggage full of books so they would not fall behind in their reading. One who did, though, was Daniel Boorstin (1934). He got a First in law and a year later a First in B.C.L. Yet he spent most vacations abroad, especially in Florence. He crammed for his exams while living in a room overlooking the Ponte Vecchio. When taking breaks from studying he roamed through the Uffizi or practiced his Italian. (Decades later he would spend a year as a visiting professor at the University of Rome, and thanks to his Rhodes Scholarship would be able to deliver his lectures in Italian.)[20]

Frank Aydelotte and others continued to warn against the dangers of too much globetrotting.[21] Nevertheless, if this wanderlust prevented many from obtaining Firsts in their B.A. exams or from completing theses for research degrees, it fulfilled Cecil Rhodes' hopes for producing future leaders who had a deep appreciation for cultures and countries besides their own.

Again, Dean Rusk provides a good example of just how rough this learning experience could be for small-town American boys. In his first Easter vacation he scurried to Paris and holed up in a decrepit hotel on the Left Bank. One day as he walked around the Place de la Concorde a sleazy little fellow approached him and asked, "Do you want to buy some French postcards?" Thinking that he would obtain some of the raunchy materials that were so hard to find at home, he paid the 10 francs that the man demanded. The stranger then looked around furtively to make sure no policeman was near, pulled out a small packet, and gave it to Rusk. When the latter arrived back at his room and opened his treasure he found that they were indeed French postcards. They contained pictures of the Arc de Triomphe, the Eiffel Tower, and the Louvre![22]

Rusk was far from alone in his gullibility. Another of the songs by Rostow and Craig, "P-A-R-I-S, Paree" declares:

Oh, New York, London, and Berlin
Are good at taking yokels in.
But these towns give a rube a chance,
Which can't be said of the jewel of France.
For Paris is a sucker town
Of more than medium renown.
And from dull care she will be free
As long as there are fools like me.

....
The girls along the gay Mon-marter
Are skilled in all the arts of barter.
They lie in wait on Montparnasse
To separate fools from their brass.[23]

Don Price explained the importance of his travels this way:

During my first sixteen-week summer, 1933, I wandered through a half-dozen countries across Europe, and the total living and travel cost amounted to twenty-one dollars a week, a necessarily economical standard made possible by third-class rail travel and living in the cheapest pensions.

This kind of travel opened up the metropolitan culture of Europe to a young American who had never heard a symphony orchestra except on phonograph records and who had never spent any time in a major art museum. I had never been in New York, or for that matter seen the Atlantic Ocean, until I traveled to take up my Oxford scholarship ... . During the spring holiday before our final Honours School examinations ... I went with my tutor and his wife and a fellow student for a stay in the old abbey of Pontigny, France, which had been converted into a center for the study of French history. That history came to seem more real to me when immersed in the architecture and rural society of Burgundy.[24]

Even more than was true of their predecessors, the Rhodes Scholars of the interwar period became internationalists. They might not enjoy every experience in Britain and elsewhere, but they came to realize that if the United States was going to be a world power it could not be isolationist. Those of the 1930s saw first-hand that the Great Depression was a global phenomenon. The vast majority of Americans in Oxford returned home fervent supporters of the League of Nations.

Sports

The Rhodes Scholar record in sports was basically a continuation of earlier years, though there was also a gradual shift in a new direction. The number who played on one or more of their college teams in Oxford remained at 70 or 80 percent, with the number obtaining a blue or half-blue around 25 percent.[25] These figures were about the same as those for British students. Tennis and swimming now joined rowing and track as the areas in which Americans did best. When Dean Rusk was at St. John's, for example, five out of the top six tennis players were Americans.[26]

The two most famous American athletes in Oxford during this period were Eddie Eagan (1922) and Byron White (1938). Eagan was a boxer. In 1920 he won the light heavyweight gold medal in the Antwerp Olympics, and in 1924 in Paris he again represented the United States. In between, he was a boxing champion in Oxford. He helped to change the nature of the sport at the college level. Previously it had been gentlemanly fisticuffs, but he made it into hardhitting mayhem as he systematically devastated his Cambridge opponents. His exploits made him an Oxford hero. His fellow student, the Marquess of Clydesdale (later the Duke of Hamilton), became one of his best friends. In 1926 and 1927 the Marquess and Eagan would tour the world taking on all comers wherever matches could be arranged.

In Oxford Eagan managed to obtain a Second in law, and he went on to a distinguished career as an attorney in New York. He was one of the few Rhodes Scholars who maintained a direct involvement in sports throughout his entire career. In 1932 he became one of the few persons ever to win an Olympic gold medal in a sport entirely different from his previous one, when he was a member of the U.S. champion bobsledding team. In later decades he headed the New York State Athletic Commission and served on the U.S. Olympic Committee. In the 1950s Dwight Eisenhower appointed him chair of the sports committee of the People to People Program.[27]

Byron White's athletic feats took place in the United States rather than in Britain. He was one of the greatest football running backs in the first half of this century. At the University of Colorado he led the nation's college players in rushing and scoring and acquired the nickname "Whizzer" (which he never liked). In 1938 he was drafted by the Pittsburgh Pirates (who later became the Steelers). By that time he had already been notified of his appointment to a Rhodes Scholarship. Frank Aydelotte and C.K. Allen agreed to let him have both worlds. He was permitted to play the entire football season in the fall of that year. His salary of $15,800 was the highest ever paid to a professional football player up to that time. He proved his worth, leading the league in rushing, with 567 yards in eleven games.[28]

At the completion of the season, in December 1938, he sailed for Britain, in time for the spring term. His American football heroics would do him little good in Oxford. Furthermore, the coming of war in 1939 cut short any opportunity he might have had to establish a record in British sports.

There were a few other remarkable athletes. John Monk Saunders swam against Cambridge and represented the United States in the

1920 Olympics.[29] William Stevenson (1922) ran track at the 1924 Olympics.[30] George Pfann (1926) was an All-American quarterback at Cornell. Frederick Hovde (1929) revolutionized the sport of rugby during the match against Cambridge in 1931, when his team used a new system of code words when passing the ball.[31] The trend after the First World War, however, was to downplay athletic prowess as a criterion for winning the scholarship. Aydelotte and the Rhodes Trustees wanted to bury the stereotype of the Rhodes Scholar as someone whose chief claim to fame was hitting or kicking a ball around a field.[32]

Even more than the pioneer scholars, those of the 1920s and 1930s soon adopted Oxford's more relaxed approach. Writing to his mother after his first game of "rugger," Bill Fulbright reported that "the English take it easy and it doesn't seem to make a great deal of difference whether they win or not."[33] Dean Rusk "horsed around" with cricket and rugby before he made the university's lacrosse squad – though he had never played the game previously. Rusk discovered that the only training rule for the team was that at lunch before a game the players were supposed to limit themselves to one pint of beer.[34] Don Price found that the training regimen for the Merton rowing crew during Eights Week consisted of breakfast each morning of "beefsteak and strong ale – no lager beer nonsense." If the crew was successful in bumping another boat, the bump supper at the end of the week would be especially rambunctious. He recalls that on the night of one of these suppers the head porter had to warn people coming into the college, "Be careful as you go through the quadrangle, sir; the young gentlemen are throwing bottles, sir."[35]

However, even these amateur(ish) athletic contests were too rigorous for some Americans. The closest that Frank Verhoek (1933) came to sports for example, was singing in the Bach Choir.[36]

Though by and large Americans did not dominate Oxford sports in this period, there was one brief protest lodged against them by British students and dons. This occurred in the fall of 1928 and resembled what had happened in 1914. After receiving complaints against the older and larger Americans, the university barred from varsity competition anyone over the age of twenty-three. Within a year, however, this action was revoked. The ostensible reason was that Cambridge continued to allow older students to participate in varsity matches. Oxford realized it was suicidal to remove older students from its squads if the Cantabs would not do the same.[37]

It also seems that the rule was revoked because saner heads came to realize that Americans generally did not dominate. Moreover, the rule against students over twenty-three discriminated against numerous British and foreign students who were not Rhodes Scholars. Even with the aid of Rhodes Scholars, Oxford's overall record against Cambridge was disappointing through the interwar period. Loud, anguished cries filled Oxford, for example, in 1936, when the Cambridge rowing crew won the annual contest for the thirteenth year in a row.[38]

In short, the 1928 controversy was an atypical blip in an otherwise harmonious relationship between Rhodes Scholars and their fellow students.

Academics

What can be said of the academic record of Rhodes Scholars in the period between the two world wars? The figures for the 1920s showed only modest improvement in the B.A. examination results. Still only about 15 percent taking undergraduate degrees were awarded a First. Significant improvement, however, came in the number of students who failed their exams, obtained a Third or Fourth, or left Oxford prior to the end of their scholarship. In fact the number of students who fell into these latter categories dropped to only one or two per year. This improvement at the bottom of the ladder can be attributed to the better selection process in place after 1919 and an increase in the number of applicants. The granting of immediate senior status also promoted better performance.

The biggest change came in the 1930s, after the adoption of the district plan of selection. The more elaborate application procedures, including several letters of recommendation, an essay, and interviews at the state and district levels, ensured that there were fewer "klinkers" among the thirty-two chosen each year. In addition to Dean Rusk, another member of the first batch selected under the new system, late in 1930, was Carl Albert. His later career in government made him more famous than the average Rhodes Scholar, but he typified the higher caliber of men being chosen.

The diminutive Albert had been born in Bug Tussle, Oklahoma. His first-grade teacher said he was the best student she had had in her fourteen years of teaching. He remained at the top of his class through high school and university. He was named valedictorian of his senior class at McAlester High School, and after he won a national oratorical contest he received a three-month trip to Europe. In the summer after graduation from high school he toured

Britain. (including Oxford) and the continent. He was one of the few Rhodes Scholars to travel so widely prior to winning the scholarship. At the University of Oklahoma he made Phi Beta Kappa, was elected president of the student council, won another national oratorical contest, and was chosen outstanding male student. The university's president called him "the most brilliant student ever to attend this university."[39]

In the 1930s, the number of B.A. students obtaining Firsts rose to 21 percent, while those obtaining Seconds amounted to nearly 60 percent. Those with Firsts included the future Librarian of Congress Daniel Boorstin, future Supreme Court Justice John Marshall Harlan (1920), and future classical scholar Richmond Lattimore (1929). The more numerous Seconds included future Senator J. William Fulbright, future Secretary of State Dean Rusk, future investment counselor John Templeton (1934), future literary critic Cleanth Brooks, future editor-in-chief of *Time* Hedley Donovan, and future Purdue University President Frederick Hovde. Among the roughly 10 percent who got Thirds were William Vaughn (1925), later Chairman of Eastman Kodak; Charles "Tick" Bonesteel (1929), later U.S. military commander in Korea; Paul Engle (1933), later Head of the Writers' Workshop at the University of Iowa; and Philip M. Kaiser (1936), later Ambassador to Senegal, Mauritania, Hungary, and Austria. Future Speaker of the U.S. House of Representatives Carl Albert managed a Second in his Jurisprudence B.A. and then declined to a Third in the B.C.L.[40]

In a trend set prior to the war, the Americans usually scored below the New Zealand and Australian scholars, but above Canadians, South Africans, Jamaicans, and others. Likewise, except for 1932, the American record did not match that of British open scholars. Aydelotte resigned himself to accepting that this was "as good as there is any right to expect." For a program that did not seek mere bookworms, these results "seem to be as good as we have the right to look for or are likely to achieve."[41] C.K. Allen admitted that few scholars met the highest standards, but at least the number who were gravely undisciplined or indolent was "microscopically small."[42]

On behalf of the Americans, one must recognize that the same problems and distractions mentioned in Chapter Five continued to hamper academic achievements. It should also be noted that the number of Americans taking research degrees rose from around 13 percent to about 30 percent in the 1930s. The fact that an increasing number of scholars felt confident enough to embark on B.Sc., B.Litt., or D.Phil. degrees spoke well for the program as a whole. Moreover, if these students had instead taken B.A. degrees, the percentage of Americans getting Firsts undoubtedly would have been higher.[43]

The pages of *The American Oxonian* and sundry books and articles written by the scholars of the interwar period indicate decisively that a higher number of scholars were happy in their studies than their predecessors had been. For every student who despised his tutor, there were two or more who found their supervisors brilliant, helpful, and sociable. In the mid-1930s one don, Dr. Arthur Compton, invited all American Rhodes Scholars each year to a Thanksgiving Day tea at his home. Each American guest was given a lapel pin showing the flag of his state. The assembled group played ping pong and other American games, ate "magnificent" pumpkin pies, and sang American ballads and spirituals "with gusto."[44]

Two of the more famous legends regarding Rhodes Scholars in their tutorials occurred, if they occurred at all, sometime between the wars. In one story, a student who had failed to write a paper for his weekly session borrowed one from another American. When reading it to his tutor, he quoted "Bophocles." "You mean Sophocles," interjected the don. After glancing at his paper again, the student confidently replied, "It says Bophocles, sir." The second concerns a scholar who read his paper to a tutor who appeared to be napping. After the student finished, the tutor still had his eyes closed. So the student read it again. Still the don's eyes remained closed. Unable to stop his game, the student then read it a third time before quietly exiting the room. Some three decades later the student returned to Oxford and sought out his now white-haired former tutor. The American stated his name and asked if the don remembered him. The old tutor nodded and grumbled, "Yes. You're the damned fool who insisted on reading me the same essay three times." Even if these stories are part fiction, they give the flavor of what must have happened on scores of occasions.

The ten or twelve Americans each year who pursued research degrees were aided by several concessions granted by the university. The requirements for obtaining a B.Sc. or B.Litt. were made less rigorous. These degrees became more like the M.A. degree in American universities. Eventually these degrees gained the reputation of being consolation prizes for students who could not complete a D.Phil. Moreover, Rhodes Scholars as well as British students working for a D.Phil. received a boost in the 1930s by the university's willingness to waive the requirement that all work be completed within three years. This meant that an American could return home after three years, continue to work on his thesis, and then return to

Oxford a year or two later for an oral defense before an examining committee. In this way Rhodes Scholars and others who commenced on doctoral work would have some assurance that they would have a degree to show for their years of study.

In addition to the D.Phil. there was a new B.A. degree that was established in 1920 partly in response to the needs of American Rhodes Scholars. This was the interdisciplinary Honours School (i.e., "major") in Politics, Philosophy, and Economics, which soon came to be called PPE. It was designed for those students who aimed for careers in public service but who did not have a sufficient command of Greek for Literae Humaniores. PPE quickly also became known as "Modern Greats." Within just a couple of years PPE rivaled law, modern history, and British literature as one of the top choices not only of Rhodes Scholars but of Oxford students as a whole.

Oxford also made improvements in its science facilities between the wars. In the 1920s the university constructed new laboratories, and in the 1930s and early 1940s Lord Nuffield donated considerable sums for additional buildings, for a science library, and for the endowment of professorships in medical research. Nevertheless, Oxford still lagged behind the top American universities in most areas of physics, chemistry, and biology. The caliber of its faculty usually far exceeded the quality of the facilities in which they worked. In 1936 one American scholar wrote of "the gradual emergence of Oxford's physical equipment from its medieval limitations."[45]

There were, however, striking exceptions to this relative backwardness. Frank Verhoek applied for a scholarship to study chemistry in Oxford even though he had already obtained a Ph.D. in that field at the University of Wisconsin. He wanted to work under Cyril Hinshelwood at Trinity College. (Hinshelwood later was knighted, and in 1956 he shared the Nobel Prize for chemistry.) Verhoek successfully obtained his D.Phil. within two years and then, with permission from the Rhodes Trustees, spent his third year studying at the University of Copenhagen. He enjoyed his relationship with Hinshelwood and other Oxford scientists. He also found the laboratory facilities on a par with those in the States. Verhoek recalls, however, that the laboratory he worked in, located at the back of Trinity, had recently been converted from service as the college latrine. Its heating system was effective but unconventional. The rooms were kept toasty by lighting a Bunsen burner at the end of a four-inch sewer pipe that zigzagged through the building.[46]

Despite curriculum reforms and upgrading of facilities, one senses that many in Oxford were dragged kicking and screaming into the twentieth century. When Don Price expressed the intention of reading PPE, the head tutor at Merton persuaded him to switch to modern history instead; Oxford, said the tutor, had been offering PPE for less than a quarter of a century and still did not know how to teach it well.[47] When Howard K. Smith arrived at Merton in 1937 a don asked if he would like to study modern history. "No," replied the student, "I'd prefer the sixteenth century." Sighing with amusement, the tutor replied, "The sixteenth century? But, my dear fellow, that is modern history."[48] Americans found their college libraries too small for their needs. The Bodleian, which was the central university library, was huge but intimidating and outmoded. It was one of Britain's copyright depositories, which meant that it received one copy of each book and periodical published in the country. Its holdings of materials printed outside Britain, however, were sadly deficient. Moreover, it still did not have a central card catalog. The methods employed for finding books on a particular topic were so cumbersome as to defeat all but the most hardy. It was big news in 1930 when electric lights were installed in the reading rooms and the library announced that it would stay open until 7:00 p.m. each night during terms.[49] An American visitor in 1934 reported the following:

> One who visits the Bodleian during the winter will find the students huddled in overcoats, their feet wrapped in rugs, their breaths rising in little clouds of fog, their faces pinched and their noses a pale blue from the cold, their fingers almost too numb to clutch a pencil.[50]

Opportunities for the study of American history, the social sciences, and business were still meager or non-existent. In 1922 *The New Republic* lamented British insularity and rejoiced at Oxford's newly endowed Harmsworth Professor of American History. This was the first professorship of American history established at any British university.[51] When John Templeton arrived in Oxford in 1934, for example, he discovered that "there were no courses on business, no professors and no books," and so he read law.[52] At least in the social sciences this situation would soon change. In 1937 Lord Nuffield donated funds for the creation of Nuffield College. This college would be revolutionary in several respects. It would concentrate primarily on the "new" fields of sociology, political science, and psychology. It would be the first Oxford college composed exclusively of graduate students. It would also be the first to admit both men and women. Finally, the college's charter committed it to working to bridge the gulf between the academic and non-academic worlds.[53]

One American who might have been expected to regret wasting his time in Oxford was John King Fairbank (1929). As a senior at Harvard he had made the decision to study the language and history of China, about which he knew almost nothing. Though his academic record had been outstanding, he almost blew his chance for admission to any of the Oxford colleges. Francis Wylie later told a friend that in his application letter to Balliol Fairbank made himself sound like "a combination of Hercules and Jesus Christ."[54] In Fairbank's memoirs, the chapter on Oxford starts off on an unpromising note:

> When I arrived at Balliol College, Oxford, in the fall of 1929, I was no closer to China than I had been in Cambridge, Massachusetts. Indeed, Oxford was not at all the place to begin Chinese studies. It offered no instruction in Chinese language or history. I spent the next couple of years approaching China obliquely in a flanking attack.[55]

What Fairbank makes clear, however, is that Oxford was not unusual in that regard. Neither Harvard nor any other American university offered much, if anything, in the way of Chinese studies at that time. Indeed, it would be Fairbank, in his long career in Harvard's Department of History, who would do more than anyone else to establish that field in the United States.

Regarding Oxford, Fairbank admitted that being there turned out to be a "blessing in disguise." He could view China as the British Empire had done through the nineteenth century. Furthermore, Oxford was more cosmopolitan than Harvard. Most of the globe seemed represented there. He regretted the primitive organization of the Bodleian, but he admired the tradition of hard work and social concern that permeated Balliol. He quickly changed from PPE to do a B.Litt., and eventually he also obtained a D.Phil. Given the lack of structure in the research degrees, he was almost entirely on his own in doing his thesis. His B.Litt. supervisor, "a kindly oldster," was a retired missionary who knew Chinese and was completing a dictionary of Chinese Buddhist terms. His supervisor put him in touch with others in England who had studied in or written about China. With their advice and with books, he taught himself the language. He worked so intensely at it that he suffered from nervous exhaustion and insomnia.[56]

Fairbank quickly made friends with British students, some of whom read *The New Yorker* and quoted Damon Runyon. He learned that British reticence was to be admired: "Spilling the beans to a chance acquaintance, in the frontier fashion that presumably helped build America, seemed repugnant as either boasting or betraying secrets. To disclose too much to a friend was in a way to invade his privacy by destroying your own, like suddenly undressing. What one friend can expect from another, in short, is to be left alone."[57] Most of all, he reported, Balliol was "an interlude of aesthetic enjoyment." He and his friends listened to and argued about classical music, and they took long walks in the perpetual cold mist.

As he was intensely goal-oriented, Fairbank did not suffer from the distractions that affected some of his fellow Americans. If anything, he went to the other extreme. During vacations, instead of seeing as much of Europe as possible, he holed himself up in the Public Record Office in London. There he perused the archives of the British Customs Service in China through the nineteenth century. Even when he did permit himself a few days in Paris or Vienna, he spent most of his time writing his B.Litt. thesis.

Upon completion of that degree, Fairbank applied to the Rhodes Trustees for permission to spend the third year of his scholarship outside Oxford – something that few scholars had been allowed to do up to then. The British consular records that he needed to consult for his D.Phil. were still deposited in various Chinese ports. Given his proven track record, the trustees quickly approved his plan. Off he sailed.[58]

Most Americans, however, were not so single-minded in their drive for academic distinction. As noted earlier, most of them quickly came to realize that their Oxford degrees and their ranking in the examinations would mean little in the United States. Those intending to be attorneys or physicians would, at most, be allowed to skip their first year of law or medical school – as recognition for the two or three they had spent in Oxford. Except for the two or three Americans per year who successfully completed a D.Phil., most who hoped for careers in academe would return to American graduate schools for their Ph.D.s.

Hedley Donovan loved his Oxford experience and later freely acknowledged that the experience left him "incorrigibly Anglophile."[59] He admired his "two first-rate history tutors" at Hertford, but he spent far more time in marathon parties and in continental travels than in libraries.[60] Decades later his children would not believe him when he told them the lectures were optional and he studied only one hour per day.[61] "Basically," Donovan wistfully remembers, "I was being paid to have a good time."[62]

Don Price found his tutorials to be stimulating, and he valued the training in writing and thinking that his weekly essays gave him. But he did not have a passion to excel: "The same Honors Schools examinations that were such a competitive strain on my British friends meant very little to me or my future career, except as a subject to study for its relation to [my future career in] governmental affairs."[63]

Daniel Boorstin has explained yet another reason for the lack of a first-rate effort by many Americans in Oxford. He calls the educational system there one of "intellectual vagrancy," but he means this as a compliment.[64] In Oxford one is encouraged to have a rich, variegated life. Spending hours browsing in Blackwell's, taking a long stroll along the Cherwell or the Isis, playing around on the sports fields for an hour or so, and then taking afternoon tea prior to socializing in a friend's room or going to a concert – this was an ideal afternoon and evening. Most American Rhodes Scholars had been top students at home, and it was a shock to experience the more relaxed style of Oxford. No one there seemed to burn the midnight oil studying – at least not until the time shortly before final examinations.

Yet, as Boorstin explains, what many Americans failed to realize was just how hard many of the British students actually did work. The ideal attitude in Oxford was that of "effortless superiority." One took things in stride and did not let on that one might be worried or anxious. Boorstin explains that this outward pose of nonchalance hid the fact that there was actually a lot more studying going on than the Americans realized. Add to this the fact that a typical British student did most of his reading during vacations. Boorstin says that when an ambitious Oxford student wanted to study in his room late into the night he would close his curtains, so his lights could not be seen. He wanted others to assume that he was asleep or out on the town. Zealous American students back in the States, however, were consumed by work and felt guilty when not doing it. Thus an American student might slip away to the movies but leave his lights on – so that others would assume he was hard at work.[65]

Another example of this facade of effortless superiority concerns J.R.R. Tolkien. The world knows him as the author of *The Hobbit* and *The Lord of the Rings*, but from 1925 to 1945 he was Professor of Anglo-Saxon and from 1945 to 1959 Professor of English Literature at Oxford. Most afternoons he could be seen in his garden at 3:00 p.m., where he gave the appearance of reading novels in leisurely fashion – thereby trying to hide the fact that he was a prodigious, serious scholar.[66]

Robert Penn Warren was also fairly typical in what the academic experience meant for him. Prior to Oxford he was obviously an intelligent young man on the fast track to success. Born in Guthrie, Kentucky, the young "Red" Warren was so gifted and hardworking that he skipped several years in school. At age fifteen he won a scholarship to Vanderbilt, but he had to delay going there for a year because university regulations called for a minimum age of sixteen. He graduated summa cum laude, majoring in English literature. One of his professors there was former scholar John Crowe Ransom. Warren then won a scholarship to graduate school at Berkeley, where he received his M.A. He failed in his first attempt at a Rhodes Scholarship and thereupon transferred from Berkeley to Yale. Before he got very far on his Ph.D. work at Yale he applied once again for a Rhodes Scholarship, and this time he won.[67]

By the time that he arrived at New College in the fall of 1928, Warren was well on the way to a solid career as a poet and critic. It would have been difficult for him to pursue American literature in Oxford, and so he did a thesis on the Elizabethan period for his B.Litt. In large part, however, Oxford seems to have been a sort of way station for him. Warren liked his "moral tutor," but barely got along with his B.Litt. supervisor. The latter was the enormously productive and erudite Percy Simpson, a fellow at Oriel College. In his first meeting with the don, Warren was treated to a cool lecture about how Australian and American students never did well at Oxford.

That encounter set the tone for Warren's relationship with the academic side of Oxford. Over the next two years Warren rarely visited the Poetry Society or any other formal lectures. Instead, he reported, "I just soaked myself" in sixteenth and seventeenth-century poetry.[68] He continued to write his own poetry and to work on a biography of the American abolitionist John Brown, while doing a thesis on the early seventeenth-century dramatist John Marston.

During his first year Warren lived with five other students in a house owned by New College. From their drafty upstairs bedrooms they could see both light and snow coming down the chimney. His reactions to the climate and the social environment echoed those of many of his fellow scholars. New College had "the temperature of an ice house." He found British women "generally ugly and uninviting" and concluded that British men fathered sons only out of patriotic obligation. He once summed up his mixed emotions this way: "There is some good company, tobacco (pretty bad), drink, books, and dulness. Great dulness [sic]. Rain. There is something like a narcotic effect about the whole dump, which is rather pleasant in its total effect."[69]

In the spring of 1929 Warren landed in a heap of trouble with New College authorities. He had been caught with an unchaperoned woman (or, as he called her, a "daughter of Britain") in his rooms, and he had returned to college late at night more than once. Such behavior had got the young Warren into trouble previously at his American universities. Now he was on the verge of being fined heavily or being sent down. If the latter occurred, Warren vowed to "give them something to send me down for before I leave."[70] Evidently Rhodes House and New College proved forgiving, for Warren was permitted to stay at the university – provided that he moved from college rooms into digs in town.

Despite all his ambivalent feelings about Oxford, Warren mixed well with British students. They did not seem to mind that he won substantial sums of money from them in poker – which he had obligingly taught them how to play. In his second year he gave many parties at his digs. Cleanth Brooks (1929) later recalled one of the last such gatherings hosted by Warren. Warren's landlord had agreed to prepare a meal for the guests. Warren asked that the menu start with dry martinis and an oyster cocktail. When the landlord triumphantly ushered in the menu's first course, the students stared at a huge bowl into which gin, vermouth, and "a huddle of raw oysters" had been mixed together. This bizarre concoction apparently did nothing to dampen the youthful revelry.[71]

In a letter written late in 1929 to a close friend, the American poet Allen Tate, Warren offers a vivid glimpse of his rambunctious lifestyle:

> I have been to five cocktail parties, two theatre parties, four dinners, one shooting party, five poker games, and to church since my return to Oxford; furthermore, I have written an astonishing amount of J.B. [i.e., John Brown], read half a dozen novels, three books on America, *The Demon of the Absolute*, Zola's *Therese Raquin*, and the comic section of the New York *American* … Also, the poker has given me a very pleasant profit of about five pounds, which helps me over an excessively lean term."[72]

When not working or socializing in Oxford, Warren was visiting London or seeing the sights around Oxford. Several times during his two years at Oxford he traveled to Paris, where he saw his friend Allen Tate and met celebrities like F. Scott Fitzgerald, Ezra Pound, Ford Madox Ford, and Ernest Hemingway.

Further complicating Warren's relationship with Oxford was the fact that in the summer of 1929 he got married. His spouse was Emma Cinina Brescia, an aspiring writer whom Warren had met in San Francisco in 1926. Warren knew that marriage meant the end of his Rhodes Scholarship, unless he kept the marriage a secret. This he intended to do. Only by returning to Oxford to complete his B.Litt. could he hope to obtain a position in an English Department at an

American university. The only people who knew of the wedding were the bride's family.[73] Not until Warren had his Oxford degree safely in hand in 1930 did he reveal the nuptial news to his friends. Indeed, the young couple created the fiction that they only then got married – after Warren's final return from Britain. During the remaining six decades of Warren's life he never summoned the courage to inform the Rhodes authorities of the deception. In the 1981 *Register of Rhodes Scholars* the wedding date was still listed incorrectly as 1930.

The New College report on Warren at the end of his first year declared him "widely read" and "respected by a small circle." In his second year the college reported him "retiring and shy." (Evidently, Warren's move to digs helped to conceal his lively goings-on from college authorities.) Francis Wylie wrote the following in the Rhodes House file on Warren: "He is not exactly the kind of ideal Rhodes Scholar of whom we sometimes think [but] I think that we may be glad in the future to claim Warren as an old Rhodes Scholar for he is certainly a man of ability and character." Like the New College officials, the Warden seems to have been ignorant of Warren's nocturnal adventures, for he noted that Warren did not mix well with other students.[74]

What did the Oxford experience mean for Warren's career? In the latter decades of his long life he granted numerous long interviews. Whenever he was asked about the early influences on his ideas and career, he stressed the impact of growing up in the South. He spoke of Kentucky, Tennessee, the legacies of the Civil War, Southern Methodism, and his friendships with professors and students at Vanderbilt and Louisiana State University. Never did he discuss Oxford.[75] (Nor did he discuss his brief stints at Berkeley and Yale.) In none of the fiction or nonfiction works that he published did he ever write of Oxford.

Oxford did grant him a B.Litt. degree. That, plus his M.A. from Berkeley, sufficed to allow him a career in academe – he never obtained a D.Phil. or Ph.D. There is no evidence, however, that his studies in Oxford had any direct impact on his style or ideas. As with many other Rhodes Scholars, the experience of living abroad for the first time in his life enabled Warren to understand more clearly the characteristic features of the United States.

Using the great freedom that he was afforded in Oxford, Warren did just enough work to complete his degree. He spent most of his time in his room writing about topics that were distinctly American. He composed poems and contributed reviews to *The New Republic*.

In Oxford he completed two novels (neither of them ever published) and his first two major prose publications: his biography of John Brown and a short story entitled "Prime Leaf." The latter concerns a tobacco farmer whose misguided effort to help his family leads instead to financial ruin and the murder of his son.[76]

As far as can be determined, Warren wrote about Oxford only once in his life – outside of the dozens of private letters that he sent to relatives and friends while studying there. Buried in the Warren papers in the Beinecke Rare Book and Manuscript Library at Yale University is an unpublished poem composed sometime between 1928 and 1930. It is entitled "Oxford City Wall." Warren was intimately familiar with the medieval wall that snaked its way through the quads and gardens of New College. The first of the poem's three stanzas rhapsodizes:

> More than to God or to the heart's last prayer
> They trusted in the stone; stone after stone,
> Parapet and port and bastion,
> They raised their wall against the timeless air.
> Three bowmen here might crouch within the deep
> Embrasures and let fly the grey goose-feather;
> In turrets all night long the sentinel
> Kept watch and called the hours, though God might
> sleep.
> Northward and stark against the autumn weather,
> Under the sad vine strung along the wall,
> Still bastion and parapet abide
> While to the stone's wind-sheltered side
> Gently the garden blooms into the fall.[77]

Why did Warren never seek to publish the poem? Perhaps because it was a youthful endeavor not up to his best efforts. After we discovered the poem we gave it to several English professors and college English majors and asked them to evaluate it – without telling them who the author was. Their unanimous verdict was that it was a decent job, with some evocative images, but not a great work. Perhaps, however, Warren chose not to publish it because it simply was not "him." The future author of *All the King's Men* and scores of other stories and poems about farmers, corrupt politicians, and other American archetypes might have felt that such a topic was a bit too rarefied for his tastes and skills.

The chief value of the Rhodes Scholarship for Warren was that it gave him time to read, reflect, and write. He enjoyed the experience, but it did not change his life in any dramatic way. Over the next sixty years of his life Warren would respond only sporadically to the yearly entreaties by his class secretary for a couple of sentences about himself for the class notes section of *The American Oxonian.* During his long career he visited and lectured in London on several occasions, but not until 1983 did he return to Oxford. He went back that year to receive an honorary degree from the university on the occasion of a general reunion of all Rhodes Scholars.

In short, the academic experience in Oxford was not central to the intellectual interests or the career goals of Warren or most other Rhodes Scholars. Hence it is remarkable that the great majority managed to do a creditable, if not spectacular, job.

NOTES

1. *People*, 11 July 1983, 61.
2. Randall Bennett Woods, *Fulbright: A Biography* (New York, 1995), 19-20.
3. Ibid., 24-25.
4. Ibid., 24.
5. Ibid., 31.
6. Rock Brower, "The Roots of the Arkansas Questioner," *Life*, 13 May 1966, 98.
7. *NYT*, 22 December 1994, D18; Dean Rusk, as told to Richard Rusk, *As I Saw It* (New York, 1990), 33-63; *TAO*, 79 (1992): 134-35.
8. Rusk, *As I Saw It*, 64.
9. Ibid., 65.
10. Ibid., 65.
11. Ibid., 79-80.
12. Ibid., 67-68.
13. Ibid., 71.
14. Reprinted with permission of Walt Whitman Rostow and Gordon Craig. Cassette recordings of all their songs are deposited in the Walt Whitman Rostow Collection, Lyndon Baines Johnson Library, Austin, Texas.
15. *TAO*, 26 (1939): 362.
16. *TAO*, 61 (1974): 222.
17. Price, "A Yank," 196.
18. *TAO*, 61 (1974): 22.
19. *TAO*, 9 (1922): 123; 11 (1924): 50; 13 (1926): 1-2; 16 (1929): 9; 17 (1930): 180; 22 (1935): 100; 23 (1936): 126, 235-36.
20. Boorstin interview, 9 June 1994.
21. *TAO*, 16 (1929): 199-200; Elton, *First Fifty Years*, 150; Aydelotte, *American Rhodes Scholarships*, 62-63.
22. Rusk, *As I Saw It*, 68.

23. Reprinted with permission of Rostow and Craig.
24. Price, "A Yank," 206.
25. *TAO,* 8 (1921): 25; 11 (1924): 26; 33 (1945): 126.
26. Rusk, *As I Saw It,* 70.
27. *TAO,* 53 (1968): 91-93.
28. *NYT,* 20 March 1993, 9.
29. *TAO,* 27 (1940): 210.
30. *TAO* 11 (1924): 181.
31. Lord Elton, "An Englishman's Audit of Rhodes Scholars," *Harper's,* May 1964, 99.
32. *TAO,* 7 (1920): 173; Elton, *First Fifty Years,* 21.
33. Woods, *Fulbright,* 25.
34. Rusk, *As I Saw It,* 70.
35. Price, "A Yank," 197.
36. Verhoek interview, 26 November 1993.
37. *TAO,* 15 (1928): 60-61; 16 (1929): 9; 18 (1931): 28.
38. *TAO,* 23 (1936): 133.
39. *TAO,* 60 (1973): 193-94; Albert interview, 30 March 1994.
40. At Oxford and all other British universities, examination results for each student are a matter of public record. For Rhodes Scholars one can consult the *Register of Rhodes Scholars.*
41. Aydelotte, *American Rhodes Scholarships,* 54, 55.
42. Elton, *First Fifty Years,* 142.
43. Aydelotte, *American Rhodes Scholarships,* 54-60, 132.
44. *TAO,* 22 (1935): 17.
45. *TAO,* 23 (1936): 25. Also see Crosby and Aydelotte, *Oxford of Today,* 136-37; and *TAO,* 22 (1935): 24; 31 (1944): 89-94.
46. Verhoek interview, 26 November 1993.
47. Price, "A Yank," 202.
48. Smith interview, 5 April 1994.
49. Price, "A Yank," 200; *TAO,* 15 (1928): 102;17 (1930): 3.
50. Kenneth Roberts, "An American Looks at Oxford," *Saturday Evening Post,* 16 June 1934, 66.
51. "American History at Oxford," *The New Republic,* 30 August 1922, 7-8.
52. Peter Fuhrman, "Reluctantly, Oxford Enters the Twentieth Century," *Forbes,* 14 December 1987, 128.
53. Harrison, *Twentieth Century,* 647-48; *TAO* 25 (1938): 19-21.
54. John K. Fairbank, *Chinabound: A Fifty-Year Memoir* (New York, 1982), 20.
55. Ibid., 19.
56. Ibid., 22-23.
57. Ibid., 25.
58. Ibid., 30-31.
59. Donovan, *Right Places, Right Times: Forty Years in Journalism not Counting My Paper Route* (New York, 1989), 61.
60. Ibid., 64.
61. *People,* 11 July 1983, 61; Donovan, *Right Places,* 66.
62. Donovan, *Right Places,* 48.
63. Price, "A Yank," 199.
64. Boorstin interview, 9 June 1994.
65. Boorstin interview, 9 June 1994.
66. David Howlett interview, 12 August 1993.

67. Joseph Blotner, *Robert Penn Warren A Biography* (New York, 1997), 69, 75.

68. Ibid., 89.

69. Ibid., 87.

70. Ibid., 92.

71. *TAO*, 78 (1991): 14.

72. Blotner, *Robert Penn Warren*, 91.

73. Ibid., 97.

74. Ibid., 92, 99.

75. Some examples of the "absence" of Oxford in Warren's life and writings: Walter B. Edgar, ed., *A Southern Renascence Man: Views of Robert Penn Warren* (Baton Rouge, 1984), 95-110; James A. Grimshaw, Jr., *Robert Penn Warren: A Descriptive Bibliography, 1922-1929* (Charlottesville, 1981); Lewis P. Simpson, ed., *The Possibilities of Order: Cleanth Brooks and His Work* (Baton Rouge, 1976), 1-124.

76. John L. Stewart, *The Burden of Time: The Fugitives and Agrarians* (Princeton, 1965): 449; Leonard Casper, *Robert Penn Warren: The Dark and Bloody Ground* (Seattle, 1960), 40; Thomas W. Cutrer, *Parnassus on the Mississippi: The "Southern Review" and the Baton Rouge Literary Community* (Baton Rouge, 1984), 28, 36, 140, 143.

77. Reprinted with permission of the Yale Collection of American Literature, Beinecke Rare Book and Manuscript Library, Yale University.

Chapter 8

INTERWAR YEARS

Fighting the World's Fight

The 1910 R.S. from Wyoming and Exeter, who shall be nameless, "has certain capabilities which would do honor to our noble class; I dare not mention facts for fear of the revenue officers, but will merely say that he is a very efficient chemist."

Esper Fitz, *The American Oxonian*

Shorty Harrold says that it is amazing to him how all of his classmates can manage in the short period of a year to fill up an entire paragraph with personal news. He can't. The same old thing in the same old way – Coca Cola, Atlanta, golf, bridge, badminton, with a little reading. Mix that with a nice home, and that's Shorty. He just hopes Mr. Hitler lets him remain the same.

Boardman Bosworth, *The American Oxonian*

Domestic Issues

Cecil Rhodes wanted his scholarships to go to the best men for the world's fight – whatever that meant. In later chapters we will analyze in more detail the careers of Rhodes Scholars. Here we will discuss their attitudes about matters of public concern in the 1920s and 1930s. To what extent were former and current scholars speaking out on topics of national or international importance?

Their chief organ was *The American Oxonian.* If Rhodes could have read its issues from the interwar period he would have found some things pleasing, and some not. He would have been happy to see that the scholarship program was solidly established. He would have liked that most scholars were mixing in well with their fellow students and their tutors while achieving a respectable academic record. He would have found evidence that numerous American scholars were playing leading roles in their professions and, in general, making their marks.

Notes for this chapter can be found on page 133.

But he might very well have been troubled by other information. From 1914 to the present day, the quarterly magazine has generally printed seven types of items: 1) Class notes, giving snippets of news about the members of each class, starting with 1904. Each class had one member designated as class secretary. It was his job once a year to round up something about his classmates. 2) A letter from Oxford. This was written by a current Rhodes Scholar, relating current events at the university. 3) Reviews of books. These were of two sorts: books written about Oxford or Britain and books on any topic written by Rhodes Scholars. 4) "Business" announcements, such as lists of newly appointed scholars and reports of meetings by the Association of American Rhodes Scholars. 5) A directory of all living Rhodes Scholars, providing addresses and occupations. There was also a list of non-Rhodes Scholar Americans who had studied in Oxford. In the early years this directory took up part of one issue per year. By the 1920s it filled an entire issue. 6) Articles written on Oxford, on the careers of Rhodes Scholars, or on general issues relating to the United States or the world. 7) Obituaries of Rhodes Scholars, usually written by fellow scholars.

If one's only source of information was this magazine, one might very well conclude that most of these "best men for the world's fight" were little more than happy-go-lucky Bertie Woosters or substantial bourgeois citizens straight from Sinclair Lewis' Main Street. Some issues contained one puff piece after another. The obituaries made most scholars seem an amazing combination of brilliant/visionary/humanitarian hero and down-to-earth, fun-loving, regular guy. The letters from Oxford devoted most space to Oxford sports, parties, and social events. At least once each year there was a multi-page summary of the bump races, complete with a full-page chart showing the performances of all the boats.

The class notes included in most issues could strike the reader as either entertaining or boring, depending on one's point of view. In the vast majority of cases each former scholar did either of two things: make a wry, satirical wisecrack about himself or the state of the world; or give a humdrum account of his expanding waist, his receding hairline, his narrow escape from matrimony, the newest birth in the family, his election to the local Rotary Club, his success as an insurance salesman or automobile dealer, the perilous condition of his golf game, or the itinerary of his most recent family vacation. In 1921 William Crittenden (of pistol-packing notoriety in 1904) does not seem to have changed much:

I suppose you want to know what I have accomplished since leaving Oxford. Briefly, these are the facts: A wife; a couple of thousand dead ducks; two blue-eyed baby girls; a few prizes at trap shoots; now and then a fee [he was an attorney]; several limits of deer; a really good stenographer; some exceptionally large steel-head trout; a few friends; many trips into the hills; some enemies; a broken knuckle; and, of recent date (this by far the most distinguished honor that I have had conferred upon me for many years) the unanimous election as president of the "Rummy Duck Club.[1]

The tone and content of most of these reports remained constant over the years: one scholar says he is "keenly interested in the commercial success of a popular song dealing with the economic and agricultural significance of a shortage of bananas"; another is "looking for an heiress with matrimonial aspirations"; another is occupied with "college tennis, private golf, dance orchestras, pub-crawls, and bridge"; one who is still in Oxford "pursuing pulchritude" plans for a career "missioneering" at "Fou Fou, near Woo Woo, Chu Chin China"; another notes that "the address is still the same, family the same, viz.: one wife (also the same) and two children; bank account the same, to speak optimistically"; another admits that he has "no wife, no children, no new job, no trips abroad, no publications ... There is, however, one positive achievement – I have borne and bred and buttered a mustache"; finally, another reveals that he has become a "city slicker" and is proud to work for "the largest printing ink concern in the world."[2]

More serious topics take up only a small portion of each issue. Prohibition, for instance, appears only in the sardonic comments in the class notes: former scholars miss the beer of Oxford, they move to regions of the country where it is easier to get a drink, or they imbibe B.V.D. style (Before Volstead Done it).[3]

Through the 1930s the magazine published only two articles that dealt specifically with the Great Depression.[4] In 1933 the magazine also gave a one-paragraph summary of a speech given by a former scholar, whose recommendations for ending the crisis included cutting government spending (i.e., abolishing the New Deal) and forcing all the urban unemployed to move to the countryside to work in agriculture.[5] At a general Rhodes Scholar reunion at Swarthmore College in 1933 the agenda did, however, feature a symposium on international cures for the Depression.

Otherwise, the only references to the economic crisis came in the class notes. There classmates traded witticisms about FDR's programs (regarding which they were about evenly divided).[6] If the scholars did mention the Depression, they simply referred to how they themselves were faring. Some reported belt tightening, and a handful lost their jobs.[7]

Most, however, managed to get by tolerably well. In 1930 George Carter (1923) seems oblivious to the situation around him: "Enjoying life tremendously; live on a ten-mile lake and within a stone's throw of a ripping golf course where I play at least four times a week; have a small stone house in the English manner. What more could one ask of life?"[8] Hard times forced William Crittenden temporarily to give up his law practice in 1932, but he and his family managed to eke out a living on their 2,500 acre ranch.[9] In 1936 Alfred James (1907) regrets that he cannot make a summer trip to Europe. The problem is not that he is unemployed but rather that he will be teaching summer courses at the University of Pittsburgh. James is not happy to live in a chaotic age, but he keeps steady with his work, contract bridge, and golf.[10]

In other words, through their magazine Rhodes Scholars as a group did not reveal any extraordinary concern or demonstrate any joint effort to remedy the problem. In 1936 Edwin Fitch (1923) upbraided his brethren for their apparent complacency:

> What's the matter with the tribe? We're all really pretty young yet, and it's too soon to lay aside the radicalism of youth for curving waist lines and stock-and-bond respectability.[11]

For dozens of young men the Rhodes Scholarships were a vehicle by which they could escape the Depression. The prospect of having a secure, princely stipend (then set at £400 per year) instead of low wages or unemployment was a tempting prize. This was the case, for example, with John Fischer, Howard K. Smith, and Don Price. Each of them had graduated from college and begun work as a newspaper reporter. Their salaries were barely enough to live on, and so simple economics was a significant part of why they applied.[12]

To be fair, one must acknowledge evidence that many Rhodes Scholars were involved in the "world's fight" in a variety of ways. In their class notes they occasionally strike a serious tone about the Depression, the League of Nations, the government, and other significant issues. Some were quick to respond to Fitch that scores of his fellow scholars were federal civil servants working on sundry New Deal programs.[13]

Nonetheless, it is surprising that this group of bright men, who ostensibly were interested in serving the general good, would publish such a "light" magazine. The magazine's reviews of works by Rhodes Scholars were so glowing that one former scholar asked if any of them had ever written a bad book. Crane Brinton (1919) served as editor of the magazine from 1936 to 1943. He had obtained a D.Phil. in Oxford and by 1936 was a respected Harvard historian and author of several books on France and England. He was determined to make *The American Oxonian* into a serious journal of opinion rather than just a bulletin board announcing new babies and books. He aimed at something along the lines of *The American Scholar*, published by Phi Beta Kappa.

Brinton's gradual introduction of more substance into the journal encountered vitriolic opposition from the many who wanted to keep it a fluffy, gossipy alumni newsletter. In 1938, for example, Brinton himself wrote a review of *Kennebec: Cradle of Americans* by the poet Robert P. T. Coffin (1916). The latter bristled at the critical tone and retorted:

> Dear Sir:
> I recently renewed my subscription to the *AMERICAN OXONIAN*. After reading your review of my *Kennebec* in the April number, I have decided that I do not care to continue my association with the magazine ... while you are in charge of its editorial destinies. I shall be grateful, therefore, if you will return to me the price of my renewal ... and I shall count it as a favor if you will trouble yourself no further with reviewing my books.
> ... I have more than once observed the spleen and deliberate misrepresentation and bad manners exhibited in some of the recent reviews ... I feel I myself have been the victim of spleen, bad manners, and deliberate misrepresentation.[14]

Brinton responded sarcastically and determined to forge ahead with more provocative and meaty articles and reviews. Many supported him. Thomas Mosley (1908) applauded the attempt to bring robustness to a "lukewarm" publication: "Its pages have been a placid pool reflecting the after-glow of one perfect idyll; around it we gather only for purposes of mutual admiration and polite retrospect."[15] But the forces of tradition and "chumminess" won out. Although in succeeding years several reviews were more than mere puff pieces, and occasionally an article offered pithy and detailed comments on important issues, these were exceptions in an otherwise tame publication.

The years following Brinton's editorship witnessed only modest headway in giving more weight to the publication. In 1964 the *Oxonian*'s editor, Carleton Chapman (1936), published a general index covering the first fifty years of publication. On the first page he admitted that he had some doubts about the significance of the magazine. He acknowledged that many scholars read only the notes for their class and no other pages. He also conceded that most issues went straight into wastebaskets.[16]

Another important question on which Rhodes Scholars took little action was that of race. The scholars of the 1920s and 1930s were, for the most part, little different from those who had shunned Alain Locke several years earlier. Indeed, Locke could have been the prototype of Ralph Ellison's "invisible man" as far as Rhodes Scholars were concerned. *The American Oxonian* mentioned him only twice in these years: the first, a brief reference to his traveling to Africa to conduct a study of League of Nations activities there; the second, a list of scholars who belonged to the League of American writers.[17] By the 1920s, however, Locke was a noted philosopher at Howard University and one of the champions of the Harlem Renaissance. He had written several books on philosophy and black culture. Yet *The American Oxonian* never reviewed any of them, and the class notes never mentioned him. It is easy to see why Locke never contributed any messages to the notes, given his treatment at the hands of his classmates. But numerous other Rhodes Scholars also never bothered to respond to the yearly entreaties, and yet their class secretaries found nice things to say about them. Edwin Hubble, for example, rarely, if ever, contributed information about himself. Despite this, every year the magazine discussed him in the class notes, reviewed his books, or mentioned the various awards he received. In short, Locke continued to be snubbed.

Locke's neglect typified the attitude of most scholars regarding non-whites in general. One has to look hard to find the issue of race discussed anywhere in the magazine or in any of the other writings of Rhodes Scholars. A few times the class notes mention that a handful of former scholars opposed local chapters of the Ku Klux Klan. In the 1930s attorney Clayton Burwell (1932) became a champion of Negro rights before the courts of North Carolina.[18] In 1936 James Saxon Childers (1921) published *A Novel about a White Man and a Black Man in the Deep South.* One of the protagonists is a college-educated black man who returns to the South and composes classical music. He suffers numerous insults and vicious threats, and a political boss falsely charges him with arson. This novel may not have been great literature, but its sympathetic portrayal of a black man made it remarkable for that era.

Several members of two overlapping groups of writers, the Fugitives and the Southern Agrarians, were often criticized in the 1930s and 1940s for racism in their novels and essays. The Fugitives, originally known as the Nashville Fugitives because of their association with Vanderbilt University, included Rhodes Scholars Robert Penn Warren and John Crowe Ransom as well as non-Rhodes Scholars like Allen Tate and Donald Davidson. Rhodes Scholar Cleanth Brooks was also closely associated with the movement, as were many other southern writers and scholars. The main focus of the Fugitives and the Agrarians was not race relations, but the longing for a time past when capitalist greed, urbanization, and industrialization were not dominant American traits.

Some early reviewers complained that the blacks in Warren's stories were always called "niggers" and relegated to Stepin Fetchit roles. That was true, but somewhat unfair to Warren. He claimed that he was simply portraying the South as it was at the time. He did not share the extreme racial attitudes espoused by many of his white characters. Admittedly, he could have striven to create some strong black personalities. Moreover, in his essay "The Briar Patch," printed in the famous Southern Agrarian collection *I'll Take My Stand,* he adopts a position that one might label "separate but equal." [19]

Warren believed that achieving economic independence was more important than integration for blacks. Although he did not encourage the mixing of the races, he urged that blacks should have access to the same compensation and security as whites.

John Crowe Ransom was a generation older than Warren. He was born eight years before the infamous *Plessy vs. Ferguson* decision of 1896 advocated "separate but equal." Ransom was an outspoken advocate for those aspects of the antebellum plantation system that promoted the quiet, easy life and allowed a man the luxury of pursuing affairs of the intellect. In his essay for *I'll Take My Stand,* "Reconstructed but Unregenerate," Ransom dismisses slavery as "monstrous enough in theory, but, more often than not, humane in practice."[20] This led many critics, especially in the North, to attack Ransom and his colleagues for resisting "progress." The Fugitives and Agrarians also were accused of idealizing a paternalistic white society that never really existed.

However, one must acknowledge that the racial attitudes of Warren, Ransom, and their partners evolved over time. By the 1950s they were outspoken opponents of segregation.

For Dean Rusk, Oxford served as the catalyst that dissipated his southern-bred prejudices. Both his high school and Davidson College had been segregated. Only when he got to Oxford did he encounter students of different races, nationalities, and religions.

There, his own racial tolerance "took root." Thanks in part to Oxford, three decades later he championed civil rights legislation in the Kennedy and Johnson administrations. In 1967 he and his wife fully supported their daughter Peggy when she married a black. "Just two people in love," he told reporters.[21]

Rusk and a few other Rhodes Scholars, however, were exceptional. In the 1920s and 1930s several former scholars wrote articles about Cecil Rhodes and nearly always adopted a reverential tone. A few visited Rhodes' tomb and made their journeys sound like pilgrimages to the Holy Land. On the anniversaries of Rhodes' death or of his settling of Rhodesia, some scholars commended him for bringing civilization to the "savages" and "barbarians."[22] In 1928 Thomas Robins (1904) became the general manager of the British South Africa Company, which had been founded by Rhodes.[23]

Walt Rostow and Gordon Craig showed some evidence of a revised attitude about their benefactor. In their song "White Man's Burden" they satirized "bloody" (used in the British sense) imperialism and the "White Man's God." They also observed that these weighty matters did not cause worries for the "ninety mad Englishmen dancing in the quad." In another song, however, they reverted to the old nursery rhyme: "Eenie, meenie, minie, moe. Catch a nigger by the toe."

Other scholars of the interwar years continued to declare the superiority of Anglo-Saxons and expressed the hope that this race would continue to lead the world. In 1924 one scholar reported that he had a "wonderful coon" in his outer office to whom he paid $25 a week to call him "judge."[24] When Buel Trowbridge (1920) announced in 1938 that he had become interested in "negro education," one of his classmates joked, "I wonder if the negroes are interested too."[25] Edwin Hubble's rising fame as an astronomer did not lead him to temper his language when referring to blacks, who were "darkies" and "pickaninnies."[26]

There is no evidence that any Rhodes Scholar in this period called for the recruitment of blacks for the scholarships. With characteristic British understatement, C. K. Allen lamented that in the 1930s "coloured" Rhodes Scholars from Jamaica and elsewhere "still produced a noticeable restraint in the company of Rhodes Scholars from certain constituencies."[27]

On the question of women's rights, Rhodes Scholars likewise remained part of their times rather than leading the vanguard of change. In *The American Oxonian* they approved of the granting of full membership to the women's colleges in Oxford in 1920. Like British dons and students, however, they placed limits on how much they would concede to women. By the late 1920s many men (including Rhodes Scholars) feared that the women's colleges were growing too fast and that Oxford would soon lose its status as a male bastion. In 1928 men succeeded in passing restrictions that would, at least for several years, limit growth so that women would not surpass 25 percent of the student body.[28]

Rhodes Scholars appear to have approved or at least accepted these instances of male territorial protectiveness. Moreover, no scholar of this period suggested that Rhodes' will be amended to permit women to apply. When one former scholar revisited Oxford in 1934 he was appalled by the extent to which women students were in evidence all over.[29]

Rhodes Scholars were not so much hostile to women as they were paternalistic and, at times, condescending. When women were admitted to full equality in 1920, Americans celebrated this, not because justice had been done, but because the "charming Portias" and "undergraduettes," wearing newly designed scholarly caps that "droop with sheer femininity," would bring more "picturesqueness" to the university.[30] Women mentioned in *The American Oxonian* never had first names; they were appendages of their husbands. Whenever a former scholar mentioned his wife he called her "Mrs. ___." In 1925 a scholar reported the birth of a new baby girl; the baby cried a lot, he joked, after she was told she could not become a Rhodes Scholar.[31] Some Americans unfairly denigrated British female students as unwashed and unattractive; this meant it was hard for a Rhodes Scholar to find a pretty girl to date.[32] Allan Seager (1930) said this of the students at the five women's colleges:

> Most of their undergraduates were going to be schoolmistresses and looked it. They wore rugged tweeds full of sticks of heather and twigs of gorse that stank in the wet weather, and they had big, frightening muscles in their legs from bike riding.[33]

One wonders what the women of that era thought of the baggy, shapeless flannels worn by the men. It is true that the women, more than the men, had to ride bicycles through town. After all, the women's colleges were located on the periphery of the university area.

Dean Rusk personified southern chivalry. As president of his JCR he was delegated to take a petition to St. John's president. The petition asked that a powder room be installed for ladies visiting the college. By the 1930s women generally could enter the rooms of male students in the afternoon, or, with special permission, in the evening for mixed parties. But, without a powder room, a male St. John's student would have to escort his guest outside the college, across the street, to an underground structure, and then put a penny in the slot of a public toilet. With two of his committee members, Rusk screwed up his courage and approached the college president, the elderly Dr. James (nicknamed the "Bodger"). After Rusk finished his presentation, Dr. James glared at them and proclaimed, "What a monstrous proposal!" That was the end of that.[34]

There was one Rhodes Scholar in the interwar period who shone in the pages of *The American Oxonian* as a champion of women's rights. In 1940 Paul Havens (1925), President of Wilson College, declared that women as well as men must be educated for all possible roles they might play in the modern world. If a college-educated woman chose to become a full-time homemaker and mother, that was fine. But if she elected to pursue a career in academe, government, or business, she should be permitted, indeed, encouraged, to do so.[35] These sentiments might seem fairly trite today, but they could spark heated disagreement at that time.

Foreign Affairs

There was one topic on which many scholars did exhibit courage and determination. That was the looming threat of Fascist Italy and Nazi Germany. Most Americans visited Germany during one vacation or another. Some studied there for brief periods. Dean Rusk, for example, took courses on the German language and economics at the universities of Hanover and Hamburg. He was in Berlin in early 1933, when Hitler took power and a mysterious fire burned the Reichstag. Like several other scholars, Rusk returned to Oxford with first-hand accounts of the Nazi horrors. Also like many scholars, he was appalled by the infamous vote in the Oxford Union in February 1933. The pacifist motion "that this House will in no circumstances fight for King and Country" won by a margin of 275 to 153.[36]

Much that has been written about the Oxford of that time implies that it was a seedbed of pacifism, appeasement, or airy indifference to serious matters. There were a fair number of woolly minded intellectuals as well as members of the "Brideshead set." But they were not a majority. While hundreds of books and articles have criticized the Oxford Union resolution of 1933, they have neglected to mention that by 1936 the Union had reversed itself. In that year the Union came out strongly for sanctions against Italy over its invasion of Ethiopia and supported a show of force by the League of Nations.[37]

Oxford's Marxists formed the October Club, which numbered in the hundreds and included at least one American – Daniel Boorstin. John Templeton recalls that about half the scholars of his class were ardent socialists.[38] The socialist, anti-fascist Labour Club had about one thousand members, or roughly 20 percent of the entire Oxford student body. Several Americans belonged to it, and in the spring of 1939 Howard K. Smith was elected its president.

Smith was one of the Rhodes Scholars of this period who made the biggest splash while in Oxford – not as a student or athlete, but as a Labour party organizer and anti-fascist protester. Prior to taking up his scholarship, he had already traveled through Germany and attended several Nazi rallies. Upon arriving in Oxford he found that he was in a minority. He quickly gained the reputation of being a "harmless but annoying zealot." In the Labour Club he helped publish a newspaper, orchestrated huge public rallies, and supported workers in local factories. With a few like-minded student radicals, he sneaked out of Merton late at night and filled the city with graffiti like "Chamberlain must go!" and "Throw out the men of Munich!" Once he picketed 10 Downing Street, walking up and down wearing a sandwich board, along with his comrades, shouting "Throw the rascals out!"[39]

Smith spent most of his vacations in Germany, but once he also spent a month in Russia. There he saw how "dirty and disorderly" the country was, but the "spirit of the thing" got to him.

He also attended one of the tea parties given for Rhodes Scholars by Lady Astor. The American-born Member of Parliament invited the Americans to her estate at Cliveden each year, to show hospitality to fellow countrymen and try to bring them over to her own conservative, pro-appeasement views. She also entertained them by sticking false teeth into her mouth and doing an imitation of an English lady imitating an American lady. Many of the foremost politicians and writers accepted invitations to her gatherings. The time when Smith was there, she draped her arm around his and asked where he was from. He gritted his teeth but managed a smile as he answered in his thickest southern accent "Louisiana, Ma'am."[40] Smith's classmate, Penn Kimball, meanwhile was busy teaching George Bernard Shaw to do a popular dance step, the Lambeth Walk.[41]

While gaining notoriety as a political activist, Smith did not distinguish himself academically. Decades later he readily conceded that Oxford "was almost totally wasted" on him. He was too engulfed in British and world affairs to concentrate on his weekly essays. Also, like many other Rhodes Scholars, "after four years of university in America I was a little weary of academic life."[42]

Nonetheless, he got on well socially. He loved his six-hundred-year-old rooms in Merton's Mob Quad. According to college legend, his rooms had once belonged to medieval scholar John Duns Scotus. Smith loved the "patinated" charm of the place but found that one old Rhodes Scholar joke still held true:

Q. – What do American students do in Oxford?
A. – The same thing they do in America but with inferior plumbing.[43]

The first students Smith met at Merton were stuffy and shallow, but within a few days he "discovered that there were also Englishmen, even in Oxford, who could be classified as human beings." By the 1930s, he recalls, Oxford's reputation as "the ultra-ultra of snobbism" was greatly out of date. Though still a minority, working-class youths were more in evidence – thanks to an increase in the number of scholarships provided by the government and the trade (i.e., labor) unions. When not attending rallies, Smith spent his days punting and his nights in smoke-filled student rooms engaged in conversation.[44]

Smith also enjoyed being invited to spend weekends at the country homes of some of his British classmates. There he could breathe "the rarefied air of the uppercrust." One of his weekends was spent at the vast Staffordshire estate of a member of the House of Lords. Upon entering the mansion he handed his bag to the butler. After enjoying a sherry near the grand fireplace, he went to his room. There he was horrified to discover that a servant had laid out all his clothing on the bed: his impressive new coat and trousers along with his ragged underwear and socks. For the rest of the weekend he could hardly move, ashamed and fearful that everyone knew his secret. The first thing he did after he got back to Oxford was purchase new undergarments.[45]

Such occasions, however, were mere interludes in Smith's obsessive drive to "Do Something!" about the international situation. To his dismay, he discovered that most Oxford students and dons supported appeasement or non-involvement, as did a majority of Americans back home. One former Rhodes Scholar labeled Charles Lindbergh a "jackass" because of his isolationist America First policies, but most Americans, if not extremely isolationist, at least favored a wait-and-see attitude.[46] They supported Lend Lease and other kinds of support for Britain after the war commenced in Europe, but they rejected more active involvement.

Not all Rhodes Scholars were vehement interventionists either. Some opposed American participation in the Berlin Olympics of 1936, but others attended the festivities and were guests in the homes of German Rhodes Scholars.[47] Beginning in 1929 Germany once again had Rhodes Scholars – though only two per year, compared to the five it produced annually until 1914. Whereas earlier ones had been appointed by the Kaiser, after 1929 the selection process was similar to that of the United States and elsewhere – with a national secretary and committees. Being in Britain during the 1930s proved to be increasingly awkward for the German scholars. Apparently none was a member of the Nazi party, but all were nationalists and patriots. They got along well with American and British students. In the fall of 1936, at the annual dinner welcoming all new Rhodes Scholars to Oxford, the chairman of the Rhodes Trustees, Lord Amery, offered a toast to both Franklin Delano Roosevelt and Adolf Hitler. No Americans protested.[48]

Though scholars were worried about Hitler and Mussolini, they expressed little concern over the Spanish Civil War. Two considered going to Spain to help the republican forces fight Franco's army, but they decided to remain in Oxford to complete their studies.[49]

The American Oxonian devoted an increasing amount of space to the European crisis in the late 1930s, but most pages still focused on sports and social life. In the spring of 1940, the magazine reported approvingly that Eights Week would continue as usual; only a German submarine in the Isis could stop the races.[50] Most American scholars in Oxford before the war left no record of their feelings. One can assume that they, like most British students, were more concerned with athletics and academics than with politics.

Howard K. Smith has said that not only the British but some of his best Rhodes Scholar friends got tired of listening to him as he warned about Hitler.[51] Byron White could not recall any militancy or feverish activity by the Rhodes Scholars whom he knew.[52]

A small number of scholars advocated appeasement or even admired certain things about Hitler. In 1941 Edward Porter (1913) declared:

I cannot join in the total condemnation of Herr Hitler urged by many, but still agree with an artillery friend in the last war who said he did not blame the Germans for trying to conquer us but would blame us if we let them do it. Our greatest danger is not from the black and brown shirts from abroad, but from the stuffed shirts within … The Nazis are the only people who have ever made a thorough and organized effort to put brains into government, and unless we learn from them as they have from us, this war is going to be a greater waste of time and effort than the first one.[53]

A few scholars favored non-involvement because they had reservations about helping Britain. F. O. Matthiessen (1923) was a pacifist and a socialist. He claimed that the Tory government's major goal was simply to preserve the British Empire. If the United States were going to aid Britain, he maintained, it must also bolster the Soviet Union.[54] Other scholars were more blunt. In 1940 several attacked Lord Lothian (then British ambassador in Washington and formerly head of the Rhodes Trustees) for trying to pull the United States into the conflict – as had occurred in the previous war.[55] At that same time a member of the class of 1932 announced:

> I find that my own attitude, while not strictly isolationist, is one of suspicion of England's endeavors to draw us into the war. My years at Oxford gave me first, a profound admiration for the British genius for government and politics, one of the principal features of which is the hard-headed ability never to do anything except in self-interest but at the same time to make it appear that in so doing they are assuming a "white man's burden"; and second, the knowledge that the English regard all Americans as rather crude and inferior people who owe them somewhat the same attitude of respect and servitude that their own lower classes properly adopt.[56]

Late in 1941 a member of the class of 1933 admitted he was pro-Britain and anti-Hitler, but nevertheless exclaimed, "England doesn't really give a hoot for democracy, was willing to see it perish in Spain and Czechoslovakia, only fought when her own imperial interests were threatened" and concluded that Britain's "majestic ineptitude" had helped to bring the war about.[57]

However, these sentiments represented a small fraction of Rhodes Scholars. Even before the United States officially entered the hostilities in December 1941, several scholars had entered the fray on the British side in one fashion or another. In the spring of 1939, just after Hitler's troops had marched into Czechoslovakia, Guy Nunn (1937) performed a clever, James Bond-ish feat of derring-do. He volunteered to journey to Prague to rescue a group of thirty-six writers and artists who were being hunted by the Nazis. With his excellent command of German, Nunn went to Berlin posing as an art dealer. His hasty reading on Hegel's theory of aesthetics was enough to persuade German officials to grant him a visa for Prague. With Nazi police sniffing his trail, he managed to find all the people on his list and give them money and British visas. All but one of the group made it safely to Britain.[58]

A handful of scholars followed the footsteps of those in the First World War and joined the British army.[59] Howard K. Smith, John Golay (1938), and Charles Collingwood (1939) became active in yet another way. Late in the summer of 1939 Smith was preparing for his third year in Oxford and Golay for his second. Collingwood had just arrived; he had come to Europe that summer, ahead of the rest of his class. None of them could stand the prospect of sitting out a war while studying in Oxford libraries. When Hitler invaded Poland on 1 September the three of them happened to be spending a few days in London. Two days later they listened to the radio broadcast announcing Britain's declaration of war. They immediately marched into the United Press office just off Fleet Street. They spoke with U.P.'s star reporter, Webb Miller, who immediately offered them jobs.[60]

Smith returned to Oxford and informed C.K. Allen that he would have to resign his scholarship. Allen was somewhat peeved, because he had just approved a third year for Smith – despite the latter's lack-luster academic performance. Nevertheless, Allen consented. Indeed, within a few days the Rhodes Trustees encouraged all Rhodes Scholars to return home for the duration of the war. Collingwood visited Oxford a few times that fall before finally quitting and turning to war reporting full time. A notorious dandy and ladies' man, Collingwood seems to have used his brief forays to Oxford mainly to socialize with the students in the women's colleges. He also went punting with two of the young female actresses in the Oxford repertory company – Deborah Kerr and Pamela Brown.[61] Golay, on the other hand, managed to continue his studies while also working in London. In 1941 he obtained his B.A. in PPE.

All three would distinguish themselves in the war. Smith left almost immediately for Berlin, where he remained for the next two years. In December 1941 he was the last American to flee from Germany just as Hitler was about to declare war on the United States – hence the name of his first book, *Last Train from Berlin*. While continuing to work for United Press through the war, Smith also served as a correspondent for *Time*, the *New York Times*, and CBS. Collingwood soon switched exclusively to CBS. Both Smith and Collingwood became part of the group known as "Murrow's Boys." Working under renowned CBS correspondent Edward R. Murrow, they dispatched radio bulletins from throughout Britain and the continent. Golay began work for the British Ministry of Labour in 1940, and in 1942 he joined the R.A.F.

By the beginning of 1940 nearly all of the Americans had left Oxford. None of the class of 1939, except for Collingwood, had even reached Britain. The Rhodes Trustees did whatever they could to make arrangements so that scholars in the classes of 1937 and 1938 whose stays were cut short could somehow complete their studies. The University of Chicago and a few other American universities agreed to accept some of them. One of these scholars later lamented, on condition of anonymity, that when he reached home his only proof that he had ever been to Oxford was his bar bills.

When Byron White arrived back in the States, he entered Yale Law School and resumed his football career, playing for the Detroit Lions in 1940 and 1941. In 1942 he joined the U.S. Navy. White has admitted always regretting having to leave Oxford after less than a full year there. He enjoyed it socially and got on well with his law tutor. His stay was so short that he felt he had not had the time to become a Rhodes Scholar.[62]

After the war all the scholars who had been compelled to return home, plus the class of 1939 that had never reached Oxford, were invited to attend the university. Nearly half accepted the offer. The others, as White has said, "moved on with their lives."[63]

From 1940 through 1945 the United States and most other constituencies suspended the appointment of Rhodes Scholars. Indeed, Oxford barely kept going as a university. Over half of the colleges were taken over by the British government for war-related purposes. The other colleges were nearly empty, except for women, the physically handicapped, and soldiers taking short courses while on leave from duty.

Approximately 250 out of the 350 former American Rhodes Scholars of military age served in the Army, Navy, or Marines. Another 150 scholars worked in the federal government in areas directly related to the war.[64] Elmer Davis, for example, headed the Office of War Information from 1942 to 1945. At least a dozen put their language skills and travel experiences to good use by serving in the secret intelligence service-the OSS. Certainly for most of these men at least part of their devotion to the cause derived from their Rhodes Scholarship experience. They had been able to see the Nazi menace close-up during vacations, and they had formed attachments to Oxford and to the British. Most of the scholars from the British Commonwealth (the name given to dominions and colonies after 1931) likewise contributed to the war effort, either in their own countries or in Britain.

In a replay of 1914, the German scholarships were revoked in 1939. This reflected no ill feelings towards the German scholars themselves. Indeed, Oxford's friendship for its German students is movingly reflected in the impressive First World War memorial in the New College Chapel. There one can find a list of all "old members" who died in the war, including the German Rhodes Scholars who were killed while fighting against Britain.

There was a total of seventy-five former German scholars (1903 to 1913 and 1930 to 1939), of whom sixty were still alive in 1939. Their record in the Second World War gave clear testimony to the impact that their British education had had on many of them. As far as can be determined, all of them were patriots, but only two ardently supported Hitler. One of these held high government office in the Nazi regime: Ludwig Schwerin von Krosigk (1905) was Finance Minister through most of the war. The U.S. Military Tribunal later found him guilty of war crimes, and he spent several years in prison. Eight German scholars, however, emigrated to the United States or Britain either before or after the fighting commenced. One of them served in the U.S. Army, and another joined Britain's. Three others actively opposed Hitler within Germany. Albert von Muller (1910) was killed by the Gestapo in 1941. Albrecht Bernsdorff (1909) and Adam von Trott zu Solz (1931) participated in the botched attempt to assassinate the Führer in 1944 and were executed.[65]

Like other British cities, Oxford enforced a blackout at night through the war. Amazingly, the city was never bombed, though the nearby Cowley automobile factory was. Many in Oxford believed that German Rhodes Scholars had exerted influence to spare their university. Other factors, however, were probably responsible for Oxford's good fortune. Hitler's penchant for Gothic architecture could have compelled him to save the dreaming spires. It was also believed by many at that time that Hitler planned to make Oxford his capital, after he conquered Britain. There was also the rumor that foreign minister Ribbentrop wanted to spare a sister of his who lived in the city.[66] The Germans may also have concluded that Oxford was not as important as dozens of other strategic targets in Britain.

Mid-Century Assessment

If one were to grade the overall success of the scholarship program, at least with regard to Americans, for the interwar period, one might assign a grade of B or B+ (or, in Oxford terms, an Upper Second).

That was up from the C+ or B- that could be assigned for the prewar years. Americans were doing better academically, and fewer of them were acting like cowboys.

The extent to which Oxford warmed to Americans was astonishing. There continued to be a small number of hidebound traditionalists and xenophobes, but compared to the earlier years there were remarkably few criticisms of Rhodes Scholars in newspapers and magazines. The great majority of dons realized that if the university wanted top-quality students to continue to "come up" then it itself would have to "keep up" with the best universities around the world. Pressure from Americans was partly responsible for the dropping of the Greek requirement, the establishment of the D.Phil., the creation of the PPE program, and improvements in the law and science curricula, but these changes were soon welcomed by most British students as well. Of the thousand or so persons who obtained a D.Phil. between 1917 and 1945, Britons outnumbered Americans by more than 3 to 1.[67]

Another sign of Oxford's approval of Americans came in its hospitality for former scholars. Several Americans returned to the university as distinguished guest lecturers. Two Americans were awarded honorary doctorates: Edwin Hubble in 1934 and Frank Aydelotte in 1937. The Latin citation for Aydelotte revealed that the university, for all its formality, also had a sense of humor. Aydelotte was a fanatic golfer. His citation said that he loved "to course the meadows and knock the ball over the grass with a club, to see if by chance it may rest in a hole."[68]

Two other Americans in this period achieved another mark of esteem: they joined the faculty at Oxford. In 1923 Henry Allen Moe (1919) was appointed Hulme Lecturer in Law at Brasenose College. He remained there for one year before returning to the United States to pursue his legal career.[69] In 1935 Charles Hitch (1932) became a fellow at the Queen's College, a position he held until 1948 – with several years off for military service.[70]

The American record during this period, however, was far surpassed by that of other Rhodes Scholars. A dozen or more Canadians, Australians, and New Zealanders became fellows at various colleges in the 1920s and 1930s. Several non-Americans, in fact, had become Oxford fellows even before the First World War. These included two Canadians and one Australian from the class of 1904. Canadian John Lowe (1922) was chosen to head a college, when in 1939 he became dean of Christ Church.[71]

If fewer Americans than other former scholars became Oxford dons, that was partly their own choice. No records survive, but undoubtedly several other Americans were offered Oxford jobs but turned them down in order to return to the United States. For non-American Rhodes Scholars, the opportunity to study in Britain meant attending a university better than any available at home. It also meant residing in a country where – at least up to mid-century – the standard of living was higher and where there were more professional job opportunities. For some Jamaicans and other "colonials" there was also the allure of residing in the home of the Empire/Commonwealth. Over the years a high percentage of non-Americans, sometimes one-quarter of Australians and New Zealanders, chose to remain in Britain – in Oxford as academics or elsewhere in other occupations.

What can be said of the general American evaluation of the scholarships? Nearly twenty years after going down, a majority of the class of 1931 asserted that the Oxford experience had been the most important part of their education.[72] However, the response of the class of 1934 was much more equivocal. Shortly after they returned home, the members of that class received a questionnaire from their class secretary. Twenty-four responded. When asked if Oxford was a valuable cultural experience, eighteen gave a definite "yes," five a qualified "yes," and one gave no answer. When asked if Oxford was a "bore," half said that it was. Half also agreed that spending two or three years there was a waste of time, so far as their careers were concerned. To the question, was the entire experience "a lot of fun?" all who answered gave a hearty, or at least a qualified, "yes." On their response sheets they penned additional comments. One said the experience was "better than expected, except for the quality of the instruction ... which was disappointing"; another called it a "painful pleasure"; and yet another deemed it "the most valuable three years of my life."[73]

There are several signs that the great majority of former scholars, regardless of what some of them felt while in Oxford, eventually came to cherish the experience. In 1928 the Association of American Rhodes Scholars established an American Trust Fund for Oxford. The purpose of this fund was to contribute to university expenses, especially for the purchase of books. Donations by alumni to their alma maters was such a novelty in Britain that the *Times* warmly praised the Americans for this "almost unparalleled event."[74] In succeeding years the fund would grow steadily, thanks to contributions from hundreds of former scholars.

In 1937 the University of Oxford initiated its first-ever fund-raising drive, which was delicately termed an "appeal." Oxford was struggling to keep up with the better American and German universities, especially in the sciences. Lord Nuffield and the Rockefeller Foundation had already given hundreds of thousands of pounds in recent years, but still more was required. Frank Aydelotte headed an American Appeal Committee, and hundreds of former scholars eventually contributed.[75] American students in Oxford at that time responded much more enthusiastically than did their British peers. Whereas only 15 percent of the British students made donations, 50 percent of the Americans did.[76] This figure for Americans includes others besides Rhodes Scholars. By the late 1930s there were about two hundred American students in Oxford at any given time, including some women. There were thirty-two Rhodes Scholars each year. Most of them remained three years, which meant that there were about eighty-five in residence each year.

The longer former scholars had been back in the United States, the better Oxford looked. In part this was a result of the mist of nostalgia, which always makes the distant past look like "the good old days." One joked that he "enjoyed Oxford no end, but never as much in reality as in retrospect."[77] Another had occasion, decades later, to look through some of the letters he had written to his mother from Oxford. "I had forgotten," he said, "how lonely and homesick I was."[78]

However, far more than mere nostalgia and forgetfulness were at work. Most former scholars recalled the frigid rooms, the soggy Brussels sprouts, the rain, and the occasional snubs, but they also remembered the fun and the positive influences. In 1939 Buel Trowbridge reminisced about his Oxford days of nearly twenty years earlier. His recollections were probably close to what most felt as they looked back:

> Oxford has been of profound intellectual advantage and stimulus to me, partly because of its tutorial method which opened my eyes to what education might be ... partly because of the travel in Europe ... and then the endless new interests which the experience exposed me to, which otherwise I might not have developed.
>
> Warnings? ... Oxford performs no miracles ... It puts it strongly up to the individual to educate himself. It won't amuse or entertain anyone. A student can be very lonely at Oxford, and very disillusioned, according to his mind-set. I have known a few Rhodes Scholars who come home belly-aching about their experience. I suspect they have some sort of emotional disturbance which would cause them to gripe, just to assert their superiority.
>
> ... I personally feel that the three years I spent at Oxford were the most colorful, delightful, and important I have ever spent ...[79]

NOTES

1. *TAO,* 8 (1921): 58.
2. *TAO,* 10 (1923): 149, 168, 171, 172; 13 (1926): 200; 17 (1930): 47.
3. *TAO,* 5 (1918): 34; 9 (1922): 181, 185; 17 (1930): 21.
4. *TAO,* 20 (1933): 97-100; 21 (1934): 17-20.
5. *TAO,* 20 (1933): 13.
6. For example, see *TAO,* 23 (1935): 204.
7. *TAO,* 20 (1933): 233; 21 (1934): 205, 250.
8. *TAO,* 17 (1930): 226.
9. *TAO,* 22 (1935): 169.
10. *TAO,* 23 (1936): 212.
11. *TAO,* 23 (1936): 251.
12. *TAO,* 21 (1934): 3; 61 (1974): 22; Price, "A Yank," 195; Smith interview, 5 April 1994.
13. *TAO,* 23 (1936): 251.
14. *TAO,* 25 (1938): 193-94.
15. *TAO,* 25 (1938): 196. Also see 22 (1935): 95-96; 23 (1936): 31-33; 26 (1939): 1, 39-50; 29 (1942): 153-54; 30 (1943): 23.
16. *TAO,* 51 (1964): 1.
17. *TAO,* 14 1927): 148; 25 (1938): 125.
18. *TAO,* 27 (1940): 279.
19. *I'll Take My Stand: The South and the Agrarian Tradition by Twelve Southerners.* Intro. by Louis D. Rubin, Jr. Biographical essays by Virginia Rock. (New York, 1962; orig. ed. 1930), 246-64.
20. Ibid., 14.
21. *TAO,* 79 (1992): 137-38.
22. *TAO,* 13 (1926): 57; 14 (1927): 81, 166; 16 (1929): 75; 20 (1933): 47; 28 (1941): 207.
23. *TAO,* 17 (1930): 13.
24. *TAO,* 11 (1924): 142.
25. *TAO,* 25 (1938): 280.
26. *NYT Book Review,* 3 September 1995, 21.
27. Elton, *First Fifty Years,* 138.
28. *TAO,* 15 (1928): 6-8.
29. *TAO,* 21 (1934): 208.
30. *TAO,* 8 (1921): 37-38; 9 (1922): 178.
31. *TAO,* 12 (1925): 182.
32. Philip M. Kaiser, *Journeying Far and Wide: A Political and Diplomatic Memoir* (New York, 1992), 50.
33. Allan Seager, "The Joys of Sport at Oxford," *Sports Illustrated,* 29 October 1962, 62.
34. Rusk, *As I Saw It,* 71.
35. *TAO,* 27 (1940): 157-59.
36. Rusk, *As I Saw It,* 73, 78; Kaiser, *Journeying,* 64, 72; *TAO,* 20 (1933): 104, 109-13.
37. *TAO,* 23 (1936): 22.
38. Templeton interview, 2 August 1994.
39. Howard K. Smith, *Last Train from Berlin* (New York, 1942), 33-35.
40. Smith interview, 5 April 1994.
41. *Washington Post,* 1 July 1983, sec. D, 1.
42. Smith, *Last Train,* 33.

43. Howard K. Smith, *Events Leading up to My Death: The Life of a Twentieth-Century Reporter* (New York, 1996), 57-58.
44. Smith interview, 5 April 1994; Smith, *Last Train*, 33; Smith, *Events Leading up to My Death*, 58-60.
45. Smith interview, 5 April 1994.
46. *TAO*, 27 (1940): 275; Smith, *Events Leading up to My Death*, 68-72.
47. *TAO*, 23 (1936): 29, 178, 233.
48. Kaiser, *Journeying*, 68.
49. *TAO*, 79 (1992): 126.
50. *TAO*, 27 (1940): 200.
51. Smith interview, 5 April 1994.
52. White interview, 11 June 1993.
53. *TAO*, 28 (1941): 230.
54. *TAO*, 28 (1941): 249.
55. *TAO*, 27 (1940): 111-12, 166-70, 194-95.
56. *TAO*, 27 (1940): 274.
57. *TAO*, 28 (1941): 296.
58. Kaiser, *Journeying*, 100-1.
59. *TAO*, 29 (1942): 36.
60. Smith interview, 5 April 1994; Smith, *Last Train*, 40; Smith, *Events Leading up to My Death*, 80-81.
61. *People*, 11 July 1983, 62.
62. White interview, 11 June 1993.
63. White interview, 11 June 1993.
64. Aydelotte, *American Rhodes Scholarships*, 104-5.
65. Giles McDonogh, *A Good German: Adam von Trott zu Solz* (New York, 1992); *Washington Post*, 23 February 1993, A18; Elton, *First Fifty Years*, 157-59; *TAO*, 32 (1945): 135- 37; 36 (1949): 22-30.
66. *TAO*, 30 (1943): 126; 34 (1947): 203.
67. Harrison, *Twentieth Century*, 52; Aydelotte, *American Rhodes Scholarships*, 57.
68. *TAO*, 21 (1934): 149; 24 (1937): 160; 29 (1942): 160.
69. *Register of Rhodes Scholars*, 114; *TAO*, 63 (1976): 352.
70. *Register of Rhodes Scholars*, 228; *TAO*, 23 (1936): 47.
71. Elton, *First Fifty Years*, 85-86, 226, 228; *TAO*, 27 (1940): 208.
72. *TAO*, 38 (1951): 227.
73. *TAO*, 25 (1938): 345-46.
74. *TAO*, 15 (1928): 97, 167.
75. *TAO*, 24 (1937): 1-13.
76. *TAO*, 77 (1990): 28.
77. *TAO*, 23 (1936): 279.
78. Elton, *First Fifty Years*, 89.
79. *TAO*, 26 (1939): 21-22.

Chapter 9

POSTWAR PROBLEMS AND ADJUSTMENTS

There has been a good deal of talk lately about the seriousness of Oxford's undergraduates. "They're all so dull nowadays," complain the old guard. "Oxford's not what it used to be; it's changed." ... Oxford, like St. Paul, has put away childish things.

Oxford Mail, 1947

At 7:45 this morning, a chipper college servant named Kimber thumped into my living room, lamented the sight of a table filled with coffee cups which my nocturnal guests had left dirty, and pushed into my bedroom to render an habitual, "Good morning, sir." As he opened the blind I noted that it was snowing, and as I reached into the frigid atmosphere to switch off my electric blanket, I wondered how I should summon sufficient courage to walk out of doors to another building containing the bathroom.

Richard Lugar, *The Denison Alumnus*

Oxford Confronts New Realities

The period from the late 1940s to the mid-1960s witnessed changes that were both evolutionary and revolutionary – for the university and for Rhodes Scholars. One of the most noticeable developments lay with the students. Prior to the Second World War the British government, trade unions, and some other organizations had been providing scholarships for working-class youth to attend universities. What had been a trickle became a flood after the war. The government and the people realized that a modern industrialized nation would require a much larger number of university-educated citizens. The forces of democratization also decreed that universities should no longer be preserves of the well-to-do and the well connected. The chief instrument of change was the Education Act of 1944. This law dealt chiefly with

Notes for this chapter can be found on page 149.

improvements in secondary education but also established the principle that all sixth-formers (i.e., high school seniors) who performed well
in their final examinations and gained admittance to a university were
eligible for state aid, based in part on financial need. The central government's University Grants Committee would pay their college fees,
and local authorities would provide a living allowance. Thus higher
education became part of the new welfare state.[1]

By 1950 the number of university students in Britain was double
the figure of the 1930s. Oxford and Cambridge each had about
seven thousand students. The other established universities – principally London, Edinburgh, and Durham – also experienced steep
rises. To meet the increasing demand – from war veterans who
wanted to return to college and from employers who clamored for a
university-educated work force – Clement Attlee's Labour government of the late 1940s called for the establishment of new universities around the country. The next two decades witnessed the creation
of about twenty new institutions, including the universities of Hull,
Exeter, Leicester, Keele, Sussex, East Anglia, York, Lancaster, and
Warwick.[2] The stark, modern appearance of many of their buildings
resulted in the label "glassplate universities," which distinguished
them from the "redbrick universities" founded in the nineteenth century. In addition, the 1950s and 1960s saw the mushrooming of poly-
technics and colleges of further education – along the lines of junior
colleges and vocational schools in the United States.[3]

The percentage of British students in universities remained small
relative to the United States: about 10 percent of all secondary
school graduates in Britain compared to almost 40 percent in the
United States. However, the British figure was comparable to that of
continental countries, where higher education was viewed more as a
privilege than as a birthright.

By 1950 there were not only more students in Oxford and Cambridge, but a larger percentage of them now came from middle and
working-class families. In the 1950s approximately two-thirds of
Oxford's students continued to be products of public schools like
Eton and Harrow, as opposed to the state-run schools. But two-thirds
of Oxford's students were also having their way paid by state scholarships. This meant that many of the public school students came
from families of modest means and might not have been able to
afford either the public schools or a university in earlier decades.
Many dons complained that a growing number of their students
were now spending their vacations working in jobs, rather than reading and traveling, because they needed money.[4]

The academic quality of the student body rose noticeably. The government was paying for most of the expenses and wanted to ensure that students merited the subsidy. Of course, scions of old Oxford families still could maneuver to ensure acceptance for their sons and daughters, but not as easily as before.

The dons in Oxford rejoiced at the improvement in the academic caliber of their charges. The college scouts, however, rued the changes. They took pride in being manservants of young gentlemen. A working-class scout did not relish serving the sons of businessmen and tradesmen. Throughout Oxford scouts mourned the good old days and complained that the new students were too serious and studious. The new breed also tipped less than the gentlemen of an earlier era. A lot of the fun and status went out of being a scout.[5]

That was one reason why from the early 1950s to the late 1960s the old-fashioned scouts gradually disappeared from the colleges. Another was that scouts, like factory employees and other members of the working class, were now demanding higher wages, shorter working hours, and paid vacations. The heads of the Oxford colleges repeatedly complained of the "servant problem."[6] Finding men to become scouts and accept low pay and long hours was becoming increasingly difficult.

By 1950 dramatic evidence of these new circumstances could be seen in nearly all the colleges. Scouts no longer brought breakfast and lunch to a student's room. Students had to take all three meals in hall. By 1953 many scouts were no longer serving as waiters, bringing food to the tables. Instead, the students had to follow the American fashion and carry their own trays through a cafeteria line. In Michaelmas term 1953 at Lincoln College, students were dumbfounded to discover that all the male scouts had been replaced by women. The women were still called scouts, but they did not dress formally. Nor did they run errands for students in college and around town. They were merely cleaning ladies who tidied up in the corridors, toilets, and student rooms.[7]

When Richard Lugar arrived at Pembroke College in 1954, he found that traditions still held sway there. His old-fashioned scout was named Clipper. Pete Dawkins (1959) likewise could luxuriate in the services of his man Reggie. Within twenty-four hours of Dawkins' arrival at Brasenose, Reggie had scurried out to purchase a bicycle and a gown for him.[8] But by 1960 there were only a few of the old-style scouts left. (The cleaning ladies/scouts remain to the present day.)

There were other transformations as well. By 1950 Oxford could no longer be described as a "college town." The stupendous growth of the Morris car works and other industries doubled the city's population to about 100,000. The city was now more than an equal partner to the university. The latter's "demotion" was confirmed when it lost the privilege of electing its own Members of Parliament. After 1950 the university lay within the districts of the two M.P.s representing the city.

The colleges likewise lost some of their power, vis-à-vis the university. It was the university as a whole, under the direction of the vice-chancellor, that controlled the ever-more-important science buildings. It was also the university that spearheaded the principal fund-raising appeals and distributed the money allocated by the government's University Grants Committee. For most students, however, the individual colleges remained the center of activity and allegiance.

There were numerous academic changes too. To meet the demands of foreign students, especially the Americans, in 1947 the university established a new degree, called the B.Phil. Similar to the B.Litt. and the B.Sc., the B.Phil. was roughly equivalent to an American M.A. It was designed for students who wanted something beyond a B.A. but were not prepared for the advanced, independent research of the D.Phil. Small groups of B.Phil. students usually met their respective supervisors in weekly seminars. In addition to writing several papers each term a student submitted a thesis of about thirty thousand words, usually at the end of two years. Though many dons scoffed at this new degree as a lowering of standards for the benefit of Americans, it also proved to be popular among British students.[9]

Signs of a dilution of standards in some areas were counterbalanced by a stiffening in others. By the 1950s the pass degree was being sought by only a tiny number of students. In the 1960s it died a natural death, and in 1967 the university abolished the Fourth class B.A. degree. As a result, by the late 1960s all undergraduate students were reading for honours degrees, aiming for a Third or higher. These reforms, however, gradually produced some grade inflation. By the 1980s it was evident that many who obtained Thirds actually should have received Fourths and many of the Seconds should have been Thirds. Hence in the mid-1980s Seconds were divided into Division I and Division II. Henceforth, a Division I Second (2:1) was equivalent to an old Second, a Division II Second (2:2) to an old Third, and a Third to an old Fourth.

By 1960 the eight thousand students in Oxford included one thousand graduate students. Every college now had at least a couple of dozen students working on a B.Phil., B.Litt, B.Sc., or D.Phil. To accommodate these older students, separate residence halls were built either inside some of the colleges or nearby. The older students wanted their own meeting rooms and a voice in college affairs, and gradually each college established an MCR (Middle Common Room) – paralleling the JCR and SCR.

The higher number of British graduate students meant that Rhodes Scholars now found it easier to meet older students with whom they could socialize. Eventually even those Rhodes Scholars working on undergraduate degrees were allowed to join the MCRs in their colleges.

The increased demand for advanced degrees led to the establishment of new colleges restricted to graduate students. In addition to Nuffield College (1937), these included St. Antony's (1948), Linacre (1962), St. Cross (1965), and Wolfson (1966).[10] Rhodes Scholars working on advanced degrees could work under supervisors at those colleges, but until the 1970s all of them continued to be assigned to the undergraduate colleges. The reason was that in the older, more traditional colleges one would find the full range of sports and social activities that were part of what Cecil Rhodes had wanted for his protégés. There were too many monastic bookworms in the graduate colleges.

In the sciences Oxford made great strides in the 1950s. It was especially strong in biochemistry and low-temperature physics. The facilities and the faculty were strong enough not only to tempt Rhodes Scholars, but also some of the top scientists from the United States. Baruch Blumberg went up to Balliol in 1955 to work in biochemistry, though he had already completed medical school in the United States. In 1976 he shared the Nobel Prize in physiology and medicine in recognition of his research leading to a vaccine against hepatitis B. His professional experience in Oxford had been so fruitful that twenty-five years later he accepted the job of master of the college. In his particular areas of specialization, he believed Oxford had been up-to-date in the 1950s and continued to be so in the 1990s.[11]

Another prominent scientist who worked in Oxford during the 1950s was George W. Beadle. A geneticist at the California Institute of Technology, he spent the academic year 1958/1959 as the Eastman Professor in Oxford. During his stay there he was named a co-recipient of the Nobel Prize in physiology and medicine for his work on genes and enzymes. While Beadle was lecturing and conducting research, his wife and son were encountering all the joys and frustrations of life in Oxford. Muriel Beadle later recounted these adventures in one of the best books ever written about the city and the university. In *These Ruins are Inhabited,* she goes from initial disappointment (at the Oxford train station she fears that the city looks like Peoria), to endless frustrations (lack of central heating, being left alone while her husband attends High Table meals to which spouses are not invited), to joy. The title of the book comes from one of the family's outings early in their stay. By mistake the Beadles wandered into the Rector's garden at Exeter College. The Rector happened to notice them from his window and glared down. Just then their son looked up and shouted, "Dad, *look*! These ruins are inhabited." By the end of the year Muriel felt so much at home that she tried to avoid being mistaken for an American tourist.[12]

In terms of prestige, Literae Humaniores continued to be the field reputed to attract the smartest students. However, that degree was in its last blaze of glory. This can be seen in Ved Mehta's book *Up at Oxford.* Born in India and blind since the age of three, Mehta had received scholarships and grants to attend a high school in Arkansas and then Pomona College in California. From childhood he had dreamed of studying in Oxford, whose graduates had so dominated the Indian Civil Service. Financial aid from private foundations and friends enabled him to go up to Balliol in 1956. Like many Rhodes Scholars, Mehta was not sure what he wanted to study in Oxford, and after doing the very un-Oxford thing of switching from law to English and then to PPE, he finally settled on history. The real academic superstars in his book are his friends reading classics. One of them, Jasper Griffin, is a veritable superman, reciting hundreds of lines from the Greek and Roman classics.[13] Yet Griffin was part of a tradition that was dying. British public and state schools were gradually reducing or eliminating their offerings in Greek and Latin. By the 1960s fewer British students had the interest or the ability to read Greats.

Like Literae Humaniores, philosophy, modern history, literature, and PPE remained strong and popular through this period. Psychology became a fully recognized Honours School, but engineering and sociology lagged behind. In the early 1950s C.K. Allen, the Oxford Secretary, displayed his traditionalism when he warned new Rhodes Scholars that "for the few who hanker after the controverted science of Sociology Oxford does not cater."[14] This remark was not precisely accurate. There were a few sociologists in Nuffield and a few other colleges by that time. Some Americans were dismayed to find that "modern" history reached only to 1914. For these reasons the future sociologist Neil Smelser opted to read PPE in Oxford.[15] Nicholas Katzenbach (1947) initially intended to write a D.Phil. thesis on the psychological preconceptions of three great political philosophers.

However, this topic sounded suspiciously newfangled and trendy to his supervisor, who thought it would involve studying things like the effects of nannies dropping infants on their heads. So Katzenbach switched to a study of perceptions of democracy in Britain, the United States, and the Soviet Union. He wrote about three hundred pages, but returned home before finishing the thesis and obtaining his degree.[16]

Though Oxford and Cambridge still reigned as the jewels in the British educational crown, they received a rude kick in the shins in the mid-1960s. In 1963 a government-sponsored committee chaired by Lord Robbins produced a lengthy study, soon dubbed the Robbins Report, outlining the current status of British higher education and making recommendations for the future. The document acknowledged the preeminence of Oxford and Cambridge, but also criticized their complacency and inefficiency. Harold Wilson headed the new Labour government in 1964, and he was determined to make all British universities more accountable to the public. Like private universities in the United States, Oxford and Cambridge were becoming more and more dependent on government funding – for research grants, for the establishment of new professorships, for the payment of student fees.

To head off further criticism from the government, early in 1964 Oxford set up its own internal investigative commission. It was headed by Lord Franks, the Provost of Worcester College. The Franks Commission issued its one thousand page report in May 1966. It caused a furor. The headline in the *New York Times* trumpeted: "Oxford Urged to Catch up with 20th Century."[17] The commission urged that the university's administration be streamlined, that its admissions policies be less secretive, and that the student body be increased from 9,500 to 13,000. Regarding the curriculum, the commission recommended that all areas of science be improved, especially the applied sciences. Finally, the commission asserted that Oxford must give added stress to research in order to retain its status as a world-class university. This would entail increasing the percentage of students pursuing graduate degrees.

Though the Franks Report produced consternation, it did not cause revolution. The commission acknowledged that Oxford was still "a fine place." Moreover, in many ways the report simply gave added support to changes that were already occurring. A close reading of the text shows that it was less radical than many newspaper headlines and letters to editors suggested. For example, one can look at the issue of women students. In 1966 about 15 percent of the students were women. The commission urged that women should make up 25 percent within the next fifteen to twenty years. If this was revolution, it was a very slow one. At any rate, the Franks commission served as an alarm. It strengthened the position of those who advocated more funding for the natural and social sciences and called for improvements in the university's administrative machinery.[18]

The American presence in Oxford grew remarkably in the 1950s. There were now three hundred or so Rhodes Scholars and other American students in the colleges. Thanks to postwar prosperity and cheaper and faster means of travel, American tourists flooded into Oxford and many other British and continental cities.

In addition, there were hundreds, and eventually thousands, of American college students who came to Oxford for summer academic programs. Though Oxford had lost its superiority over the best American universities, it retained an aura that was unmatched in the United States. Most dons either left the city in summer or holed up in their rooms to avoid contact with the noisy invaders. Like universities on the continent, Oxford and other British universities never offered summer sessions for their regular students. Thus in summer the only students working in Oxford were graduate students busy with their research. To replenish their depleted treasuries and make use of the rooms left empty in summer, some of the colleges began to welcome the three to six-week summer programs operated by American universities – a trend that by the 1990s had expanded to include nearly all the Oxford colleges and dozens of American programs. Sidewalk vendors and shops started selling Oxford University T-shirts and sweatshirts – items that no ordinary Oxford student would be caught dead in, but that the Americans and other visitors snatched up by the armful. (Ordinary Oxford students might wear sweatshirts or other items signifying their colleges, but not the university as a whole.)

Like Muriel Beadle, many of the Rhodes Scholars who happened to be in Oxford in the summer months cringed at the sight of armies of their fellow citizens and hoped that they themselves would not be mistaken for mere tourists. The scholars also regretted other signs of Americanization: the appearance of fast food restaurants (predecessors of the McDonald's, Pizza Hut, and Kentucky Fried Chicken that appeared in the 1980s), launderettes, and a Woolworth's. To maintain "their" Oxford, they supported the Oxford Preservation Trust and joined protestors in a successful drive to block construction of a highway through Christ Church Meadow.[19]

Americans Face a Battered Britain

The Rhodes Scholars of the late 1940s and early 1950s were remarkable for their number and their age. The first postwar class was that of 1947. To compensate for the lack of appointments during the war, the classes of 1947 and 1948 each had sixteen extra Americans. Moreover, for the benefit of those who normally would have applied in the early 1940s, the age restrictions were waived. Prior to obtaining his Rhodes Scholarship, Nicholas Katzenbach had already served in the Army Air Corps, spent two years in a German prisoner-of-war camp, and obtained a law degree at Yale. His classmate Bernard Rogers had spent four years on active duty in the Army (and was still in the service during his three Oxford years). Martin Rush (1949) also had served in the Army Air Corps, started medical school, and celebrated his thirtieth birthday before he reached Oxford in 1949.

Along with nearly fifty other American Rhodes Scholars of this period, Katzenbach, Rogers, and Rush also brought their wives with them. In Katzenbach's case, it was the spouse who had displayed the keener interest in going to Oxford and filled out the application for the scholarship.[20] As had happened after the First World War, the trustees temporarily bent the rules on marriage – at the risk of making the founder shudder in his grave.

C.K. Allen and his wife Dorothy cheerfully did their best to make the couples feel at home. The married scholars had to find living accommodations out of college, but they all managed to find suitable flats – either in the college areas or in places like Boar's Hill. Several later admitted that living out of college excluded them from a lot of the student activities, but they managed to socialize with each other as well as with many Britons. These older, married students were not as out of place as one might assume, for during the late 1940s and 1950s Oxford had a large number of married British students – war veterans or those who had completed their mandatory military duty prior to going up to the university. The Rhodes stipend was sufficient for just one person, but the American war veterans also had funds from the G.I. Bill. Katzenbach recalls that the combined sources of income made him and his wife feel quite comfortable.

Dorothy Allen gave frequent teas for the wives and helped to get perambulators and other supplies for the two dozen or so American babies born in the Radcliffe Infirmary. C.K. Allen paternalistically complimented the women, stating that "being real comrades and helpmates of their Rhodes Scholar husbands … is the highest destiny any woman can fulfill." He further commented that Rhodes Scholars had "always been good pickers" (i.e., of pretty women).[21]

Despite their close wartime collaboration, sometimes the Americans and the British still acted as if they came from different planets. British reserve continued to befuddle many Americans. Perhaps more than previously, however, the Americans accepted British quirks and even found them a source of amusement. Bernard Rogers provides a telling example. In 1950 he sat for Schools in PPE. One afternoon when he glanced at his page of essay topics he noticed that one of the questions was in Greek. That would have been expected if the examination were in Literae Humaniores, but knowledge of Greek was not a requirement for PPE. The intrepid Yank marched to the front of the hall to ask the proctor for a translation. Rogers was told to return to his seat. A few minutes later the proctor announced to the entire assembly of students that, as Greek was not a central part of the exam, he would provide a translation for all of them. When the exam was over Rogers was thanked by many of his fellow students. They told him that an Englishman would have been too shy to ask.[22]

Frank Sieverts (1955) has offered another illustration. Soon after he had settled into Balliol he attended a formal gathering for freshers in the college hall. He was assigned a seat next to a young man who called himself Clydesdale. Sieverts introduced himself and chatted away with typical American openness. Later he discovered that the college had intentionally picked him to sit next to the young Briton, who was the Marquess of Clydesdale, son of the Duke of Hamilton and scion of one of the oldest and wealthiest noble families in the country. College officials told Sieverts that English students would have been afraid to talk to Clydesdale but that an American could be counted on to keep the conversation going.[23]

One of the things that made the Rhodes Scholar experience of this period different from earlier decades was the altered status of Britain and the United States in world affairs. Britain emerged from the war with many cities ravaged and its economy reduced to bare necessities. Britannia no longer ruled the waves. India and Pakistan would be granted independence in 1947, and most of the rest of the old empire would break away over the next twenty years. In its "special relationship" with the United States, Britain was now the junior partner.

Rhodes Scholars from 1947 through the mid-1950s got a vivid taste – literally – of Britain's weakened condition. A long series of consumer items continued to be in short supply. Scholars were

shocked to find that their orientation packets included ration book-
lets. Philip Zabriskie (1950) recalls that he could have only one small
bucket of coal per day for his fireplace – enough for just a few
hours.[24] Bernard Rogers and his wife had just enough coal to make
their radiator warmer than the rest of the room.[25] Students could
purchase only one bottle of whiskey per term, though the pubs had
all the beer they wanted.[26] The dons at the wealthier colleges did not
suffer in this regard, for huge supplies of wine, sherry, and port had
been stored in the cellars before the war.[27] John Brademas (1950)
remembers having to take his own margarine or butter to hall at
mealtime.[28] Other rationed items included meat, cheese, tea, sugar,
jam, eggs, soap, candy, dried fruits, fuel, most kinds of clothing, and
all cereals except oatmeal.[29] There was, however, plenty of bread
and soggy vegetables. As one scholar lamented, the basic result was
that English food went from dull to duller.[30] Scholars who were in
the military, like Bernard Rogers, escaped the rigors of this monot-
ony by traveling to London to shop in the commissary of the American embassy.[31] As late as 1953 Americans were advised to take tins
of meat and butter with them; if they did not use these themselves
they could give them as presents to others.[32] Ronald Dworkin (1953)
vividly recalls his mother stuffing his luggage with cans of food
before he left for Oxford.[33]

For a country that had possessed the richest economy, largest
navy, and greatest empire, it was difficult to accept a decline that was
both absolute and relative. What made it harder was that one of the
two emerging superpowers was a former colony. Everywhere the
British looked they now encountered signs of American dominance.

This was made doubly irksome because of a sharp political diver-
gence between the two countries. With the growth of the welfare
state after the war, nearly all political parties in Britain and on the
continent came to accept a high degree of government intervention
in citizens' lives – in the form of a national health program, state-
owned mass transportation, state funding for university students,
and guarantees of workers' rights. Willie Morris (1956) got a taste of
this one day when he and some friends were visiting E.T. Williams
in Rhodes House. In 1952 Williams had succeeded Allen as Oxford
Secretary and Warden. Morris asked Williams what his politics
were. The Warden responded, "I'm right-wing Tory, which I understand is considerably farther to the left of anything you have in the
United States."[34] The result of this leftward shift in British politics
was that increasingly the United States looked like a militarist,
imperialist, arch-capitalist behemoth. The future journalist Paul

Craig Roberts came to realize this in the early 1960s, when an Earhart Fellowship permitted him to work on a D.Phil. at Merton College. Like most other Americans, he was struck by how socialist Britain appeared.[35]

The great majority of the Rhodes Scholars of this period got along well, person to person, with most British students, dons, and others. Martin Rush and Nicholas Katzenbach said that Americans were very popular in Oxford in the late 1940s. Ronald Dworkin reported that Americans were still a kind of novelty in the early 1950s, and Oxford dons knew little about American scholarship. Dworkin became a sought-after speaker in several colleges because he could instruct British dons and students about William Quine and other current American philosophers.[36] Frank Sieverts blended into the Oxford scene so well that he contributed numerous articles and movie reviews to the student magazine *Isis*. Sieverts and his classmate Reynolds Price helped to stage one of the most important and controversial theatrical events of the 1956/1957 season in Oxford. They participated in a public reading of Tennessee Williams's *Cat on a Hot Tin Roof*. (It was a reading rather than a full production, because Britain's Lord Chamberlain judged the play scandalous and temporarily banned stage performances.)[37] James Woolsey (1963) likewise enjoyed himself immensely in Oxford. He encountered absolutely no animosity from the people he met, and he was surprised even to be asked about it.[38]

A sizable majority of scholars, however, did face occasional anti-American snubbings or sneers. In 1946 Crane Brinton wrote in *The American Oxonian* that most Britons liked the United States, but that they were not accustomed to being a nation in debt. They feared that the United States would revert to isolationism. Upper-class Englishmen and intellectuals had an additional concern: they worried that all the world would become a vast, homogenized Hollywood as a result of the pervasive American influence.[39]

Neil Smelser (1952), Robert Rotberg (1957), and Gary Noble (1958) reported that they had to endure sporadic attacks on their country but that these episodes were minor and did not put a blight on their overall experience.[40] Eugene Burdick (1948) depicted a subtle sort of antipathy, saying that some of his British friends occasionally said things like, "Look, old chap, I'm not anti-American and, God knows, some of my best friends are American, but …" Burdick also acknowledged, however, that this mild resentment was counterbalanced by the fact that it was fashionable for Oxford students to have an American friend.[41]

One Oxford acquaintance assured Willie Morris that, although most students criticized America, secretly they liked it.[42] In the early 1950s a study of current British usage of the word "American" showed that it had negative overtones in the context of politics and diplomacy, but positive ones regarding economic and technological developments. A newly remodeled bathroom or any newfangled gadget was thought to be "American."[43] But this technological and economic superiority could also be oppressive. Many called it "Coca-colonization." In 1960 one of the most hotly contested debates in the Oxford Union concerned the motion: "Resolved: That this house holds America responsible for spreading vulgarity in Western society."[44]

The potential for friction was increased by the fact that British economic and imperial decline occurred just as the United States entered a prolonged period of growing prosperity. Rhodes Scholars personified this affluence. The dollar seemed almighty in the 1950s. Jason McManus (1958) recalls that his Rhodes Scholar stipend (by then £750 annually) made him relatively wealthy.[45]

The conspicuous consumption of some of the scholars did not help to assuage British envy. Hamilton Richardson (1955) chose Trinity College because he had been told it served the best food. It did not, however, have the best heating. After the young man from Louisiana complained of the cold, damp climate, the college bursar permitted him to purchase an electric heater for his rooms. When Richardson plugged it in, the lights went out all over college. The American then paid a princely sum to upgrade the wiring and install a new outlet. Some twenty years later Richardson revisited Oxford and took his family to see his old quarters. He proudly pointed to the outlet and the venerable heater. One of the British students then occupying the rooms looked up fearfully and asked, "You haven't come to take it away, have you, sir?"[46]

Soon after Pete Dawkins moved into Brasenose, his bicycle was stolen. (Petty larceny remains frequent today. Many students prefer to ride old, rusted bicycles that will not tempt thieves.) Instead of obtaining another bike, Dawkins purchased an Alfa Romeo so that he could tour Britain and the continent in style.[47] Dawkins was able to splurge because, as a West Point graduate, he was also receiving a salary as a second lieutenant. Other, less affluent, scholars bought motorcycles, old taxis, and jeeps for vacation travels as far away as India. David Boren (1963) probably holds the Rhodes Scholar record for wanderlust; he claims to have visited sixty countries during vacations.[48]

Frank Wells and Vince Jones (both 1953) enjoyed the most daring hobbies in their travels: flying and mountain climbing. Early in 1955 they pooled their resources ($600) and bought an old single-engine, two-seat airplane that had no navigation equipment or radio. After teaching themselves to fly, they set out during spring break for Cape Town. When they reached the outskirts of Nairobi they noticed the sun glistening on Mount Kilomanjaro. On a spur of the moment impulse they landed and climbed the mountain. Eventually they reached Cape Town and then headed back to Britain. They had not flown far when their plane's engine began to fail. They made an emergency landing in a farmer's field, with their plane flipping upside down. They emerged unscratched and managed to hitch a ride back to England in a British military transport.[49] This experience left Wells with an appetite for adventure. He especially wanted to be the first person to climb the highest peak on each of the seven continents. In 1982 he and a friend decided to put their careers on hold in order to carry out their Walter Mittyesque dream. He quit his job as president of Warner Brothers in Hollywood. During the months that followed he succeeded on six expeditions, but a turbulent storm forced him and his Sherpa guide to turn back three thousand feet from the summit of Mount Everest.

At the time of his death in April 1994 Wells was president and chief operating officer of the Disney Corporation. The man who had defied death on many earlier occasions died in a helicopter crash while returning to California from a skiing holiday in Nevada.

James Billington (1950), Richard Lugar, and others in the early and mid-1950s complained that they had to defend the United States against the charge that Senator Joseph McCarthy was leading the country into a reign of intellectual terror.[50] Just as McCarthyism was dying, the Suez crisis in the fall of 1956 reignited anti-American passions. President Dwight D. Eisenhower and Secretary of State John Foster Dulles condemned the joint British-French-Israeli assault on Egypt – a response to the latter's seizure of the Suez Canal. The assault was abruptly ended. Britain lost honor and blamed the United States for the humiliation. Rhodes Scholars became a target of abuse. John Sears (1955) recollects that for several weeks Americans had a hard time getting served in pubs.[51] By the summer of 1957, however, the crisis had been forgotten, and attention in Oxford turned to more important issues, like Eights Week.[52]

In the early 1960s criticism of American politics arose again. There were protests against the nuclear weapons stored at the American Strategic Air Command base twenty miles from Oxford. Many Britons decried the American Bay of Pigs fiasco as naked imperialist aggression.

It would be wrong, however, to exaggerate the impact that these tensions had on the daily lives of Rhodes Scholars and other Americans living in Britain. At the same time that many dons and students objected to the U.S. government's policies, they generally liked individual Americans. One sign of this came in 1965, when University College renamed its music room in honor of James F. Ray (1959), a young Rhodes Scholar who had been killed in Vietnam.[53]

NOTES

1. Harrison, *Twentieth Century*, 48-49, 71, 186-88.
2. Some of these "new" institutions had already existed as educational bodies of some sort but now were raised to the status of university. For a masterly account of the educational, health, and other welfare state programs of Clement Attlee and later prime ministers, see Nicholas Timmins, *The Five Giants: A Biography of the Welfare State* (New York, 1995).
3. Harrison, *Twentieth Century*, 577-83.
4. *TAO*, 45 (1958): 60.
5. *TAO*, 34 (1947): 177; 37 (1950): 3, 124.
6. *TAO*, 41 (1954): 93; 46 (1959): 103.
7. Interviews with Sieverts, 11 January 1994, Nye, 6 June 1994, and Sarbanes, 8 June 1994; *TAO*, 37 (1950): 3; 40 (1953): 43, 92.
8. "Pete Dawkins Writes from Oxford," *Cosmopolitan*, September 1960, 68.
9. Harrison, *Twentieth Century*, 222; *TAO*, 33 (1946): 177-78; 34 (1947): 23-24.
10. One additional graduate student college came later: Green College (1977).
11. Blumberg interview, 26 July 1993.
12. Muriel Beadle, *These Ruins Are Inhabited* (Garden City, NJ, 1961).
13. Mehta, *Up at Oxford*, 277-344.
14. Elton, *First Fifty Years*, 157.
15. Smelser interview, 30 March 1994.
16. Katzenbach interview, 30 March 1994.
17. *NYT*, 12 May 1966, 47.
18. Harrison, *Twentieth Century*, 227-29, 721-36, and passim; *TAO*, 53 (1966): 109-16.
19. *TAO*, 34 (1947): 105; 35 (1948): 1-17; 43 (1956): 130-31, 109; 47 (1960): 75-80.
20. Katzenbach interview, 30 March 1994.
21. *TAO*, 34 (1947): 165.
22. Rogers interview, 19 April 1994.
23. Sieverts interviews, 11 January and 9 June 1994.
24. Zabriskie interview, 30 December 1993.
25. Rogers interview, 19 April 1994.
26. Zabriskie interview, 30 December 1993.
27. *TAO*, 32 (1945): 70.

28. Brademas interview, 28 December 1993.
29. *TAO,* 33 (1946): 106-08.
30. *TAO,* 47 (1950): 1.
31. Rogers interview, 19 April 1994.
32. *TAO,* 40 (1953): 134.
33. Dworkin interview, 19 November 1993.
34. Willie Morris, *New York Days* (Boston, 1993), 44.
35. "The Oxford-American Connection," C-Span, January 1993.
36. Dworkin interview, 19 November 1993.
37. Sieverts, letter to authors, 16 June 1997.
38. Woolsey interview, 9 June 1994.
39. *TAO ,* 33 (1946): 81-87.
40. Interviews with Smelser, 30 March 1994, Rotberg, 31 August 1994, and Noble, 16 October 1994.
41. *TAO,* 37 (1950): 26.
42. Morris, *New York Days,* 43.
43. *TAO,* 38 (1951): 131.
44. *NYT,* 19 January 1960, 71.
45. McManus interview, 6 April 1994.
46. *NYT,* 20 November 1983, magazine, 118.
47. "Dawkins Writes," 73.
48. Interviews with Lee Donne Olvey , 25 June 1993, and Lester Thurow, 28 April 1994; *People,* 11 July 1983, 61.
49. Dick Bass and Frank Wells, with Rick Ridgeway, *Seven Summits* (New York, 1986), 10-13; *Hollywood Reporter,* 5 April 1994; *TAO,* 83 (1995):102-7.
50. Interviews with Lugar, 11 June 1993, and Billington, 12 January 1994.
51. Sears interview, 25 August 1994.
52. *TAO,* 44 (1957): 133.
53. *TAO,* 53 (1966): 42.

Chapter 10

THE COLD WAR AND THE SILENT GENERATION

At Oxford I led, by the standards of the University of Texas, a quiet and detached four years. My first tutorial in 1956 had been on the Reform Act of 1832; I had stayed up straight through one fog-filled night applying the finishing touches. My next-to-last sentence said, "Just how close the people of England came to revolution in 1832 is a question that we shall leave with the historians." I read this to my tutor, and from his vantage point in an easy chair two feet north of the floor he interrupted: "But Morris, we *are* the historians."

Willie Morris, *North toward Home*

At Oxford I had time to experiment with every aspect of my life. For the first time since I was fourteen I took chances with my body – hiking, racing cars, and playing contact sports – without fear of injury. Eating five meals a day I even gained 30 pounds. I questioned my religious faith and sought workable moral values instead of simply rules. I became more playful and rebellious, responding to events in a way that discipline and obligation had outlawed before. I began to enjoy people more, at first only if they were interesting foreigners and then even a few of the less serious-minded Americans. I traveled widely in Russia, the Middle East, and western Europe. Specific studies were neglected without guilt. I stopped taking myself so seriously, recognizing that life is as much a good laugh as a stirring sermon. I began to see how far I had to grow and change if I was to become a person that even I would like to know.

Bill Bradley, *Life on the Run*

Winners and Losers

Despite the many possible sources of conflict with Britons from the late 1940s to the mid-1960s, most Rhodes Scholars enjoyed the experience. Nevertheless, each year there were at least a couple of nervous breakdowns and one or two who quit before the end of the first year. At least one in the 1950s and three in the 1960s commit-

Notes for this chapter can be found on page 167.

ted suicide soon after returning home. Yet there is no evidence that Oxford alone was responsible for the mental or emotional problems of these individuals.[1] Most Rhodes Scholars were over-achievers. The pressures they placed on themselves, the unaccustomed freedom of Oxford, homesickness, and loneliness made such incidents less than surprising.

Word-of-mouth favorable publicity in the United States contributed to a steady rise in the number and caliber of applicants. The machinery that Frank Aydelotte had set in motion in the 1930s was well greased by now. The grueling interview process, at the state and district level, began to achieve widespread notoriety. From its beginnings the scholarship program acknowledged that intuition played a large role in decision making. A candidate needed to look good on paper, but he also needed to display a special kind of spark when confronted face-to-face with his committee.

In addition to the questions about proposed studies in Oxford and about current events around the world, committee members lobbed bizarre queries designed to test mental acuity. John Wofford (1957) was asked "What's the difference between a fly and a tree?" Fortunately for him, the chair of the committee was Milton Eisenhower, who disliked such silly questions. Eisenhower interrupted the questioner and saved Wofford from delving for a clever response. Moments later another person, recalling that Wofford's essay spoke of a fondness for opera, asked him to sing his favorite aria. Eisenhower again came to the rescue of non-singer Wofford.[2] Richard Lugar was asked something about Ingmar Bergman, which led to a discussion of the movie *Gaslight*, which then ricocheted into queries about stromboli.[3] Donne Olvey (1955) remembers that a fellow West Point cadet had to face this proposition: "Imagine that you are stranded on a desert island. Which two people from all history would you want to be with you?" The quick-witted candidate replied, "Leonardo da Vinci at age sixty-five and Sophia Loren at age seventeen."[4]

Erwin Canham (1926) sat on one of the selection committees in Massachusetts in the 1950s and witnessed how a candidate handled this query: "How would you spend a week in New York if supplied with unlimited funds?" The bold answer: the young man would take his girl friend to the Versailles Restaurant to hear Edith Piaf sing. Then he would go to Goody's music shop and buy all the records he could not afford previously. Following this he would purchase Columbia University and appoint himself president; thereby he could reorganize the university's rotten philosophy department.

Finally, he would invite three of the world's top tennis stars to play a match with him at the West Side Club. There he was: a gourmet, a music lover, an educational reformer, and an athlete. "Of course he was elected," commented Canham.[5]

The interviewers did not always pick the best, and everyone agreed that relying on intuition and the search for that "special something" was sometimes an arbitrary method. Numerous unsuccessful applicants went on to distinguished careers. Some of the "losers" of the 1920s and 1930s included George Gallup (the pollster), Walter Heller (later Chairman of John F. Kennedy's Council of Economic Advisers), Alger Hiss (a top State Department official before he was accused of treason), David Lilienthal (future head of the Tennessee Valley Authority and the Atomic Energy Commission), and Robert S. McNamara (Secretary of Defense under Kennedy and Lyndon Baines Johnson).

In the years immediately after the Second World War, the most famous non-winner was Jimmy Carter. Both he and Stansfield Turner were Annapolis graduates applying for the class of 1947. Turner won, but Carter never held this against him. That was partly because Carter acknowledged that all the midshipmen were in awe of Turner. Also, Turner and Carter applied from different districts – Turner in Illinois and Carter in Georgia – and thus did not compete against each other. It was no surprise decades later when Carter appointed Turner Director of the CIA. However, Carter has always borne a slight grudge against the district committee that passed over him. He later wrote that in preparation for the interview he had tirelessly read up on current events and world history. "They couldn't ask me any question in *Newsweek* or *Time* that I couldn't answer. But they chose him." The winner was an English major who specialized in the Elizabethan period and knew little about current events. Decades later Carter peevishly noted that the winner "became, I am told, a good teacher."[6]

Those who did win the scholarships discovered that Oxford was accommodating itself to Americans and to the twentieth century in ways beyond curriculum changes and improved laboratories. Many of the unpopular restrictions on student life were disappearing. By the mid-1950s students could enter pubs and go out at night without their gowns, though they could not play billiards before 1:00 p.m. or visit any of the race tracks in the area. The rule about returning to college before getting locked out had become a farce. While Pete Dawkins lived in Brasenose the college decided that the usual route taken by students climbing in was too dangerous. Therefore the college posted a notice revealing a new location where the barbed wire and broken glass above a wall had been removed.[7] The dean of Balliol went out of his way to tell Ved Mehta of a ground-floor window that he could climb through to get in after midnight.[8] James Woolsey discovered that the usual entry into St. John's was through the ground-floor room of one of the students. That student left a hat on the floor. Anyone passing through was expected to drop a coin into it.[9]

Changes could also be seen on the streets of the city. In addition to the increasing traffic congestion, there were beat poets, folk singers, and rock-and-roll music. Students let their hair grow long, and wild clothing replaced the old flannel "bags." Erwin Fleissner (1957) remembers seeing Allen Ginsberg at a poetry reading. Ginsberg offered marijuana to the students, and most of them (but not Fleissner) joined him in smoking it.[10]

On the other hand, many of the traditions that attracted or amused Americans remained in place. Students were still considered gentlemen, and they could run up tabs at shops. After he returned to the United States, Willie Morris needed three years to pay off the book bill he had accumulated at Blackwell's. Bump suppers were just as rowdy as before. Woolsey witnessed one in which dons and students, all dressed in gowns, dipped their rolls in gravy and threw them at each other. After the food fight, everyone went to the SCR, stacked all the furniture to make a tunnel, and then forced each other to crawl through it.[11] Gary Noble observed a similar dinner at Balliol. At the end of it a large bottle was passed around. Dons and students urinated in it and then dumped the contents onto the grounds of Trinity College next door.[12]

Oxford likewise continued to be a place eminently tolerant of eccentric behavior and ideas. One evening in the early 1950s at a private student dining club, the featured guest was T. S. Eliot. James Billington was there and remembers that a student asked Eliot what he thought about the growing menace of Red China. The poet responded that one did not need to worry about a country that had never been able to produce an indigenous cheese.[13] A few years later Willie Morris attended a dinner at which W. H. Auden was the special guest. Auden wagered Morris a one-pound note that he could drink a large carafe of red wine within a minute. The poet then accomplished the feat and collapsed on the floor.[14]

In a trend that started before the war, sports declined as a criterion for winning a scholarship. A smaller percentage of winners had played in the major varsity sports in their American universities, though more than three-quarters continued to participate in rowing and other Oxford college sports. By the 1960s someone like William Frerking (1966) seemed close to the norm rather than an amusing oddball; in his interviews for the scholarship he unabashedly acknowledged that his favorite sport was bridge.[15] Jonathan Kozol (1958) was shocked to learn that he won a scholarship, for he had flunked a mandatory swimming test at Harvard.[16]

This period did, however, send some top athletes to Oxford. One was tennis player Hamilton Richardson (1955). He was a member of the Davis Cup team from 1951 to 1958 and men's doubles champion in 1958. The Rhodes Trust allowed him to fit his Oxford studies around his sports schedule.

Another was Heisman Trophy winner Pete Dawkins. Like most other Americans, when he arrived at Brasenose in 1959 he took a bemused attitude toward the more amateurish Oxford approach to athletics. A *Cosmopolitan* article described how his gung-ho cheering during rugby matches departed from standard etiquette. The article also featured a photograph showing Dawkins breaking another rule by tackling opposing players.[17]

Basketball was introduced to Oxford by American Rhodes Scholars who went up in 1947. At first it was an informal club sport, and until the mid-1960s the nearest decent basketball court where the team could practice was at the SAC base twenty miles away. From the start the Americans dominated the team, but Oxford dons and students never seem to have objected. After the game became a formal college sport in the early 1950s, the American and Canadian Rhodes Scholars ensured that Oxford beat Cambridge in most years. In the fall of 1954 the team included two future U.S. senators: Paul Sarbanes and Richard Lugar. "Tyke" Sarbanes was the captain. Several times in this decade the American-led team won the British amateur national championship and toured Europe.[18]

The most famous basketball player during these years was Princeton All-American Bill Bradley. He had turned down a $100,000 offer to play in the National Basketball Association in order to study in Oxford. But the lure of the sport proved overwhelming. He played for the Oxford team against Cambridge, and the Rhodes Trust also permitted him to play for a professional Italian team during vacations.

In general, however, athletic prowess declined to such a degree that several scholars of this period had physical defects that almost surely would have excluded them in earlier years. Charles Bolté (1947) was missing most of his right leg. He had gained national attention in the spring of 1941 when, as a Dartmouth undergraduate, he wrote an open letter to Franklin Roosevelt calling for American entry into the war. The letter was published in the *New York Herald Tribune*. Impatient with American slowness to act, Bolté joined the British Army and fought under British commander Bernard Montgomery in North Africa. After an 88 mm. shell shattered his right leg, the limb was amputated above the knee.

George Steiner (1950) had been born with a withered right arm. James Barnes (1954) was sight-impaired and, in later years, became legally blind. What impressed the selection committees in these cases and others was that the individuals were still vigorous and, because of their disabilities, were compelled even more than other persons to demonstrate their stamina. Steiner, for example, was an avid hiker.

Ved Mehta was blind and yet his professors at Pomona had wanted to nominate him for the class of 1956. His blindness was no obstacle, but other impediments prevented him from applying. He was caught in a sort of Catch-22. As a citizen of India he could not apply for a scholarship from the United States. But because he attended a university outside his native country he was also ineligible to apply from India. Fortunately, other grants enabled him to reach Balliol.[19]

Many Rhodes Scholars eventually went into careers that won them national or international fame, but few Rhodes Scholars have ever been celebrities while they were still students. The exceptions have tended to be the athletes: Eddie Eagan, Byron White, Pete Dawkins, and Bill Bradley, to name a few. Only a handful have become celebrities in Oxford for feats outside of sports. Two belong to this period: Roger ("Denny") Hansen (1957) and Kris Kristofferson (1958).

Hansen's tale has been poignantly chronicled by his Yale classmate and friend Calvin Trillin in the book *Remembering Denny*. Denny Hansen was everyone's "all-purpose boy hero," a young man of "stunning completeness" with "a million-dollar smile." In his California high school he was the top student and president of his senior class. At Yale he was a varsity swimmer, member of Scroll and Key (one of the exclusive secret societies), and owner of a Phi Beta Kappa key. He graduated magna cum laude. Most of his friends assumed he would some day be President. It was also taken for granted that he would win a Rhodes Scholarship.

In the spring of 1957 *Life* magazine decided to run a story on an ideal student graduating from one of the nation's universities. The magazine asked Yale's publicity department to recommend someone. Yale had two upcoming Rhodes Scholars that year: Hansen and

Erwin Fleissner. The P.R. office rejected Fleissner and sent two names to *Life*: those of Hansen and a football star named Ackerman. Trillin speculates that Fleissner was rejected because his name sounded Jewish. Yale was exuberant when WASPish *Life* opted for the all-American boy with the all-American name: Denny Hansen.[20]

Hansen's graduation from Yale was covered by the era's most famous photographer, Alfred Eisenstaedt. In those days *Life* carried an impact far greater than any of today's magazines or television shows. Being featured in a *Life* photographic essay was tantamount to anointment for high office and permanent celebrity.[21]

Hansen attracted renewed attention five months later, when the magazine reported on his first term in Oxford. This sequel humorously suggested that Hansen was a typically naive, gauche American set down in the refined eyrie of Oxford. Hansen is described as "staggered" by the erudition of his British classmates. He beseeches his tutor not to assign him books in German and French. He drinks Ovaltine and orangeade instead of ale. He fumbles in his first attempt to make tea.[22] For understandable reasons, Erwin Fleissner has remarked that he has always been grateful that Yale chose Hansen over him for *Life*.[23]

Despite the jokes at Hansen's expense, this second article was favorable. His fellow Rhodes Scholars had the impression that his two years at Magdalen were "ebullient," though it must have been a disappointment when he managed to obtain only a Second in modern history. Both Hansen's fame and the upward spiral of his career trajectory were to be short-lived.[24]

Kris Kristofferson's notoriety would be more lasting. Many people today are shocked to learn that he was a Rhodes Scholar. The shaggy actor and country-western singer- song-writer is about as far as one can go from the usual stereotype for Rhodes Scholars. Yet in the 1950s Kristofferson matched the ideal almost perfectly. At Pomona College he was a top student, won election to Phi Beta Kappa, was an all-conference football end, commanded the ROTC battalion, was a Golden Gloves boxer, and won four prizes in a short-story writing contest sponsored by *The Atlantic Monthly*. During summers he worked with railroad crews and firefighters in Alaska.

At Oxford he played rugby for Merton and won a blue in boxing. In his free time he started a novel – "a sort of complicated thing, in which I look at the same episode through five different points of view."[25] Soon after he arrived at Merton his English literature tutor, Hugo Dyson, judged him "one of the most favorable specimens of Rhodes scholarship" and was sure that the young man would have a sparkling career as a writer.[26] Warden E.T. Williams, Rhodes classmate Jason McManus, and many others imagined that within a few years Kristofferson would become one of the greatest novelists and short-story writers America had ever produced.[27] (Even today, whenever Kristofferson gives a career description of himself he offers "writer.")

Years later Kristofferson admitted that he "never felt like a scholar or part of the academic world" while in Oxford. Yet he had always been a "word junkie." In Oxford he developed his passion for poetry in general and for the works of Shakespeare and Blake in particular.[28]

However, there were signs that he would soon become one of the most atypical Rhodes Scholars. Jason McManus and Joseph Nye (1958) recall that Kristofferson seemed to be deeply introspective, restless, trying to "find himself."[29] He spent as much time away from Oxford as he could. Some scholars of that period who knew Kristofferson were surprised when we told them that he finished his two years in Oxford and obtained a Second in his English literature B.A. They saw so little of him that they assumed he had quit and gone to live in France or the United States.

The things that made Kristofferson the most unusual were his musical abilities and ambitions. He accompanied himself on guitar as he sang his own folk songs. Indeed, a London promoter named Paul Lincoln signed up Kristofferson when he was halfway through his first year at Oxford. Within weeks Kristofferson had a contract with J. Arthur Rank's recording firm. Lincoln renamed the young singer Kris Carson – a moniker that stuck only briefly. Lincoln was confident that if Carson's entertainment career faltered the scholar could become a successful professional wrestler. *Time* picked up the story of this unusual Rhodes Scholar and predicted that the "well-muscled" Kristofferson was on his way to becoming a wealthy "teen-agers' guitar-thwonking singing idol."[30]

Kristofferson shocked everyone after he left Oxford. He entered neither show business, nor academe, nor the wrestling arena. Instead, he joined the army and for the next two years piloted heli-copters in Germany. One of his classmates bemoaned the fact that someone who had a "habit of excelling in everything" should waste his time in the military.[31] His fellow scholars were even more befud-dled when Kristofferson left the army and settled down in Nashville to compose country music. Perhaps this explains why Kristofferson has never contributed to the class notes of *The American Oxonian* or remained close to his fellow scholars. For the past three decades the annual notes for the class of 1958 have habitually joked about Kristofferson "sightings."[32]

Academic Vagaries

One of the most fascinating persons ever connected with Rhodes Scholars was E.T. Williams – later Sir Edgar, though he asked nearly everyone to call him Bill. Williams served as Oxford Secretary and Warden of Rhodes House from 1952 to 1980. Prior to that job he had a distinguished career in both the military and academe. In the late 1930s and again after the war he was a fellow and history tutor at Balliol. Shortly before accepting the position at Rhodes House he had also assumed the co-editorship of the multi-volume *Dictionary of National Biography*. During the war he served as chief intelligence officer to General Montgomery, who later credited Williams with the tactics that led to victory at El Alamein in Egypt. From North Africa, Williams followed Montgomery to Italy, France, and Germany. At age thirty-three he became the youngest brigadier in the British Army. In 1946 and 1947 he served as a director on the Security Council Secretariat of the United Nations.[33] Years later it was widely rumored that he was one of the models for Ian Fleming's spy-master "M" in the James Bond thrillers.

Until shortly before his death in 1995 he remained a healthy octogenarian who still took a bus to dine frequently at Balliol. He remembered vivid details of all the Rhodes Scholars who had come up during his twenty-eight-year "watch." Scholars from his period have offered conflicting views about him. Given his military background, it is not surprising that some found him gruff and intimidating. His obituary in the *Daily Telegraph* said that Rhodes Scholars "came to appreciate his pithy, elliptical and above all candid comments on their progress."[34] Others, however, insisted that he and his wife, Gillian, were models of graciousness. Rhodes House in their years could always be counted on to provide one of the things that Americans missed most: ice water.[35] When Frank Sieverts had his tonsils removed during the winter of 1956, the Williams family invited him to recuperate in Rhodes House. There he could enjoy another rare commodity in Oxford: central heating.[36] Furthermore, Williams was known to lend his own money to scholars in desperate need. Such a loan permitted Willie Morris to fly home to Texas to see his dying father.[37]

Williams admitted that he was blunt with some of the young men, those who posed behavioral problems or who were drifting aimlessly in their course of studies. He went so far as to tell one Canadian scholar, Norman Cantor (1954), that his selection had been a mistake. Four decades later, Cantor concedes that he still harbors some ill feelings toward Williams, but he agrees that the Warden's assessment had been correct. Outside of intellectual brilliance, the young man had none of the other Rhodes criteria. Additionally, Cantor now confesses that in Oxford he had treated dons and fellow students abrasively, partly because he was desperately in need of a girlfriend.[38]

When analyzing Rhodes Scholars as a whole, it is impossible to see any strong tendencies linking later careers with scholarly performance in Oxford. One might assume that those destined for academic careers would tend to do better in Oxford, and that the "political types" were the ones who devoted too much time to sports, pubs, and travels. Yet this assumption does not correlate with the facts. Admittedly, some future politicians had less than stellar records. Among future U.S. senators, Larry Pressler (1964) settled for a diploma rather than a full-fledged degree, Richard Lugar got a Fourth, Bill Bradley a Third, and David Boren a Second. (It was widely believed at the time that Lugar would have scored higher but that his steadfast opposition to the dominant left-wing political views of the day led his examiners to mark him down.)[39] Future Ohio Governor Richard Celeste (1960) worked toward a B.Litt. but obtained no degree. Future Supreme Court Justice David Souter (1961) obtained a Second in law. Yet future Senator Paul Sarbanes got a First, and future Democratic Whip in the House of Representatives John Brademas (1950) obtained a D.Phil. after completing a thesis on Spanish anarchists in the 1930s.

Many scholars who eventually achieved distinguished academic or research careers sparkled in their Oxford essays and theses. Robert Darnton (1960) completed both a B.Phil. and a D.Phil., and his doctoral thesis turned into his first book: *Mesmerism and the End of the Enlightenment in France* (1968). Today he is on the faculty at Princeton and has written several of the most influential books on modern French history. He sums up his experiences this way:

> [Oxford dons] Robert Shackleton and Richard Cobb got me started in French history; and thanks to their initial shove, I never stopped. I learned even more from my tutor in Worcester College, Harry Pitt, who never published much but read everything and was the greatest teacher I ever encountered. I loved my years at Oxford, both as a student and later [for one year] as Eastman Professor. I loved the beauty of the place. I loved its foreignness. And when it became somewhat more familiar, I loved the intellectual life inside its walls.[40]

Darnton has returned often to Oxford, where he says the opportunity to chat with scholar/raconteurs like Isaiah Berlin (who died in 1997) has been a genuine intellectual "feast."

Poet Guy Davenport (1948) found the British to be "the rudest and the most insufferably snobbish" people he had ever met. Nevertheless, he persevered and completed his B.Litt. in English literature. Along the way he also enjoyed attending lectures by J.R.R. Tolkien, C.S. Lewis, Thomas Mann, T.S. Eliot, Enid Starkie, and other worthies. By the time he returned home he had purchased 774 books, a number fixed in his mind from having to declare them through customs.[41]

Poet, novelist, and short-story writer Reynolds Price (1955) admits that he just barely completed his B.Litt. thesis on Milton:

> ... a project conceived in anxiety, delayed by personal pleasure (the delights of early love and continental travel when I should have been chained to a clammy desk in the misty Bodleian library), and completed two years later in a near-panic of duress literally one hour before deadline.[42]

Yet one could cite other future academics who failed to obtain Firsts or who returned home before completing all the work for an advanced degree. William Jay Smith (1947) resigned his scholarship after one year, though this did not prevent him later from becoming a distinguished university professor, author, and poetry consultant to the Library of Congress. Historians Robert K. Massie (1950) and Robert Paxton (1954) got Seconds in modern history. Wesley Posvar (1948) got a Third in PPE, though he eventually became president of the University of Pittsburgh. Gary Noble went on to become one of today's most important medical researchers, especially in the area of AIDS, and yet he obtained only a Third in physiology.

Of course, many factors besides intelligence and perseverance affected one's final record in Oxford. Erwin Fleissner found the study of history and philosophy at Brasenose to be thin intellectual nourishment. He had to go over many of the same things he had already learned at Yale. Moreover, he found his dons to be chauvinistic and preoccupied with word games rather than with finding solutions to real world problems. Yet Fleissner loved much about Oxford, and he is thankful that his studies there convinced him that he did not want a career in philosophy.[43] He got a Third in PPE and then returned to the United States to become a leading cancer researcher.

The experiences of Thomas Bartlett (1951) and James Woolsey were typical of many others. One of Bartlett's PPE tutors sat him down soon after he arrived in University College. The tutor told him he could obtain a First, but only if he set all else aside for the next two years. Or he could aim for a solid second and do "all the rest."

Bartlett took the second option. The son of a poor family from a small town in Oregon, he saw thirteen plays in his first eight weeks and performed in one or two of them. He also played rugby and tennis for Univ. and traveled throughout Britain on a used motorcycle that he had bought.[44]

Woolsey had majored in history at Stanford and planned to become a college professor. At St. John's he hoped to complete a D.Phil. Soon after he arrived, he realized that he wanted a career in law rather than academe. Thus a D.Phil. would be of no use to him, and he would need to attend law school in the United States regardless of what he did in Oxford. He switched to PPE, where he finally obtained a Second. The tutorial experience helped him immensely in his writing and thinking. Though he worked hard, he did not have that extra little drive needed for a First. Instead, he rowed in Torpids and Eights, played rugby and tennis, saw plays in London, attended Oxford Union debates, played guitar in a folk singing club, and chased Somerville women.[45]

E.T. Williams has observed that the two Rhodes Scholars of the 1950s and 1960s who struck him as most different from the others were George Steiner and Jonathan Kozol. Steiner was born in Paris in 1929. His father was a Jew who had emigrated from Czechoslovakia to Vienna and then, with his wife, to France. Young George was raised speaking three languages: French, German, and English. His mother would often start a sentence in one language and finish in another. In Paris he attended the American School. After 1940 the family lived in the United States., where Steiner graduated from the Lycée française in New York City in 1947. He then went to Yale, where he encountered a pervasive tone of anti-Semitism. He quit Yale and transferred to the University of Chicago, where he thrived in the polyglot, high-powered, energetic atmosphere nourished by President Robert Hutchins. From there he went to Harvard. He found the environment there too patrician, though he completed his M.A.

When he arrived in Oxford in 1950 there were already several characteristics that set him off from most of his classmates. One was his cosmopolitanism. This was no small-town rube staring glossy eyed at the marvels of Europe. Steiner had never considered himself American, and he deplored the crassness and shallowness of American culture – a feeling that deepened in his later years. He was also unusual in his intellectual seriousness and ambition. This was not an American who would spend two or three years in raucous bump suppers, pub crawls, and carefree wandering across the continent in his vacations. He wanted to get on with his career and not waste two years "finding himself."

In Oxford Steiner developed a new approach to literary criticism. He opposed the reigning doctrine of New Criticism, which advocated looking at a novel or poem on its own terms, with no regard for the personal life of the author or the social context in which it was written. Moreover, Steiner was interested in comparative literature rather than the traditional approach of sticking to one author, country, or period. He aimed to complete his D.Phil. thesis in the shortest time possible.

His supervisor told him that his ideas were unacceptable in Oxford. Nevertheless, Steiner pursued his reading and writing independently for the next two years. Finally he presented his thesis and sat for a three-hour examination. This was a disaster. Steiner later claimed that his supervisor (whom he declined to name) never read even a line of the work. The examiners told him that his thesis was too subjective, too speculative, too unorthodox, and insufficiently documented. They said he might get it published and become famous, but that it was not acceptable as a doctoral thesis. Rather unceremoniously, they also expressed the hope that the assertive young man would never set foot in Oxford again.[46]

Unfazed by this experience, Steiner was determined to find a way to remain in Europe rather than return to the United States. He marched to the offices of the *Economist* in London and brazenly asked for a job. Thinking to deter the applicant, the editor assigned him to write an article on David Ricardo, John Maynard Keynes, and Alfred Marshall within one week. Steiner completed the piece within two days and was promptly offered a job.

A few weeks later a distinguished-looking old gentlemen, dressed in a Victorian suit, showed up at Steiner's *Economist* office (actually, a desk in a hallway). It was the celebrated Oxford don Humphrey House. The latter had heard of Steiner's plight and thought that Oxford had treated him abominably. He told the young man that if the university agreed to take in foreign students it must at least work with them and make sure they understand the requirements for theses. House told Steiner that if he was willing to revise the thesis that he, House, would serve as his supervisor. Steiner agreed, and over the next two years, on evenings and weekends, he did additional research and forced himself to conform to the "system." He learned that an Oxford doctoral thesis must be difficult to read, filled with footnotes, and padded with a long bibliography. Steiner's revised thesis passed the examination, and Humphrey House died forty-eight hours after seeing it through.[47]

Steiner hoped no one would ever go to the Bodleian to read the copy of the thesis deposited there, for it would put them to sleep. Eventually, his original, rejected thesis was published by the distinguished publishing house Faber & Faber. *The Death of Tragedy* (1961) helped to cement his reputation as one of the most important and original literary critics and general men of letters in the English-speaking world. His admirers have praised him extravagantly with phrases like "puissant majesty," "polymathic virtuosity" and "shocking massiveness of ... learning."[48] They have also called him "one of the great, restless wanderers of modern criticism" and "one of the towering intellectual figures of our time."[49]

In his essays and novels Steiner has attacked inhumanity, totalitarianism, and the low appreciation of high culture in contemporary post-industrial capitalist societies. As a public intellectual fighting for worthy causes, he is fulfilling Cecil Rhodes' dream, but he remains stoutly iconoclastic and different from of any of the usual stereotypes of Rhodes Scholars. He has contributed hundreds of reviews to the *New Yorker* and the *New York Review of Books*, but virtually all of these have been on European themes. From 1956 to 1958 Steiner was a member of the Institute for Advanced Study in Princeton, and he has held temporary and part-time appointments at several American universities. He has spent most of his career, however, in Britain and on the continent. In 1961 he accepted an appointment as fellow at Churchill College in Cambridge. Since 1974 he has split his time between Cambridge and the University of Geneva.

Steiner eventually forgave Oxford for the shabby way he had been treated, and in 1994 he became the first person appointed to Oxford's Lord Weidenfeld Visiting Professorship in European Comparative Literature. Steiner has remained on close terms with several of his Rhodes Scholar classmates, and he has contributed to the class notes regularly over the years. Nevertheless, his impatience and bluntness have shown through on numerous occasions, as he has bemoaned what he considers the failure of Rhodes Scholars to do enough in fighting the world's fight.[50]

Jonathan Kozol was like Steiner in his drive to accomplish serious work rather than daydream in Oxford's serene time warp. E. T. Williams was happy that the American selection committee had seen something special in Kozol and awarded him a scholarship. Williams also perceived immediately, however, that Kozol was not suited to the frivolities and expansive social and athletic life that accompanied academic work in Oxford. Kozol later recounted that all through his youth he seemed to be glued to a course charted by his elders. Even before he thought of applying for a Rhodes Scholarship, the master of his house in Harvard asked him, "Will it be Balliol or Magdalen?" (The young man eventually opted for the latter).[51] After a decade in an English-style prep school and Eliot House at Harvard, Kozol felt that he had been living in Britain for years before he even reached Oxford.[52]

Kozol felt stifled in Magdalen's cloistered walls and lasted less than one term. Late one night near the end of 1958, he grabbed his typewriter and a small bag of personal effects, climbed over the Magdalen wall, and fled to Paris. There he hoped to become a serious novelist of books that would change the world. Two of the occupants in his Left Bank hotel were William Burroughs, then writing *Naked Lunch,* and Allen Ginsberg. Kozol also came to know other American expatriates, including Richard Wright and James Baldwin. The only trouble, he gradually discovered, was that he had not lived through anything worth writing about. "It's hard to write a novel about being in writing class."[53] After four anguished years in Paris, he returned to Massachusetts.

After reading news accounts of the civil rights movement, Kozol was stirred to action. He took a job as a substitute fourth-grade teacher in Boston's Roxbury ghetto and suddenly confronted what would be his mission in life: teaching and writing books condemning the ills of society. He was fired from his teaching job two weeks before the end of the school year when his principal discovered he was trying to open the minds of his black pupils by teaching them the angry poetry of Langston Hughes and showing them posters of Paris. Teachers in that school were expected to stick to the rigid curriculum and mete out corporal punishment in generous doses.

Kozol chronicled the deadening environment of a segregated ghetto school in his first book, *Death at an Early Age: The Destruction of the Hearts and Minds of Negro Children in the Boston Public Schools,* which received a National Book Award in 1967. His later books have included *Illiterate America* (1985), *Rachel and Her Children: Homeless Families in America* (1988), *Savage Inequalities: Children in America's Schools* (1991), and *Amazing Grace: The Lives of Children and the Conscience of a Nation* (1995). He has become one of his nation's most perceptive and incendiary social critics.

Decades later Kozol acknowledged that his resignation from his Rhodes Scholarship had not been Oxford's fault. In Oxford he found himself "among some of the brightest and most likeable people I had ever known." During his brief stay at the university he had befriended several fellow scholars plus Ved Mehta and E.T. Williams.[54]

Kozol's reforming zeal in itself does not make him different from numerous other Rhodes Scholars. But his single-minded serious-ness, his perpetual impatience with stupidity and intolerance, his abhorrence of laxness, his lack of a "good ol' boy" quality, made him, like George Steiner, unable to fit in at Oxford with other Rhodes Scholars. Not until the 1980s did Kozol begin to contribute, at irregular intervals, to the annual class notes. Though *The American Oxonian* had become a more substantial and serious journal, in 1993 Kozol accused it of being "bewilderingly detached from the realities of life today. It reads like the newsletter of a gentleman's club from the Victorian age."[55]

Despite the bad experiences of a few Americans – through their fault or Oxford's – the great majority from these years had an extremely positive academic and social experience. In summing up his own years in Oxford, Neil Smelser voiced the feelings of many when he said, "The vaccine took."[56]

One of the biggest changes in the history of the scholarship pro-gram came late in 1962, with the announcement that two black Americans had been selected for the following year's class. They were the first African Americans since Alain Locke's controversial nomination fifty-six years earlier. The appointment of J. Stanley Sanders and John Edgar Wideman reflected dramatic changes in American society. The story of these and other black scholars will be discussed in a later chapter.

NOTES

1. Interviews with David Alexander, 23 May 1995; John Alexander, 4 August 1994; Thomas Allen, 20 November 1995; James Billington, 12 January 1994; Erwin Fleissner, 29 December 1993; Joseph Nye, 6 June 1994; Donald Rivkin, 27 December 1993; and Richard Schaper, 22 August 1994.
2. Wofford interview, 22 April 1994.
3. Lugar interview, 11 June 1993.
4. Olvey interview, 25 June 1993.
5. Elton, "Englishman's Audit," 99.
6. Funari interview, 11 October 1993; *NYT Magazine*, 20 November 1983, 113; *NYT*, 14 January 1993, C1, C10.
7. Dawkins, "Dawkins Writes," 70.
8. Mehta, *Up at Oxford*, 73.
9. Woolsey interview, 9 June 1994.
10. Fleissner interview, 29 December 1993.
11. Woolsey interview, 9 June 1994.
12. Noble interview, 16 October 1994.
13. Billington interview, 12 January 1994.
14. Willie Morris, *My Two Oxfords* (Council Bluffs, IA, 1989), 7.
15. *St. Louis Post-Dispatch*, 6 June 1993, 1C.
16. Kozol interview, 18 January 1996.
17. Dawkins, "Dawkins Writes," 74.
18. Interviews with Jason McManus, 6 April 1994, and Bernard Rogers, 19 April 1994; Willie Morris, *New York Days* (Boston, 1993), 44-45; *TAO*, 43 (1956): 16-19;, 44 (1957): 135; Harrity, "63 Years of Yanks," 82-83.
19. Mehta, *Up at Oxford*, 4.
20. Calvin Trillin, *Remembering Denny* (New York, 1993), 81-89.
21. "A Farewell to Bright College Years," *Life*, 24 June 1957, 130-36.
22. "Man of Eli at Oxford," *Life*, 2 December 1957, 81-82.
23. Fleissner interview, 29 December 1993.
24. *TAO*, 78 (1991): 216; 79 (1992): 117-19. Hansen will be discussed further in a later chapter.
25. *Time*, 6 April 1959, 69.
26. Ibid.
27. Interviews with McManus, 6 April 1994, and Sir Edgar Williams, 1 July 1994.
28. *People*, 11 July 1983, 63.
29. Interviews with McManus, 6 April 1994, and Nye, 6 June 1994.
30. *Time*, 6 April 1959, 69.
31. *TAO*, 48 (1961): 247.
32. For example, *TAO*, 83 (1996): 296.
33. *TAO*, 38 (1951): 113. Many books on the British Army in the Second World War frequently mention Williams' role. Most major British and American newspapers carried long obituaries. Examples: (London) *Times*, 29 June 1995, features section; *Independent*, 7 July 1995, 18; *NYT*, 30 June 1995, 17D. Rhodes Scholars eulogized him in *TAO*, 83 (1996): 4-17.
34. *Daily Telegraph*, 28 June 1995, 27.
35. *TAO*, 40 (1953): 133.
36. Sieverts, letter to authors, 19 September 1996.
37. Morris, *North toward Home*, 196.

38. Interviews with Cantor, 28 December 1993, and Williams, 1 July 1994.
39. Sieverts, letter to authors, 19 September 1996.
40. Darnton, letter to authors, 31 March 1994.
41. Davenport, letter to authors, 30 June 1995.
42. Reynolds Price, *A Common Room* (New York, 1987), x.
43. Fleissner interview, 29 December 1993.
44. Bartlett interview, 13 December 1995.
45. Woolsey interview, 9 June 1994.
46. George Steiner and Ramin Jahanbegloo, *Entretiens* (Paris, 1993), 21-42.
47. Ibid., 43-44.
48. Nathan A. Scott, Jr., and Ronald A. Sharp, eds., *Reading George Steiner* (Baltimore, 1994), 1.
49. *New York Review of Books*, 12 May 1994, 33.
50. *TAO*, 71 (1984): 67; 73 (1986): 47.
51. *TAO*, 72 (1985): 79.
52. Kozol interview, 18 January 1996.
53. *TAO*, 83 (1996): 34.
54. *TAO* 72 (1985): 79; Kozol interview, 18 January 1996.
55. *TAO*, 80 (1993): 186.
56. Smelser interview, 30 March 1994.

→ Chapter 11 ←

BILL CLINTON AND FRIENDS

[Oxford, 8 June 1994]. President Clinton returned today for a sentimental journey to the university where he didn't inhale, didn't get drafted and didn't get a degree.

Maureen Dowd, *New York Times*

Bill Clinton was an eager pupil, reading copiously for each tutorial and writing thorough though not always very polished essays. There was no doubt in my mind, even at the very beginning of his Oxford career, that he would pass the B.Phil. exam without any problems. He enjoyed his tutorials hugely and shone in discussion. He had a natural feel for politics which made me certain even at that stage that he would one day become a politician.

Zbigniew Pelczynski, *Pembroke College Record*

The Rhodes Scholars of the late 1960s and early 1970s were products of one of the most tumultuous periods in American history. These years witnessed a long series of divisive events and developments: the assassinations of Robert Kennedy, Martin Luther King, Jr., and Malcolm X; race riots in dozens of large American cities; violent student-police confrontations at the 1968 Democratic National Convention in Chicago; the climax of student radicalism, with its accompanying atmosphere of flower power, marijuana, and iconoclasm; growing disenchantment with the status quo in government, as evidenced by the popularity of political mavericks like Eugene McCarthy; and, finally, the growing national opposition to U.S. involvement in the Vietnam War.

This painful cycle of national traumas inevitably had an impact on the Rhodes Scholars of the period. The particular scholar who best exemplifies all that was going on at that time also happens to be the one who eventually became President of the United States.

Notes for this chapter can be found on page 214.

The Making of a Southern Scholar

Bill Clinton's first twenty-two years were so remarkable that his winning of a Rhodes Scholarship was almost anti-climactic.[1] Many aspects of his childhood might have caused personal and professional failure for other individuals, but Clinton managed to rise above the problems life presented him. William Jefferson Blythe III was born in the small town of Hope, Arkansas, in August 1946. His mother Virginia was a flirtatious, widowed nurse who would eventually rise to become a nurse anesthetist. When not at work, she enjoyed parties, card playing, and betting on horses. Virginia was an energetic American original, who took pride in her heavy makeup, false eyelashes, and loud jewelry. The boy's father, Bill Blythe, had been a restless, scheming sort; he died in an automobile crash a few months before the birth of his namesake. Blythe had neglected to tell Virginia that he had been married two (or perhaps three) times previously and that he was the father of several children born in and out of wedlock. These facts became public only in the 1990s, when reporters began delving into the family history.[2]

Little Billy Blythe spent his first four years living with his mother and his maternal grandparents in Hope. In 1950 Virginia Blythe married Roger "Dude" Clinton, who owned the local Buick car dealership. Virginia married him over the protests of her parents, for Roger Clinton had a well-earned reputation as a nattily attired, gambling, hard-drinking philanderer. It was not long before Billy and his mother also discovered that the man was a wife-beater and an inept businessman. In 1952 Roger Clinton sold his dealership and moved the family to his hometown of Hot Springs. There he could get financial support from his brothers and also enjoy the nightlife. Hot Springs was a resort town and sported numerous illicit casinos and brothels as well as a race track.

Billy's legal surname was Blythe, but everyone knew him as Clinton. Not until he was 16 years old did he formally adopt the latter name. He did it to show love and protection for his young half-brother, Roger (born in 1956), rather than to display any affection for his stepfather.[3] Indeed, on more than one occasion as a teenager Bill had to rescue his mother and brother from the father's violent, alcoholic rampages.

Despite his troubled home life, young Bill Clinton shone in the classroom. He was the smartest boy in his elementary school and one of the top two or three students in his class at Hot Springs High School. Though his mother and stepfather were not churchgoers, he joined a nearby Baptist congregation. A tall, burly, outgoing youth, he acquired the nickname "Bubba."[4] He excelled in Latin, physics, and math, and his saxophone playing in the school band won him "All State" accolades. As the best saxophone player in Hot Springs, he frequently performed in the local night spots. He was also popular with many of the girls.

The most famous episode of his high school days came in the summer of 1963, when he was selected one of Arkansas's two senators at the annual Boys Nation in Washington, DC. Sponsored by the American Legion, this "mock Congress" was a five-day program in which high school students from around the nation debated national issues, met "real" senators and congressmen, and toured government agencies. Clinton lunched with Arkansas Senators John L. McLellan and J. William Fulbright. That meeting helped to instill in the young man a desire to be a "citizen of the world," with Fulbright as his first political role model.[5]

During the debates in the mock assembly Bill Clinton distinguished himself by being one of the few southern delegates to push for civil rights legislation. For several years already he had been expressing dismay at the legacy of segregation and discrimination in Arkansas.

The incident from that year's Boys Nation that has become most famous, however, is the trip to the White House for a brief visit with President John F. Kennedy. Clinton rushed to grab a seat in the front row of the Rose Garden. As Kennedy was finishing his talk to the students, Clinton jumped up and shook the President's hand. A photographer caught the handshake, and that picture has become one of the icons in the Clinton political odyssey.

After Kennedy was assassinated a few months later, Clinton, as one of the few residents of Hot Springs ever to have seen the President, became a sought-after speaker in the Kiwanis, Rotary, and other clubs in town. In fact, Clinton was so busy with extracurricular affairs that his high school principal prohibited him from running for senior class president. She feared the youth was spreading himself too thin. Despite all his activities, he managed to graduate fourth in his class of 363 students.[6]

In the fall of 1964 Clinton entered the School of Foreign Service at Georgetown University. At first he appeared an astonishing misfit. When he joined friends in local bars, he drank soft drinks rather than beer – his stepfather's alcoholism had led him to become nearly a teetotaler. Clinton's Southern Baptism and Arkansas accent made him even more of an oddity amidst a sea of mostly Catholic, east coast, preppy types. But the young man was adept at working any crowd, and within a few weeks he had become one of the best known and most popular students on the East Campus, site of the School of Foreign Service. He accomplished this not by blending in but by openly boasting of his small-town, southern roots and by making "aw' shucks" self-deprecating jokes. Rather than rooting for the Georgetown basketball squad or the Washington Redskins football team, Clinton unabashedly cheered for the "Razorback" football and basketball teams of the University of Arkansas.

In the cosmopolitan Georgetown atmosphere, Clinton flowered and determined more than ever before to succeed on a world stage. One of his favorite professors was Carroll Quigley, who taught a popular survey of Western Civilization. One trait that all great leaders possessed, Quigley told his classes, was the ability to get along on less sleep than that required by ordinary mortals. This notion inspired Clinton to discipline himself likewise. To the annoyance of his roommate, he set his loud wind-up alarm to ring early each morning – regardless of how late he had turned in the night before.

At Georgetown Clinton outdid his high school performance in the variety of his activities. He joined the Air Force ROTC program for a short time in his freshman year (a fact that has gone unnoticed by his later critics who accused him of being anti-military). He was elected class president in his freshman and sophomore years. At various times he chaired the freshman orientation committee, organized Sports Week, headed Interdenominational Services, edited the first-ever college student directory, and gained an entry in *Who's Who in American Colleges and Universities.* He also served in the university's volunteer program in the inner city. During one summer he worked as a camp counselor and in another served as a campaign aide to a Democratic gubernatorial candidate in Arkansas. When he was not engaged in these sorts of affairs, he could be found late at night or early in the morning reading books – fiction by Faulkner, philosophy by Kierkegaard, history by Arthur Schlesinger, Jr., almost anything.

At the start of his junior year he won a part-time job as clerk in the Senate Foreign Relations Committee, chaired by J. William Fulbright. Clinton loved being in a position to mix with Washington's movers and shakers, and he relished the fact that a senator from Arkansas held such a prominent position. Later Clinton recalled, "People dumped on our state and said we were all a bunch of back country hayseeds, and we had a guy in the Senate who doubled the IQ of any room he entered. It was pretty encouraging. It made us feel pretty good, like we might amount to something."[7]

Originally a sponsor of the 1964 Gulf of Tonkin Resolution, Fulbright had broken with Lyndon Baines Johnson by the time Clinton started to work for him. Fulbright maintained that the President had deceived the people and that U.S. involvement in Vietnam was a tragic mistake. Clinton soon came to agree. Through the remainder of his Georgetown days, Clinton and his roommates spoke out against the war. By the standards of that day, however, they were straight-arrow moderates. Clinton debated the issue with friends, but he did not participate in sit-ins or protests.

Despite his many extracurricular activities, he managed to keep his grades at the cum laude level or higher. He had an amazing facility for last-minute cramming and essay writing, and he never shrank from challenging his professors in conversation. He was one of only two students in a class of 230 to get an "A" in his history class with Quigley. He so impressed one of his philosophy teachers, a young Jesuit named Otto Heinz, that on one occasion the latter tried to talk him into becoming a priest. Clinton was flattered but replied that, as a Southern Baptist, he was ineligible. Heinz was flabbergasted: "I saw all the Jesuit traits in him – serious, political, empathetic. I just assumed he was Catholic." Clinton's work in the Senate undoubtedly helped him in one graduate-level course he took on American foreign relations in Asia; his twenty-eight-page paper on the Gulf of Tonkin resolution contained ninety-two footnotes.[8]

In the spring of 1967, near the end of his junior year, he lost the election in his bid to become student council president for the senior year. One of the major factors working against him was that he had come to be seen as too moderate, too favorable to the university's administration. A student viewed as more radical won the race.

Ironically, that loss may have been the key element giving Clinton the extra free time and the inspiration necessary for winning something even better. During that summer he stayed in Washington to work for the Foreign Relations Committee. It was also at this time that he took up jogging. He told friends that he started running in order to be able to eat more without gaining weight. The principal reason, however, may have been that Senator Fulbright had encouraged him to apply for a Rhodes Scholarship.[9]

Clinton had never played a varsity sport in high school or college, and the Rhodes Scholarships were still widely – and erroneously – believed to require athletic prowess. Clinton was healthy, but bulky and clumsy. His friends joked that whenever he played touch football his chief talent was winning arguments about whether someone had been touched.[10]

He therefore determined to remove the bulges around his midriff and do whatever he could to become the "all-rounder" Cecil Rhodes had wanted. Early in his senior year he won the chairmanship of the Student Athletic Commission. Only afterwards did he realize this had probably been unnecessary. Several of the Rhodes Scholars in the class of 1968 were decidedly non-athletic. George Butte announced in his regional interview that playing the concert piano was his main sport. Another, Robert Reich, boldly told his interviewers that he was an "anti-athlete who vigorously avoided athletic events."[11]

In his state and regional interviews Clinton declared that he intended to return to Arkansas after his education was completed. He wanted to pursue a career in government service. This declaration, coupled with his incredibly diverse range of activities, his impressive academic record, and his letter of recommendation from Fulbright, made him a seemingly ideal candidate. After the selection committee in New Orleans told him he had won, he phoned his mother and asked, "Well, Mother, how do you think I'll look in English tweeds?"[12] When his appointment was made public in December 1967, newspapers and radio stations across Arkansas trumpeted the story of this home-town boy who made good.

In the spring of 1968, after graduation from Georgetown, Clinton returned to Arkansas to spend the summer working on Fulbright's reelection campaign. Clinton deplored the senator's opposition to civil rights legislation, but admired the man's courage in opposing the Vietnam War. (Years later Fulbright admitted his diffidence in the area of civil rights but contended that a southerner would have been voted out of office if he had done anything else in the 1960s.) Clinton also felt gratitude to the senator for sponsoring his Rhodes candidacy.

During one week Clinton served as Fulbright's driver, and the duo traveled the back roads from one small town to another. That week proved disastrous and nearly wrecked their relationship. Fulbright was aloof and scholarly, Clinton gregarious and informal. What was worse, Clinton was a horrible driver. He sometimes got lost and once caused a monumental traffic jam at a hotel when he neglected to leave the keys with the parking valet. On another occasion Fulbright had to phone his office and ask an aide, James McDougal, for help. The floor of his car was filling with water. After asking several questions, McDougal figured out what was causing the problem: Clinton was running the air conditioner at full blast while keeping the vents closed. After hanging up, McDougal exclaimed, "Two goddamn Rhodes Scholars in one car and they can't figure out why they're making rain!"[13] Fulbright's biggest complaint, however, was that Clinton never shut up. The following week the senator set out with a different driver.

One of the standard jokes among Rhodes Scholars goes like this: immediately after one is selected, one is shell-shocked and wonders, "How in the world did I win it?" After the new scholar meets the others his class, he asks, "How in the world did *they* win it?" During the crossing of the *S.S. United States* to Britain in October 1968, the new scholars had ample time to size each other up. Large though his swath had been in Hot Springs and at Georgetown, Clinton did not immediately stand out as greater than the others. To most journalists and other observers at that time, two other scholars seemed to shine brightest: Strobe Talbott and Robert Reich.

Nelson Strobridge Talbott III came from a wealthy Ohio banking family. At his birth his parents had registered him for Yale. Once he reached the university, he became "Mr Inside." Yale's president, Kingman Brewster, regularly consulted him regarding student issues. He was the star in his graduating class: an avid squash player, a classical guitarist, a gifted scholar of Russian literature and history, chair of the *Yale Daily News*. He spent most of the summer before Oxford working as an intern for *Time* in London. After a quick trip home to see his family, he boarded the ship in New York. On the high seas Talbott emerged as unofficial leader of the group.[14]

Robert Reich, however, struck most of the ship's passengers as the most impressive. Ironically, Reich himself thought otherwise. Surveying the others, he felt "overwhelmed by the intellectual firepower and felt grossly inadequate." The others "seemed ready to launch their careers in the direction of ambassadors or presidents or university professors." He believed "a great mistake had been made by the selection committee in picking me."[15] To his Rhodes classmates, Reich was a giant in every way but height. He was four foot ten, his growth having been stunted by a genetic ailment called Fairbanks Disease. During his years at Dartmouth, Reich had campaigned for Robert Kennedy and then for Eugene McCarthy. By the time he was a senior, Dartmouth's president, John Sloane Dickey, had come to rely heavily on his advice for dealing with antiwar protesters and black-power militants. In the spring of 1968, *Time* ran a cover story on the class of 1968, and Reich was featured as one of the top student leaders in the nation. What he lacked physically, he more than made up for with his piercing eyes, his quick wit, and his grand theatrical command of an audience.[16]

Never one to be daunted by a challenge, Clinton worked this group the way he had done in Hot Springs and Georgetown. Not everyone was won over. As would be true throughout his life, some people were turned-off by his hearty friendliness. They could not believe that anyone could be this sincere, this concerned about others, this desirous of trying to make everyone happy. A few insisted on believing that the "innocent hick" was merely using them.

Most of the initial doubters, however, were quickly won over. They realized that Clinton was ambitious, but at least he was up-front about it. Rick Stearns recalls that within forty-five minutes of meeting Clinton aboard ship the southerner had told him of his dreams of becoming governor or senator and then a national leader.[17] Any qualms Reich may have had were dissipated when Clinton played nursemaid to him. Like many passengers during the rough crossing, Reich became seasick and spent much of the trip in his cabin. Clinton stopped by frequently, bringing hot chicken soup and crackers. At first Reich was put off by the over-eager, ever-helpful fellow American. Soon, however, the two became inseparable. The sophisticated Dartmouth graduate was won over by the Arkansas hick who unabashedly exclaimed, "Isn't this amazing? ... Being on this ocean liner. Heading to Europe. I never thought it would happen to me. Bet you never thought it would happen to you either."[18]

Tom Williamson initially was loathe to meet Clinton. Williamson had been a standout football player at Harvard, holder of a lucrative General Motors scholarship, and member of a special honors program. Williamson also was black, the only African American in the class of 1968. After years of watching southern politicians and policemen on television barring university doors to blacks or chasing them with clubs and dogs, Williamson instinctively put up his antenna whenever he heard a southern accent. Within just minutes, however, Clinton had won him over. Clinton said he was ashamed of the South's race record that he was determined to compensate for it. The two became lifelong friends.[19]

Clinton the Student

Bill Clinton's stay in Oxford has received far more attention from historians, journalists, and political opponents than has the Oxford career of any other Rhodes Scholar. Much of what has been said has been negative. What was his academic record there? Did he lead a dissolute life of drugs and free love? Did he use Oxford to avoid the military draft? Did he act unpatriotically in Britain and during a trip to the Soviet Union? Did he dislike the English and, as a result, adopt anti-British attitudes later in his life?

While doing research for this book we had many conversations with our friends and acquaintances in Oxford. Almost invariably, when Bill Clinton's name came up, their comments were something like, "Oh, but you know, he wasn't a very good Rhodes Scholar." Several Rhodes Scholars we interviewed, especially the older ones, voiced disappointment about the fact that when one of "their own" finally made it to the Presidency it happened to be one who did not do well academically in Oxford.

After the *New York Times* published a review of David Maraniss' *First in His Class: A Biography of Bill Clinton*, a reader named John W. Wood, writing from London, contributed a letter to the editor that declared in part:

> One place where Bill Clinton did not stand out in any way was at Oxford.
>
> The first year he was there, he attended a few lectures and wrote one or two papers. The second year, he was hardly in evidence and made no impression whatsoever. Most dons who would have had contact have only the vaguest recollection of him, if that; he passed no exams and got no degree.
>
> Indeed, so little was the impression that he made, and so low the private opinion of him at Oxford, that Sir Maurice Shock, his tutor, remarked before he became President, that "Bill Clinton would never have been elected governor of a serious state." So much for the myth of "first in his class."[20]

The fact that Clinton left Oxford without obtaining a diploma continued to haunt him even when he returned there in June 1994 to receive an honorary degree. The *New York Times'* Maureen Dowd was not the only journalist to bring it up. One widespread joke was that the only way Clinton could get an Oxford degree was to become President of the United States first. The headline in the *Independent* referred to Clinton's return to Oxford twenty-four years after "dropping out." The article that followed quoted one American tourist currently in Oxford, who said of Clinton's years as a student there, "Oh, sure, he picked up a book, but he didn't read it."[21]

This "received wisdom" about Clinton's record in Oxford is, however, seriously misleading. No, he did not obtain a degree. But was he a good student nonetheless? The answer to the latter question cannot be a simple "yes" or "no."

When Clinton and his classmates arrived in Oxford they were escaping a United States rocked by race riots and anti-war protests. Fifteen years later, when, as governor of Arkansas, Bill Clinton revisited Oxford, he recalled his first trip and admitted "a lot of us felt a little strange to jump on a boat and go to idyllic Oxford and escape."[22] Given this, it is little wonder that Clinton and many other Americans in Oxford found it difficult to concentrate on academic studies.

Initially Clinton had hoped to study at Balliol, but the tutors there were not sufficiently impressed by his application for reading PPE. They rejected him. Such an action was not unusual, for several Rhodes Scholars each year usually fail, for one reason or another, to win membership in their first choice of college. University College quickly accepted the young Arkansan. A quarter-century later Clinton told Sir Anthony Kenny that, in retrospect, he was happy about the Balliol rebuff, for he ended up being very happy at Univ. Kenny had been one of the tutors in question in 1968. Eventually Kenny became master of the college and then Warden of Rhodes House.[23]

Once ensconced at Univ., Clinton signed up to do a B.Litt., which was an advanced degree just below a D.Phil. He proposed a long thesis on Western imperialism, in order better to understand the roots of U.S. involvement in Vietnam. Within a few weeks he switched to a slightly less demanding B.Phil. in politics.[24] The B.Phil. required regular tutorial essays, a thesis of about thirty thousand words, and a battery of examinations in four separate areas. (In the 1980s, to reflect the fact that this degree was higher than an undergraduate one, "B.Phil." was changed to "M.Phil." in politics and most other fields.)

Though he was a member of Univ., he was assigned a supervisor at Pembroke College. His tutor was Zbigniew Pelczynski, a Polish resistance fighter during the Second World War who had ended up in Oxford as a student in 1946. After completing his studies, Pelczynski stayed on as a lecturer and soon became a fellow at Pembroke. He wrote and lectured about the political systems of eastern Europe and the Soviet Union. From the 1950s to his retirement in 1993 he tutored hundreds of American undergraduate and graduate students – perhaps more than any other Oxford don.[25] The Americans were assigned to him because his specialties (European political theories and practices) fell within what many of them wanted to study and because, as a foreigner himself in Britain, he could empathize with them. Clinton was not the only Pelczynski student who would go on to a prominent political career. Another was U.S. Senator Paul Sarbanes, who preceded Clinton by fourteen years.

Nearly a quarter of a century after his Oxford days, Clinton reminisced about his former tutor, affirming that "I loved him; I thought he was terrific. I really enjoyed my tutorials with him."[26] During the

1992 presidential campaign, Pelczynski was sought out by many journalists, and he responded with several newspaper articles and interviews. He retained vivid memories of the young Bill Clinton – contrary to what John W. Wood and others have said about Clinton leaving no mark in Oxford. Pelczynski "was not disappointed … and from the beginning Bill Clinton made a very good impression on me."[27] Clinton, as his tutor recalls, had a nice smile and good manners. Pelczynski thought the young American an "agreeable chap."[28] More important, Clinton was "very shrewd and good at processing information" and had "the makings of a statesman."[29]

During the fall term of 1968 and winter term of 1969 Clinton met with Pelczynski every week, turning in essays that showed impressive insights – even if the writing itself was not always of the highest levels. Pelczynski has pointed out, however, that most Americans were inferior to British students in their writing ability; this was to be expected, for British undergraduate students had far more prior experience in submitting weekly essays. He also recalls that Clinton was able to argue his position effectively, both on paper and in oral discussion. Pelczynski perceived that his student "had a sharp analytical mind and an impressive power to master and synthesize complex material."[30] It was also evident to the tutor that Clinton "had the mind of a politician, trying to figure things out, rather than the patience of an academic." Even though Clinton did not have the temperament of an academic, Pelczynski thought he clearly had the ability to obtain a B.Phil. Clinton submitted papers on topics such as the presidential versus the cabinet system of government, the separation of powers, and the relative merits of democracy and totalitarianism.[31]

Has Pelczynski painted a flattering picture of his former pupil merely because the latter has become President of the United States? There is substantial evidence to show that his words are sincere. There are, for example, the general reports he wrote about Clinton in March 1969. At that time, Pelczynski was departing Oxford for a sabbatical leave. He would spend the upcoming spring and summer writing a book on Polish Communism while residing in an old *palazzo* near Lake Varese in Italy. He wrote reports on all his students, and in his summary for Clinton he noted solid progress and recommended that he be permitted to continue for a second year.[32]

Although Pelczynski was popular among the students, this does not mean he was a soft touch in matters academic. Several years earlier, in November 1955, fresher Frank Sieverts read his essay on Edmund Burke to a clearly unimpressed Pelczynski. After finishing it, Sieverts admitted that his composition was "complex." "Complex hell," Pelczynski retorted. It was "a botch." Pelczynski allowed that some of Sieverts's subsequent essays were "O.K." Eventually Sieverts became one of Pelczynski's favorites and completed his B.Phil. in the standard two years.[33]

Perhaps the finest paper Clinton wrote for Pelczynski was one entitled "Political Pluralism in the USSR." It was eighteen pages long and based on some thirty books and articles. It presents an astute, prophetic analysis of the Soviet system and notes severe signs of decay in the monolith created by Stalin. Pelczynski thought so much of this paper that he made copies and handed them to students in later years, so they could use the essay as a model for their own. One of these later students, Walter Isaacson (1974), recalls that Pelczynski told him of "this brilliant former student."[34] At that time Isaacson had barely heard of Clinton, who in 1974 was an obscure assistant professor of law at the University of Arkansas.

Pelczynski remembers that on one occasion in the mid-1970s he was invited to speak at McGill University in Montreal. He took along a copy of that same paper by Clinton, so that he could refer to it during his talk.[35] In December 1979 Pelczynski saw in *Newsweek* that his former student had just been elected governor of Arkansas. He wrote to Clinton to congratulate him, and Clinton invited him to Little Rock for the inauguration – a trip that the don was unable to make. From that point on the two corresponded occasionally. In short, Pelczynski's favorable reminiscences are not the product of a sudden desire to cash in on his student's later fame.

One Oxford authority told us, on condition of anonymity, that he suspected Clinton was not the author of the essays so highly praised by Pelczynski. This person suggested that Strobe Talbott, Clinton's friend, roommate, and authority on the Soviet Union and eastern Europe, was the true author. When we asked Pelczynski about this he laughed at the ridiculousness of the charge. First of all, Talbott was working on a different degree, reading things entirely different from those Clinton had been assigned. Second, Clinton spent his first year residing in University College. That was the time of his essays for Pelczynski. Talbott was at Magdalen. Clinton and Talbott did not become roommates until their second year, when they and a third scholar, Frank Aller, rented a house at 46 Leckford Road. Third, it would be impossible in a one-on-one tutorial to fake authorship of an essay. Pelczynski prided himself on his thoughtful probing of a student in the discussions that accompanied the reading of a paper. If Clinton had not done all the work himself, Pelczynski would have spotted the fraud immediately.[36]

Clinton was making steady progress toward his B.Phil, but something derailed him. That something was Vietnam. From the moment he arrived in Oxford, he was convinced that he would be drafted before he could complete his studies. After Pelczynski left on sabbatical, Clinton lost the friendly mentor with whom he had established such a close rapport.

He seems to have fallen between the cracks in the Oxford administrative machinery. None of the committees or tutors who would have had responsibility for checking his work seems to have known much, if anything, about his whereabouts. One of the dons who might have filled in for Pelczynski was likewise on sabbatical. No one appears to have contacted Clinton from the spring through the fall of 1969, to check up on his thesis work and set times for tutorials. Everyone assumed he was working with someone else or that he had been drafted and called back to the United States. Nor did Clinton make much, if any, effort to contact them.[37]

What did he do for the next year? He spent the summer of 1969 back in the United States. After his return to Oxford the following October, when he was not engaged in lengthy debates with friends about Vietnam and other international issues, he read books. Of the latter there can be no doubt. He later claimed:

> I probably read 300 books a year the two years I was at Oxford. I read just about everything I could get my hands on. I was constantly in motion with a book. I traveled a lot, and when I traveled by train, I was always inhaling books.[38]

There is plenty of evidence to bear this out. His friends recall that he always had a book with him, often stuffed into the back pocket of his jeans. Records at the Univ. library list scores of volumes he checked out. He also ran up substantial bills at Blackwell's. (During his one-day return in 1994, Blackwell's was one of the places he made sure to visit. On this occasion the bookshop refused to charge him for the three books he obtained.) His reading tastes were wide-ranging: John Locke's *Second Treatise of Civil Government*, Thomas Hobbes' *Leviathan*, all the works of Dylan Thomas, Eldridge Cleaver's *Soul on Ice*, John Steinbeck's *The Moon is Down*, Willie Morris' *North toward Home*.[39] During a journey with Rick Stearns to Spain in the spring break of 1970 he read an astonishing number of works on the Spanish Civil War: George Orwell's *Homage to Catalonia*, André Malraux's *Man's Hope*, Ernest Hemingway's *The Sun Also Rises*, Franz Borkenau's *The Spanish Cockpit*, and Hugh Thomas' *The Spanish Civil War*, among others.[40]

When Pelczynski arrived back in Oxford late in 1969 he checked up on Clinton and discovered that other politics tutors had assumed Clinton was serving in the U.S. Army. Pelczynski quickly met with Clinton and got him back on track. From March through May 1970 Clinton participated in a seminar designed for B.Phil. politics students who needed to cram for their general examinations.[41]

During these same months Clinton also came under the supervision of Univ. politics tutor Maurice Shock. Later in his career Shock would become Sir Maurice and rector of Lincoln College. We interviewed him just before his retirement from that post and asked him about his widely quoted remark about Arkansas not being a serious state if Clinton were its governor. He admitted saying it but argued that it was a part of a casual conversation overheard by a third party who took it out of context. When Shock said it, in the 1980s, he intended no snide denigration of his former student. Much the reverse. He was impressed with Clinton's claims to being a "New Democrat." Shock thought that traditionalists in the Democratic Party would oppose Clinton, allowing him to become a governor only because Arkansas was not an important state. Moreover, Shock maintained that Clinton showed great academic promise while in Oxford. If not for Vietnam and other distractions, Shock is certain Clinton would have obtained his degree with great distinction.[42]

Shock's actions in the spring of 1970 confirm that he held Clinton in high regard. By the end of May it was clear that Clinton, quick study though he was, would not be ready for the June exams. Shock was so impressed by Clinton's hard work and ability that he suggested Clinton not take the exams. Instead, Shock recommended that Clinton stay on for a third year and transform his B.Phil. into the more demanding D.Phil.

Initially this appealed to Clinton, but soon he changed his mind and decided to push on with his life in the United States. He and fellow scholars Bob Reich and Douglas Eakeley had already been accepted into Yale Law School. He informed Shock that he would not return to complete a doctoral thesis. Shock did not admonish him, for "it was clear he had gotten a lot" out of Oxford.[43]

Does the fact that Clinton failed to obtain a degree mean he was a failure as a Rhodes Scholar? No. It should be clear from earlier chapters that many earlier scholars either did not complete their studies, settled for Thirds or Fourths, or acquired lesser diplomas or certificates. In addition to the distractions encountered by scholars of earlier years, the scholars of the late 1960s and early 1970s faced the turmoil of the Vietnam issue.

Not only Clinton, but eight other members of his class "failed" to get degrees. The 1968 cohort had the lowest graduation rate of any since the Second World War – and one of the lowest in the history of the program. Those who were able to keep focused on their studies and complete their work included some of Clinton's closest friends: Reich (a Second in PPE), Talbott (M.Litt. in Russian literature), and Rick Stearns (B.Litt. in politics). Bosom companions who did not obtain degrees included Frank Aller, Alan Bersin, and Tom Williamson.

It is hard to consider the non-finishers as failures when the Warden of Rhodes House, E.T. Williams, did not think of them as such. Williams could be blunt if he thought a student simply was slacking off. On the other hand, he took a realistic approach to what the Rhodes Scholarship meant to many of them:

> If you were an American and entirely on the make, you would do well in college, try for the Rhodes, get your name in the newspapers for winning one, and then resign it and go to Harvard or Yale Law School ... The motivation is to get it. What you do here doesn't really matter so long as you enjoy yourself. Don't fail to take notice that it's a free trip to Europe. Make friends. And, we hope, don't grow to dislike the English.[44]

Williams was one of those not captivated by Clinton's down-home charm. He thought Clinton a "bumpkin."[45] When Clinton let his hair grow long during his second year, the Warden wryly commented that "he wanted to look like a cavalier."[46] Yet Williams was impressed enough with the reports from Pelczynski and Shock to approve the optional third year.[47]

Tom Williamson had decided to leave Oxford midway through his second year. He was eager to see other parts of the world, especially Africa. When he informed Williams of his decision, the Warden was gracious rather than resentful or angry. Williams told him that there was a restlessness in many Americans, and that for some of them one year in Oxford was sufficient to give them the experience Cecil Rhodes had envisioned. The Warden even offered to let Williamson resume his scholarship, should the latter ever wish to do so (he did not).[48]

Ira Magaziner, from the class of 1969, likewise did not obtain a degree. This is somewhat ironic, in view of Magaziner's legendary accomplishments as an undergraduate at Brown University. Cecil Rhodes had hoped that his scholars would fight the good fight and improve the world after they attended Oxford. Of all scholars from the entire history of the program, Magaziner probably did more than any other to make a lasting mark *before* he reached Oxford. The son of a bookkeeper at a tomato-packing house, the Long Island native organized a strike for better wages among counselors at the summer camp where he worked. When he reached Brown University he rattled the establishment on a larger scale. In his freshman year he campaigned successfully to make the administration abolish the disliked meal contract system, whereby students had to pay an annual fee, regardless of how many times they ate in the school cafeterias. As a sophomore he led a group of students studying curriculum reform, and the university paid him to spend the following summer writing a general analysis. The resulting 415-page "Magaziner Report" was hailed by Harvard sociologist David Riesman as "a herculean effort, an impressive document."[49]

Because the university was slow to implement his ideas, he organized student rallies and lobbied every professor over the next two years. The fact that he was elected class president in each of his four years and student body president in his senior year gave him added clout. As he was about to graduate in May 1969, the university announced implementation of the "Magaziner curriculum" for an experimental period of two years. Eventually, many other universities around the country would adopt all or parts of his program.

His educational ideas were not totally original, but he defended them with uncanny logic and flair. He called for more flexibility, allowing students greater freedom to depart from a narrow spectrum of courses in a core curriculum. He also advocated more freedom for students to take courses on a "pass/fail" basis rather than with conventional grading. Finally, he called for professors to give more stress to concepts and reasoning rather than to memorization of facts. Magaziner's friend Derek Shearer claims that as a result of these reforms Brown became "one of the hottest schools in the country."[50]

When he was not campaigning for curriculum reforms, he fought for other causes. These included more scholarships and financial aid for minority students. He participated in protests for civil rights and against the Vietnam War. He also exhibited entrepreneurial flair. He established a small company that hired out students as temporary workers. With the profits from that venture he funded a variety of activities on campus. The most famous was a spring break festival that featured performers James Brown, Dionne Warwick, and the Yardbirds, poet Allen Ginsberg, and a twenty-four-hour marathon of Marx Brothers movies. "We had the best collection of stars pre-Woodstock," he proudly remembers.[51]

Magaziner was a "super nerd," but one who cast a charismatic spell on all sorts of people. He was notorious for his addiction to junk food. Before entering college he had won a pizza-eating contest on Long Island. During his years at Brown one center of his operations was a hamburger joint just off campus, the Beef and Bun. For several years after his graduation that establishment honored his memory by holding an "Ira Magaziner Day." In this yearly event his customary seat was roped off to reserve it for him, in the event that he would return to his old haunt (he never did).

Despite all these activities, he was also a model student. He made Phi Beta Kappa and graduated magna cum laude with a major in an interdisciplinary program called Human Studies. His senior thesis was entitled "The Decline of Metaphysical Religion and Values in the West."

When he graduated from Brown, both *Time* and *Life* ran stories on him. *Time* hailed him as a "peaceful revolutionary" and quoted a common graffito that could be found scribbled on walls throughout the Brown campus: "Ira, please see me – God." "You come to see me – Ira."[52] *Life*'s article "The Class of '69" focused on several of the valedictorians from campuses around the country. Featured on the same page, with photos and excerpts from their speeches, were Magaziner and the valedictorian at Wellesley College – Hillary Rodham.[53] Magaziner's speech garnered headlines around the country. In protest against the Vietnam War, he persuaded virtually the entire graduating class to stand and turn their backs on one of the honorary degree recipients, National Security Advisor Henry Kissinger.

Magaziner's impact on Brown was so enormous that more than a quarter century later he remains a cult figure there. When future Rhodes Scholar Jeff Shesol (1991) was admitted to Brown in 1987 he got the impression that Ira Magaziner had been some sort of god.[54]

From the time he arrived in Oxford, Magaziner had no intention of working for a degree. Officially, he was preparing for a B.Litt. in Social Studies. Primarily, however, he saw the scholarship as a time to absorb new experiences and to read. He spent two years at Balliol, doing independent reading under various dons. He also attended economics seminars at Cambridge and the London School of Economics and helped to organize some anti-Vietnam rallies in London. Mostly he just sat in his rooms and perused all the works of Adam Smith, Thomas Malthus, David Ricardo, John Stuart Mill, Alfred Marshall, John Maynard Keynes, Emile Durkheim, and Max Weber, among others. Never before or after would he have the free time to do such serious reading. Moreover, Magaziner says that E.T. Williams did not pressure him to direct his readings toward a particular degree program.[55]

Williams verified this when we spoke to him. He said that Magaziner would sometimes hardly be seen for days on end. The quirky American kept his curtains closed and occasionally emerged for meals – looking pale and rumpled, like a piece of shriveled green cheese.[56]

Clinton thus was far from alone in his "failure" to obtain a parchment.

Mixing In

After Bill Clinton won the presidential election in November 1992, fellow Rhodes Scholar James Fallows (1970) announced on National Public Radio that this did not bode well for Britain. Fallows himself had not enjoyed his two years in Oxford, and he assumed that Clinton and most of his friends shared the same sentiments. According to Fallows, "Brideshead Revisited types … [still] set the tone for the place. Moreover, Warden E.T. Williams viewed the Americans as "provincial yeomen" who had "just come in from eating woodchucks or inbreeding up in the hills." One of Fallows' tutors, knowing that he came from California, "always seemed disappointed that I did not have a sixshooter, like a figure from the Old West." Fallows lampooned the "Oxford-style premise that to become an honorary Englishman is a huge step up from American yokelhood." Finally, he declared that "the young Clinton was, in fact, exactly the kind of Yankee Oxford most loves to mock – the fresh-faced, small-town self-improver determined to like everyone he meets."[57] In short, Fallows concluded that the Anglo-American "special relationship" would now be endangered because of the bad memories that Clinton and his classmates retained of Oxford.

In a 1993 article in *GQ*, Rhodes Scholar Jacob Weisberg (1987) states that Clinton's outgoing charm did not go over well among a nation known for its reserve. Clinton's admiration for the British went "unrequited." In reaction to this, says Weisberg, Clinton retreated into a Rhodes Scholar cocoon, associating mostly with other Americans. Whereas some Rhodes Scholars adopt fake British accents and sport English tweeds, Weisberg notes that Clinton became, if anything, even more American. He sometimes wore a pink poplin suit, and it took little prompting for him to pull out his saxophone for impromptu performances. His southern drawl became more pronounced. According to Weisberg, Clinton's friends joked that he could make "shit" into a four-syllable word. In short, he did not get along well with the British and came to know few of them very well.[58]

On 8 June 1994, during Clinton's one-day return to Oxford to receive an honorary doctorate, BBC television interviewed Richard Stengel, a journalist at *Time* and Rhodes Scholar of 1977. Stengel had disliked his Oxford days as well, for the same reasons as Fallows. Moreover, like Fallows, he maintained that the same must have been true of Clinton. When pressed by the interviewer, Stengel said that Clinton and his roommates hung out together so much that they could not have liked the English very much. Stengel acknowledged that Clinton has never admitted this publicly. Stengel observed, however, that as a politician Clinton had to be diplomatic. Stengel's concluding remark was that Clinton always liked everyone and everything and would have had fun even being cooped up in a cave.

Going further, one of Clinton's best and most recent biographers, Martin Walker, has asserted that most Rhodes Scholars of the late 1960s tended to dislike the experience:

> Clinton and his fellows felt, on the whole, only limited affection and nostalgia for Britain as a result of their time in Oxford. As much as pellucid May mornings punting on the Isis and sunsets gilding the dreaming spires, they recalled snooty undergraduates, languid dons, cold rooms, and bad food. From the vantage point of an elite enclave, they experienced Britain as a country in palpable decline. The contradiction was acute between the snobbish complacencies of Oxford and the wider realities of shriveling British grandeur.[59]

What can one make of these conjectures about Clinton's "evident" dislike of Oxford? In contrast to the above writers, the overwhelming majority of the scholars from that era who have spoken about their experiences have asserted that they *did* enjoy living in Oxford. Strobe Talbott's memories of E.T. Williams, for example, differ sharply from those of Fallows. In the spring of 1969 Talbott suffered a serious eye injury during a game of squash. Williams and his family benevolently insisted that he live with them in Rhodes House during his several weeks of recuperation. In those comfortable surroundings his friend Clinton visited him nearly every day. Talbott has called his three years in Oxford "happy and productive."[60] Robert Reich has said that his Oxford experience was "terrific."[61] Robert Earl (1968) recalls that Oxford introduced him to a whole new cultural universe; he became an opera fanatic and helped introduce his friends Clinton and Talbott to the joys of Covent Garden.[62]

Mark Janis (1969) says that some of his most pleasant memories concern the annual croquet tournaments, complete with tea and biscuits, hosted for Rhodes Scholars by the Warden and Mrs.

Williams.[63] Kurt Schmoke (1971) likewise enjoyed his relationship with Williams. Schmoke lived in Balliol, where the Warden often took lunch. Schmoke was dazzled by Williams' ability to imbibe several dry sherries and still remain alert for a full afternoon of work.[64]

Ira Magaziner agrees that many of the British he encountered were quirky, but he was amused rather than offended by their sometimes odd behavior. He was amused, for example, by Oxford's occasional preference for form over substance. Once during his period in Holywell Manor (a Balliol residence hall mostly for graduate students) a male student welcomed a woman friend who was visiting from France. The man wanted to put her up for the night, and he asked his scout if he could borrow a cot from the college. The scout was horrified at this suggested breach of policy. Officially, no student was to have overnight guests. Unofficially, however, the college merely closed its eyes at such transgressions. Winking slyly, the scout told the student to sneak his friend into the room. The result was to force the student and his guest to share the same bed, which had not been the student's original design.[65]

Thomas Allen (1967) says that Oxford was everything he had hoped it would be.[66] Mark Janis had some of the same tutors as Fallows, and yet Janis never found them condescending or snobbish.[67] Moreover, Janis married a British woman whom he met in Oxford. His experiences as a Rhodes Scholar were so positive that in 1993 he left his position as a law professor at the University of Connecticut and, with his family, moved to Oxford. For the next three years (until he returned to Connecticut) he was a fellow at Exeter College, where he tutored Rhodes Scholars as well as other students.

Douglas Eakeley did not meet his future wife in Oxford, but he and his bride spent their honeymoon there in 1973. He found the town "even more idyllic" than he recalled from a few years earlier.[68] (More than two decades later Eakeley admitted, however, that taking his new bride to Oxford was a mistake. She was not eager to spend the time visiting his old haunts and wallowing in his reminiscences.)[69]

Bob Reich was one of four from the class of 1968 who entered University College. The three others were Clinton, Eakeley, and John Isaacson. Immediately after arrival Reich became active in all the theatrical productions at Univ. He acted in or directed nearly every play. A few weeks into his first term, outside an audition room, he spotted a beautiful young British student. He was "too timid to ask her name." After she left he feared he might never see her again, and so he decided to direct his first play. He posted notices all over Oxford and was overjoyed when the girl showed up for an audition.

He assigned her the leading female role. Clare Dalton eventually married him, the ceremony taking place in the Univ. chapel in 1973. She became an attorney and law professor in the United States.[70] During the 1992 presidential campaign, Dalton worked as an assistant to her friend Hillary Rodham Clinton.

What of Bill Clinton himself? Are Fallows, Weisberg, and Stengel correct in their assumptions? In a 1992 interview Clinton said the following about Oxford:

> ... it exceeded my expectations. It was more beautiful, more steeped in history, more hospitable to what I wanted to do at that point in my life: just take some time to read extensively and think and be totally taken out of the routine that had dominated me for years. I just loved it... . The first two weeks I was there I bet I walked fourteen hours a day. I visited all the colleges, went in all the churches, walked through all the parks ... It was simply incredible.[71]

Clinton then goes on to admit one reservation about the English. He says that class distinctions were much more visible there than in the United States. That was why he went out of his way to meet ordinary citizens. Like several earlier Rhodes Scholars, he frequented the distinctly unfashionable, working-class Brown's Cafe in the covered market near the center of town. Nonetheless, his overall impression of British society was positive:

> I thought they were very generous, good people who were tough as nails. I could really see how Churchill had rallied them and why they had survived for two years without winning a battle. Once I had lived there, I could see the underlying toughness that's often lost in their polite manners and their well-spokenness. So I was very impressed. I liked England; I was a real Anglophile when I was there.[72]

Are these merely the rose-colored, self-edited memories of a politician who must avoid offending people and nations? Perhaps, to a very limited extent. However, there is much contemporary evidence to show that Clinton did have a good time in Britain. At least one of his classmates, James Crawford, has staunchly rejected Weisberg's portrayal of a naive yokel who never quite felt at ease in Britain.[73] Another, Douglas Eakeley, has said if Clinton did not enjoy living in Britain "it's news to me."[74]

During Clinton's first year he lived within the college walls, in Helen's Court, an old, converted almshouse. Univ. was one of the few colleges that still had the old-style scouts, and Clinton's was named Arch. College legend had it that many years earlier one of

Arch's students had been Prince Feliks Yusupov, who had helped to assassinate Rasputin.[75] During this first year in Oxford, Clinton and Reich seemed almost inseparable. Reich was Clinton's companion in several of the fourteen-hour walks that came soon after their arrival. By the end of the first term they were the two best-known undergraduates in the entire college. British student Chris McCooey says they:

> were kind of a double act, those two – Bill was big and lumpy and over-weight, and Reich I guess was kind of a certified dwarf. It was like Laurel and Hardy. And they were very good value. They added a lot of fun to the college.[76]

Reich has always been the first to make self-deprecating jokes about his lack of height. Though he underwent painful hip replacement operations in 1992, he continues to find humor in his situation. Early in 1993, as Secretary of Labor, he appeared on the Tonight Show with Jay Leno. At one point Reich stood up and asked the audience, "Does this look like big government?"

Reich possessed just the sort of urbane wit that was prized in Oxford. John Albery, then a chemistry don and later master of the college, considered him "small and twinkly, and very clever, very clever indeed."[77]

Clinton was not a typical Oxonian – Fallows is certainly correct on that point. But that did not prevent him from making friends and becoming as popular as Reich. It is true that he occasionally wore a pink suit and that he made no effort to speak or dress as an Englishman. But he also had played the role of a proud, corny, good ol' boy southerner prior to Oxford, at Georgetown, and after Oxford, at Yale Law School. With Clinton the old adage was true: "what you saw was what you got." Most of his Rhodes Scholar classmates came from Ivy League schools. Some, like Talbott, had also gone to ritzy prep schools. A few – again, like Talbott – came from extremely wealthy families. Among these friends Clinton never tried to hide his modest origins. Late in 1968, for example, he unabashedly shared the news that his mother was about to get married again. Roger Clinton had died during Clinton's senior year at Georgetown, and now Virginia was going to take a third husband. The new spouse was Jeff Dwire, proprietor of one of the best hair salons in Hot Springs. Clinton had no qualms about telling his friends that "Mother's marrying a man who runs a beauty parlor."[78]

Thomas Allen and other scholars often were astounded, when passing by the lodge in Univ., to hear the porters swapping stories about Arkansas – yarns recounted to them by Clinton.[79] Douglas Eakeley recalls typical lunch and dinner scenes in the Univ. dining hall. Clinton would sit at a long table, surrounded by British under-graduates, chatting for hours after the meal had ended. The younger English students "were in constant fascination with Bill and he with them. It was expected that you would not just eat and run but eat and talk and debate the great issues of the day until you were thrown out of the dining hall. Bill was always in the thick of it."[80] Jack Zoeller (1972) took up residence in Univ. two years after Clinton had left Oxford. He soon discovered that students and dons were still telling stories about the exploits of the gregarious, popular Arkansas scholar.[81]

Clinton enrolled in a dining club, attended debates at the Union, and participated in sports. What he lacked in physical dexterity, he made up for in heft and team spirit. Univ.'s top rugby player, Chris McCooey, affirms that Clinton:

> wasn't very good, but it didn't matter because what he contributed was wonderfully American enthusiasm. Actually, a bit much enthusiasm. He flattened a guy in the first lineup that didn't have the ball. When the ref said you don't do that I had to explain, "Sorry, he's from America, where you can flatten anyone."[82]

When, more than twenty-five years later, a reporter asked about sports in Oxford, Clinton recalled:

> I played a year for the University basketball team... for the second team, which shows you how weak basketball was at Oxford. If I wasn't over-weight, I was slow, and I wasn't in good shape. It was a period in my life when I didn't have the discipline to show up and do the practice.
>
> What I really liked was rugby. It was pretty tough. I remember we played one of the Cambridge colleges. I got a mild concussion. There were no substitutions in rugby, so our coach told me to go back in. I asked what I was supposed to do, since I was dizzy. He said, "Just get in somebody's way." ... I think it's a terrific game. I just loved it.[83]

After athletic matches and other events, he could often be found with British or American students in any of several pubs and restau-rants: the Turf, the King's Arms, the Bear, and the Taj Mahal. Along with friends he also sometimes hiked along the Isis a couple of miles north of the city to two picturesque riverside pubs, the Perch and the Trout. In Oxford Clinton developed a taste for beer and for a British concoction called shandy – half beer and half lemonade. However, he never became more than a moderate, social drinker. Not known to be a picky eater, he quickly took to steak and kidney pie, shepherd's pie, Scotch Eggs, greasy eggs and sausage, and other standard dishes.

Just after the November 1992 election, an *Oxford Times* reporter interviewed George Cawkwell, who had been dean of graduates at Univ. in the late 1960s. He readily asserted that Clinton "was an amiable person whose record at the college was absolutely impeccable. Some of the things I heard during the campaign from President Bush made me gawp."[84]

Though he mixed well with the British, he became particularly close to a band of other Rhodes Scholars. In addition to Reich, these included Strobe Talbott, Frank Aller, Rick Stearns, Tom Williamson and a handful of others. They tended to be the most "political" members of the class, the ones who planned for government careers and who spent hours on end engrossed in debates about American domestic issues and foreign policies. This group became known as a "floating seminar" engaged in "the conversation" on ways in which they would change the world. In a seamless, nonstop fashion their discussions carried on from their rooms, to pubs, to college quads, and to wherever else they might be. Talbott remembers that on Thanksgiving day in 1969 at the Leckford Road house Clinton and Aller got so involved in a discussion about Vietnam that they stayed four hours talking near the stove, occasionally stopping to baste the turkey.[85]

It was these friends who were Clinton's companions on trips. Like nearly all Rhodes Scholars since 1904, Clinton saw as much of Europe as he could before returning home. Two of his classmates had even brought their transportation with them aboard the *S.S. United States*: Daniel Singer, a Volvo, and James Crawford, a Porsche. At virtually the drop of a hat Clinton was willing to drop everything else and spend a weekend hitchhiking throughout England, Wales, or Scotland. He also toured Ireland, Germany, Austria, Czechoslovakia, France, Spain, Norway, Finland, and the Soviet Union.

Early in the first year Clinton and Tom Williamson visited Ireland. In Dublin they visited a girl whom Williamson had befriended aboard the ship. They also hitchhiked around the Emerald Isle. The black Williamson and the southern, white Clinton had a rollicking good time playing a practical joke on the unsuspecting motorists who picked them up. Whenever a car would stop, Williamson looked sternly at Clinton and ordered, "Boy, get in back." Clinton obediently hung his head down and shuffled into the back seat.[86]

Another interesting story concerns a trip to Wales about a year later, in October 1969. One Friday afternoon Clinton and Rick

Stearns discovered that they both loved the poems of Dylan Thomas. On an impulse, they decided to make a pilgrimage to the writer's birthplace. They grabbed their coats plus a dog-eared copy of the poems and started hitch-hiking west. Their rides ended up taking them all over Wales, but nowhere near their goal. On Saturday evening, drenched by nonstop rains, they retreated back over the English border.

Rick Stearns retains two touching memories of that expedition. One involves the twosome entering a pub in Bristol and hearing Tom Jones's version of "Green, Green Grass of Home" playing on the jukebox. That saccharine tune always filled Clinton with tearful homesickness. The second concerns the following day, a Sunday, when the duo spent their remaining money in a grocery shop, buying a pint of milk and some steaming hot fresh bread. The grocery woman feared they would get indigestion by devouring the bread, and so she gave them some butter to go with it. Clinton so captivated the lady that she and her husband closed their shop for the rest of the day. The English couple invited the young Americans into their living quarters for a traditional English Sunday lunch. Following that the couple gave Stearns and Clinton a tour of the city. At the end of the afternoon they deposited the two students at the local bus station and paid for their tickets to Oxford. Stearns further remembers that the grocers had two small children. Once back in Oxford, Clinton bought gifts for the children and sent them notes.[87]

Did everyone in Oxford like Clinton? A small number of British and American students found him to be, quite simply, too much. No one, they thought, could be that friendly, that concerned about others. Some thought he was just "full of bull." Others suspected that the future politician was merely using them, notching up friendships that could help him in his later career. He made no effort to hide his desire for a prominent role in Arkansas, and perhaps national, politics.

It was widely known that nearly every night he retreated to his room to work on his index cards. These cards contained the names of nearly all the people he had ever met. On each one Clinton added notes about when they had met or corresponded and topics they had discussed. Clinton was, in short, the consummate networker. By the time he first ran for office, in an unsuccessful 1974 bid for a seat in the House of Representatives, his cards numbered at least ten thousand. These files formed the nucleus of his mailing lists for contributors and campaign volunteers. Therefore, yes, he was to some extent using people. Such is the life of nearly anyone who succeeds in electoral politics.[88]

In spite of this, just about all the Americans in Oxford either liked Clinton immediately or quickly were won over. They willingly agreed that this energetic southerner, who survived on catnaps, would one day become governor, or maybe even a senator.[89] One who never overcame his suspicions, however, was fellow Arkansas student Cliff Jackson. The latter was a Fulbright Scholar studying at St. John's College. In many ways Jackson and Clinton were similar. Both played on the Oxford basketball team. Neither was very agile or fast, but each was hefty and more than six feet tall. Both were their hometown "golden boys." Both had been class presidents, Clinton at Georgetown, Jackson at Arkansas College. Both aspired to high public careers in Arkansas. Jackson was a Republican, but that in itself did not cause any friction between them. Like Clinton, Jackson did not want to go to Vietnam and was using all available means to avoid it.

The real cause of their eventual rift may never be known. Some journalists have suggested that Clinton may have stolen a girlfriend from Jackson or in some other way slighted his fellow southerner. Clinton has never spoken about the matter, and Jackson denies that there is anything personal involved. Clinton biographer David Maraniss has demonstrated that much of what Jackson has said about Clinton in later years cannot be trusted.[90] All that is clear is that Jackson's feelings eventually developed into an obsessional hatred. Since 1992 Jackson has gone out of his way to dig up dirt on his rival, doling out to reporters any tidbits that he has found about Whitewater, marital infidelities, and possible misuse of public authority.[91]

David Maraniss and several other political observers have conjectured that the root of the hatred is envy.[92] Jackson wanted to rise high in politics, but early on he could see that Clinton's star would ascend higher. Jackson had to settle for a career as a fairly prosperous attorney on the relatively small stage of Little Rock.

Jackson argues, unconvincingly, that personally he likes Clinton. His actions to thwart Clinton, he says, simply result from Clinton's dishonesty. Jackson maintains that in Oxford he could see that his opportunistic friend was merely exploiting people for his own ends. To be sure, there are a couple of letters from that period in which Jackson expresses some misgivings about Clinton. Yet there is even more evidence demonstrating friendship and a relationship of mutual benefit. In several letters from 1969 Jackson expressed hope that both he himself and Clinton could avoid Vietnam. Jackson even placed calls to the office of the governor of Arkansas, Republican Winthrop Rockefeller, asking for help in obtaining a deferment for his friend. Rockefeller's office obliged, making several calls to the Garland County Draft Board. It is hard to reconcile these facts with Jackson's later claims that he distrusted Clinton from the start. Moreover, if Clinton sometimes "used" people, so did Jackson. In November 1971, by which time both men were law students in the United States, Jackson sought advice from Clinton regarding how to win a White House Fellowship (a prestigious award usually given to up-and-coming men and women aspiring to careers in government).[93]

There is also abundant evidence to demonstrate that Clinton's friendliness was more than just a way of hatching a network of friends who would support his future political campaigns. Many of the people with whom he spent time in Oxford were unlikely ever to be of any "use" to him in the future.

The prime example of this was Douglas Millin, the head porter at Univ. Douglas was a middle-aged Second World War veteran notorious for his surly temperament and lexicon of expletives. Most students feared him, and even dons tried to stay out of his way. The college was his domain, and he the house dragon protecting it. When Clinton, Reich, Eakeley, and Isaacson first arrived at the main gate in October 1968, he glanced at the diminutive Reich and exclaimed, "They told me I was getting four Yanks and here they send me three and a half! You're the goddam bloody shortest freaking American I've ever seen in my life! I didn't know it was possible for America to produce someone that freakin' small."[94]

Where other students retreated, both Clinton and Reich saw a challenge to be surmounted. Reich won Douglas over with his jokes and stories. Clinton, however, reached an unparalleled intimacy with the curmudgeonly porter. Within weeks Douglas and the folksy young American were bosom buddies. Most students entered Douglas's lair with trepidation, checked for mail in their pigeon holes, and then beat hasty retreats. Clinton, however, spent hours there. Other students and dons incredulously noticed that Douglas let the American sit at his desk, feet propped up, answering the phone and distributing mail. This unlikely twosome blissfully spent entire afternoons and evenings trading tall tales and gossip.

Douglas would be of no conceivable use to Clinton's later political career, but the porter was able to help his protégé in the college. He allowed Bill to get away with things forbidden to others. This included letting friends stay in Clinton's rooms overnight and permitting his parties to get boisterous. The supreme mark of Douglas' affection came in June 1969. Clinton was about to depart for the United States, and everyone expected him to enter the army rather than return to Oxford for a second year. Douglas permitted Clinton's British and American friends to throw a party that went on for some three days. Among other things, the fête called for a barbecue grill on college grounds – which must have made Max Beerbohm shiver in his grave. Many of the attendees climbed out on rooftops to drink beer and eat. Being caught on the roofs was an offense that would have got most other students gated or sent down. Douglas, however, was willing to permit almost anything for his Bill.[95]

Clinton never forgot his old friend. When, against all expectations, Clinton did return for a second year, he resided in digs outside college. But often he could still be found visiting in the porter's lodge. After Clinton won the presidential election in November 1992, he invited Douglas to attend the Inauguration. Douglas was the only person in Oxford to receive such an invitation. If Clinton were merely using people, he would also have invited Oxford dons and former Oxford students who were now prominent in British politics. Instead, he singled out this working-class, retired porter who had been a sort of surrogate father to him many years earlier.[96]

Douglas by then was in his mid-seventies and in frail health. He did not make the trip. However, when Clinton returned for his honorary degree in 1994, he set aside time to have tea with Douglas. The duo sat in Clinton's old rooms in Helen's Court and relived old memories.

There is no evidence that Clinton ever went out of his way to cultivate friendships in Oxford with students or dons who seemed likely to be able to help him in his later career. Among Rhodes Scholars, he was close to those who, like Talbott, Reich, and Stearns, shared his obsession with public affairs. However, he also befriended the non-political ones. One of these was the comparatively shy Paul Parish. An English major from the University of Mississippi, Parish had a rough time in Oxford. He agonized about the draft and finally applied for conscientious objector status. In Oxford Parish also fell in love with Sara Maitland, an undergraduate British student at St. Anne's College. That relationship would be an on-again-off-again affair that tormented both Parish and Maitland.

Parish frequently sought out Clinton for late night soul searchings. One reason he chose Clinton was that the latter never seemed to sleep; he was always to be found somewhere, and always willing to talk. It was not just that Clinton talked, but that he was easy to talk to. Parish observed that very often people ended up telling Clinton their life histories and their darkest secrets soon after they met him. "People's souls shined in their faces when they were talking to Bill," he remembers.[97]

It was to Clinton that Parish turned when he sought help in applying for conscientious objector status and when he needed solace after spats with Maitland. Eventually Parish realized that his problems with Maitland stemmed at least in part from an unsuspected problem. It was in long talks with Clinton that Parish first openly came to realize and accept his homosexuality. By the time he left Oxford, Parish had adopted a British accent and a more "artsy" persona.

In the years since Oxford Parish has had a rather checkered career, spending several years "finding himself." At different times he has been a waiter, danced ballet, and written about ballet. All the while he has remained a friend of Clinton and of no "use" to the latter's career.

Clinton also became close to numerous British female students. In addition to the several American girlfriends with whom he kept in contact – at least a couple of them visiting him in England – he dated perhaps a dozen British women and hung around with many others. Looking back, Sara Maitland says Clinton was not alone in this regard:

> A lot of Rhodes Scholars had a hard time at Oxford because of a shortage of females … it was before the colleges were mixed. Bill liked female company and found the boys' world that was Oxford more difficult than [British] men who had come from public schools. We became such good friends; it wasn't just S-E-X.[98]

Since Clinton's rise to prominence in 1992, there have been many rumors about his love life in Oxford. Two British writers have even published thinly fictionalized novels about it. Robyn Sisman's *Special Relationship* concerns Jordan Hope (note the "coincidental" choice of Clinton's birthplace). Hope is an earnest, saxophone-playing, Baptist Rhodes Scholar. While in Oxford he opposes the Vietnam War and displays outrage at America's heritage of Jim Crow laws. After Oxford he marries a brainy, blond, ambitious American woman and eventually wins election to the Presidency. His "special relationship" involves a one-night stand more than two decades earlier in Oxford. That brief flirtation produced a male child, and the revelation of this son's existence threatens Hope's political career. Tim Sebastian's *Special Relations* is a spy thriller that likewise concerns a British female student who has a brief affair with an American in Oxford. Some thirty years later he is elected President (albeit as a Republican) while she becomes the first female prime minister from the Labour Party.[99]

The available facts are less sensational. Clinton and other Rhodes Scholar pals frequently attended tea parties in Sara Maitland's rooms. A quarter-century later Clinton recalled that in these delicate surroundings he witnessed all the young British men and women "talking about this and that, just being clever about something."[100] Though he may have seemed a bull amidst fine china, he impressed Maitland as "quite easily the most gregarious human being" she had ever met.[101]

There was much casual sex among his fellow students, and Clinton was frequently seen with one or another of his female friends. However, all of his British and American acquaintances have remained close-mouthed with prying journalists in later years. Maitland has coyly remarked that Bill always slept with his saxophone.[102]

Clinton helped Maitland overcome her political innocence. One night she, Frank Aller, and Clinton were sitting in a pub discussing Vietnam. When Aller started describing the horrible effects of napalm on people, Maitland began to cry. Aller responded, "That's the only correct response." Clinton, however, argued, "No, it's not. If something makes you cry, you have to do something about it. That's the difference between politics and guilt."[103]

Another close female friend was Mandy Merck, a Smith graduate studying English at St. Hugh's College. She often visited the Leckford Road house during Clinton's second year and noticed that he was always "reading and tootling the sax." She could also see that he was a serious, troubled young man.[104] Merck found Clinton to be so thoughtful and sympathetic that he became the first man to learn she was a lesbian. When an affair with another woman went sour, she turned to him for help and understanding.[105]

It was with Merck and Maitland that Clinton one night attended a lecture at Ruskin Hall by the celebrated feminist author Germaine Greer, whose new book *The Female Eunuch* had achieved phenomenal notoriety. In his typical down-home fashion, Clinton said he wanted to see Greer because he had heard she was more than six feet tall, had great legs, and was going to talk about sex. Greer arrived wearing a tight rawhide miniskirt that confirmed Clinton's hopes about her physical charms. In her lecture Greer shocked many in the audience with her frank discussion of sex and social classes. She maintained that sex with middle-class intellectual men was worthless, for they were no good at it. It was better with lorry drivers and other working-class men. Clinton piped up, "Miss Greer, in case you ever change your mind about bourgeois men, can I give you my phone number?" Greer cheerfully retorted, "You should be so lucky."[106]

Maitland says of this light-hearted moment:

> It was very Bill-like, that exuberance of what a good time he was having, and it was so much what every man there was feeling at the meeting, and Bill was so unembarrassed about it … Mandy and Bill and I were all very pleased with ourselves walking home that night.[107]

Maitland was also involved in another typically Clinton episode. In the spring of 1970 she and Paul Parish had their final falling out. Maitland was so distraught that she was admitted to the Warneford psychiatric hospital on the edge of town. Clinton and Aller took a bus to see her several times, and they brought her packets of exotic teas. After she left the hospital, Clinton thought that a hair makeover would cheer her up. He made an appointment for her in a beauty parlor. Because she was terrified of being trapped in the electric dryers, he paid extra to have her hair dried by hand. This kindness further confirmed her belief that Clinton was "one of the good guys."[108]

All eyewitnesses agree that Clinton's unkempt appearance and the slovenly living conditions at the Leckford Road house smacked of hippie bohemianism. Some drugs were in evidence. Did Clinton himself take marijuana? Yes, as he finally acknowledged during the 1992 campaign. Rather than eliciting admiration for his candor, however, the admission evoked snickers from millions of Americans. Clinton said he had smoked pot on a few occasions, but that he had not inhaled.

His apparent "halfway" admission was curious. By the 1990s it had become acceptable for middle-aged politicians to confess that they had dabbled in drugs when young. In 1995, for example, Newt Gingrich was asked about his own past and forthrightly announced that, yes, he had smoked marijuana. But all that proved, he claimed, was that he "had been alive and in graduate school in that era."[109]

Was Clinton being less than candid in his "partial" admission? Yes and no. It is true that he never inhaled, but he never adequately explained why. Perhaps he believed that giving the whole truth would bring even more ridicule and disbelief than the partial truth would. The complete truth is that when pot was passed around, his friends tried to make him inhale. However, he physically was not able to do so. He could not tolerate tobacco or cigarettes of any kind. One of his friends recalls many scenes at parties where Clinton could be found choking, sticking his head out a window for fresh air.[110] (Given this, it is not surprising that Clinton was the first President to prohibit smoking anywhere in the White House.)

Vietnam

The Vietnam War inevitably affected the Oxford experience of all Rhodes Scholars of the late 1960s and early 1970s. More than a dozen years after he returned home, Bill Clinton admitted in an interview that:

A lot of us felt a little strange to jump on a boat and go to idyllic Oxford and escape ... the emotional conflict because of the war put a cloud over it all. It wasn't bad, but it was always there. As a result, we Americans probably clustered in groups more than was usual before or after.[111]

By the time Bill Clinton and his class reached Oxford in the fall of 1968, a majority of Americans of all ages and political persuasions had come to question their government's involvement in the Vietnam War. The TET offensive in January of that year was a military defeat but a psychological victory for the North Vietnamese, as it demonstrated that American firepower could never prevent supplies and men from reaching the South. American military commanders were unable to guarantee that the war could be won with anything less than the nuclear destruction of all of the North. After his own Secretary of Defense, Clark Clifford, turned against the war, President Lyndon Baines Johnson announced in March 1968 that he would not seek reelection. Yet direct U.S. military involvement would continue for another five years. Still ahead lay the secret bombings of Laos and Cambodia, the deaths of students at Kent State, and scores of other violent confrontations across the United States.

Did Clinton oppose the war? Yes, he had come to that decision after he started to work for Senator Fulbright in 1967. Did he try to avoid the draft? Yes, but so did millions of other young men at the time. They sought student or medical deferments; they applied for conscientious objector status; they joined the navy (where there was less chance of going to Vietnam); they joined units of the National Guard or ROTC; when all else failed, thousands of them fled to Canada or Scandinavia. Most of the men who sought these avenues of escape were white and middle class; they tended to have the education and the connections needed to obtain these escape routes. Besides Bill Clinton, others of his generation who used these safety nets included Republicans Dan Quayle, Newt Gingrich, Phil Gramm, Dick Cheney, and Steve Forbes.

Were these millions of American men traitors or cowards? Undoubtedly many of them were less than brave. However, only a handful can justifiably be labelled treasonous anti-Americans. Most history books have now tended to vindicate the anti-war protestors. Not only was this war unwinnable, but U.S. involvement resulted from a tragic misunderstanding of Asian history, a stupid rejection of friendly overtures from Ho Chi Minh in 1945, and a Cold War mentality that exaggerated the possible threats from "monolithic" Communism.[112] The Americans who suffered most from the war were the soldiers who patriotically obeyed commands from a government that should have known better.

The Rhodes Scholars of the late 1960s and early 1970s were representative of most college-educated young men of those years. If anything, they were probably, as a group, less vocal in their opposition than were most students back home. This resulted from the fact that Rhodes Scholars tended to be part of the establishment. They obtained their scholarships partly because they were good at pleasing their superiors and working within the system. Most of them aimed for top jobs in government, academe, law, and business. Only a few were long-haired iconoclasts, and even these shunned violence and inflammatory language.

If the conflict had been the Second World War, instead of Vietnam, they probably would have been gung-ho volunteers. On several occasions in later years Bill Clinton has said that he was raised watching patriotic John Wayne westerns and war movies.[113] During the 1992 campaign, national security expert Michael Mandelbaum strongly defended his friend in this regard. Mandelbaum had been a Marshall Scholar studying in Cambridge in the late 1960s and had come to know Clinton, Talbott, and many of the other Rhodes Scholars. Mandelbaum pointed out, "What people don't understand about this guy is that he's rather pro-military ... Virtually the only mementos he has of his father are his military decorations from World War II."[114] Moreover, as a native of the South, Clinton came from a part of the country where the military in general was revered most highly. One should also recall his brief stint in the Air Force ROTC program at Georgetown. His quitting of that program seems to have resulted more from his clumsy inability to keep up with the drill team than from any hostility to the military. There is also no evidence that he was a physical coward. His standing up to his violent, drunken stepfather and his volunteer work in rough sections of Washington during his Georgetown days show that he did not run from danger. The decision to oppose the war thus did not come easily for him.

Even before Clinton reached Oxford, Rhodes Scholars had won national attention for questioning the war. In January 1967 newspapers across the United States carried stories about a letter that fifty Rhodes Scholars had sent to President Johnson, expressing concern about American involvement in Southeast Asia. This story was newsworthy because it was from Rhodes Scholars, the "anointed" leaders of tomorrow, rather than because of what it said. In restrained, polite words, the letter simply asked the President to explain the rationale for the war. The letter made clear that the scholars were not opposing the war or calling for American withdrawal. They simply asked for a clearer explanation of American motives and plans. In short, these "militants" were perfect gentlemen in their deference to authority.[115]

The scholars from the mid-1960s to the early 1970s were consumed with the national passion of those years: debating the options in Vietnam. James O'Toole (1966) says they talked about Vietnam "only about twelve hours a day, seven days a week."[116] This obsession bored most British students. Thus the scholars of this period, as a whole, bonded less with British students and more with each other than had been true earlier.

The class of 1968 was predominantly antiwar and more vocal than its immediate predecessors. Strobe Talbott freely admits that "from the moment the thirty-two of us got on the boat and sailed to England, Topic A was Vietnam and Topic A-1 was Vietnam and me."[117] Two members of this group were Annapolis graduates, Dennis Blair and Robert Earl. Every Rhodes Scholar class generally had two or three graduates of the military academies. These scholars were permitted to pursue their degrees in Oxford, having all the same freedoms as any civilians, though they were considered to be on active duty. Not until 1971 did Blair and Earl enter actual military service, Blair aboard a destroyer and Earl in the Marines. By all accounts these and other military Rhodes Scholars of the Vietnam era got along well with their classmates.[118] Certainly there were arguments about the war. But the military scholars were not ostracized. Earl became an opera fanatic while in Britain and on at least one occasion took his friends Bill Clinton and Strobe Talbott to Covent Garden with him.[119] West Point's Timothy Lupfer (1973) became secretary of his class, charged with rounding up yearly reports for *The American Oxonian.* Scott Barker (1970) of the Air Force Academy worried about how he and others would be accepted by the non-military scholars and was pleasantly surprised by the cordial acceptance he received. Barker admits that he and most other military scholars generally were not "keen" on the war either.[120] The civilian scholars were not anti-military or anti-American, they were simply anti-Vietnam.

Before he left Hot Springs for Oxford, Bill Clinton got some help from one of his uncles. Raymond Clinton was one of the wealthiest and most influential businessmen in town, and he got the local draft board to delay Bill's draft notice so that the boy could finish at least one year in Oxford. Bill Clinton's case was by no means unusual. Draft boards around the country performed similar favors for their own "golden boys" – whether they be Rhodes Scholars, top athletes, or simply well-connected. In his biography of Clinton, David Maraniss demonstrates how pervasive these kinds of favors were:

> The draft board in Alameda County, California, was so impressed by the achievements of the only black Rhodes winner that year, Tom Williamson of Harvard, that they granted him a graduate school defer-ment even though such deferments supposedly no longer existed. Darryl Gless, whose small home town in Nebraska was so proud of him that they strung a banner across the Main Street bank welcoming him back from his successful Rhodes interview, also was given a special deferment. Dartmouth scholar John Isaacson visited his draft board in Lewiston, Maine, and pleaded with them to let him go to Oxford, which they did. University of Iowa scholar Mike Shea went to England "happily but erro-neously 2-S" [i.e., with a student deferment] for the first year. Paul Parish's mother in Port Gibson, Mississippi, received a letter from the governor telling her that Paul should go to England because they were trying to get an exemption for Rhodes Scholars. For virtually every mem-ber of the Rhodes class of 1968 there was a similar story.
>
> Willie Fletcher, a Harvard graduate from Washington State … cut a deal with the Navy, signing up for a four-month officer candidate school that summer on the condition that when he finished in October they would defer his commission for two years and let him go to Oxford.[121]

Both at that time, and years later, Clinton admitted that he felt guilty about going to Oxford, knowing that several Hot Springs boys were in Vietnam. By 1968 two of his high school friends had already died there. Only one Rhodes Scholar of 1968 was so overcome with guilt that he did something about it. Walter Pratt's draft board in Jackson, Mississippi, benevolently promised him a deferment. Before that could come about, however, Pratt marched to the nearest army recruiter and signed up for officer candidate school. As his class-mates boarded the ship for Britain, he departed for basic training in Louisiana.[122] The Rhodes Trust obligingly told him that he could take up his scholarship at a later date. After three years of active duty, Pratt did just that and entered Balliol in 1971.

The details of Clinton's opposition to the Vietnam War and his escape from the draft have been recounted in too many books and articles to need full treatment here. He received his induction notice in April 1969 but was given permission to finish his first year in Oxford. A few months later he gained admission to the ROTC pro-gram at the University of Arkansas, with the assumption that he would start law school at that university in the fall of that year.

In October 1969 Clinton returned to Oxford rather than enter law school in Arkansas. There is ample evidence from friends in

Arkansas and Oxford that the young man was genuinely in torment as to what he should do. Because he had not anticipated returning to Oxford for a second year, he had not made arrangements for living quarters. For a few weeks he slept on a rollaway bed in the rooms of fellow scholar Rick Stearns. Then he moved into a house on Leckford Road, about two miles north of the center of town, where he joined his classmates Strobe Talbott and Frank Aller.

Soon after his return to Oxford he notified his draft board that he wanted to restore his draft eligibility status, thereby giving up his ROTC deferment. At about the same time President Richard Nixon announced that there would be a national lottery on 1 December 1969. Each day of the year would receive a number, corresponding to the order in which it was drawn by lot. The higher one's number, the lower one's chances of being drafted. Clinton's birthday, 19 August, was number 311. The likelihood of his ever being drafted was virtually nil. If his birthday had been picked among the first several dozen, he would have been inducted. There is no reason to doubt that he would have served – even if that meant the rice paddies of southeast Asia.

Clinton's efforts to avoid Vietnam were no more remarkable than those of most other scholars of that period. Several scholars checked themselves into the nearby Warneford psychiatric hospital, hoping to gain 4-F status because of mental problems. Others tried to induce physical illness so they would flunk their medical examinations. Strobe Talbott's salvation was a "gimpy knee" that won him a 1-Y deferment. He had hurt the knee years earlier playing football at his prep school, Hotchkiss. He was relieved that his injury "was enough to keep me out of the Mekong Delta but not off the squash courts and playing fields of Oxford."[123] Others from the class of 1968 were equally lucky in flunking their physicals. Bo Jones had high blood pressure, Rick Stearns was asthmatic, and John Isaacson suffered from migraines. Doug Eakeley had a dislocated shoulder, though, like Talbott, he could still play his fill of Oxford sports. Robert Reich just barely escaped service. During his army physical a sergeant spotted him and cried out, "Hallelujah! We got ourselves a tunnel rat." "What'd you say?" asked the befuddled Reich. Thereupon the sergeant explained that the army needed short men to enter tunnels and toss in grenades, to flush the Viet Cong out. Reich's life was flashing before his eyes when another sergeant measured his height and said, "I'm sorry, son." To his immense relief, Reich discovered that he was an inch and a half below the five foot minimum.[124]

Two members of the class obtained conscientious objector status: George Butte easily gained his from his local draft board before he left the United States, and Paul Parish was granted his in the summer of 1969. Just as he was about to be drafted, Tom McFadden managed to win a slot in the Army Reserve. Mike Shea joined a ROTC program at the University of Iowa Law School. He developed bad knees, however, and was discharged. Shea returned to Oxford in 1970. Warden E.T. Williams, a Second World War hero and by no means a pacifist, wrote letters to draft boards on behalf of many of his scholars, supporting their applications for deferments of various sorts.[125]

Scholars of the years before and after 1968 used some of the same stratagems. Tom Ward (1967) got help from his father, a prominent Republican lawyer in Meridien, Mississippi. Thanks to his father's intercession, he got into a local National Guard unit. Ward's military duties were so light that he had plenty of time to coach basketball for a nearby junior college.[126]

James Fallows took a different approach. On 1 December 1969, when he was a senior at Harvard, he learned that his birth date had drawn the low number 45, which almost guaranteed that he would be drafted. With what he calls "a diligence born of panic," he commenced to starve himself, so that when he was called for his physical his emaciated six-foot-one frame tipped the scales at only 120 pounds. When the examining physician asked him if he had ever contemplated suicide, Fallows admitted the he had been "feeling very unstable and unreliable recently."[127] With a sigh a relief, Fallows saw the physician write "unqualified" on his folder. Four out of five Harvard and MIT students used similar ruses – if not starving themselves then overeating, or intentionally botching their eye exams, or faking violent psychiatric problems, or pretending to be gay. Most of them probably shared Fallows's genuine hatred of what they considered an immoral war. Most of them also probably shared his guilt feelings about their ersatz ailments, for they knew that most working-class youths would not be so lucky.

The story of Clinton's Leckford Road roommate Frank Aller would end in tragedy. When notified in early 1969 that he should report for induction, he told his draft board that he would not fight in an immoral war. He refused to return to the United States and thus became an outlaw. He stayed in Oxford to continue his studies in Chinese literature and history. The pressure of being a draft resister gradually evaporated his sunny disposition. In December 1970 he finally returned home to Spokane, Washington, where he was immediately indicted for his crime. Soon thereafter he took his draft physical, which he flunked – perhaps because of a bad ear. The government then dropped its case against him. On 12 September

1971 he committed suicide. None of his friends or relatives could completely understand that action. Obviously the turmoil of Vietnam had at least something to do with it. The death of their friend at such an early age had a profound impact on Clinton, Talbott, and other Rhodes Scholars. They elevated him to martyr status, seeing him as one of the "unseen" victims of the war in southeast Asia. During his years in the governor's mansion in Little Rock, one wall in Clinton's study featured a poster-size enlargement of a photo of Aller, Talbott, and himself taken during their year at Leckford Road.[128]

During the 1992 presidential campaign, George Bush and his supporters again and again tried to use Clinton's Oxford days against him. Once the election was over, John Albery, master of University College, complained that "George Bush tried to make Oxford a dirty word."[129] Republicans compared Bush's valorous exploits during the Second World War to Clinton's shunning of military service. They also criticized Clinton for participating in anti-war rallies while he was in Britain. As Bush explained, Americans are free to criticize their government here at home; but doing so while abroad is not quite acceptable. The clear implication was that Clinton had acted in unpatriotic fashion.

It is important to place Clinton's behavior in context. During his two years in Oxford, he became notorious for his marathon bull sessions – in the Univ. dining hall, in pubs, in his rooms, everywhere. He and most other Rhodes Scholars opposed the war. Their most vitriolic comments about American policies, however, were reserved for discussions among themselves. Again and again Clinton's friends observed that whenever British students attacked the United States, he defended his country.[130] He admitted that its policy in Vietnam was wrong, but he argued that by and large the United States pursued moral foreign policies. He also pointed to the imperialist vices of European countries.

Though the topic of Vietnam consumed Clinton and his friends, for the most part they were mere talkers rather than actors. Ira Magaziner and Strobe Talbott had gained reputations as student radicals back home, at Brown University and Yale. In Oxford, however, they often were considered shut-ins and non-joiners. They participated in only a handful of public discussions or polite marches. Magaziner stayed in his rooms reading the great economists and sociologists. Talbott tried to stay focused on his degree work. In his second year Talbott was even less in evidence, as he holed up in his bedroom and asked his roommates, Clinton and Aller, to keep people away from him. Clinton kept his reclusive friend supplied with scrambled eggs, biscuits, and coffee. The source of this mystery was a special project on which Talbott was working for *Time*. During the summer of 1969 he had worked as an intern in the magazine's Moscow bureau. He had so impressed the bureau chief there that, when *Time* came into possession of hundreds of hours of taped recollections by ousted Soviet leader Nikita Khrushchev, the editors asked Talbott to prepare a translation. The following year *Time* printed excerpts of them, and eventually Little, Brown, published the entire collection as *Khrushchev Remembers*.[131]

For Clinton too the amount of time actually devoted to protesting against Vietnam was minimal. Quite by coincidence he happened to pass by and witness an anti-war rally in London in March 1969. In October and November of that same year he and other Americans studying in Oxford helped to organize two demonstrations outside the American Embassy in London's Grosvenor Square. Thomas Allen recalls that all the Americans present were obsessively determined to remain polite, moderate, and peaceful.[132] These rallies were prayer vigils and "teach-ins," not violent, seditious attacks on America.[133] One can further underscore the peaceful, moderate tone of these rallies by noting some of the other Americans in attendance. Three of the Rhodes Scholars in the November rally were members of the armed services: J. Michael Kirchberg (1967), Willie Fletcher, and Robert Earl. Annapolis graduate Kirchberg eventually obtained conscientious objector status. Some fifteen years later Earl worked under Lieutenant Colonel Oliver North in the Reagan White House. Yet another American at the November demonstration was Michael Boskin, who two decades later served as Chief of the Council of Economic Advisers under George Bush.[134]

Yet another Oxford episode that political adversaries used against Clinton in 1992 was his trip to the Soviet Union and Eastern Europe during Christmas vacation in December 1969. Some of George Bush's supporters suggested that during this trip Clinton conspired with Communists and tried to give up his American citizenship. On 7 October 1992 Bush himself appeared on "Larry King Live." Radio host King obligingly asked him, "What do you make of the Clinton Moscow trip thing?" Bush responded, "I don't want to tell you what I really think ... I don't have the facts. But to go to Moscow one year after Russia crushed Czechoslovakia.... . [Clinton should] level with the American people ... Level, tell us the truth, and let the voters decide who to trust or not."[135]

Throughout the 1992 campaign, and again in 1996, the conservative *Washington Times* and *American Spectator* fueled these speculations with unsupported articles about "Boy Clinton" being financed on this "vacation" by either the CIA or the Communist Party (depending on which article one reads) and slipping away from Russia for a clandestine side trip to Hanoi.[136]

During the 1992 campaign Clinton repeatedly maintained that he simply had been on a Christmas vacation trip, seeing the sights, and occasionally staying with friends or the families of people he had got to know at Georgetown and Oxford.

All the available evidence corroborates his story. There was nothing mysterious about a Rhodes Scholar visiting eastern Europe or the Soviet Union at that time. Traveling through Europe during vacations was a standard practice that had been enjoyed by Rhodes Scholars since 1904. Prior to this trip, Clinton had made numerous excursions through Scotland, Wales, England, Ireland, Germany, France, and Austria. Several of his classmates had already been to Moscow, and most would do so prior to the end of their scholarships. Strobe Talbott was not alone among Rhodes Scholars when he declared that the insinuations of the Bush campaign team had been "ludicrous," "shameful," and "egregious."[137]

Indeed, thousands of American businessmen and tourists were visiting the Soviet Union each year by the late 1960s. Republican political commentator George Will studied at Magdalen College as a Fulbright Scholar in the early 1960s and traveled widely before returning home. William F. Weld, former Republican Governor of Massachusetts, spent the academic year 1966/1967 studying in Oxford on a Knox Fellowship. Like Clinton, he visited Moscow and Prague. After Will and Weld heard the Bush charges in 1992, both had the good sense to dismiss them as nonsense.[138]

Oxford's Impact

Some political commentators have claimed that Bill Clinton's actions as President reveal an anti-British bias that reflects old wounds from his Oxford days. Clinton's cool relationship with Conservative Prime Minister John Major, the granting of visas for Sinn Fein leader Gerry Adams to visit the United States, and American prodding of Great Britain to negotiate for a peaceful solution to the Northern Ireland question have all been seen as "revenge" for slights suffered in Oxford.[139]

However, there are other, more convincing explanations for these actions. Given the fact that John Major's government tilted in favor of George Bush during the 1992 campaign, it is not surprising that Clinton's first meeting with Major was rather icy. In addition, the Clinton family's Irish background plus the long tradition of Irish-American nostalgia for the Emerald Isle make it no surprise that he has taken strong steps to further the peace process.

Clinton biographer David Maraniss sums up his subject's Oxford experience by saying that, on the whole, the minuses outweighed the pluses. Anxiety over the Vietnam issue, he says, cast a cloud over the entire experience. Maraniss concludes that:

> Many of those who eventually left without degrees, including Clinton, later expressed regret and wished that they could go back and complete that unfinished period of their lives. Although later in his career Clinton never spoke bitterly about his Oxford experience, he rarely extolled those years, either. One reason was a touch of embarrassment: Oxford represented unfinished business. Perhaps that sense of mild regret and ambiguity served as the fitting metaphor for an extraordinary, unrepeatable era.[140]

It is true that, over the years, Clinton has occasionally expressed mild regret at not having completed his degree. He has joked about requesting the optional third year of the scholarship so that he could return to Oxford. It is hard, however, to detect any sign of embarrassment. Most of the scholars of the Vietnam era had difficulty staying focused on their degrees. Furthermore, Clinton has never voiced misgivings about his decision to enter Yale Law School in the fall of 1970 rather than returning to Britain.

Robert Reich's final assessment of Clinton in Oxford varies significantly from that of Maraniss:

> This is the part of him I remember best from our student days – the good-natured prankster, the fun-loving storyteller, the fellow who could spend hour upon hour trading jokes, playing cards, gossiping about politicians, taking delight in himself and those around him. That's how he spent most of his two years in Oxford and then the next three at Yale Law School, I think. I remember being envious of his capacity for sheer, exuberant joy.[141]

Over the past two decades, Clinton has rarely brought up Oxford and his Rhodes Scholarship in speeches and interviews. However, a glance at his public pronouncements from the 1980s and 1990s shows that seldom has he mentioned Georgetown and Yale either. What he has continually brought up are stories about his childhood and career in Arkansas. If Clinton has rarely mentioned Oxford, there are two good alternative explanations. One is the fact that the overwhelming majority of Rhodes Scholars find it "bad form" to boast about Oxford – though they might be pleased when others bring it up.

The second is that being a Rhodes Scholar is a mixed blessing for an American politician. In his classic book *Anti-Intellectualism in American Life* (1963) historian Richard Hofstadter perceptively depicted a strong tendency for many Americans to distrust public leaders tainted as cultural and academic highbrows. In the 1950s, Democratic presidential candidate Adlai Stevenson was hurt by his reputation for being an egghead who read serious books, whereas Dwight Eisenhower's folksy, grandfatherly charm was enhanced by the knowledge that he favored Zane Grey western shoot-em-ups. More recently, Russell Jacoby's *The Last Intellectuals: American Culture in the Age of Academe* (1987), has labeled intellectuals a marginalized "endangered species."[142] In a recent *Time* essay, Jeff Greenfield observed that "American politicians show genius at pretending to be modest, homespun heroes … the distrust of the intellectual hustler with his airs and his high-flown language runs deep."[143]

Is Bill Clinton an "intellectual"? If one uses prestigious academic degrees and scholarships as a gauge, he is. If one includes love of reading fine literature and serious nonfiction, he is. If one regards an interest in theory and grand ideas as an important trait, he is. Perhaps we can let *U.S. News & World Report* be the final arbiter. In February 1988 the magazine devoted nearly an entire issue to analyzing "The New American Establishment." Separate articles gave a veritable "Who's Who" list of top leaders in the following fields: Business, Foreign Policy, Politics, Intellectuals, Science, Media, Culture, and High Society. The Governor of Arkansas not only was listed but was one of the few to be featured in a photo. He was included, however, not under "Politics" but rather "Intellectuals." Echoing Russell Jacoby, the magazine called those individuals who could speak knowledgeably and broadly about the issues of the day an "endangered modern species." Clinton's picture was nestled between those of *New York Review of Books* co-editor Robert B. Silvers and University of Chicago President Hannah Holborn Gray.[144] (Clinton was not the only Rhodes Scholar deemed a member of the "New Establishment." Several others made the list. Under "Politics," for example, the magazine named Bill Bradley. Besides Clinton, the "Intellectuals" included James Billington, Daniel Boorstin, John Brademas, Ronald Dworkin, and Robert Reich.)

Some Rhodes Scholars who have run for political office have testified that being an Oxford alumnus has occasionally been used against them by opponents. The most famous example came in the 1992 presidential campaign. Several times George Bush tried to paint himself as the "ordinary" American and Clinton as the over-educated, polished elitist. Bush declared that he was not the world's greatest debater, for he had not been to Oxford. This argument was rather dubious, given the fact that Bush was the scion of a wealthy family, the son of a U.S. Senator, and a graduate of Yale.

Years earlier Clinton had witnessed close-up how being an Oxford intellectual could damage a political career. In 1974 J. William Fulbright lost his bid for reelection and retired from politics. Clinton could see that Fulbright's cerebral aloofness had gradually created a rift between him and the average Arkansas voter.[145] Fulbright's stiff, tweedy demeanor also alienated some of his fellow Democrats in Washington. Harry Truman called him "Senator Half-Bright" and "an overeducated Oxford son-of-a-bitch."[146] Lyndon Baines Johnson coined even more evocative expletives for the professorial senator who turned against his Vietnam policies. Clinton determined that he himself would never lose touch with Arkansas citizens the way Fulbright had. Among other things, this meant that he would not allude frequently to Georgetown, Oxford, and Yale.

Over the years, whenever he has been asked about Oxford, he has responded favorably. He has said he found the people friendly and the university beautiful. Moreover, he has claimed that his Oxford experience gave him "an invaluable perspective on our diverse world" and convinced him that, as a great power, the United States should never return to its former isolationism.[147]

In saying such things is he using the vague, diplomatic language of an astute politician? It should be clear from the pages above that he made many friends and enjoyed himself in Oxford – despite Vietnam.

There is also solid evidence from later years that he has maintained a genuine affection for the university and its people. He has done things not required of him as a careful politician. If a person has disliked his experiences at a university, there are things that he generally will not do. He will not revisit the university while on private vacations, will not keep in contact with many fellow students and former professors, will not attend alumni reunions, and will not make contributions to fund-raising drives. Yet Bill Clinton has done all these things.

On at least three occasions in the 1970s and 1980s Bill and Hillary Clinton vacationed in Britain. (Robert Reich had introduced Hillary to Bill early in the fall of 1970 at Yale Law School.) During a visit in 1978 the Clintons were joined by several Rhodes Scholar classmates in a sentimental return to their alma mater. A few years later the Clintons spent the Christmas holidays with his old friend Sara Maitland, who had become a prominent novelist and feminist critic.[148]

In the summer of 1983 Clinton attended a general reunion of all Rhodes Scholars in Oxford. When the governor of Arkansas arrived at the gates of Univ. he found his old friend Douglas still commanding the porter's lodge. Curmudgeonly as ever, Douglas greeted him by saying, "I hear you've become king of a place with two men and a dog."[149]

On numerous occasions through the 1970s and 1980s Clinton happily agreed to serve as mentor for students from his home state or from Georgetown University who were applying for Rhodes Scholarships. He helped the Georgetown seniors at the request of his friend, Georgetown President Reverend Timothy S. Healy, who himself had attended Oxford many years earlier. At least one student intern on his staff in Little Rock applied for and won a scholarship.[150] Clinton also served for several years in state and regional selection committees.[151]

Like thousands of Oxford graduates around the world, Clinton was solicited for financial support during the most recent Oxford appeal. When the fund-raising drive was concluded in 1994, the university triumphantly announced that it had exceeded its goals and raised more than £340 million. In a newsletter of November that year, the university printed an exhaustive list of the nearly sixteen thousand individuals and organizations who had contributed. There, in tiny print, almost buried in the sea of names, is "President of the United States."[152]

In June 1993 a large gathering of North American Rhodes Scholars convened for a weekend reunion at Georgetown University. (The date and location had been selected before Clinton's election to the presidency.) More than a thousand former scholars participated, along with many of their spouses. Clinton attended a Saturday evening reception at the British embassy and shook hundreds of hands. He also hosted a Sunday brunch at the White House for scholars who had been in Oxford during his time there.

In October of that same year, more than a hundred Americans who had studied under Zbigniew Pelczynski at one time or another organized a reunion in his honor in Washington, DC. Several dozen were former Rhodes Scholars; the others had studied in Oxford with the help of Fulbright, Marshall, or other scholarships. The gathering was organized by Thomas Herman, a Boston attorney who had studied at Pembroke College in the early 1970s. Clinton's presidential schedule prevented him from attending the main reception, but he invited his old tutor to the Oval Office later that day. The photo taken by the White House photographer of the teacher and his pupil is now one of Pelczynski's most precious possessions.[153] Between 1994 and 1997 during three trips to Europe Clinton made room in his hectic schedule for private meetings with his former tutor.[154]

Clinton's decision to visit Oxford in June 1994 to receive an honorary degree was not something he had to do. Every President of the United States receives many invitations for such awards, only a few of which can be accepted. Given the negative publicity that Clinton's Rhodes Scholarship had received in the 1992 campaign, he must have realized that he had little or nothing to gain politically by returning there. Indeed, much of the reporting done during this brief stopover was negative, dredging up stories about draft resistance, marijuana, and dropping out without a degree. The *Washington Post* declared that by visiting Oxford Clinton was "defying the ghosts of his youth."[155] The headlines in many newspapers also trumpeted the fact that his visit was marred by the presence of hundreds of noisy student protestors.[156] Only in the smaller print did one find that most of the protestors were not attacking Clinton. They were merely using the occasion of his visit to mount public demonstrations about issues having nothing to do with him – for example, a recent hike in their college fees.

By all accounts Clinton enjoyed himself during the short visit. He attended a reception with current Rhodes Scholars, and both he and Hillary cheerfully signed autographs for dons and students who surrounded them after the awards ceremony. The citation for his honorary degree was delivered in Latin. The university's public orator lauded Clinton for ending "impeditissimas omnium" (government gridlock) and hailed his wife as "feminam praestantissimam" (a most outstanding woman).

In his acceptance speech, Clinton light-heartedly joked:

> I always felt a mixture of elation and wariness, bordering on intimidation, in your presence. I thought if there was one place in the world I could come and give a speech in the proper language, it was here, and then I heard the degree ceremony. And sure enough, once again at Oxford I was another Yank a half step behind ...
>
> I am ... deeply honored by this degree you have bestowed on me, as well as the honorary fellowship I received from my college today. I must say that, as my wife pointed out, I could have gotten neither one of these things on my own. I had to be elected President to do it – with her help.[157]

This confident, self-deprecating banter demonstrated that Oxford had left its stamp on him.

In 1995 Clinton agreed to sit for two portraits that would be housed in Oxford. One is a sketch of his face by the Oxford-trained, American-born artist F. Kitaj; this work now belongs to University College. The other, by Michael Noakes, shows Clinton at his desk in the Oval Office. Perched on the desk are several personal mementos, including a bust of Winston Churchill. The desk itself is one that Queen Victoria donated to the White House a century earlier. This painting now hangs in Rhodes House.[158]

In the summer of 1996 Rhodes House Warden Sir Anthony Kenny mailed copies of a new, updated *Register of Rhodes Scholars* to the approximately three thousand American and other scholars who are still alive. Several months later Kenny reported that only three scholars had written to thank him for the gift. One of them was the President of the United States.[159]

NOTES

1. By far the most thorough and balanced account of Clinton's early life that has appeared thus far is David Maraniss, *First in His Class: A Biography of Bill Clinton* (New York, 1995).
2. Maraniss, *First in His Class*, 26. In her posthumously published autobiography Virginia candidly discussed such matters: Virginia Kelley, *Leading with My Heart* (New York, 1994).
3. Maraniss, *First in His Class*, 41.
4. Ibid., 40, 49.
5. Ibid., 17.
6. Ibid., 48.
7. Ibid., 84.
8. Ibid., 58, 61, 94.
9. Ibid., 93.
10. Ibid., 101.
11. Ibid., 101.
12. Ibid., 105.
13. Ibid., 114-15. It was during this campaign that McDougal and Clinton came to know one another. Several years later McDougal asked his friend to join him in the ill-fated Whitewater investment project.
14. Charles Lane, "The Master of the Game: Strobe's World," *The New Republic*, 7 March 1994, 19ff.; Maraniss, *First in His Class*, 101-2, 127-28.
15. Maraniss, *First in His Class*, 123.
16. Ibid., 124-25.
17. Ibid., 124.

18. Robert B. Reich, *Locked in the Cabinet* (New York, 1997), 4-5; Weisberg, "Clinton at Oxford," 174.
19. Williamson interview, 6 June 1994.
20. *NYT Book Review*, 23 April 1995, 35.
21. *Independent*, 9 June 1994, 3.
22. Margaret Osmer-McQuade, "The Legacy of Rhodes," *NYT Magazine*, 20 November 1983, 119.
23. Anthony Kenny, *A Life in Oxford* (London, 1997), 32.
24. Pelczynski interview, 4 July 1994.
25. After retiring from Pembroke, Pelczynski became head of the Soros Foundation's office in Oxford.
26. Pagan, "Bill Clinton at Oxford," 78.
27. Zbigniew Pelczynski, "Oxfordzkie dni I noce Billa Clintona," *Obserwator Codzienny* (Warsaw), 7 May 1992. The authors thank Krzysztof Lubkiewicz for his translation.
28. Pelczynski interview, 4 July 1994.
29. *Oxford Today*, Hilary Issue, 1993, 2.
30. Zbigniew Pelczynski, "My Pupil Bill Clinton," *Pembroke College Record* (1992): 40.
31. Pelczynski, "My Pupil," 40.
32. Anthony Kenny, Warden's Christmas letter, December 1994, 6-7.
33. Sieverts, diary and letter to authors, 19 September 1996.
34. Isaacson, letter to authors, 10 December 1993.
35. Pelczynski, "Oxfordzkie dni I noce Billa Clintona."
36. Pelczynski interview, 4 July 1994.
37. Pelczynski interview, 4 July 1994; Maraniss, *First in His Class*, 186.
38. Pagan, "Bill Clinton at Oxford," 78.
39. *Independent*, 9 June 1994, 3; Alessandra Stanley, "Most Likely to Succeed," *NYT Magazine*, 22 November 1992, 84; *NYT*, 9 June 1994, A8; Maraniss, *First in His Class*, 164.
40. Maraniss, *First in His Class*, 220.
41. Pelczynski interview, 4 July 1994.
42. Shock interview, 4 July 1994.
43. Maraniss, *First in His Class*, 223.
44. Maraniss, *First in His Class*, 223.
45. Williams interview, 1 July 1994.
46. *NYT*, 30 June 1995, 17D.
47. Shock interview, 4 July 1994; Maraniss, *First in His Class*, 223.
48. Williamson interview, 6 June 1994.
49. *Time*, 4 July 1969, 52-53.
50. Jacob Weisberg, "Dies Ira: A Short History of Mr. Magaziner," *The New Republic*, 24 January 1994, 18ff.
51. *People*, 11 October 1993, 61; Magaziner interview, 8 June 1994.
52. *Time*, 4 July 1969, 53.
53. *Life*, 20 June 1969, 31.
54. Shesol interview, 26 February 1996.
55. Magaziner interview, 8 June 1994.
56. Williams interview, 1 July 1994.
57. NPR commentary, 23 November 1992. The authors thank Fallows for providing a copy of the transcript.
58. Weisberg, "Clinton at Oxford," *GQ*, June 1993, 174-76.

59. Martin Walker, *The President We Deserve. Bill Clinton: His Rise, Falls, and Comebacks* (New York, 1996), 62.

60. C-SPAN, "Oxford/American Connection," January 1993.

61. Ibid.

62. Ibid.

63. Janis interview, 7 July 1994.

64. Schmoke interview, 2 August 1994.

65. Magaziner interview, 8 June 1994.

66. Allen interview, 20 November 1995.

67. Janis interview, 7 July 1994.

68. *TAO*, 65 (1978): 297.

69. Eakeley interview, 3 July 1996.

70. Reich, *Locked in the Cabinet*, 6; Maraniss, *First in His Class*, 142.

71. Pagan, "Bill Clinton at Oxford," 78.

72. Ibid., 80-81.

73. Crawford interview, 18 August 1994.

74. Eakeley interview, 3 July 1996.

75. Maraniss, *First in His Class*, 131.

76. Ibid., 142.

77. Ibid., 142.

78. Ibid., 146. Dwire died in 1974 as a result of complications from diabetes. In 1982 Virginia wed Hot Springs food broker Richard Kelley, who survived her following her death from breast cancer in January 1994.

79. Allen interview, 20 November 1995; *New Yorker*, 8 February 1993, 77.

80. Maraniss, *First in His Class*, 140; Weisberg, "Clinton at Oxford," 175.

81. Zoeller interview, 14 September 1995.

82. Maraniss, *First in His Class*, 141.

83. *New Yorker*, 12 August 1996, 22.

84. *Oxford Times*, 6 November 1992, 1.

85. Stanley, "Most Likely to Succeed," 40.

86. Williamson interview, 6 June 1994; Weisberg, "Clinton at Oxford," 177.

87. *U.S. News & World Report*, 19 October 1992, 36; Maraniss, *First in His Class*, 195.

88. Stanley, "Most Likely to Succeed," 40; Maraniss, *First in His Class*, 260, 284.

89. Maraniss, *First in His Class*, 124, 144.

90. Ibid., 169, 175-76.

91. *NYT*, 2 January 1994, 16; Maraniss, *First in His Class*, 464.

92. Maraniss, *First in His Class*, 156-57, 169; *NYT*, 24 December 1993, A18 and 2 January 1994, 16.

93. Maraniss, *First in His Class*, 157, 166, 168-69, 172-73, 181, 239, 261.

94. Ibid., 130.

95. Ibid., 135; Weisberg, "Clinton at Oxford," 176.

96. *Financial Times*, 4 January 1993, 27.

97. Maraniss, *First in His Class*, 144, 152.

98. *Evening Standard*, 18 June 1993, 11.

99. Robyn Sisman, *Special Relationship* (London, 1994); Tim Sebastian, *Special Relations* (London, 1994). Most reviewers have praised the latter while finding the former trite. For example, *Independent*, 7 February 1994, 15; *NYT Book Review*, 13 August 1995, 14.

100. Pagan, "Bill Clinton at Oxford," 80.

101. Maraniss, *First in His Class*, 153.

102. *Evening Standard*, 18 June 1993, 11.

103. Ibid.

104. Maraniss, *First in His Class*, 217.

105. *Evening Standard*, 18 June 1993, 11; Maraniss, *First in His Class*, 219; Weisberg, "Clinton at Oxford," 229.

106. Eyewitnesses give slightly different versions of what Clinton and Greer said. Some recall Clinton asking for her number; others say he offered to give her his own. Weisberg, "Clinton at Oxford," 173; Maraniss, *First in His Class*, 218-19; *Evening Standard*, 18 June 1993, 11.

107. Maraniss, *First in His Class*, 219.

108. *Evening Standard*, 18 June 1993, 11.

109. *Time*, 17 July 1995, 64.

110. Maraniss, *First in His Class*, 154.

111. *NYT Magazine*, 20 November 1983, 119.

112. Two of the better general introductions to the Vietnam War: Robert S. McNamara, *In Retrospect: The Tragedy and Lessons of Vietnam* (New York, 1995); Robert D. Schulzinger, *A Time for War: The United States and Vietnam, 1941-1975* (New York, 1997).

113. Stanley, "Most Likely to Succeed," 38; *NYT*, 9 June 1994, A8.

114. *U.S. News & World Report*, 19 October 1992, 36.

115. *NYT*, 27 January 1967, 1, 3.

116. O'Toole interview, 3 July 1996.

117. *Washington Post*, 14 February 1992, A16. "1-A" meant eligible for induction.

118. Interviews with James O'Toole, 3 July 1996, and James Crawford, 18 August 1994; *TAO*, 63 (1976): 311.

119. C-SPAN, "Oxford/American Connection"; Crawford interview, 18 August 1994.

120. Barker interview, 28 August 1995.

121. Maraniss, *First in His Class*, 120.

122. Ibid., 120.

123. *Time*, 6 April 1992, 37.

124. Maraniss, *First in His Class*, 176.

125. *TAO*, 65 (1978): 302; Maraniss, *First in His Class*, 152, 164-65, 243.

126. Maraniss, *First in His Class*, 178.

127. James Fallows, *More Like Us: Making America Great Again* (Boston, 1989), 125.

128. Stanley, "Most Likely to Succeed," 58, 84-85.

129. *NYT*, 13 December 1992, 41.

130. Maraniss, *First in His Class*, 135.

131. *Time*, 1 October 1990, 4; 1 February 1993, 12.

132. Allen interview, 20 November 1995.

133. Maraniss, *First in His Class*, 186-89.

134. Ibid., 189-90.

135. CNN transcript.

136. For a concise litany of these allegations, see *American Spectator*, July 1996, 30. Also see Meredith L. Oakley, *On the Make: The Rise of Bill Clinton* (Washington, DC, 1994), 83.

137. C-SPAN, "Oxford/American Connection."

138. *Chicago Sun-Times*, 22 October 1992, 42; ABC News, "This Week with David Brinkley," 11 October 1992.

139. *Evening Standard,* 3 March 1994, 49; *Sunday Times,* 27 February 1994, sec. 4, 6, and 13 March 1994, Style and Travel sec., 17.

140. Maraniss, *First in His Class,* 223-24.

141. Reich, *Locked in the Cabinet,* 83.

142. In the past several years numerous books and articles have examined the rise in political and economic clout of well-educated, ambitious young Americans. Terms like "meritocracy," "overclass," and "Mandarins" have gained currency. Nevertheless, many Americans have remained suspicious of these self-made, mostly Ivy League new leaders. Three perceptive discussions of this topic can be found in *Newsweek,* 31 July 1995, 32ff.; *Time,* 26 February 1996, 42-44; *and Atlantic Monthly,* November 1996, 109-16.

143. *Time,* 10 June 1996, 88.

144. *U.S. News & World Report,* 8 February 1988, 64.

145. Maraniss, *First in His Class,* 114, 322.

146. Kaiser, *Journeying Far and Wide,* 67, 108.

147. *Oxford Today,* Trinity Issue, 1995, 57; Pagan, "Bill Clinton at Oxford," 79.

148. *Evening Standard,* 18 June 1993, 11; Weisberg, "Clinton at Oxford," 230; *TAO,* 65 (1978): 301.

149. *NYT,* 13 December 1992, A41. Also, John Brademas, letter to authors, 12 January 1994; Thomas A. Bartlett interview, 13 December 1995.

150. That was Roosevelt Levander Thompson (1984), who died in an automobile crash in New Jersey before he reached Oxford. *TAO,* 71 (1984), 251.

151. *TAO,* 80 (1993): 93; Walter Isaacson, letter to authors, 10 December 1993; Healy obituary, *NYT,* 1 January 1993, A21.

152. Campaign for Oxford, "Campaign Benefactors," November 1994, 3.

153. Thomas Herman interview, 9 August 1994, and letter, 23 August 1994; Pelczynski interview, 4 July 1994.

154. Zbigniew Pelczynski, letter to former students, 17 December 1997.

155. *Washington Post,* 9 June 1994, A19.

156. *Oxford Courier,* 9 June 1994, 1; *Oxford Times,* 10 June 1994, 1; *Independent,* 9 June 1994, 3; *Washington Times,* 9 June 1994, A4; *Chronicle of Higher Education,* 15 June 1994, A35.

157. *Oxford University Gazette,* 16 June 1994, 1,259-60.

158. *Oxford Today,* Trinity issue, 1996, 37.

159. Warden's Christmas letter, December 1996, 4.

Cecil Rhodes, c. 1894
Courtesy of de Beers

Members of the class of 1904 aboard the *Ivernia* on their way to Britain.
Courtesy of the Association of American Rhodes Scholars

Frank Aydelotte
(class of 1905)
receiving an
honorary degree
in Oxford in 1937
*Courtesy of the
Association of American
Rhodes Scholars*

The High Street, Oxford, c. 1915
Courtesy of the Association of American Rhodes Scholars

J. William Fulbright (front, right) and the Oxford lacrosse team of 1926
Courtesy of the J. William Fulbright Papers, University of Arkansas Libraries

Dean Rusk (class of 1931) in his lacrosse uniform
Courtesy of the Dean Rusk Papers, Russell Library of the University of Georgia

Walt Whitman Rostow, Philip M. Kaiser, and Gordon A. Craig, all from the class of 1936
Courtesy of Philip M. Kaiser

" RHODES SCHOLAR, NO DOUBT ! "

Drawing by Robert Day; copyright 1936, The New Yorker Magazine, Inc.

Robert Taylor starred in MGM's 1938 film *A Yank at Oxford*. The screenplay was written by John Monk Saunders, class of 1918.
Courtesy of Turner Entertainment Co., all rights reserved

The caption that accompanied this UPI photo ran as follows: "It is Byron 'Whizzer' White, 21 year old American Pro football star who is a Rhodes Scholar at the famed English University. White is shown being duly admired by Miss Betty Nolan at Hertford College, Oxford. The 'Mortarboard' looks strange to those who have seen the Whizzer only in football helmet. He was a University of Colorado grid star before he turned pro."
Courtesy of the Bettmann Archive

Stansfield Turner and his parents celebrate graduation (Encaenia) in 1949
Courtesy of Stansfield Turner

The Oxford basketball team in 1954 included five American Rhodes Scholars: Erling Skorpen (#1), Alan Illig (#2), Richard Lugar (#6), Paul Sarbanes (#7), and Albert Utton (#10)
Courtesy of Richard G. Lugar

Former President Harry S. Truman is escorted by American students during his visit to Oxford in June 1956. To his right is Frank Sieverts (class of 1955), and to his left is Paul Sarbanes (class of 1954).
Courtesy of Frank Sieverts

Kris Kristofferson (class of 1958) completed his degree in English literature while also launching his singing career.
Courtesy of Oxford & County Newspapers

John Edgar Wideman (class of 1963). Along with classmate Stan Sanders, he helped to reopen the doors to Rhodes Scholarships for African Americans.
Courtesy of the Bettmann Archive

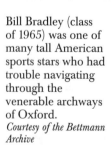

Bill Bradley (class of 1965) was one of many tall American sports stars who had trouble navigating through the venerable archways of Oxford.
Courtesy of the Bettmann Archive

American and other Rhodes Scholars in the class of 1968. Among those pictured here: Robert Reich (#1), James Crawford (#2), Douglas Eakeley (#3), Bill Clinton (#4), Warden E.T. Williams (#5), Alan Bersin (#6), Strobe Talbott (#7), Rick Stearns (#8), and Tom Williamson (#9).

Courtesy of Douglas S. Eakeley

LOCAL BOY MAKES GOOD

Shortly after Bill Clinton won the 1992 election, *The American Oxonian* published this cartoon by Jeff Shesol (class of 1991).
Courtesy of Jeff Shesol and the Association of American Rhodes Scholars

OTHERS WERE LESS SUBTLE.

TONIGHT I ANNOUNCE MY CANDIDACY FOR THE PRESIDENCY OF THE UNITED STATES OF AMERICA...

THOSE OF US WHO'D BEEN TRAVELLING BEGAN TO PONDER **OUR** POLITICAL VIABILITY...

I APPLIED FOR CHINESE CITIZENSHIP. IS THAT BAD?

BUT ANGST GIVES WAY TO ELATION AS THE RETURNS FLOOD IN. FRIENDS EMBRACE, CHAMPAGNE IS UNCORKED...

IS THIS STUFF OZONE·FRIENDLY?

...AND SOON THE WEARY REVELLERS RETURN HOME, VISIONS OF SOCIAL PROGRAMS DANCING IN THEIR HEADS.

GROUP HUGS FOR THE INNER CITIES! SMILE SUBSIDIES FOR THE UNHAPPY! A ROUND OF APOLOGIES TO JIMMY CARTER!

AS THE SUN RISES, THE AMERICAN FLAG IS HOISTED OVER UNIV. ALL IS SILENT BUT FOR THE SOUNDS OF THE EARLY MORN...

THE SOUND, THAT IS, OF THE CLICKING OF COMPUTER KEYS.

Dear Bill:
You will no doubt consider yourself fortunate that I, a fellow Rhodes Scholar, am prepared to join your innermost circle of advisers...

Rhodes Scholars revisit the Perch, an inn on the Isis just north of Oxford, in 1978. From left: Michael Shea and his wife La Donna, Rick Stearns and his wife Patricia, Bill Clinton and his wife Hillary, and James Crawford.
Courtesy of James E. Crawford III

During a Rhodes Scholar reunion in Oxford in 1983, Marjorie Billington greets Prince Philip while her daughter Susan (class of 1981) shakes hands with Queen Elizabeth II. Susan's father James Billington (class of 1950) is to her right. Thus far the Billingtons comprise the only father-daughter team among Rhodes Scholars.
Courtesy of Association of American Rhodes Scholars

Chapter 12

NEW VOICES, NEW FACES I

Blacks and Other Minorities

All of us black Scholars attended predominantly white colleges, where we were schooled in the ways of "cultured" white folks. The likelihood is remote of a black winning a Rhodes Scholarship who cannot adapt reflexively to the tribal mores of white upper-middle-class society. Moreover, he must prune the argot of the black community from his conversation – at least while talking with whites – and replace it with the clipped, preppie glibness appreciated by the sort of men and women who sit on the Rhodes Scholarship selection committees. It is, then, only a certain kind of black who succeeds – or probably even attempts to succeed – in winning a Rhodes: the black who is middle-class in ethos if not in income, and who wants to "make it" even if that entails playing ball by rules he opposes but hopes to alter.

Randall Kennedy, The American Oxonian

In short, as an African-American Rhodes Scholar, I face the same sorts of emotions that any Rhodie faces, only from a different perspective. We are all amused, relieved, comforted, lonely at Oxford because such emotions make up life. We are all involved with certain communities and demands from our home-life, wherever that may be. There *is* something peculiar, however, about having a background that is sensitive to racial oppressions, being on a scholarship that bears the name of the previous century's most renowned racist, and being in an environment where you are, once again, a racial minority, but where you expect to, and are expected to be, unaffected by that.

David P. White, The American Oxonian

The Emergence of Non-White Scholars

In December 1962 newspapers and magazines across the United States trumpeted the news that two "Negroes" had been selected as Rhodes Scholars for the class of 1963. J. Stanley Sanders of Whittier College in California and John Edgar Wideman of the University of

Notes for this chapter can be found on page 241.

Pennsylvania would be the first black American scholars since Alain Locke more than five decades earlier.

The breaking of this informal color barrier by Sanders and Wideman had more to do with their own individual accomplishments than with any civil rights crusading by former Rhodes Scholars. Indeed, until the mid-1960s, the record of white Rhodes Scholars as a whole in race matters was decidedly mixed.

If one looks at the careers and writings of scholars from the 1940s through the 1960s, one can see dozens of cases of courageous zeal in the drive toward racial equality and tolerance. By mid-century Robert Penn Warren had progressed remarkably in his attitudes. In books like *Band of Angels* (1955), *Segregation: The Inner Conflict* (1956), and *Who Speaks for the Negro* (1965) he castigated slavery, segregation, and the long legacy of humiliation of blacks by whites.

Several Rhodes Scholar attorneys gained renown – or opprobrium – by championing the cause of civil rights before state and federal courts. One of the most courageous was Clifford Durr (1918), who defended Rosa Parks and Martin Luther King, Jr., in the bus boycotting case of 1955 in Montgomery, Alabama.[1] Other scholars, like Armistead Boothe (1929), worked in local school boards and state legislatures to end segregation.[2] Journalists Willie Morris and Edwin Yoder (1956) became so vocal in support of civil rights that by 1961 both were sure they were on the blacklist of the right-wing John Birch Society.[3] Morris Abram (1939) fought for black voting rights in Georgia, helped to build subsidized housing for blacks and other indigents, and for several years chaired the United Negro College Fund.[4]

One of the Rhodes Scholars who did the most for civil rights on a national scale was Oliver Cromwell ("Mike") Carmichael (1913). From the 1930s until his death in 1966 he held a series of important posts in education: chancellor of Vanderbilt University, president of the Carnegie Foundation for the Advancement of Teaching, chair of the board of trustees of the State University of New York, president of the University of Alabama, and educational consultant for the Ford Foundation, among others. Throughout his career he fought not only for high standards in all levels of education but also for full equality of blacks. He ignited numerous controversies with recalcitrant boards of education, state governors, and university administrators. When a faculty member at a southern state university was fired because of his pro-black sentiments, Carmichael succeeded in withdrawing accreditation for that institution.[5]

For every scholar who distinguished himself as a proponent of civil rights, however, there were one or two others who vocally opposed this movement. In 1952 Robert Preston Brooks (1904) published a collection of essays entitled *Georgia Studies*. In it he lamented the backwardness of his home state and asserted that one cause of its poverty was its large number of Negroes. He believed that, with a few brilliant exceptions, blacks were incapable of progress. Francis Lester Patton (1913) reviewed the book approvingly in *The American Oxonian* and called Brooks "the ideal Rhodes Scholar."[6] In 1956 Philip Jones (1918) declared proudly, "I am an isolationist, a segregationist, and a conservative," and complained that both the Republican and Democratic parties were "racing each other toward socialism."[7] In 1965 Clarence Spaulding (1908) criticized the extension of voting rights to "ignorant" persons of "low moral standards."[8] In 1966 one scholar complained about "colored riots" and another about "contamination of the electorate."[9]

Through the 1950s *The American Oxonian* published several articles or brief notes about Cecil Rhodes, South Africa, and Rhodesia. With the exception of a couple of places where a contributor admitted that "change" was needed, these pieces continued to heap praise on Cecil Rhodes for his vision and civilizing mission. The articles and class notes pointed out that apartheid was a reasonable, workable, paternal system that was fair to the "boys" (i.e., black men). In 1953 Rhodes Scholars applauded Rhodesia's decision to celebrate the centenary of the birth of Cecil Rhodes, who had done so much to bring civilization to that part of the world. One scholar visited Salisbury, Rhodesia in 1957 and came away impressed by the "air of breathless excitement, of buoyant optimism, of bursting energy" that overwhelmed the "omnipresent color problem."[10]

Two Rhodes Scholars who were in a position to make significant contributions to racial toleration in the 1950s and 1960s were John Marshall Harlan and J. William Fulbright. Harlan served on the Supreme Court from 1954 to 1971. Throughout those years he maintained a staunch reputation as a conservative non-activist. He voted against reapportioning state legislatures to conform to the principle of "one man, one vote." He supported the right of southern states to charge fees for the right to vote (known as poll taxes in the United States). These discriminated against the poor (especially blacks). He opposed requiring police to give suspects the "Miranda rulings" regarding their right to counsel and silence. He also fought against allowing convicted indigents to have free lawyers during appeals of their convictions. On a few occasions, however, Harlan did make exceptions in his record of judicial non-involvement in civil rights issues. In 1955, for example, he voted to enforce all previous desegregation decrees. In 1963 he agreed with the majority in granting free counsel to indigents accused of major crimes.[11]

Fulbright's civil rights record was even more paltry. Like several Rhodes Scholars in the early 1950s, Fulbright courageously denounced McCarthyism. In the mid-1960s he again displayed steadfast adherence to principle when he broke with Lyndon Baines Johnson over Vietnam. On the issue of race, however, he was less valorous. He filibustered against nearly every civil rights reform bill that came before the Senate during his years there. His record on civil rights was not only politically prudent for a politician from the South but also reflected his true feelings about the abilities and rights of black citizens. After John F. Kennedy won the 1960 presidential election, most observers agreed that Fulbright, chair of the Senate Foreign Relations Committee, was the obvious candidate for Secretary of State. When he did not get that appointment, it was widely rumored in Washington that Fulbright's lackluster record in civil rights was the principal cause.[12]

The great majority of former scholars from the 1940s to the mid-1960s, however, were neither strong supporters nor opponents of the civil rights movement. They were simply silent. At a reunion of American Rhodes Scholars held at Princeton in 1947, Clarence Streit (1918) complained that more should be done to appoint blacks, as well as young men from working-class families. American Rhodes Trust Secretary Frank Aydelotte and others calmly pointed out that the scholarship program had never discriminated on the basis of race or social class. The assembled scholars unanimously passed a resolution reaffirming the policy of non-discrimination.[13]

From the vantage point of the 1990s that resolution appears something less than zealous. By denying that any problems existed, the scholars in effect were prolonging the policy of inaction. A few white youths from working-class families or from less prestigious universities continued to win scholarships each year, as they had from the beginning. There is no evidence, however, that anything was done to recruit and appoint black applicants. The sole mention in *The American Oxonian* of any concern about the absence of black scholars came in the 1954 obituary for Alain Locke. This piece was written by Karl Karsten (1911), who had never met Locke. The obituary represents one of the few times Locke ever received attention in the magazine. Karsten praises Locke's literary output and his popularization of African culture, and ends by saying:

> It is probable that he will be accounted one of the three greatest Americans of his color in history. Certainly we can be proud that he was a

Rhodes Scholar and regret that we do not have more Rhodes Scholars of his race to carry on his work in the times of world peril ahead.[14]

There is no evidence that Rhodes Scholars as individuals or as a group ever did anything in the 1950s to compensate for the complete absence of blacks, Native Americans, or other minorities among their numbers. Indeed, when questioned about this today, older scholars admit that the issue of admitting blacks was simply nonexistent before the 1960s.[15]

In part this situation existed simply because in the half-century after Locke there were few, if any, blacks who applied for the scholarship. The Rhodes Trust in Oxford and the office of the American Secretary have never kept records on the race, religion, or gender of applicants, but it seems safe to say that if any blacks did apply none made it to the interview stage.

The fact that more than a half-century passed with probably no black applicants resulted from two factors. The first is that Rhodes Scholarships were viewed as being a "white man's club."[16] The imperialistic, racist legacy of Cecil Rhodes tainted the program. When Randall Kennedy (1977) won a scholarship, some relatives and friends joked that he was an "Oreo" – black on the outside, but white on the inside.[17] The second factor is that extremely few blacks attended the "better" American universities prior to the 1960s, and it was these "better" schools that produced most Rhodes Scholars. Until mid-century, most blacks who managed to attend college went to predominantly-black institutions. Harvard had only a handful of blacks in the late 1940s, and Tom Williamson recalls that his Harvard graduating class of 1968 could count only about thirty.[18] Ira Magaziner has said that the situation at Brown in the mid-1960s was equally stark: blacks constituted one percent of the student body.[19] In 1967 only fifteen out of 820 Princeton freshmen were black.[20]

In other words, most Rhodes Scholars were accustomed to seeing mostly whites among their fellow students in the United States. The fact that no black Americans won the scholarships therefore did not seem an aberration from the norm.

In short, when two blacks did apply for scholarships in the fall of 1962, they did not benefit from any affirmative action program instituted by the former scholars, all white, who ran the selection committees. Most Rhodes Scholars joined the civil rights bandwagon when most other Americans did, from the mid-1960s onward. They were no better and no worse than most of their fellow citizens – except that one might have expected these "best men for the world's fight" to have taken an earlier, more prominent role in fighting for a just cause.

Stan Sanders and John Wideman were perfectly cast for the pioneering roles that fate had given them. It would have been hard even for the most adamant racist to argue that they did not admirably fulfill all the qualities Cecil Rhodes had wanted. Sanders came from Watts, the notoriously poor and volatile Los Angeles ghetto. His older brother Ed had taken one road to fame: sports. Ed had won a gold medal in boxing in the 1952 Helsinki Olympics, but died in 1954 from head injuries after being knocked out in his ninth professional fight. Stan's father (a garbage truck driver) and mother made him promise that he would choose academics over sports.

A star athlete in high school, Sanders won a full athletic scholarship to Richard Nixon's alma mater, Whittier College, in the Los Angeles suburbs. There he maintained an A- average as a political science major, twice made small-college All American as an end on the football team, and became student body president. As he was registering for courses for his junior year, the chair of the political science department called him aside, looked at his academic record, and declared, "You will apply for a Rhodes Scholarship next year. We think you will be Whittier College's first Rhodes Scholar."[21]

That prophecy came to pass. But the week in December 1962 when Sanders was awarded the scholarship was a hectic one. Three professional football teams had told him they wanted to draft him. He learned of his Rhodes award on a Saturday night, and on the following Monday he was drafted by the Chicago Bears. To the astonishment of many sports fans, he chose Oxford over Chicago. He did this for several reasons. The first was his promise to his parents. Another was that he felt it important to set an example for fellow blacks. Sanders was aware that he and Wideman would be the first black Rhodes Scholars since Alain Locke. Just before he departed for Oxford, his neighborhood in south-central Los Angeles declared a "Stan Sanders Day." A final reason was that he felt a compelling need to show the white world that blacks could be more than sports stars and entertainers.[22]

John Wideman's background was just as remarkable. He came from a poor family in Pittsburgh's rundown Homewood neighborhood. His father was a waiter. In the 1950s his parents moved the family to nearby Shadyside, so that their children could attend Peabody High School, one of the state's best public institutions. At Peabody, John was captain of the basketball team and valedictorian in his graduating class. He won a full athletic scholarship to the University of Pennsylvania, where he likewise rose to be captain on the basketball team and was named to the All-Ivy League squad. He made Phi Beta Kappa and majored in English literature. In his spare time he wrote poems and plays.

As was the case with Sanders, sports and academics combined to make Wideman's Rhodes interview week hectic. Without waiting to find out if he had won a scholarship, he left Baltimore immediately after his final interview. The reason for the hasty departure was that he had to return to Philadelphia, where Penn was playing Vanderbilt that night. He played the first half in a mental fog, but his fourteen points in the second half led his team to a 74-70 victory. That capped an undefeated season for Penn. As the game ended he received a call from the secretary of the Rhodes selection committee, who asked, "How did the game go?" "We won," Wideman answered. "Well, you won the game down here, too," he was told.[23]

After the dramatic selection of Wideman and Sanders, the story of black Rhodes Scholars lost much of its drama. By 1970 the American Secretary of the Rhodes Trust, William J. Barber (1949), was able to boast that the Rhodes Scholarship program as a whole had become "impressively" multi-racial.[24] This resulted mostly from the creation of additional scholarships from the late 1940s through the 1960s for the newly-independent countries of India, Pakistan, Malaysia, Kenya, and Zambia. From 1963 through the class of 1969, however, there were only eight black Americans. To many, both blacks and whites, this was unsatisfactory. Tom Williamson, for example, was dismayed to find that he was the only black in the class of 1968.[25]

The classes of 1970 and 1971 each had five blacks, and in the quarter century since then each class has, on average, had two or three. A few classes have had none, whereas others have had four or five. In short, the percentage of Rhodes Scholars who have been black has come to be roughly equal to the percentage of blacks among Americans as a whole: about 10 percent.

It is difficult to give a precise figure for black Rhodes Scholars from 1963 to the present, given the Rhodes Trust's steadfast refusal to keep records on such matters.[26] Some journalists who have played the "numbers game" have come up with varying statistics. In 1971 several wire services and newspapers featured a story on the new black Rhodes Scholar who hailed from New Orleans and played a hot jazz clarinet. Reporters were later embarrassed to discover that Thomas Sancton was white. (Throughout his subsequent career at *Time*, Sancton has continued to play Dixieland music and make recordings.)

The entry of women into the program will be covered in the next chapter. Here, however, one can note that the first black woman belonged to the class of 1978. Karen Stevenson received the same sort of national publicity that had been showered on Sanders and Wideman. Like the two men, she eminently displayed the sort of well-rounded excellence that Cecil Rhodes desired. She had won a Moorehead Scholarship to attend the University of North Carolina, in the first year that those scholarships had been open to women. At North Carolina, she made Phi Beta Kappa and starred on the women's track team. She set the state record in the women's 400 meter dash and the university record for the 60 and 100 meter hurdles. She majored in American history and by graduation had become fluent in French and Russian. By the time she won a Rhodes Scholarship, she had already been accepted by Yale Law School – which granted her a postponement.[27]

The 1970s gradually brought another kind of racial diversity as well. Starting slowly and increasing as the years passed, immigrants or the children of immigrants have won Rhodes Scholarships. Over the past two decades, on average, two or more new scholars each year have names that bespeak an Asian or African background. Stan Sanders has served on Rhodes Scholar selection committees in California for over a quarter of a century, and he reports that nowadays roughly half of the applicants from that state are of Asian descent.[28] This development parallels what is happening in American higher education in general, as highly-motivated children of immigrants win a disproportionate number of top awards.

A glance at the list of Rhodes Scholars printed in the Appendix to this volume will illustrate some of the dramatic social transformations of recent decades. Through the first half of this century, many Rhodes Scholars had first names like John, Tom, and Mike, but there were also many with names like Chauncy, Farnsworth, Beverly, Stringfellow, and Thornton. In recent years, however, there has been a regular stream of names like Atul Gawande (1987), Wen-son Hsieh (1988), Reza Gandjei (1990), Rujuta Bhatt (1993), and Rinku Chandra (1995).

The influx of blacks and first or second-generation immigrants into the program has been accompanied by a smaller number of two other minority groups: Hispanics and Native Americans. Like blacks and Asian Americans, several of these scholars have seen the award as an important victory not only for themselves as individuals, but for their ethnic groups in general. When Cornell University senior Eduardo Peñalver got word in December 1993 that he was a finalist for a scholarship, he was in the midst of organizing a four-day occupation of the institution's administration building. The sit-in was aimed at calling attention to the lack of Hispanics on the faculty and the library's paucity of books on Hispanic culture. He left the protest in the hands of his lieutenants, went to his interviews, and emerged a winner. He hoped that his Rhodes Scholarship would give him more clout in his fight for Hispanics at Cornell.[29]

In the early 1990s Rhodes Scholars then in Oxford overwhelmingly agreed that the most charismatic and colorful among them was Deacon Turner (1991), an Oklahoma Cherokee who had graduated from Harvard. As Turner went down, one of the new scholars going up in 1993 was Montana's Scott Bear Don't Walk.

Although the Warden in Rhodes House and the scholars sitting on the selection committees have denied it, some people have speculated that an informal affirmative action program has led to the selection of blacks, Asian Americans, and other minorities. Some critics have suggested that there might indeed have been a lowering of standards in some cases. It is true that in recent years the American Secretary of the Rhodes Trust has explicitly urged universities to encourage women and minorities to apply.[30] The reason given for this is that the Trust is simply trying to increase the candidate pool and ensure that all top-notch students are encouraged to become candidates.

The American Secretary has also striven to guarantee that there is geographical balance in the program. In 1996 his office succeeded in getting Rhodes Scholars and the trustees to agree to a realignment of the eight districts – each of which appoints four scholars per year. Since the district plan had been adopted in 1930, applicants from several less populous states had always had a great advantage, for they competed against fewer rivals. In some years, states like Wyoming and the Dakotas produced only one applicant, or even none. Students applying from states like California, New York, and Massachusetts, on the other hand, had a much more difficult time becoming finalists in their more populous districts. The new district plan, in effect for the class of 1997, offers "affirmative action" of a sort for students from the larger states. Henceforth, the reconfigured districts will be closer to each other in total population.[31]

In December 1993 publicity concerning newly elected scholars highlighted the fact that for the first time ever candidates had been appointed from two small Georgia institutions: Berry College (Joanna E. Grant) and historically black Morehouse College (Nima A. Warfield).[32] Here too, cynics might be tempted to assume that some well-meaning affirmative action zealots dipped below the cream of the crop to reward black institutions. However, a look at publicity from the American Secretary's office from the past couple of decades shows that the program has become increasingly concerned about diversity among institutions – not just among states and among racial and ethnic groups. Since the beginning of the program early in this century, a couple of dozen universities have dominated the competition. Harvard has a commanding lead over everyone else. In 1988 Harvard graduates picked up ten of the thirty-two scholarships. This was a source of pride for Harvard, but of some embarrassment for many associated with the program. Over the past twenty years, Harvard, Princeton, and Yale have produced over 30 percent of all U.S. scholars. For the decade 1988 through 1997 the top universities, in terms of Rhodes Scholarships, have been the following:

Harvard University	61
Yale University	21
Princeton University	18
Stanford University	15
Georgetown University	12
U.S. Military Academy at West Point	8
Duke University	6
University of North Carolina	6
Massachusetts Institute of Technology	6

In response to this seemingly exclusionary "elitism," the American Secretary and the Rhodes House Warden have endeavored to encourage applicants from smaller, less prestigious schools. Whenever any college or university has produced its first-ever Rhodes Scholar, the American Secretary has tried to publicize that fact. Thus the special mention given to Berry and Morehouse resulted more from this general drive to receive applications from every campus, rather than from any unusual steps to help black colleges.

A survey of the backgrounds of the 150 or so blacks, Hispanics, Asian Americans, Native Americans, and other minority scholars further confirms that they equaled or exceeded all the criteria used for whites. To be sure, some minority scholars were what Rhodes officials call "diamonds in the rough." Those are candidates whose credentials on paper might not seem as glittering as those of some other candidates, but who demonstrated in their interviews that they might have a special spark of greatness. Sometimes this method has proved remarkably prophetic; at other times, however, it has picked persons who turned out to be "duds."[33] Even so, if some minority scholars were "rough" diamonds who never developed a shine, so were several whites.

From the inception of the program, selection committees have often let their intuition guide them – going beyond a mere tabulation of grade point averages, student organizations, and athletic feats. This process works for blacks and other minorities as well as for whites. Selection committees tend to be extremely impressed if a candidate has had to overcome major obstacles. In the case of a black applicant, this could be growing up in an urban ghetto and attending inner city schools. For an Asian-American applicant, it might mean being a political refugee and learning English in adolescence. The cases of Randy Berholtz (1985) and Adam Ake (1997) demonstrate that the same sort of consideration applies to whites. Berholtz's candidacy was helped by the fact that he came from a poor region in northeast Pennsylvania; his father worked in the coal mines and his mother in a dress factory. Berholtz also impressed his committee with his determination not to let a slight speech impediment deter his ambitions. Adam Ake (1997) had to overcome a far more unusual problem. When he applied for the Rhodes Scholarship, he and his family were still grappling with the torment of a personal scandal. His father was in prison in Anchorage. The elder Ake was one of Alaska's most notorious criminals, a renowned gynecologist convicted of raping many of his patients. The Rhodes committee admired the way in which Ake openly discussed this ordeal. Ake graduated first in his class at West Point and was offered Truman and Marshall scholarships prior to his acceptance of a Rhodes. His instructors at West Point praised his character and maturity and called him the most talented cadet they had seen in decades.[34]

By and large, blacks and other minority applicants have been superlative all-rounders. In addition to Wideman, Sanders, and Stevenson, one could cite dozens of other examples. Richard Joseph (1966) had already spent a year at the University of Grenoble in France on a Fulbright Scholarship before arriving in Oxford to take up his Rhodes.[35] Tom Williamson had been accepted into Yale, Princeton, and Dartmouth, before he finally chose Harvard, where his tuition was covered by a General Motors Scholarship. At Harvard he played football and obtained his degree in a special honors program. Before he won his Rhodes, he had already been admitted to Berkeley's law school – to which he eventually returned.[36]

Prior to Oxford, Jerome Davis (1971) had coordinated Princeton's black student association, worked as student manager of the university dining halls, and served as president of the student body. Like numerous black scholars, Davis had misgivings about accepting Cecil Rhodes's "blood money." Soon after he arrived in Oxford, he declared:

> When you accept money from a source and aren't sure what people went through to make it, you have to ask questions. I don't feel I can waste time here; black people may have died for this money, and I have to have a greater justification for being here than just enjoying sitting in oak-paneled rooms sipping sherry.[37]

Despite the rhetoric, Davis remained in Oxford for two years, traveled extensively, and obtained his B.A. in PPE.

One of Davis's classmates was Kurt Schmoke, the product of a solid middle-class Baltimore family. By the age of five he was already telling people he hoped to become mayor of the city. In high school he was only a B student, partly because he was so active in student organizations, in lacrosse, and in football. In his senior year he led his school's football team to the state championship while also serving as student body president. When he decided to attend Yale, the news made page one of the *Baltimore Sun*'s sports section. At Yale he got good, but not spectacular, grades. His real celebrity came in sports and in student leadership. He befriended Yale's president, Kingman Brewster, and persuaded him to initiate projects to improve relations with the poor neighborhood that bordered the campus. His most celebrated moment came in the spring of 1970, when the Yale campus was about to explode into riots, due to the murder trial of Black Panther Bobby Seale, which was then taking place in New Haven. Faculty were pitted against students. The faculty agreed to hear one student representative, and Schmoke was designated to address them. The faculty had anticipated a barrage of expletives and abusive charges. Instead, Schmoke addressed them in calm tones, presented the student grievances, and explained that young, confused students needed the wise counsel of concerned faculty. When he finished, the entire faculty rose and applauded. His speech made headlines across the country and was featured in a book by Pulitzer prize winning Yale professor John Hersey, entitled *Letter to the Alumni.* Schmoke's residential college dean, Bob Chambers, later recalled the event and said, "It was at that moment, I think, that he won his Rhodes Scholarship."[38]

Asian-American scholars have likewise "earned" their awards. Hoang Nhu Tran (1987) provided one of the most dramatic examples. His father was a major in the South Vietnamese Airborne Division. The Tran family were among the last people to escape from Saigon in April 1975 as it was taken over by the North Vietnamese and Vietcong. They joined the ragtag flotilla of "boat people." After their rescue, and their passage through refugee camps in the Philippines and Guam, they were admitted to the United States. A Lutheran church in Fort Collins, Colorado, agreed to sponsor them. At his arrival in America, the nine-year-old Hoang's command of English was limited to "hello." Soon he not only mastered the language but excelled in school. He won admittance to the United States Air Force Academy, where in 1987 he graduated at the top of his class and was named valedictorian. When he applied for a Rhodes, he said his goal was to "do something great" and serve mankind to pay back "many times more" for all that America had given him.[39] In Oxford he read PPE and then went on to Harvard Medical School.

The family of Surachai Supattapone (1988) moved from Thailand to the United States when he was a small boy. He could not speak any English at first. After an elementary school teacher took a special interest in him, he rapidly advanced. At age eighteen he graduated from Johns Hopkins with a degree in chemistry. Along the way, he also participated in the university's swimming team and earned a brown belt in karate. When, at age twenty-two, he won a Rhodes Scholarship, he was in his final year of medical school at Johns Hopkins.

Like Karen Stevenson, Nnenna Jean Lynch (1993) might have been suspected of favored treatment on two accounts: she was black and female. Yet her record could hardly have failed to dazzle the selection committee. New Yorker Lynch attended Villanova University, where she graduated summa cum laude, majoring in sociology. Her athletic feats won national acclaim. She was a member of Villanova's four consecutive national champion cross country teams and in 1992 won the NCAA Division I outdoor track title in the three thousand meter race. In 1993 she was named the NCAA Woman of the Year.

In addition, Lynch managed to help found Athletes Against Alcohol, serve in a Philadelphia soup kitchen, and speak at local hospitals and youth centers. As if that were not enough, she worked part-time as a model, appearing in *Vogue* and *Glamour* as well as in advertisements for The Gap. *Sports Illustrated* and numerous other magazines featured stories on her. Her track coach, Marty Stern, was constantly hounded by reporters wanting to know more about her. His usual response to all of them was, "She should be President."[40] In her Rhodes interviews, she said she wanted to study social anthropology and then return to the United States and establish a network of community centers for underprivileged youth. Villanova proudly broadcast the news when she became the first Rhodes Scholar in the 150-year history of the institution.

The accolades continued to shower on Lynch after she reached Oxford. In its special double issue of 9 May 1994, *People* named the "fifty most beautiful people in the world." Nnenna Lynch was among them, sharing the spotlight with celebrities like Paul Newman, Denzel Washington, Julia Roberts, Al Gore, Meg Ryan, and John F. Kennedy, Jr. About Lynch the magazine said:

> Never mind those luscious legs or that smoldering gaze: Lynch's real grab is her gray matter. "From the minute she opens her mouth, you're captivated," says longtime track pal Paul McCabe.[41]

Lynch just missed qualifying for the U.S. Olympic track team in 1992 and again in 1996. In part these "failures" resulted from a chronic asthmatic condition. During her three years in Oxford working on a M.St. degree in social anthropology she continued to run, winning numerous cross country races, including the 1996 British national championship.[42]

Life in Oxford

The most amazing part of the story regarding blacks and other minorities is that, once they reached Oxford, there is not much story to tell. In virtual unanimity, minority and white scholars have agreed that there were extremely few racial problems in Oxford. Stan Sanders, Tom Williamson, Kurt Schmoke, and others have vigorously concurred that they encountered no opposition from other American Rhodes Scholars – not even those from southern states.[43] Virtually all the white scholars who have spoken on the subject have likewise asserted that they heard no racial epithets used behind the backs of blacks and other minorities. One white southern scholar from the mid-1980s (who wished to remain anonymous) admitted that at first he suspected standards had been lowered for minorities. But he quickly changed his mind. He now admits that his stay in Oxford was the first time he came to know blacks who were smarter than he was.

Blacks and other minority scholars of the past thirty years likewise have had extremely few racial problems with British students and dons in Oxford. In part, this has been due to Oxford's famed indifference to newcomers. All students who "go up" receive the same treatment – or lack of treatment. During his first six months at Balliol, Randall Kennedy walked by the college dean each morning and received no acknowledgment of his greeting. The don remained silent, not because Kennedy was black, but because the two had not yet been properly introduced.[44]

In part, the scarcity of racial problems has also been due to the fact that Oxford has been accustomed to African and Asian students for several decades. These students, including Rhodes Scholars, have come to Oxford from across Asia and Africa. When Karen Stevenson arrived in Oxford, she was impressed by "the different races and cultures and backgrounds, which created a wonderful kaleidoscope."[45]

This does not mean, of course, that racism is nonexistent in Oxford or in Britain as a whole. A disproportionate number of lower-paid jobs are held by immigrant minority groups. In recent decades the country has witnessed several violent race riots. Whereas many Americans want to stop the flow of Latin Americans and Asians into their country, many Britons want to exclude immigrants from the Caribbean, Africa, Pakistan, and India. The point here is simply that minority students in Oxford have largely escaped these problems.

A handful of black American scholars have not liked Oxford. Some have occasionally experienced piercing stares, slight rudeness, or other fleeting signs of racism.[46] Franklin Raines (1971) admitted that blacks were "treated pretty well" in Oxford but nevertheless concluded that the British "were even less prepared for cultural pluralism than the U.S. ever was."[47] Some blacks were upset to learn that there were no black studies programs in Oxford.[48] Of course, long-time Oxford observers could have told these Americans that this resulted not so much from racism as from the university's stubborn resistance to new academic trends.

Other blacks encountered smaller kinds of irritations. In the 1960s and 1970s blacks discovered that white barbers and hair dressers did not know how to cut their hair. Bonnie Saint John (1986) was relieved to find that by the time she arrived in Oxford a salon called Janet's Afro Hair had opened.[49] In general, however, the 10 percent or so of blacks and other minority scholars who have not enjoyed Oxford have given the same reasons as the roughly ten percent of whites who also disliked it: homesickness, primitive plumbing and heating, backward curriculum or facilities in some areas of study, restless desire to get on with their careers in the United States, inability to get along with the reserved British, and so on.

As the pioneering American blacks, Stan Sanders and John Wideman might have been expected to encounter some resistance. Instead, both enjoyed the experience immensely. Like many earlier scholars, Sanders did not "need" an Oxford degree. He settled for a Third in PPE and spent most his time traveling, socializing, and reading. He claims to have read a book a day – Shakespeare, novels, politics, and other kinds of works for which he had no time at Whittier or (later) at Yale Law School. Perhaps most of all, the entire experience helped him to grow in self-confidence. In later years he has revisited Oxford several times.[50]

Wideman, on the other hand, did "need" his Oxford degree. He aimed for a career in academe, and after three years of study his thesis was approved for a B.Phil. – an advanced degree, above an American M.A. While in Oxford, he married an American, Judith Ann Goldman, whom he had met at the University of Pennsylvania, and had his first novel – *A Glance Away* – accepted by an American publisher.[51]

For three years Wideman also led the Oxford basketball team to the finals for the British national championship. On the first two occasions Oxford lost. The third time, in March 1966, Oxford played the Aldershot Warriors – the latter composed of British soldiers, some of whom had been flown in from around the world to play in this game. Wideman served as both captain and coach of the Oxford squad. His team might have included Bill Bradley, but the latter was away playing for an Italian team. This match was Wideman's last chance for the championship, and yet he took a magnanimous and risky gamble in its closing minutes. One-by-one, he removed himself and the other American players from the game and put in their less skillful British teammates. Wideman thought that the British second-stringers deserved a chance to play in the championship. His gamble paid off, and Oxford hung on to win. What struck all observers as more spectacular than the victory, however, was Wideman's magnificent gesture of comradeship for his teammates. He was voted the game's most valuable player.[52]

From the time of Sanders and Wideman to the mid-1980s, black Americans (both Rhodes Scholars and others) discovered that they were curiosities in Oxford. The British were accustomed to seeing blacks and Asians from the former Empire, but American blacks were a novelty. Tom Williamson recalls many people asking him about the violent race riots of the 1960s in the United States and offering him their sympathy.[53] Robyn Hadley (1985) noticed that British people lost their famous reserve when they heard her American accent. They engaged her in conversation and wanted to know everything about being black in America. Many Oxonians were perplexed when she told them she intended to return to the South after completing her education. She enjoyed playing the role of an informal educator. (Moreover, she kept her resolve to return to the South. Today she works in Virginia as vice president of business development for a black-owned import-export company.)[54]

Williamson brought together a small discussion group of black Americans, Caribbeans, and Africans living in Balliol. They sponsored a Soul Party and introduced Balliol to Motown music. Williamson was happy to discover that the British students "thought this was real cool."[55] By the late 1980s signs of black culture had gone from being rarities to regular occurrences all over Oxford. Black History Month was celebrated, and student productions of plays by and about blacks were staged each year. In 1987 the new black Gospel Choir gave its first performance in the Balliol Chapel. Robyn Hadley sang in that debut and reported:

> I had a lot of reservations about how the English would respond to Gospel music since I'd never heard more than a whisper at an Anglican service .... Sure enough, at the beginning of the Choir's first performance, the audience was very stiff, but by the end people were on their feet. Afterwards, I was approached by people who said they didn't even believe in God, but they loved the music.[56]

The choir's second performance was sold out, and a few weeks later the singers were asked to perform at the Christ Church Ball.

Several other black scholars have had equally happy and fruitful experiences. Christopher Brown (1990) completed a D.Phil. in modern history in Oxford. A scholarship that he won while at Balliol enabled him to remain there for four years. While in Britain he experienced three incidents when racial insults were hurled at him, but these occurred outside of Oxford. He did not let these episodes destroy his life abroad, and he affirms that, compared to the United States, there is little racism in Britain. Moreover, he feels that his Oxford D.Phil. is more important for him than a Ph.D. from an American university could be. Conquering the British educational system boosted his self-confidence. Moreover, with a Ph.D. from an American university, there might always have been the suspicion that he got his doctorate through special favors. People familiar with

Oxford, on the other hand, would know that he earned it through his own intelligence and hard work.[57]

In 1992 *The American Oxonian* published a revealing article by black scholar David White (1990). The article is entitled "To Be a Black Rhodes Scholar: Balancing Race and Psyche." After he arrived in Oxford, he discovered that being "an African-American and a Rhodie" was radically different from being "just an American" and a Rhodie. In the United States he had been raised to think of everything from the vantage point of his race. He always thought and acted as a black American. In Oxford he slowly tried to think of himself as just a person, not a black person. Some black students (mostly non-Rhodes Scholars from the United States and elsewhere) ostracized him because he did not attend meetings of the Africa Society. They joked that he was "white" in fact as well as in name. The psychological problems he and other minority scholars faced thus had as much to do with the "mental baggage" they carried with them as with any things that actually happened to them in Oxford. White concludes his essay by saying that the legacies of racism will never disappear from Britain or anywhere else, but that for him "Oxford will remain a haven for academic rigor and joy."[58]

The fact that racial frictions have been scarce for Oxford students is exemplified in the story of Bill Bradley. One of the recurrent themes in his book *Life on the Run* (1977) is his growing awareness of the indignities imposed on blacks by a white majority. He did not witness this intolerance at Princeton in the early 1960s (where there would have been few minority students for him to see) or at Oxford in the middle of the decade. Rather it came in the late 1960s, when he joined the New York Knicks. In city after city where his team traveled, the blacks on the team regularly suffered insults in hotels, restaurants, and taxicabs.[59]

Black African Scholars

Although the story of African-American Rhodes Scholars in Oxford has been a rather placid one, there was one racial issue that became explosive through the 1970s and 1980s: the problem of South African Rhodes Scholars. By 1970 non-white Rhodes Scholars had been coming from constituencies like Jamaica, Malaysia, Bermuda, Zambia, Ghana, Nigeria, Singapore, Pakistan, and India for several years. By this time countries like Canada, Australia, and New Zealand also were appointing a few non-whites. Two countries, however, were conspicuous by the all-Caucasian character of their awardees: Rhodesia and South Africa. Rhodesia was allotted two per year and South Africa nine.

There was nothing much, outside of informal pressure, that the Rhodes Trust could do about Rhodesia. The selection process there was controlled by white-dominated committees made up mostly of former scholars. In reaction to world pressure for change in its political structure, Ian Smith's Rhodesian government unilaterally declared its independence from Britain in 1965. From that time until 1980, when white supremacy came to an end and Britain officially recognized the renamed Zimbabwe, the country was a virtual outlaw on the world stage. Rhodesian Scholars continued to come to Oxford through that period, but few persons blamed the Rhodes Trustees for the all-white composition of that delegation.

The issue of South Africa's Rhodes Scholars was more controversial. This was so because of stipulations in Cecil Rhodes' will. In every other constituency, it was up to former Rhodes Scholars and the national secretaries to determine eligibility for application. In South Africa, however, there was a restriction. Rhodes' will stated that each year four of the country's scholars should be chosen from among graduates of four private boys' secondary schools. These schools admitted only whites. Of course, apartheid also guaranteed that South Africa's other scholars also were white.

Until the 1960s this situation did not raise any international controversy. After all, until that decade nearly all the scholars from the United States, Canada, Australia, and New Zealand were also white. Once the color barrier had been broken in these countries, however, the attention turned to South Africa and Rhodesia.

The Rhodes Trustees might not be accountable for Rhodesia's selection process or for the process involving five of South Africa's nine annual appointments. But starting around 1970 many current and former scholars did criticize the trustees on the matter of the four South African scholars from the named schools. The trustees and the Warden of Rhodes House were sympathetic but argued that they did not have the authority to take the scholarships from the four schools, for that would violate Rhodes' will. Permission to do that could come only from a British government agency, the Charity Commission, which had authority over all philanthropies. The Charity Commission and the British Parliament expressed dismay at the racial discrimination in South Africa, but they balked at changing the will. That would have set a precedent leading to requests for changing the wills of thousands of other people. Moreover, the government pointed out that it was not Cecil Rhodes' will itself that was racist, but rather the all-white admissions policies of the four schools.

The result of this impasse was that for nearly twenty years a rancorous controversy brewed within the Rhodes Scholarship program. Many scholars (both white and non-white) asserted that the genteel, "old boys" trustees did not want to alter the status quo. The trustees and the Warden, on the other hand, maintained that they were doing all they could but were powerless to act on their own. Any violation of the will could endanger the future of the entire program.

The two decades of debate had several emotional high points. In March 1971, some 120 Oxford dons and 80 of the 145 Rhodes Scholars of all nationalities then in residence signed a petition demanding that some non-whites be appointed from Rhodesia and South Africa. If nothing happened, they threatened to do all they could to prevent scholars from those two countries from being admitted into any of the colleges. The petition garnered international headlines but brought no immediate results.[60]

In 1972 the Rhodes Trustees submitted a petition to the Charity Commission, but permission to alter the will was denied. That same year American Grant Crandall (1969), a white, resigned his scholarship in protest against the exclusion of women in general and of blacks from South Africa. He never did complete the D.Phil. thesis on which he was working. He was the first person ever to relinquish his scholarship for what might be called political reasons.[61]

Throughout the 1970s and 1980s many white scholars vociferously condemned Cecil Rhodes' "blood money." Some wondered whether all Americans should refuse to apply for the scholarships until the South African and Rhodesian problems were solved.[62] To their credit, the American selection committees of these two decades not only appointed minority Rhodes Scholars but also selected several outspoken, iconoclastic white candidates who openly vented their disdain for Cecil Rhodes. Caucasian applicant Richard Schaper both exasperated and impressed his state and regional selection committees in December 1966. In his interviews he lectured former scholars on his plans for changing the unjust social structures that allowed someone like Cecil Rhodes to amass his African fortune. The regional selection committee called him back for an unprecedented third time, demanding assurance that if he were selected he would not publicly repudiate his scholarship. Schaper assured them that, although he detested Cecil Rhodes, he would accept a scholarship and try to put some of the "blood money" to good use. The committee thereupon chose him for the class of 1967.[63] Over the years several blacks have used the same reasoning in accepting the "tainted" money.[64]

The Warden in Oxford (E.T. Williams until 1980 and then his successor Robin Fletcher) repeatedly told Rhodes Scholars that they were doing everything they could to bring pressure on South Africa as well as on the Charity Commission. They beseeched Rhodes Scholars not to show "bad form" and upset the applecart, but to let them proceed in their more quiet, behind-the-scenes fashion.[65] Williams reproved black scholar George Keys (1970) and some others for not "acting like one of the chaps." Keys and his friends, however, "didn't feel like one of the chaps – and we couldn't feign it."[66]

In the early 1970s the Rhodes Trustees made one reform they hoped would demonstrate a firm resolve to bring progress. South Africa received nine scholarships each year – four going to the named schools, one to Natal, and four that were allotted to various provinces. The trustees transformed the four provincial scholarships into "at-large" scholarships, meaning that candidates could apply from anywhere in the country and be selected by a national committee. In addition, the trustees did their best to ensure that this selection committee was staffed with blacks plus white South Africans who opposed apartheid. The South African government sometimes tried to suppress the multi-racial committee meetings. On several occasions, therefore, the committees evaded government prohibitions by meeting in the international transit lounge of the Johannesburg airport.

This was progress, but not enough. At the 1983 general reunion in Oxford, George Keys created a ruckus when he gave a speech lambasting Rhodes officials for not working hard enough to change the will. The establishment of at-large scholarships had brought only minimal improvement. Since their creation a little over a decade earlier, there had been nearly one hundred South African scholars. Keys damningly pointed out that these included only one Asian, two coloreds, and one black South African. Going further, Keys called for abolition of all the South African scholarships until apartheid ended. He cited as precedent the trustees' decision on two occasions to cancel the German scholarships: from 1916 to 1925 and from 1939 to 1970. Most of Keys' audience applauded enthusiastically, but some white South African scholars defended their country. The result was a series of loud discussions and icy stares through the remainder of the festivities.[67]

Keys' bluntness must have struck a chord. In 1984 the Rhodes Trustees voted to withdraw the several million pounds that were still invested in South African companies – about four percent of the Rhodes Trust total. At about that same time, the University of Oxford as a whole also ended its investments there.[68]

Through the latter half of the 1980s the American Association of Rhodes Scholars lodged several protests with the Rhodes Trustees and urged that more pressure be brought to bear on the Charity Commission. The Rhodes Trustees began to donate sizable portions of their discretionary funds to benefit black South Africans. By the 1990s the trustees were providing scholarships to about 150 non-white South Africans each year.[69] These scholarships paid for studies in South African secondary schools and universities. The aim was not only to help those particular students but also to enlarge the pool of black South Africans who would make good candidates for Rhodes Scholarships.

These steps still were not judged adequate by some scholars. In 1986 white scholar Douglas Jehl (1984) attacked the trustees and American Secretary David Alexander in the very pages of *The American Oxonian.* Jehl complained that the actions they had taken thus far were "disappointingly small" and accused them of avoiding the issue so as not to bring bad publicity to the program. Alexander vehemently defended himself and the trustees and charged Jehl with "ill-disguised innuendoes."[70]

With the failure of the Charity Commission or the Rhodes Trust to bring significant change, some American Rhodes Scholars themselves took action. Led by Daniel Bloomfield (1982), in 1986 several former scholars established the American South African Scholarship Association. The goal was to raise money for the educational needs of blacks in South Africa. In its first ten years of operation the ASASA has, in its modest, independent fashion, enabled a dozen students to receive a university education.[71]

The controversy over the all-white South African Scholarships finally resolved itself without any action by the Charity Commission. It was South Africa itself that ended the dispute. The release of Nelson Mandela from prison in 1990, and the growing influence of his African National Congress, ushered in the abrupt end to apartheid in 1991. Since that time both whites and non-whites have won some of South Africa's nine scholarships each year.

The entry of blacks and other non-whites into the ranks of Rhodes Scholars thus has ended on a happy note, despite the fact that white scholars from the United States and other countries were slow in picking up the cause of civil rights. After minorities began frequently to win scholarships in the 1960s, however, white scholars accepted them with open arms. Moreover, Rhodes Scholars of all colors joined the crusade to help blacks in Rhodesia and South Africa.

In a remarkable reversal of much of what Cecil Rhodes represented, the library at Rhodes House has recently become the repository of the archives of the British Anti-Slavery Society and also of the South African Anti-Apartheid Movement.

NOTES

1. *TAO*, 64 (1977): 61-73.
2. *TAO*, 37 (1950): 93; 50 (1963): 42-44; 59 (1972): 216; 77 (1990): 222-23.
3. *TAO*, 48 (1961): 242-43.
4. *TAO*, 38 (1951): 248; 53 (1966): 231; 58 (1971): 231-32; 69 (1982): 133-39, 149-50.
5. *TAO*, 54 (1967): 48-50.
6. *TAO*, 40 (1953): 63-64.
7. *TAO*, 43 (1956): 192.
8. *TAO*, 52 (1965): 178.
9. *TAO*, 53 (1966): 171, 184.
10. *TAO*, 38 (1951): 99; 39 (1952): 95, 141-43; 40 (1953): 174-85, 214-16; 42 (1955): 13-15; 44 (1957): 114; 45 (1958): 21-23.
11. *NYT*, 30 December 1971, 29.
12. *NYT*, 10 February 1995, A1, A27; Woods, *Fulbright*, chaps. 7, 12, 27 and passim.
13. *TAO*, 34 (1947): 201.
14. *TAO*, 41 (1954): 259. Karsten does not name the other two individuals whom he counts among the greatest black Americans.
15. For example, interviews with Jason McManus, 6 April 1994, and Lester Thurow, 28 April 1994.
16. *TAO*, 59 (1972), 2-3.
17. *TAO*, 66 (1979): 253.
18. Williamson interview, 6 June 1994.
19. Magaziner interview, 8 June 1994.
20. *TAO*, 59 (1972): 2.
21. Sanders interview, 20 October 1994.
22. Sanders interview, 20 October 1994; *Time*, 28 December 1962, 39; *Newsweek*, 31 December 1962, 56.
23. *Newsweek*, 31 December 1962, 56; *Time*, 28 December 1962, 39.
24. Barber interview, 22 December 1993. Frank Aydelotte retired as American Secretary in 1952. His successors have been: Courtney Smith (1938), 1952 to 1969; William J. Barber, 1970 to 1980; David Alexander (1954), 1981 to 1998; Elliot F. Gerson (1974), starting in 1998.
25. Williamson interview, 6 June 1994.

26. William J. Barber interview, 22 December 1993; David Alexander, letter to authors, 23 January 1995.
27. *Ebony*, December 1979, 45-50; *Redbook*, November 1979, 48- 49.
28. Sanders interview, 20 October 1994.
29. *Chronicle of Higher Education*, 15 December 1993, 29A; *TAO*, 82 (1995): 136.
30. David Alexander, letter to institutional representatives, 1 April 1994, 15 April 1995, 7 August 1995; Alexander, letter to authors, 23 January 1995.
31. David Alexander, letter to institutional representatives, 8 April 1996; Alexander interview, 23 May 1995.
32. *Chronicle of Higher Education*, 15 December 1993, 29A.
33. Elton, "Englishman's Audit," 104; *TAO*, 67 (1980): 171; Frank Sieverts interview, 10 January 1994; David Alexander interview, 23 May 1995.
34. *NYT*, 15 January 1997, B1; *Sunday Times*, 19 January 1997, World News sec., 13.
35. Harrity, "63 Years," 83.
36. Williamson interview, 6 June 1994.
37. *TAO*, 59 (1972): 3.
38. *Washington Post*, magazine, 27 May 1990, 12ff.; Schmoke interview, 2 August 1994.
39. *People*, 15 June 1987, 45.
40. *Sports Illustrated*, 22 November 1993, 10.
41. *People*, 9 May 1994, 141.
42. The *Observer*, 10 March 1996, 8; The *Guardian*, 12 April 1996, 23; (New York) *Daily News*, 20 June 1996, 88.
43. Interview with Sanders, 20 October 1994; Williamson, 6 June 1994; Schmoke, 2 August 1994; and Caroline Minter Hoxby (1988), 2 July 1995.
44. *TAO*, 66 (1979): 256.
45. *People*, 11 July 1983, 62.
46. *TAO*, 66 (1979): 256-57.
47. *TAO*, 74 (1987): 165.
48. *TAO*, 74 (1987): 168-69.
49. *TAO*, 74 (1987): 166.
50. Sanders interview, 20 October 1994.
51. Wideman's wedding in 1965 occurred shortly after Rhodes Trustees had decided to allow scholars to marry following their first year.
52. *Look*, 4 October 1966, 83.
53. Williamson interview, 6 June 1994.
54. Hadley interview, 30 July 1995.
55. *TAO*, 74 (1987): 166.
56. *TAO*, 74 (1987): 167.
57. Brown interview, 26 June 1997.
58. *TAO*, 79 (1992): 243-48.
59. Bill Bradley, *Life on the Run* (New York, 1977), 17-19, 47, 98, and passim.
60. *NYT*, 14 March 1971, 39; *TAO*, 59 (1972): 3-4.
61. *Newsweek*, 14 August 1972, 74.
62. *TAO*, 70 (1983), 184-85.
63. Schaper interview, 22 August 1994; *TAO*, 77 (1990): 89-90.
64. *Washington Post*, 1 July 1983, D1.
65. *NYT*, 5 January 1966, 3; *Chronicle of Higher Education*, 29 January 1986, 29; *TAO*, 59 (1972): 3; 77 (1990): 162-63.
66. *TAO*, 74 (1987): 165.

67. John Funari interview, 11 October 1993; *Washington Post*, 1 July 1983, D1; *TAO*, 70 (1983): 184-85; 71 (1984): 173-74; 72 (1985): 7-13.
68. *TAO*, 70 (1983): 185; 72 (1985): 7; 73 (1986): 4.
69. *TAO*, 74 (1987): 28-29; Anthony Kenny, speech at Rhodes Scholar reunion, Georgetown University, 13 June 1993; Warden's Christmas letter, December 1994, 7, and December 1997, 5.
70. *TAO*, 73 (1986): 2-4, 153; 74 (1987): 23-24.
71. *TAO*, 74 (1987): 94; 82 (1995): 342-43; 84 (1997): 263-69.

Chapter 13

NEW VOICES, NEW FACES II

Women, Gays, and Lesbians

We are women who have been "selected," which means we may continue to be analyzed, quoted, watched, weighed, quantified and numbered – "This one got a first; this one barely passed; this one is married" – and so on, forever.

God knows we'll be great food for some computer in years to come: Are our kids neurotic? Do we even have kids? Do our secretaries like us? Do our husbands resent us? Are we "happy"? ... .

We are 13 Rhodes women – an ominous number.

Alison Muscatine, *Working Woman*

Women Rhodes Scholars are just like the men – only more so.

Oxford don to Mary Norton

Gay and Rhodes Scholar – that's a very strange combination. They never seem to come together in my life.

Gay Rhodes Scholar (name withheld), *The American Oxonian*

Breaking the Gender Barrier

By the 1960s some of the rougher edges of Oxford's predominantly male atmosphere had worn away. Students from the five women's colleges had been receiving full-fledged degrees since 1920. Earlier American students, like Dean Rusk in the 1930s and Frank Sieverts in the 1950s, had discovered the hard way that merely mentioning a woman's name while in the dining hall was cause to be sconced.[1] That no longer occurred. Likewise, by the 1960s there were few Oxford dons as aggressively misogynistic as C.R.F.M Cruttwell, popularly known as "Crutters." Cruttwell was principal of Hertford College when Hedley Donovan arrived there in 1934. Cruttwell usually called his female housekeepers "you drab." Any female students

Notes for this chapter can be found on page 273.

who happened into his lectures on classical or modern history were chased away with a volley of obscenities.[2]

In the early 1960s one of Oxford's graduate colleges, Nuffield, admitted women students to full membership. In 1965 New College spoke of accepting women, but the university administration quietly nixed the idea.[3] The Franks Commission Report of 1966 recommended that Oxford increase its percentage of female students, who at that time comprised only about one-sixth of the total. However, the report said this increase should come from enlarging the women's colleges, not from making the men's colleges coeducational.[4] In general, the dons and students in the twenty-six men's colleges were content to preserve their unisexual domains.

When former scholar Ronald Dworkin returned to Oxford in 1969 to accept a position as a fellow at University College, his wife found the anti-female air so thick that she insisted they take up residence in London. To the present day, Dworkin spends half of each year in the School of Law at New York University and the other half in Britain. He commutes to Oxford from London.[5]

No Rhodes Scholar from the start of the program until the late 1960s ever publicly voiced any objection to the stipulation in Rhodes' will that only men could apply. As late as the mid-1970s, the entry of women into the program was not an issue for most former and current scholars. Male scholars were consumed with Vietnam and with the restrictions against blacks in South Africa and Rhodesia, but the prohibition against women bothered few of them. Numerous scholars from the 1950s and 1960s have admitted, sometimes sheepishly, that women were a non-issue at that time.[6] David Howlett (1965) says there was "not even a whisper" about women, and James Woolsey affirms that the question of granting them scholarships was "off the radar screen."[7]

One might, at first glance, assume that if women were not an issue this was because nothing could be done about it – given the clear instructions in Rhodes' will. However, as we have seen, Rhodes' will did not prevent scholars from crusading on behalf of blacks in South Africa.

The fact that male Rhodes Scholars did not mount a major crusade on behalf of women resulted in part from traditional male attitudes about men and women each having their proper, separate spheres of activity. The very qualities that Cecil Rhodes called for seemed to describe men: academic accomplishment, professional advancement, leadership, athletic vigor. Also, many of the top universities in the United States were still all-male establishments until the 1960s. It was only in that decade that coeducation came to most of the Ivy League. Thus many Americans, both male and female, accepted the notion that some universities, scholarships, private clubs, and the like could remain masculine preserves. Most of the top universities likewise had few blacks, Jews, or Asians.[8] Finally, Rhodes Scholars observed that American women who wished to study in Oxford were free to do so. Of course, they were limited to the less prestigious women's colleges, and they had to pay for their studies with their own funds or with other scholarships. Perhaps a couple of hundred American women had studied in Oxford through the decades, in this system that definitely was separate but not equal.

Even more than American universities, Oxford retained its male ethos – despite the tolerance of women's colleges. These five institutions were minor appendages – located on the geographic fringes, containing only about one-eighth of the total student body, possessing tiny endowments, and offering few athletic facilities and other such amenities. Given Oxford's disdain for trendiness, it is remarkable that the university was not far behind American universities in moving toward coeducation. In 1974 five undergraduate colleges admitted women – Jesus, Brasenose, Hertford, St. Catherine's, and Wadham. Over the following thirteen years every other college followed suit. It was perhaps fitting that the last college to accept women was Cecil Rhodes', Oriel, in 1987.[9]

The real pressure for change came not from men, but from women in America and Britain. Books like Betty Friedan's *The Feminine Mystique* and Germaine Greer's *The Female Eunuch* ignited the flames of the women's liberation movement. In 1962 women Oxford students won the right to wear trousers when attending university lectures. In that same year women were admitted to the Oxford Union, although not until several years later could they run for office in that august debating society.[10] By the late 1960s the British and American governments were supporting women's rights and exerting pressure – especially the threat of decreased funding – to any institutions that resisted change.

A handful of Rhodes Scholars demonstrated that they were still unreconstructed male chauvinists. In 1974 Harris Hudson (1911) commented in *The American Oxonian*'s class notes that:

> Oxford is not what it used to be and never was, to paraphrase a comment on that old publication, *Punch*, what with co-education insinuating itself into the ancient amenities of life there. Five colleges, I hear, have taken up this aberration ... the old place has lost much of its charm.[11]

Several other scholars, in contrast, did start to complain about the absence of women. In 1970 Ira Magaziner joined a small group of current scholars in submitting a petition to the Rhodes Trustees.[12] In that same year Steve Brush (1955) called on Rhodes Scholars to unite in pressing for change, rather than waiting for governments to act.[13] As noted in the previous chapter, Grant Crandall resigned his scholarship in protest against the exclusion of women and South African blacks. In 1973 Mark Killingsworth urged the Rhodes Trustees to end a "morally reprehensible and utterly unjustifiable discrimination against half the population" in the countries who elected Rhodes Scholars.[14]

Yet most scholars voiced no opinion on the issue. When Duane Krohnke in 1973 spoke up for the appointment of women, he was the first in his class of 1961 to do so.[15]

During this period, the Rhodes Trustees insisted that they were powerless to act on their own. It would take the British Parliament or the Charity Commission to grant authorization to break the gender restriction in Rhodes' will. In the fall of 1968, however, the trustees did take one action that they hoped would appease their critics. They announced that they would use part of the Trust's income to fund Rhodes Fellowships for women. These women would come from the United States and all other Rhodes constituencies.

These fellowships never proved especially popular or successful. Between their establishment and their gradual elimination in the early 1980s, about two dozen women "fellows" from various countries studied in Oxford. From the beginning, many women and men decried the new awards as mere tokenism. The awards were limited to five per year, and the winners had to join the women's colleges. Moreover, the women had to engage in serious postgraduate degree work; they did not receive the same encouragement given to male scholars for travel and socializing. The first American woman to win a fellowship turned it down in 1972 and never went to Oxford.[16]

Beginning in the late 1960s, Warden E.T. Williams assured all past and present scholars that he was working behind the scenes to effect change. As with the issue of black Africans, he said he wanted to follow proper form and not rattle the teacups.[17]

Change finally did come in 1975, when Parliament passed an Equal Opportunities Bill. The new law prohibited gender discrimination in employment. A rider to the bill permitted universities and charities to petition the Minister of Education and Science for permission to break any restrictions in their charters that discriminated against women.[18] The Rhodes Trustees immediately applied for, and received, authorization, and in the fall of 1976 women from all Rhodes constituencies applied for scholarships. The thirty-two Americans in the class of 1977 included thirteen women. For Rhodes Scholars as a whole that year, women comprised twenty-four out of seventy.

To a significant extent, it was pressure from American women and from the U.S. government that prompted Parliament to add the rider that affected the Rhodes Trust. Beginning in the early 1970s American female students were making free-swinging threats that kept American Secretary William J. Barber on the defensive. From 1972 through 1975 the University of Minnesota, Fisk University, La Salle College, Harvard University, and several other institutions nominated female students for Rhodes Scholarships. None of these women made it to the interview stage, and some of them threatened to sue their universities for participating in a discriminatory scholarship program. Moreover, they asked the U.S. Department of Health, Education, and Welfare (HEW) to cut off government funding for all universities that participated. Such a move would effectively put an end to American Rhodes Scholarships and possibly threaten the existence of the entire program.[19]

The next two years involved a lot of tense, behind-the-scenes negotiating by William J. Barber in the United States and E.T. Williams in Britain. Barber successfully managed to delay any actions by the HEW. Williams, on the other hand, had to let Parliament know how serious the situation was without making it seem that Britain was being pressured by the United States – which could have caused the whole campaign to backfire. Everyone associated with the scholarships breathed an immense sigh of relief when the bill was passed in Parliament, along with the relevant rider.

In quintessentially British fashion, E.T. Williams reacted to the good news by announcing:

> The men in most of our constituencies, especially the states, have been used to competing with women throughout their academic careers, and I felt and the trustees agreed that by definition the type of chaps we wanted for the scholarships would not want any unfair advantage.[20]

Though the American selection committees in 1976 denied any formal affirmative action program for women, everyone was pleased that in their first year of eligibility women won thirteen of the thirty-two slots. As the class of 1977 sailed to England, the male scholars acknowledged that the thirteen women were a genuinely remarkable group.[21]

Most former male scholars also expressed contentment. Some, like Austin Faricy (1931), reacted with arch humor:

> 1. I have nothing against women personally, and some of my best friends are women. 2. Women are all right in their place, but why must they push in everywhere? 3. When it comes right down to it, would you want your daughter to marry one?[22]

A few male scholars offered a kind of patronizing gallantry. John Bodine (1933) contributed a brief description of the 1977 sailing party to *The American Oxonian.* He lauded the women as an "attractive and accomplished group" who "brought unprecedented charm and excitement to the party."[23]

The first hurdle that the women of 1977 had to overcome was E.T. Williams. As a relic of the old school, Williams believed in chivalric tradition and thought men should give women equality rather than have women grab it on their own. Some of these pioneering women insisted on being called "Ms.," which Williams considered trite but amusing. He graciously acceded to their request.[24] Several years after his retirement, Williams still harbored raw feelings about some of these women, branding them "militant radicals" who "wanted everything."[25] Eventually, however, most of the women came around to liking the gruff Warden. After Williams died in 1995, Caroline Alexander (1977) and Ann McAllister Olivarius (1978) contributed warm testimonials to *The American Oxonian.*[26]

The inaugural crop of women certainly did receive intense scrutiny – during and after Oxford. Soon after her arrival in Oxford, Michigan State graduate Mary Norton was featured in a glowing tribute in her university's alumni magazine. In an interview for the article, Norton described herself as a "limited feminist" – an unfortunate choice of words that brought ridicule but that Norton laughs about today.[27] R.J. Apple, Jr., of the *New York Times,* tracked the thirteen female pioneers closely through their initial weeks in their new home. He called them "poised without seeming pushy, youthfully winsome without seeming immature." Alison (Lissa) Muscatine admitted that she felt pressure from all the attention. Denise Thal, who had been Muscatine's roommate and tennis team partner at Harvard, was awed by the venerable buildings and peaceful gardens. On the other hand, Thal was appalled by the horrible food and lack of vegetables at Jesus College, and she was taking lots of vitamin pills in order to compensate. Sue Halpern was so appalled by the "roast grease" that passed for roast pork that she immediately set up a cooking cooperative in her residence hall. Maura Abeln, on the other hand, saw something positive in the unappetizing fare: it "means I'm going to get thin."[28]

Sue Halpern and Lissa Muscatine were bemused by the vagueness and breadth of the first essay topics they were assigned: a general analysis of Keynsian economics and "reasons for believing that the pursuit of equality is illusory." Daryl Koehn was swamped with work during her first week: ploughing through a microeconomics textbook, writing two essays, and meeting with her tutor six times. Her tutor wanted to do things "rigorously," but Koehn declared, "I guess I'm game for that."[29]

Abeln was one of the most insecure of the group. Her working-class background had already made her feel that perhaps she did not belong in such a grand setting. Things were not helped when her hometown newspaper trumpeted the news of her award with the headline "Dumb Blonde Wins Rhodes Scholarship." The new-found freedom that Oxford offered all its students left her feeling directionless. When she plugged in her typewriter and blew a fuse she nearly decided to pack her bags and head home.[30] (Instead she remained and obtained her M.Phil. in economics.)

Halpern, on the other hand, was one of the boldest of the thirteen. At the end of her second week she shunned the formal sherry party being given for all Rhodes Scholars. Instead she went out on a date with the plumber who had visited her Brasenose room several times to fix her troublesome radiator. The two of them spent the evening visiting five pubs. Halpern liked the British but was resolutely determined to go her own American way. She continued to wear her cowboy boots.[31]

While still studying in Oxford, future Washington journalist Lissa Muscatine contributed an article entitled "Confessions of an Ex-Rhodeo Queen" to the magazine *Working Woman.* In it Muscatine said that one thing all thirteen of the women had was a desire to avoid the stereotypes that people were forming about them. "Some people," she said, "see us as overachieving bookworms, others imagine us to be militant feminists with unshaved armpits." The truth, however, was that some wore jeans and sneakers, liked to gamble, and drank Bloody Marys; others wore expensive clothing, wrote poems, and were deeply involved in diets and hair styles. They were thirteen intelligent women who had "all the traditional feathers in their caps," but who were also full of self-doubt.

Muscatine also described the occasional agonies of being hounded by photographers and television crews. One photographer, eager for a lead story, hissed at Muscatine: "Stick your chest out. C'mon, don't be afraid to show some breasts. Look at me like you want to come on to me." Dons were aghast when some cameramen wanted to invade the gloomy privacy of the one-on-one tutorial sessions.

Like male scholars, these first women had to learn that the Queen's English was not always the same as Uncle Sam's. Muscatine quickly learned that "fags" were cigarettes. Another woman blew her cool when a male undergraduate approached her in the Bodleian and asked for a "rubber." Only later did she discover that the unfortunate lad had merely wanted an eraser.

Despite these problems, Muscatine concluded that she and her female classmates had had "a grand experience" that had "been executed with the utmost ease."[32] Many of the joys and frustrations they experienced were the same as those faced by male scholars over the past three-quarters of a century. Like some of the men, Nancy Coiner got married after her first year – as was now permitted. Her husband came to live with her in Oxford.[33]

Measuring Up to Men

Have the women elected since 1976 been any different from their male counterparts? In general, their profiles have been similar. Nearly all of the women have: graduated at or near the top of their American university classes; made Phi Beta Kappa; been active in student government and other campus organizations; displayed interest in their fellow human beings; and demonstrated leadership potential.

Like many of the men applicants, many of the women impressed the selection committees with a dazzling array of accomplishments. In addition to the examples of Nnenna Jean Lynch and Karen Stevenson cited in the previous chapter, one could cite dozens of others. Michelle D. Johnson (1981) was the first woman student to be named Cadet Wing Commander at the Air Force Academy.[34] Nina T. Morishige (1982), the daughter of Japanese immigrants, was a concert pianist and flutist, an expert fencer, and a national junior amateur golf champion. At the age of eighteen she obtained both a B.A. and an M.A. in mathematics at Johns Hopkins, with a perfect 4.0 average. In her spare time Morishige worked as a classical disk jockey and played chess and softball.[35] Stephanie Dangel (1984) learned to be an overachiever and "a perfectionist to the extreme" by overcoming a physical obstacle. At the age of thirteen she was a top hurdler on the girl's track team at her school. A tumor led to a loss of sight in one eye. Her doctor told her she would never run hurdles again. This prognostication gave her the drive not only to rejoin the track team but to overcome many other sorts of "hurdles" later in life. While in high school and later at the Wharton School of the University of Pennsylvania, she tutored inmates at three different prisons. During summers she worked as a laborer on an oil pipeline, and she spent one year as an intern in the office of U.S. Supreme Court Chief Justice Warren Burger.[36]

Monica Salamon (1995) moved to the United States from Hungary in 1977, when she was four. At Harvard she worked as an officer of the Harvard Civil Liberties Union, made Phi Beta Kappa, produced plays in the student theater, and tutored children in some of Boston's ghettoes. She spent one summer writing legal briefs for the U.S. attorney's office in Boston and another working as a legal assistant in an international law firm in Boston. In addition to English and Hungarian, she was fluent in Spanish and French.[37]

It is impossible to compile a precise statistical comparison of the academic, leadership, and athletic achievements of male and female applicants. There is every reason to believe the American selection committees, however, when they say that for women – as for racial minorities – there has never been any quota system or informal program of affirmative action.

One indication of this impartiality is that for the decade after 1977 the annual number of new women scholars disappointed many observers. The number achieved in 1977, 13, seemed to be a sort of ceiling. Numbers over the following years were: 12 in 1978, 11 in 1979, 8 in 1980, 13 in 1981, 12 in 1982, 9 in 1983, 8 in 1984, 7 in 1985, 12 in 1986, 11 in 1987, 10 in 1988, and 12 in 1989. In part the failure to reach numeric equality with men resulted from the fact that only one-third of the applicants from one year to the next were women. Many top-notch female college seniors declined to apply for the Rhodes Scholarships, thinking that they were a "male thing" meant for candidates who were "Mr. Renaissance."[38]

Those women who did apply often faced some problems not encountered by male candidates. As all former scholars had been men, there were no former female scholars to sit on the selection committees. The American secretaries in the late 1970s and early 1980s, William J. Barber and David Alexander, did their best to recruit some women who had studied at Oxford to serve on the committees. Through the first half of the 1980s, however, several women applicants were interviewed by all-male committees.

Rather than giving special favors to women, some of these committees actually seemed to give women a more difficult time. During interviews several women had to contend with questions that never would have been posed to men. In the fall of 1984 Naomi Wolf faced her all-male committee, which conducted its interviews in an all-male social club. She was asked questions like: Do you intend to marry? Will you have children? If you have children, how will you continue to be a leader and fight the world's fight?[39]

After successfully fending off such questions and having to meet standards at least as high, if not higher, than those set for men, Wolf was further incensed to discover that many journalists and even some of her acquaintances implied that she won the scholarship because she was not just a female, but an attractive one. This assumption of lower standards for women set her on the path toward becoming one of today's most influential feminist writers. In *The Beauty Myth* and other works she has attacked the general American obsession with the youthful appearance and physical attractions of women – as opposed to their brains and other qualities.

By the late 1980s several former women scholars were sitting on selection committees. They were also serving on the board of directors of the Association of American Rhodes Scholars and acting as class secretaries for *The American Oxonian*. These factors, plus the growing realization that the scholarships were no longer inherently masculine, led to a breakthrough in women's numbers. The figure rose to 14 in 1990, declined to 5 in 1991 and 9 in 1992, but then regained solid momentum: 16 in 1993, 17 in 1994, 18 in 1995, 16 in 1996, 15 in 1997, and 13 in 1998.

In recent years the number of female winners has actually outpaced their percentage as applicants. Only about one-third of candidates are women. Their success in winning scholarships is probably not due to affirmative action but rather to a phenomenon working for black and other minority scholars also. In competing for a "white man's prize," women and minorities often have felt that they must outperform the traditional type of winner. The Oxford don who said the women were like the men, only more so, was therefore on to something.

There is one area in particular where this appears evident: sports. When asked if there is any difference between men and women scholars, the one thing that a majority of male scholars have suggested is athletics. In speaking of the women scholars of the late 1970s, American Secretary William J. Barber said they were "jockier" than the men.[40] His successor in that position, David Alexander, has agreed, noting especially that most of the scholars in recent years who have won national fame in sports have been female.[41]

A few women scholars, like Caroline Minter Hoxby (1988), have rejected the idea that they have been more athletic than the men.[42] Others, like Renee Lettow (1990) have agreed that they were.[43] In describing the women of 1977, Lissa Muscatine observed that one of their distinguishing characteristics was "an overabundance of physical coordination."[44] The roster of female scholar-athletes has been impressive. In addition to Karen Stevenson and Nnenna Jean Lynch, other track stars have included Caroline Alexander (1977), Molly Brennan (1982), and Rebecca Spies (1995). Alexander was an award-winning cross country runner; for several years both before and after Oxford she was a top competitor for the U.S. pentathlon championship. Brennan led the Oxford ladies track team in beating Cambridge. She became the second American to be elected President of the Oxford University Athletics Club.[45] (The first had been Rhodes Scholar Lawrence Hull more than seventy years earlier). Rebecca Spies followed in the tradition of her former teammate, Nnenna Lynch, by leading the Villanova women to national cross country championships, garnering individual All-American honors for four consecutive years, and being featured often in *Sports Illustrated* and other national magazines.[46]

When Bonnie Saint John was selected for the class of 1986, she seemed tailor-made for national press coverage: she was a woman, she was a champion skier, she was black, and she had only one leg. Due to a birth defect, her right leg had been amputated just below the knee when she was five. By the time she obtained her B.A. in government at Harvard, she had competed in several national competitions for handicapped skiers and placed second in the world championships in Innsbruck.[47]

The class of 1997 included one woman who had competed in the 1996 Olympics in Atlanta. UCLA chemistry major Annette Salmeen won a gold medal in freestyle relay swimming.

To be sure, there continue to be some top male athletes who become Rhodes Scholars. In the 1970s the three most famous were John Misha Petkevich (1973), Tom McMillen (1974), and Pat Haden (1975). Petkevich won the men's world championship in figure skating in 1971. He skated for the U.S. Olympic team in 1968 (when he finished sixth) and again in 1972 (placing fifth).

In a 1970 cover story, *Sports Illustrated* proclaimed the 6' 11" McMillen "The Best High School Basketball Player in the Country." He was recruited by 270 colleges and chose the University of Maryland. That school's proximity to Washington, DC, would enable him to make valuable contacts for his ultimate goal: a top job in government. He won All-American honors at Maryland and played for the U.S. Olympic team in 1972. Upon graduation, McMillen turned down first-round draft offers from the National Basketball Association and the American Basketball Association in order to go to Oxford. E.T. Williams obligingly made arrangements for McMillen to study during the summers in Oxford, so that he could earn $100,000 each winter playing basketball for the Bologna team in Italy.[48] After McMillen obtained his PPE diploma he returned to the United States and played pro basketball until 1985. Conveniently, he was able to end his sports career playing for the Washington Bullets. That gave him added publicity in the capital area and helped him to win election to Congress from a Maryland district.

Even more than McMillen, Haden was able to have his cake and eat it too while in Oxford. He had starred as quarterback for the University of Southern California while maintaining a 3.8 average and obtaining a Phi Beta Kappa key. He had not planned to enter professional football, partly because many had told him he was too small to survive in the pros. But when the Los Angeles Rams drafted him, E.T. Williams gave him permission to play each season for them, thereby skipping Oxford's Michaelmas term. The Rams also made their concessions, allowing Haden to board a plane for Britain as soon as the season ended. The Rams periodically shipped boxes of fresh footballs to him in Oxford, so that he could practice on his own. A few times each academic year Haden would depart from Oxford and spend long weekends at short training camps in the United States. Haden managed to keep up both halves of his life: retaining his spot as starting quarterback and obtaining his PPE degree.[49] He attributed his ability to keep up such a regimen to the discipline instilled by his mother. She awakened him early every morning, saying there would be plenty of time to sleep when he was dead.[50] When he finished at Oxford, he continued his dual career, taking courses in the School of Law at Loyola Marymount University at night and playing for the Rams during the day.

Since the late 1970s, there has been no male Rhodes Scholar with athletic accolades to match those of Haden, McMillen, Petkevich, or the women mentioned above. A handful have played on major varsity teams for powerhouse universities. In football, these have included West Point guard Rick Waddell (1982), Ohio State wide receiver Mike Lanese (1986), and Stanford tight end Cory Booker (1992).

Although the number of male scholars who have won national acclaim in sports has steadily shrunk, it must be pointed out that most women scholars also have not been All-American athletes. The class of 1988 was remarkable in that none of the thirty-two new scholars had been a college varsity athlete in a major sport.[51] Melissa Burch (1981), Robyn Hadley, Lisa Backus (1986), and Janice Hudgings (1991) were fairly typical Rhodes women athletes. Burch helped to establish a women's soccer team at Swarthmore. Like nearly all women and most men scholars, she rowed for her college in Oxford.[52] Backus played tennis and rugby at Harvard and basketball in Oxford.[53] Hadley played basketball for the University of North Carolina and was both captain and coach of the Oxford squad.[54] Hudgings played basketball and soccer at Swarthmore in her freshman and sophomore years. In Oxford she not only rowed for her college, but made the university crew.[55]

There are several explanations that Rhodes Scholars and Rhodes officials have offered for the drop-off in the athletic caliber of men applicants. One is the near impossibility nowadays of remaining both a top athlete and a top student in American universities. The number of hours spent in practice or in training has increased exponentially in most college sports. Many of the men and women Rhodes Scholars of the past twenty years have entered college as golden student-athletes but have realized early that they could not excel in both areas. They may have played on the football, track, tennis, or other teams as freshmen or sophomores, but many have dropped sports by the time they applied for the Rhodes Scholarship. This decline in sports is mirrored in *The American Oxonian.* Through the first half of this century, as many as half the pages of each issue concerned sports. Nowadays, the articles and letters from Oxford largely concern academics and world issues. It has been decades since the magazine published a full-page chart showing the fate of each college's boats in the bump races.

Another factor contributing to the sharp decline in top male Rhodes Scholar sports heroes is the lure of money. During the first three-quarters of this century, the starting salaries of professional athletes had not yet soared to stratospheric heights. As late as the 1960s and 1970s, Bill Bradley, Tom McMillen, and Pat Haden were being offered "only" about $100,000 to enter pro sports. By the 1990s, however, it had become common for top college basketball and football stars to obtain initial contracts in the millions. In short, some male scholar-athletes of the caliber of Byron White, Pete Dawkins, and Bill Bradley have not bothered to apply for Rhodes Scholarships. Top women scholar-athletes, however, generally do not receive lucrative sports contracts. Thus more of them apply for the scholarships.

Though few nationally known male athletes nowadays apply for the scholarships, Rhodes House is quick to point out that sports still are important. The percentage of American scholars who participated in varsity sports in their undergraduate schools is actually higher now than in earlier decades. In the first half of this century, there were three or four varsity athletes among each year's crop of thirty-two. In the 1980s and 1990s, the average has been five or six.[56] Most of this increase, however, is due to the presence of women scholars since 1977. One factor in the relative decrease in athleticism among men is that since the 1980s Rhodes officials have increasingly stressed that "physical vigor" rather than "manly sports" is what they seek.[57] Robert Edge, the current president of the Association of American Rhodes Scholars, has insisted that over the years the importance of sports for the scholarship has always been misunderstood.[58] All applicants for the scholarship must submit a physician's report. As long as the physician detects no debilitating illness, and as long as the candidate appears healthy during the interview, an applicant can fulfill the physical vigor criterion. (Of course, being a star athlete can be a great bonus in the eyes of a selection committee.)

It appears, however, that this message has reached male applicants more than female ones. During the past three decades many male candidates have openly flaunted their non-athleticism or even their disdain for sports. In addition to Robert Reich, who declared to his committee that he was an "anti-athlete," one could cite the owlish Michael Kinsley (1971), who made no effort to hide the fact that "I was your classic nonathlete."[59] Tom Williamson played football for Harvard, but during his Rhodes interviews he discovered that one could fulfill the "manly sports" criterion as long as one "could walk and chew gum at the same time."[60]

Bruce Reed (1982) joined Princeton's bicycle team as a freshman, but gave that up after breaking his collarbone in the first race. Thereafter he limited himself to exercising on a stationary bicycle. When he won his Rhodes Scholarship, he admitted that sports were "not a major part of my personality."[61] Reed's fellow Princetonian and Rhodes classmate Barton Gellman had played intramural tennis, but realized that the selection committees were looking for healthy people "who won't die of office fat by the age of thirty."[62]

Though most women scholars have not won All-American sports awards, most have played varsity or intramural sports. The biggest difference between the "average" male scholar and the "average" female scholar in the area of sports is that many of the men have been able confidently to downplay sports during their interviews. There is no recorded instance, however, of a woman scoffing at athletics in her application essay or interviews. The reason for this probably lies in the fact that women have not had the luxury of taking things for granted. They had to fight against the male-only clause, and when that was overturned they felt a need to demonstrate that they more than equaled male candidates in all the selection criteria.

Adapting to Oxford

How have women scholars fared while in Oxford? As noted above, many of their likes and dislikes about academic and social life were the same as those of the men. But, for the women as women, were there any differences in what had formerly been a notoriously male domain?

In general, women scholars can be divided into three roughly equal categories. First, there are those who experienced all sorts of male chauvinism or discrimination and consequently had difficulty remaining in Oxford to complete their degrees. Second comes the group that experienced some signs of male snobbery or resistance to women but found that these were minor irritations in an otherwise pleasant experience. Finally, many women have reported that they experienced absolutely no problems in Oxford from male dons or students.

Into the first group one can place Lynn Enterline (1978), who arrived in Oxford when most of the colleges had not yet gone coeducational. She studied at Somerville College. Writing for *The American Oxonian* while still a student there, she stated:

> ... a woman will face an indifferent, unenlightened, or sometimes hostile environment. For many of the American women who have come to Oxford, it has been a cruel step back to the days before feminist activism ...[63]

She noted that Somerville and the other women's colleges had no sports fields of their own and could barely provide rickety old boats in which their students could compete in the bump races. What was worse, she said that "contempt – and fear – of intellectual women flourishes yet at Oxford."[64] She was appalled to find anti-female graffiti on stone walls throughout Oxford – put up by male students resisting the move to coeducation by their colleges. (In 1992 and 1993 Enterline might have been interested to see the boisterous protests and graffiti erected by female Somerville students when their college decided to admit men.) For Enterline, the final insult came when the

Cherwell, then a male-dominated student newspaper, published a centerfold picture of a nude woman in its final issue of the 1978/1979 academic year. Enterline did admit, however, that the *Cherwell* photograph simply may have been part of a clumsy parody of a "sensational girly newspaper" rather than a direct attack on women.

Several women scholars of the 1970s and 1980s complained that whenever they were in seminars or small tutorial group sessions, their male dons and the male students spoke to each other and completely ignored the women present. Some dons insisted on calling the women "sir."[65] Though such behavior was insensitive, what the women apparently did not guess was that in many cases it was caused not by male chauvinism but by fear. The traditionalist dons – many of whom were still bachelors who lived in college – and the public school male students simply were unaccustomed to dealing with women in an academic setting and were afraid to talk to them.

In 1983 Nicholas Kristof (1981) wrote about the plight of women in *The American Oxonian.* He noted that some Oxford men were like some American men: they assumed all feminists were lesbians. Kristof says this discovery shocked him into understanding why so many American and Canadian women "complained that sexism was as much a part of Oxford as boating and afternoon tea."[66] Mary Murphy (1981) found that:

> More than anything else, the condescending attitude so many men have towards women makes this a frustrating place. The striking absence of women dons perpetuates this insular single-sex lifestyle many dons lead.[67]

Evelyn Windhager (1981) focused on another villain:

> Although devastatingly charming, articulate, gentlemanly and often exceptionally entertaining, that British monster, the public school male, must be singled out as one of the worst enemies of feminine consciousness at Oxford. Accustomed to purely male company from his short-trousered prep school days, he is likely to treat the female of the species as either his nurse-maid, his school matron, the headmaster's wife, or his haughty "mum." Intimate friendship does not come easily.[68]

When Naomi Wolf attended one of her introductory tutorials at New College in the fall of 1985, she was verbally humiliated by a misogynist anecdote. In February 1996 she returned to Oxford and was one of the guest speakers in the university's Amnesty Lectures series. After she recounted her experiences of a decade earlier, several current women students in the audience declared that similar incidents continue to occur.[69]

When Susan Craighead went up to Merton in 1986, she found that limited progress had been made in a few areas. Women Rhodes Scholars and other women students in Oxford now were not likely to face open hostility, and the JCRs no longer appointed student officers in charge of pornography. However, a faded notice at the entrance to the college library still admonished "gentlemen" to remember to sign out their books. She and other "PPE men" were invited to a sherry party. A letter from one don congratulated her for being a "talented young man." She heard stories about another don who still refused to tutor women, and about yet another who recommended that Oxford's feminists should go to Morocco so they could see how good they had it in Britain. She reported that Oriel women, when barred from the men's dining societies, formed one of their own: the Blessed Virgins.[70]

Donna Roberts (1987) likewise reported that she and several other women in her class noticed that Oxford's pace of change had remained glacial. Some women scholars were outraged when dons tried to compliment them by calling their essays "sweet." Oxford was still at least twenty years behind the United States, they concluded.[71]

Jennifer Bradley (1992) was perhaps overreacting when she was offended by being called "luv" by various college officials, porters, and other men in Oxford. (The male half of the team writing this book has been similarly addressed by dozens of British women.) She had a more substantial grievance when she complained about how Balliol reacted to an ugly incident that occurred in college during her stay there. Some young men from outside the college had entered the college bar and made improper advances to some of the Balliol women there. The next day the college dean posted a letter to "Balliol men" in the porter's lodge. The dean called the loutish invaders "miserable worms" and called on all Balliol men to defend Balliol women if any such events occurred in the future. The dean may have been exhibiting gallantry, but Bradley felt completely "disempowered" by the implication that weak women needed to hide behind strong men.[72]

The second group of American women, those not terribly offended by Oxford's slow path toward gender equality, includes those like Susan Billington (1981), Melissa Burch (1981), Elizabeth Sherwood (1981), and Renee Lettow. Billington (daughter of former scholar James Billington), realized when she moved into Balliol that the college was still adjusting to coeducation. She was amused rather than upset to find that she was considered a "Balliol man." When Balliol "men" excluded her from their dining societies, she and other "female Balliol men" cheerfully formed their own.[73]

Melissa Burch was amused rather than upset when Exeter College asked her to fill out a form, one line of which asked if she was the eldest son in the family. Both she and Elizabeth Sherwood believed that if women's liberation was less advanced in Britain than in the United States this was at least partly the fault of British women, who were "disturbingly passive," "complacent," and "afraid to challenge or threaten men."[74]

Renee Lettow was not in the least offended by some of the signs of chivalry that she witnessed in Oxford. She found Oxford men "old-fashioned" and enjoyed some of the special attention she received as a female.[75] Former scholar Neil Smelser has had occasion to meet numerous women scholars over the years and reports that several of them have reported being taken somewhat aback by Oxford's chivalry. The women were accustomed to "come ons" from men on American campuses and had difficulty accepting simple politeness from male British dons and students.[76]

Jennifer Barber (1978) experienced no problems herself, but she heard many stories about male dons making passes at female students. She adds, however, that she also heard stories about male dons making passes at male students.[77]

Deborah Jacobs (1981), Michele Warman (1982), and Stephanie Dangel have agreed that women scholars up to the mid-1980s tended to have it rougher than men, but for reasons only obliquely related to British sexism. Through the early 1980s women made up only a small percentage in the men's colleges that had recently become coeducational. Some of the American women scholars who opted for the women's colleges like Somerville and St. Hilda's felt strange in an all-female environment (after attending coed American colleges). On the other hand, they felt outnumbered and shunned if they were members of Balliol, Magdalen, and Merton, where women were still "gentlemen." Jacobs says that many of the early women scholars lacked a "critical mass" of female companionship. Only two of the eight American women in the class of 1980 stayed in Oxford long enough to complete a degree. Jacobs noted, however, that her class had thirteen women and thus did attain a sufficient critical mass. All thirteen obtained their degrees.[78] Warman did not feel "out of place" in the formerly all-male Magdalen, but she did observe that some of the public school male students felt ill-at-ease around women.[79] Moreover, Warman found that her being a woman caused absolutely no problems with any of her tutors. Dangel has stated that women of her era had to deal with a problem that male scholars did not: listening to all the problems of the men. Both men and women Rhodes Scholars had to cope with homesickness, adjusting to a different environment, and having a long period of complete freedom in which they had ample time for introspection. There were many more American men than American women in Oxford, and the men tended to seek out the women and bare their souls to them. Thus, says Dangel, she had to deal with her own personal problems plus console the many men who needed surrogate mothers in Oxford.[80]

Caroline Alexander never felt that she was treated differently because she was a woman, except in one respect. She lived in all-female Somerville College.[81] During her second year there she was stalked daily by a British man. The male college porter took steps to protect her, but the female bursar of the college upbraided her for causing the problem herself through her skimpy attire. At that time track star Alexander took long runs each day, wearing what Americans considered typical running clothes. She was shocked to discover that tradition-loving Oxford considered such clothing provocative when worn by women.[82]

The final group of women constitutes the third or so who claim never to have experienced any social or academic problems related to their gender. Mary Norton's international relations supervisor enjoyed having Americans in his seminars and had absolutely no hesitation in accepting women too. Because Norton was so willing to speak up and enliven discussions, one day the tutor invited her to participate in all seven of his tutorial sessions with British students.[83] Deborah Jacobs obtained an M.Sc. in physiology and was the first female student that her supervisor ever had; the male don expressed absolutely no embarrassment or hostility and treated her as he did all of his other students.[84] By the time Janelle Larson arrived in Oxford in 1990 she discovered that virtually every college had a "women's officer" to take care of the special needs or problems of female students. In her research field, agricultural economics, two of the six faculty members were female. Gender, says Larson, was not an issue for any of the dons or students with whom she worked.[85] Numerous other women have likewise reported that they had no problems with tutors as a result of gender.[86]

By the 1990s the situation of American, British, and other women in Oxford had improved markedly from a quarter-century earlier. To be sure, there are still some male dons who seem positively Neanderthal on women's issues. In 1994 Worcester College's Norman Stone, one of Britain's most prominent political commentators and historians, was asked why women undergraduates tended to produce fewer Firsts than did the men. He responded that he would need to be an expert in genetics to explain that phenomenon. That answer outraged women and embarrassed the university. Many Oxford women complain that they still labor in a hostile environment; this hampers their performance in tutorials and final examinations.[87] Other British and American women, however, have found male dons and students to be sensitive to feminist issues. Susan Bruns (1989), for example, was pleased when Magdalen asked her to participate in the drafting of its new sexual harassment code.[88]

Women today comprise only 15 percent of Oxford's overall faculty and 4 percent of its senior professorships.[89] These figures, however, are not far below those of many top American universities. Late in 1993 Oxford trumpeted the news that three new heads of formerly male colleges were women: Marilyn Butler at Exeter, Averil Cameron at Keble, and Jessica Rawson at Merton.[90] The fact that this made headlines showed that Oxford still had far to go regarding gender equality, but the appointment of women presidents at major American universities is also a rare, newsworthy phenomenon. Witness the publicity surrounding the appointments of Nannerl Keohane at Duke in 1993 and Judith Rodin at the University of Pennsylvania in 1994.

By the mid-1990s all of the men's colleges had been coeducational for at least a decade, and all but one of the women's colleges had begun to admit men. The lone holdout today is St. Hilda's. About 45 percent of Oxford's undergraduate and graduate students currently are women.

American women in Oxford who wish to pursue degrees in some field of women's studies continue to be disappointed.[91] There are extremely few opportunities, especially for undergraduates, to tailor their academic work toward gender studies. In part, this may reflect a lingering male ethos. In large part, however, it simply illustrates Oxford's preference for tradition over novelty. Through the previous century, the same inertia greeted the introduction of research degrees, the establishment of new undergraduate programs like PPE, the abolition of Greek and Latin requirements, and the introduction of American history and twentieth-century history as suitable topics for study.

To be sure, Oxford and Britain as a whole continue to lag behind the United States in the liberation of women. There are still several clubs on London's Pall Mall that exclude women, except on coronation day. The Queen, however, is an "honorary man" and can dine in them whenever she wishes – though there is no record of Elizabeth II ever doing so.[92] When the tradition-bound, all-male

United Oxford and Cambridge University Club in London decided early in 1996 finally to admit women as full members, the event received coverage in newspapers and magazines throughout the United States and Europe. Lest one condemn this as just one more example of troglodytic British males being dragged into the twentieth century, one should note that several male American Rhodes Scholars were members of the club. These Americans, former scholars who visited London often on business or government affairs, defended the all-male social club and said they joined it "just for the booze." This explanation did not satisfy those women who argued that they were being excluded from a meeting ground where valuable networking occurred.[93]

Rhodes House itself also was slow in dealing with gender equity. In 1981 it published a new *Register of Rhodes Scholars,* listing scholars of all nationalities since 1903. Each scholar received a one-paragraph biographical entry. Each entry contained the name and profession of the scholar's father, with nothing on the mother. Except for scholars who were raised by their mothers in single-parent households, mothers were omitted even for the women scholars chosen since 1977. A new *Register,* published in 1996, avoids this problem by omitting all references to parents for scholars of recent years.

Homosexuals

By 1980 the Rhodes program had passed some important hurdles: the entry of blacks and other minorities in increasing numbers and the admission of the first women. The decades of the 1960s and 1970s witnessed another milestone also: the first homosexual scholars.

The previous sentence needs immediate clarification. Were there gay Rhodes Scholars prior to 1960? Yes, certainly. Were there any Rhodes Scholars prior to 1960 who were known to be gay when they won their scholarships? Absolutely not. Were there any scholars prior to 1960 who "came out" while in Oxford? Perhaps a handful.

As was the case with women and minorities, so also regarding gays and lesbians, Rhodes Scholars as a whole have reflected the mores of society at large rather than play a major role in changing those norms.

Even though Cecil Rhodes himself was in all likelihood homosexual, his public persona was that of a rugged, aggressive, heterosexual man. His call for "manly sports" further contributed to the stereotype of Rhodes Scholars as "normal," "healthy," all-American scholar-athletes who would make great marks in their chosen professions. Of course, in the United States as in most other countries, until at least the 1970s, any man or woman who wished to become a leader in government, education, business, or other fields, was expected to be heterosexual. Homosexuals were deviants who could never be respected or trusted in positions of authority. Homosexuality was okay, perhaps, for some artists and writers – for Oscar Wilde, the Bloomsbury and Brideshead sets, "artistic" types, and so on, but not for mainstream leaders of society. The result was that in the United States and elsewhere many people with homosexual proclivities hid them from others and went through life feeling ashamed of their "abnormal" desires.

Many clinical studies have now demonstrated that in society as a whole perhaps as many as ten percent of all men and women are homosexual or bisexual. The inescapable conclusion is that since the beginnings of the program, there have been, on average, between two and four homosexuals in each year's new class of American Rhodes Scholars. Only in the 1960s, however, can one start to identify them in significant numbers.

Because Rhodes Scholars, from the beginning, have been the "anointed" future leaders of society, there has been an extra pressure on them to grapple with their situation. The plain fact is that even today, in the eyes of society at large and in the eyes of many Rhodes Scholars themselves, being a Rhodes Scholar and being a homosexual seem to be mutually exclusive.

Only a few scholars from the first half of the century can be identified as gay. Furthermore, none of them was openly gay while in Oxford, and some of them lived their entire lives "in the closet." It is not our purpose here to "out" anyone, alive or dead, whose homosexuality is not already a matter of public record. In the first half of this century, gay scholars included Alain Locke and F.O. Matthiessen (1923). Whereas Locke became one of the leaders in the Harlem Renaissance, Matthiessen was a well known literary critic at Yale and Harvard. Several gay scholars from the period up to 1950 are still alive, and they continue to request that their names be kept private.[94]

Until the 1960s, *The American Oxonian* was not anti-gay so much as oblivious to the possibility of gay scholars. The class notes each year resounded with hearty, masculine jokes. Secretaries tallied the number of their classmates who had married and often poked fun at those who were still lucky enough to be bachelors "playing the field."[95] Though Locke's and Matthiessen's homosexuality was no secret by the time they died in the 1950s, their obituaries in *The*

American Oxonian omitted any mention of that topic. Locke's obituary innocently mentions that "like many of the early Rhodes Scholars, he never married."[96] Matthiessen's testimonial notes that he was a socialist who was depressed by the Cold War. The fact that Matthiessen had been terribly lonely since the death of his companion in 1945 is not mentioned.[97] In these places and elsewhere through the many issues of the magazine, the thought never seems to have occurred to any of the heterosexual Rhodes Scholars that some of their brethren might be gay. Off the record, some older Rhodes Scholars have asserted that selection committees in those days would have rejected immediately any candidate suspected of being gay.

In interviews, scholars from the 1930s through the 1960s have repeatedly asserted that they knew of no gays from their classes and would not have guessed that there were any.[98] James O'Toole (1966) has admitted that he never contemplated the notion of gay Rhodes Scholars until he read an article about them in a 1994 issue of *The American Oxonian*.[99]

Ironically, gay scholars themselves have tended to share this view. More often than not, it was only later in life that they fully realized their proclivities. John Funari (1951) discovered many years after Oxford that four of his Rhodes classmates were gay. The four men may not have realized it themselves while in Oxford, for each of them eventually married and had children before "coming out."[100]

Only a handful of scholars of the 1950s and 1960s "went public" discreetly while in Oxford. These included Del Kolve (1955), Reynolds Price, and Michael Rice (1963).[101] Frank Sieverts, John Funari, and other heterosexual scholars recall that most men of that era could not imagine that some of their own might be gay.[102]

Therefore Reynolds Price's Oxford friends viewed his sometimes extravagant behavior as "campy" rather than gay. During one vacation odyssey, Price traveled to Venice. There he met British poet Stephen Spender. Back in England, Spender invited the young American to fashionable parties where the guests included writers like Cyril Connolly and W.H. Auden and actors like Laurence Olivier and Vivien Leigh. As a boy in North Carolina, Price had attended the opening of *Gone with the Wind*. He quickly developed a romantic passion for the film and, in particular, for Scarlett O'Hara (played by Leigh). Price was even more smitten by Leigh after meeting her in person. One night he left Oxford and made a pilgrimage to the actress's residence in London. There he prostrated himself overnight on her doorstep.[103]

The stories of John Wofford (1957) and W. Scott Thompson (1963), however, are more typical for Rhodes Scholars and many other American men of their generation. From the late 1950s through the 1970s, Wofford obtained his law degree at Harvard, married, had four children, and held several jobs in the federal government as well as in the Kennedy School of Government. *The American Oxonian*'s class notes in 1984 revealed that something new was up: separation from his spouse.[104] The 1989 class notes contained the real bombshell: Wofford's casual reference to his partner Chuck.[105] In the years since then, Wofford has always mentioned his partner. He has also openly discussed his leadership in various gay and lesbian advocacy groups.

Unlike Wofford, Thompson had dilemmas about his sexuality early on. Nevertheless, his career trajectory pointed ever upward in a "straight" world. When John F. Kennedy met Scotty Thompson at Stanford in 1960, the Senator joked that the student might make it to the White House before he did. Following Oxford, Thompson married a daughter of foreign policy nabob Paul H. Nitze, had three children, served as Assistant Secretary of Defense, and professor at the Fletcher School of Law and Diplomacy. In the early 1980s, like Wofford, Thompson finally abandoned his life's repression and came out. He held a variety of posts in the Ford and Reagan administrations, causing no small amount of discomfort for Reagan Republicans when he became the first member of their team to declare his homosexuality. Thompson chronicled his life and the plight of gays in general in his 1995 book *The Price of Achievement: Coming Out in Reagan Days.*

Gay and lesbian Rhodes Scholars have had a veritable coming out party in *The American Oxonian* in the 1990s. Many of them now discuss their partners and mention their participation in gay-rights marches. Paul Parish has disclosed his ups and downs in finding a significant other and reported his participation in a new ballet, "Revolutionary Nutcracker Sweetie."[106] Mark Agrast (1978) announced his fifth anniversary with his partner and the arrival of their new dependent, a terrier.[107] John Crandon (1989) made a historical first when he took his partner to the formal Rhodes Ball in Oxford; they wore matching bow ties, cummerbunds, and boutonnieres.[108] Christopher Elwell (1990) fell in love with an Englishman in Oxford, escorted his companion to the Rhodes Ball, took his partner back to America, and beseeched fellow scholars to support gay marriages.[109]

Selection committees have adapted to social changes and given scholarships to candidates who were openly gay. Numerous applicants nowadays list their gay-rights activities on their résumés. The class of 1989 held perhaps the record, with at least six openly gay men.[110] The most outspokenly open homosexual applicant to date has probably been a Canadian woman, Carellin Brooks (1993). While a student at McGill University she hosted a radio program called "Dykes on Mikes." When she applied for a Rhodes, she did so as an openly lesbian candidate.[111]

A few gay and lesbian scholars have asserted that going to Oxford helped them deal better with their sexual proclivities. Christopher Elwell declared that:

> Oxford is a good place to come out. There are a lot of gay people there. It is a new and anonymous and temporary place – one that does not have all the self-conscious questions as at home. One can feel a lot freer there.[112]

Scott Pretorius (1989) has said "getting a Rhodes Scholarship gave me the courage to face being gay ... and made me feel good about myself."[113]

All of the above might lead one to conclude that gay and lesbian scholars have fully come to terms with their sexuality and that heterosexual scholars fully accept them. But such is not the case. Several homosexual scholars have gone on record complaining that they face the same doubts and career obstacles that affect homosexuals in general. John Wofford, for example, contributed the 1994 article "On Being a Gay Rhodes Scholar" to *The American Oxonian*.[114] He made sure, however, that the article would not be published until after the political elections in November of that year. He did not want to cause any embarrassment for his brother, Harris Wofford, who was running in Pennsylvania for reelection to the U.S. Senate.[115] (At it turned out, the brother lost the election.) West Point scholar Andrea Hollen (1980) quit the Army in 1992 after spending more than a decade concealing her lesbianism and worrying about how its discovery could lead to discharge.[116] Mark Agrast experienced a host of problems while working in a corporate law firm. He had to learn that being gay meant some career options were closed to him. "Ordinary" scholars, he discovered, might aim to be President, but not gay ones.[117] At present Agrast works as a staff assistant to Massachusetts Democrat Gary Studds, one of the three openly gay members of the U.S. House of Representatives. W. Scott Thompson has conceded that "living a life as a gay man in a straight society is a perpetual run up a down escalator."[118] Thompson maintains that some, like himself, "with training and a bit of skill," learn how to do it. Others, however, do not.

Several gays and lesbians have discovered that being a Rhodes Scholar has added to their burdens. James Steffensen (1952) expressed this problem clearly when he said recently:

> There is a fair load of guilt being a gay Rhodes Scholar. Rhodes Scholars aren't supposed to do that. You try to keep your gay identity from people who had invested a lot in you, but you still act on it. For a long time I compartmentalized things very considerably, and hoped the barriers between them wouldn't develop any holes.[119]

This situation persists even for numerous younger scholars. Ten years after winning her scholarship, Susan Biemesderfer (1982) ruefully recalled:

> At one point I was on track for the American Dream. "You will never have to worry about having a job, or your place in the world," a distinguished man told 32 Rhodes scholars as we departed for England in 1982. But I have surmised that this elder Rhodes scholar must have really been speaking to the Bill Clintons among us – probably not to the women ..., probably not to other minorities and certainly not to gays or lesbians ... .
>
> When Bill Clinton talked about his Oxford days and his personal conflict over the Vietnam War, I was reminded of my own battle fought in an Oxford dorm room. There, I strained to reconcile the image I projected – straight-A student and championship athlete – with my realization about my sexual orientation: Was I a lesbian, or a Rhodes scholar? I despaired over the seeming incongruity.[120]

Biemesderfer's inability to see herself as both a lesbian and a Rhodes Scholar helps to explain her complete disappearance from any Rhodes Scholar networks. Apparently none of her classmates has maintained contact with her, and for the past several years the annual address list of all living American scholars has simply listed her as "address unknown."

Several gay and lesbian Rhodes Scholars have led troubled lives. Some have had nervous breakdowns, and a few have committed suicide. At least a half-dozen have died of AIDS. Perhaps the most prominent among the latter was Michael Rice. At the time of his death in 1989 he was general manager and vice president of WGBH in Boston, a position that made him one of the nation's driving forces in public television.

Biemesderfer is not the only one to drop from sight. Another was Philip Ritterbush (1958). Ritterbush performed brilliantly in Oxford, completing his D.Phil. thesis on eighteenth-century biology in under three years and having it published by Yale University Press. After stints as a legislative assistant in Congress, a lecturer at Yale, and a staff member in the White House Office of Science and Technology, in 1964 he was appointed assistant for policy analysis and planning at the Smithsonian Institution. Over the next several years he had an enormous impact on that body. His abrasive, anti-bureaucratic temperament led him to resign in 1971 and become a free-lance consultant and writer. Through the 1970s and 1980s his friends heard less and less about him, until finally the rumor spread that he had died. His obituaries are among the most peculiar ever published, in that no one was sure when or where he had died. Upon learning of his death, his friends shared two assumptions: that he had died of AIDS and that "his life was no doubt complicated by his having been gay."[121] Only in the 1990s did Rhodes Scholars determine the date of his death: 8 May 1986.[122]

The most famous suicide by a gay scholar was that of Roger "Denny" Hansen in 1991. He was the California golden boy featured in *Life* before and after his arrival in Oxford. Like that of Ritterbush, Hansen's early career seemed to fulfill all the expectations people had of him. Following a brief stint in broadcasting, Hansen obtained a Ph.D. in international relations at Johns Hopkins. His dissertation, *The Politics of Mexican Development*, was published by Johns Hopkins University Press in 1971 and quickly became one of the most influential studies of recent Mexican political and economic history. In 1970 and 1971 he served on the President's Commission on International Trade and Development. By 1976 he was a tenured faculty member at the Paul H. Nitze School of Advanced International Studies. Eventually he also served on the senior staff of the National Security Council during the Carter presidency and was Deputy Special Trade Representative.

By the 1980s, however, his friends could see that something was wrong. His career stalled, and he published little. His colleagues found him cranky and abrasive and started to avoid him. His antisocial behavior, like that of Ritterbush, undoubtedly stemmed in part from his difficulty in coping with his homosexuality.

Following Hansen's suicide, *The American Oxonian* published an obituary by a scholar who knew him in Oxford. Van Doorn Ooms (1956) etched a rose-colored portrait of his friend's life, speaking of glowing successes in Oxford and a rapid rise through the ranks of academe and government. According to Ooms, the only problem Hansen faced resulted from chronic back pain. That physical torment, according to Ooms, eventually pushed Hansen to take his own life. Numerous Rhodes Scholars – Scott Thompson in particular – were incensed by this obituary. It totally ignored what had become a major component of Hansen's personality in his later years – that is, his homosexuality.[123]

Some Rhodes Scholars, especially gay ones, were also dismayed by Calvin Trillin's 1993 bestseller, *Remembering Denny*. Trillin had known Hansen at Yale, and after he attended the funeral he set out to trace what had gone wrong with the glittering promise of the Yale superstar. Trillin's answer was that Hansen suffered from chronic depression aggravated by a mental burden that afflicts many Rhodes Scholars and other high achievers: the challenge of living up to exceedingly high expectations. With telling effect, Trillin quotes the English literary critic Cyril Connolly: "Whom the gods wish to destroy they first call promising."[124]

Though most Rhodes Scholars found Trillin's book sympathetic and poignant, John Wofford, Scott Thompson, and others charged that it did not adequately depict the degree to which Hansen's homosexuality had come to color his entire personality. Trillin conducted few interviews with Hansen's gay friends. Nor did Trillin realize that Hansen had come peacefully to accept his sexual inclinations during his final years.[125]

Hansen's life and death illustrate two signal facts about homosexual Rhodes Scholars. First, being a Rhodes Scholar can sometimes add to the anxieties a young person faces as he or she tries to live up to career expectations while grappling with sexual identity. Second, the inability to reconcile homosexuality with being a Rhodes Scholar has led Hansen, Ritterbush, Biemesderfer, and others to dissociate themselves from their Oxford classmates.

The ambiguous existence of gays and lesbians within a larger Rhodes Scholar network became clear at the 1993 Georgetown reunion. John Wofford and Scott Thompson decided to host a "tea, wine, and peonies" reception for gay, lesbian, and bisexual scholars during the three-day event. They sent invitations to all of the nine hundred or so North American Rhodes Scholars who were attending the reunion. Only about thirty people attended their gathering, and some of the older ones insisted that Rhodes Scholars as a whole not learn of their homosexuality.

Wofford and Thompson were not surprised that the attendees did not include some of the best-known scholars who are, privately, known to be gay.[126] One of the best-known people who fall into this category is Reynolds Price. Price's friends have known of his sexual inclination for decades, and yet he has never publicly discussed or admitted it. When the topic came up in a *Time* interview, his evasive response was

I would think that anyone who has seriously read my work could come up with a sense of my interests. But I resent the demand of our times that one is compelled to provide the Polaroids of intimate moments.[127]

Scott Thompson's book *The Price of Achievement* created shock waves throughout Washington corridors in 1995 as a result of its vituperative attacks on some of the author's personal enemies. Two of Thompson's special targets were his father-in-law Paul Nitze and fellow Rhodes Scholar David Boren. The book declares that both Nitze and Boren are gay. Thompson writes, for example, that Boren's entire career in Oklahoma and Washington, DC, has been dogged by rumors of affairs with pageboys and other "gay imbroglios." Even gay-rights groups have admitted, however, that Thompson appears to be settling personal scores in the most bitter fashion. Gay activists have also acknowledged that Thompson's titil-lating revelations are based on flimsy, hearsay evidence. Both Nitze and Boren have denied the charges, and there is no reason why an impartial observer should not believe them. The relevant point here is that Rhodes Scholars – as evidenced by Thompson – can occa-sionally be just as petty and vindictive as anyone else. Moreover, the fact that Boren was a friend of Thompson's in Oxford did not stop the latter from trying to ruin the reputation of a fellow member of the "old Rhodes boy network."[128]

It should be clear from all of the above that gay and lesbian Rhodes Scholars face all the same external problems and internal torments of homosexuals in general. Despite the fact that American selection committees have welcomed homosexual candidates into the fold, a strident minority of scholars have raised homophobic objections. Off the record, several have bitterly criticized *The Ameri-can Oxonian* for permitting homosexuals to "parade" their sexuality in the class notes. A noisy few also protested the publicity given to "that party for gay Rhodes Scholars" during the 1993 reunion.[129] In general, however, heterosexual Rhodes Scholars appear to be far in advance of society at large in accepting homosexuality as a natural and acceptable inclination.

NOTES

1. Rusk, *As I Saw It,* 70; Frank Sieverts diary, 19 December 1955.
2. Donovan, *Right Places, Right Times,* 50.
3. *TAO,* 49 (1962): 190; 52 (1965): 21-25.
4. *TAO,* 53 (1966): 112.
5. Dworkin interview, 19 November 1993.
6. Interviews with Ronald Dworkin, 19 November 1993; Erwin Fleissner, 29 December 1993; Josiah Bunting III, 31 March 1994; Lester Thurow, 28 April 1994.
7. Interviews with Howlett, 12 August 1993, and Woolsey, 9 June 1994.
8. *TAO,* 52 (1965): 18-19; 78 (1991): 258.
9. *NYT,* 29 April 1972, 9; *TAO,* 63 (1976): 167; 71 (1984): 195. Still today there are six all-male permanent private halls that have collegiate status and are part of the university. All six are religious institutions staffed mostly by clergy of various denominations. They are Blackfriars, Campion Hall, Greyfriars, Regent's Park College, St. Benet's Hall, and Wycliffe Hall.
10. *TAO,* 49 (1962): 189.
11. *TAO,* 61 (1974): 67.
12. Magaziner interview, 8 June 1994.
13. *TAO,* 57 (1970): 510.
14. *TAO,* 60 (1973): 176; 61 (1974): 23.
15. *TAO,* 61 (1974): 185.
16. *NYT,* 24 November 1968, 49; 17 March 1972, 47; 20 January 1973, 30. *TAO,* 58 (1971): 248; 59 (1972): 56-57, 293-95; 64 (1977): 1-2. We wish to thank Sherrill Pinney for providing additional information on the women fellows.
17. *TAO,* 61 (1974): 17; 83 (1996): 13.
18. *NYT,* 20 December 1976, 16.
19. *NYT,* 24 December 1972, E3; 8 October 1973, 39; 17 September 1975, 1, 36; 6 November 1973, 43. *TAO,* 60 (1973): 176.
20. *NYT,* 30 October 1977, 62.
21. Andrew Rosenheim interview, 11 August 1993.
22. *TAO,* 64 (1977): 130.
23. *TAO,* 64 (1977): 240.
24. *TAO,* 83 (1996): 17. It should be noted that very few British women have ever used "Ms."
25. Williams interview, 1 July 1994.
26. *TAO,* 83 (1996): 15-17.
27. Norton McConnell interview, 12 June 1996.
28. *NYT,* 30 October 1977, 62.
29. Ibid.
30. Ibid.
31. Ibid.
32. Muscatine, "Confessions," 64-67.
33. Coiner interview, 19 July 1994.
34. *NYT,* 22 December 1980, 21.
35. *NYT,* 21 December 1981, 14; 13 February 1982, 20.
36. Dangel interview, 26 April 1995; UPI report, 25 December 1983.
37. *Dallas Morning News,* 12 December 1994, 17A.
38. *TAO,* 78 (1981): 284-90; Janice Hudgings interview, 28 July 1993.
39. Wolf, speech to Rhodes Scholars reunion, Georgetown University, 12 June 1993.

40. Barber interview, 22 December 1993.
41. Alexander interview, 23 May 1995.
42. Minter Hoxby interview, 2 July 1995.
43. Lettow interview, 8 February 1994.
44. Muscatine, "Confessions," 63.
45. *Michigan State University Alumni Magazine*, Summer 1984, 16.
46. For example, *Sports Illustrated*, 20 February 1995, 148.
47. *People*, 17 March 1986, 127.
48. *NYT*, 27 March 1975, 21; *TAO*, 65 (1978): 175.
49. *NYT*, 27 February 1978, C10.
50. Haden interview, 13 May 1994.
51. UPI, 6 December 1987.
52. Burch interview, 23 July 1994.
53. Backus interview, 6 August 1994.
54. Hadley interview, 30 July 1995.
55. Hudgings interview, 28 July 1993.
56. Warden's Christmas letter, December 1996, 6-7.
57. David Alexander in UPI report, 6 December 1987; Alexander interview, 23 May 1995; Warden's Christmas letter, December 1993, 4.
58. Edge interview, 9 July 1996.
59. *New Yorker*, 13 May 1996, 59.
60. Williamson interview, 6 June 1994.
61. *NYT*, 28 February 1982, 7.
62. Ibid.
63. *TAO*, 66 (1979): 271.
64. *TAO*, 66 (1979): 273.
65. Interviews with Jennifer Bradley, 13 August 1993, and Andrew Nussbaum, 27 December 1993). *TAO*, 70 (1983): 21-22.
66. *TAO*, 70 (1983): 20.
67. Ibid., 21.
68. Ibid., 21.
69. *Oxford Today*, Trinity issue, 1996, 26.
70. *TAO*, 74 (1987): 84-87.
71. *TAO*, 76 (1989): 119-25.
72. Bradley interview, 13 August 1993.
73. Billington Harper interview, 22 July 1994.
74. *TAO*, 70 (1983): 23.
75. Lettow interview, 8 February 1994.
76. Smelser interview, 30 March 1994.
77. Barber interview, 19 November 1995.
78. Jacobs interview, 10 July 1996.
79. Warman interview, 29 December 1993; *TAO*, 70 (1983): 24- 25.
80. Dangel interview, 26 April 1995.
81. Following Somerville's decision to admit men in 1993, St. Hilda's remains the only all-women's college.
82. Alexander interview, 11 September 1994.
83. Norton McConnell interview, 12 June 1996.
84. Jacobs interview, 10 July 1996.
85. Larson interview, 5 July 1994.

86. Interviews with Caroline Alexander, 11 September 1994; Ila Burdette, 8 July 1994; Michele Warman, 29 December 1993.

87. *TAO*, 81 (1994): 280.

88. Susan Bruns Rowe interview, 4 April 1996.

89. *Financial Times*, 18 May 1993, 17; *Washington Post*, 5 August 1993, A24.

90. *Sunday Times*, 2 January 1994, Style & Travel, 21.

91. *TAO*, 81 (1994): 279-80.

92. *NYT*, 13 March 1994, E4.

93. *TAO*, 81 (1994): 279; *Chronicle of Higher Education*, 27 January 1995, A41; *Chicago Tribune*, 10 March 1996, womanews section, 9.

94. John Wofford interview, 22 April 1994; *TAO*, 81 (1994): 245-49.

95. Examples: *TAO*, 21 (1934): 224; 22 (1935): 202; 28 (1941): 286-87.

96. *TAO*, 41 (1954): 259.

97. *TAO*, 37 (1950): 142.

98. For example, interviews with Josiah Bunting III, 31 March 1994; Martin Rush, 8 April 1994; Bernard Rogers, 19 April 1994; Lester Thurow, 28 April 1994.

99. O'Toole interview, 2 July 1996.

100. Funari interview, 11 October 1993.

101. Mehta, *Up at Oxford*, 203-6; W. Scott Thompson, *The Price of Achievement: Coming Out in Reagan Days* (New York, 1995), 222.

102. Funari interview, 11 October 1993; Sieverts, letter to authors, 19 September 1996.

103. *Washington Post*, 18 January 1995, C1; Price interview on National Public Radio, 31 January 1996.

104. *TAO*, 71 (1984): 160.

105. *TAO*, 76 (1989): 177.

106. *TAO*, 78 (1991): 83; 81 (1994): 91; 83 (1996): 186.

107. *TAO*, 81 (1994): 195.

108. *TAO*, 81 (1994): 254.

109. *TAO*, 81 (1994): 208, 254.

110. Janelle Larson interview, 5 July 1994.

111. *The Gazette* (Montreal), 7 January 1993, A1.

112. *TAO*, 81 (1994): 250.

113. *TAO*, 81 (1994): 263.

114. *TAO*, 81 (1994): 240-66.

115. Wofford interviews, 22 April and 20 May 1994.

116. *Denver Post*, 15 January 1995, C1.

117. Agrast interview, 24 August 1994.

118. Thompson, *Price of Achievement*, 16.

119. *TAO*, 81 (1994): 257.

120. *Los Angeles Times*, 27 December 1992, M3.

121. *TAO*, 77 (1990): 341.

122. *Register of Rhodes Scholars, 1903-1995*, 234.

123. *TAO*, 79 (1992): 117-19; Frank Sieverts interview, 11 January 1994.

124. Trillin, *Remembering Denny*, 208.

125. *TAO*, 81 (1994): 244; Thompson, *Price of Achievement*, 16; *NYT Book Review*, 4 April 1993, 9.

126. Thompson, *Price of Achievement*, 19.

127. *Time*, 23 May 1994, 68.

128. Thompson, *Price of Achievement,* 222-23; Trey Graham, "Insider Out," *The Advocate*, 5 September 1995, 37-40.

129. *TAO*, 81 (1994): 245.

Chapter 14

CAREERS AND ACCOMPLISHMENTS

Grand that you young people have all this education – but the best is the use you make of it.

Harry S. Truman, speaking to Rhodes Scholars

[Rhodes Scholars] are just ordinary people, no geniuses, but people who are good citizens, and you look where they ended up. Few are world figures, but most are good, substantial people.

George C. McGhee, *New York Times*

Settling In and Spreading Out

In his final will, Cecil Rhodes stipulated that each of his scholars should be truthful, brave, and unselfish. Moreover, each scholar should protect the weak, exhibit leadership qualities, and, above all else, "esteem the performance of public duties as his highest aim." The ultimate goal was to bring peace, prosperity, and civilization to the entire globe. Given the fact that the application materials distributed throughout the United States and other constituencies each year continue to stress these criteria, it seems fair to judge Rhodes Scholars by them.

This task is made easier by the fact that, from the beginning, Rhodes Scholars have been obsessed with analyzing and evaluating what they have achieved, both individually and collectively. More than the recipients of any other academic award, Rhodes Scholars have repeatedly asked whether they have accomplished enough in life to show they deserved winning the scholarships.

From 1904 to the present, about 2,800 Americans have held Rhodes Scholarships. A little over 1,900 of them are still alive.[1] Any attempt to divide them into categories, according to careers or other accomplishments, is complicated by the fact that some individuals cannot easily be classified. In the pages that follow, we have some-

Notes for this chapter can be found on page 315.

times counted a particular person in more than one group. In most cases, however, we have endeavored to place each person in the category that best seems to represent his/her long-term interests. William Hunter (1977) illustrates one of the more extreme cases. In the annual Rhodes Scholar address list, he humorously, but accurately, bills himself as "publisher/politician/professor/lawyer." Kris Kristofferson also presents problems. In the annual address list and in various *Who's Who* types of directories, he invariably lists himself as a writer. As such he is best known for the songs he has composed, like "Me and Bobbie McGee" and "For the Good Times." Most people, however, would think of him as an actor or singer. (We have counted him as a writer and as an entertainer.) Bill Clinton, on the other hand, offers an easier choice. He clearly belongs in the "government" category, despite his short stints as a law professor and private attorney. Numerous scholars played professional sports, but we have placed Byron White, Bill Bradley, Pat Haden, and others like them in the occupations that came to dominate their overall careers – government for White and Bradley, business for Haden. Any errors that we have made are likely to cancel themselves out, thus not negating our overall figures.

Through the first half of this century, the principal record keeper and publicist for Rhodes Scholars was Frank Aydelotte. As American Secretary and editor of *The American Oxonian*, Aydelotte was an indefatigable promoter and statistician. From the 1920s through the 1940s he produced numerous tabulations and analyses of the careers into which Rhodes Scholars had settled. These pieces appeared in *The American Oxonian* as well as in mass-market national magazines. His final summaries appeared in his book *The American Rhodes Scholarships* (1946) and his chapter in *The First Fifty Years of the Rhodes Trust and the Rhodes Scholarships* (1955), edited by Lord Elton, the head of the Rhodes Trustees.

The statistical breakdowns compiled by Aydelotte and others indicated a fairly constant career pattern. Through the first half of the century, the number-one choice for American Rhodes Scholars was education. This category includes teachers and administrators in high schools, colleges, universities, as well as educational foundations or museums. Number two was law and number three business, with all other professions trailing far behind.

From 1950 to the present the career choices have remained remarkably steady and diverse. (See table 14.2). Education remains the leader, though its percentage has declined. Law and government have stayed the same, but business and medicine/science have

Table I

Occupations of Rhodes Scholars, 1904-1950

Education	40%
Law	20%
Business	13%
Medicine and Science	8%
Government	7%
Journalists, Writers, Broadcasters	5%
Clergy	3%
Entertainment (music, films, art)	1%
Military	1%
Other Occupations	2%

Sources: A Register of Rhodes Scholars, 1903-1981; Aydelotte, *American Rhodes Scholarships*, 81-133; Elton, *First Fifty Years*, 219-66; *TAO*, 5 (1918): 107-8; 8 (1921): 28-33; 25 (1938): 46-47, 37 (1950): 139-42.

risen slightly. Not surprisingly, the percentage for clergy has declined. This parallels a drop in clerical recruitment and church-going in society at large. Through the first half of this century dozens of scholars worked as lay or clerical missionaries in China. The two most prominent Rhodes Scholar clerics were Episcopalians: Beverley Tucker (1905), who rose to become Bishop of Ohio, and Arthur Lee Kinsolving (1920), who served as rector of Trinity Church in Boston and St. James Church in Manhattan. The Rhodes Scholars for the period after 1950 include a variety of missionaries and parish ministers as well as one Jesuit priest, two Benedictine monks, and one Zen Buddhist monk.

From the establishment of the scholarships to the present day, American secretaries, Rhodes Trustees, and the wardens in Rhodes House have optimistically – and sometimes defensively – declared that former scholars were making significant marks in their chosen professions and serving the public good in remarkable ways. In 1918 Aydelotte said that Rhodes Scholars could be proud, for in their careers thus far a majority of them were "distinctly successful and a few brilliantly so."[2] Ten years later he boasted that nearly two hundred scholars had already achieved "national prominence," despite the fact that the oldest among them was then not yet fifty years old.[3] In 1932 Sir Francis Wylie announced that Oxford "had no reason to

Table II

Occupations of Rhodes Scholars, 1951-1997

Education	32%
Law	20%
Business	15%
Medicine and Science	10%
Government	7%
Journalists, Writers, Broadcasters	6%
Clergy	1%
Entertainment	1%
Military	4%
Other Occupations	4%

Sources: annual address lists in *The American Oxonian, Register of Rhodes Scholars, 1903-1995;* speech by Sir Anthony Kenny, Rhodes Scholar reunion, Georgetown University, 11 June 1993; interviews with Rhodes Scholars. Dozens of recent scholars are still students – either in Oxford or the United States – and have not been included in this tabulation.

be dissatisfied," for scholars had achieved "as much as we had any right to expect."[4] Recently-retired American Secretary David Alexander, his successor Elliot F. Gerson (1974), and current Oxford Warden Sir Anthony Kenny have declared themselves, by and large, to be happy with what Rhodes Scholars have done with their lives. Kenny has said, for example, that "Cecil Rhodes' scheme seems to be working pretty well."[5]

Individual Rhodes Scholars also have come to their own defense. In 1992, for example, Philip M. Kaiser was angered when the Bush presidential campaign and conservative pundits repeatedly suggested that Rhodes Scholars were elitists who had never done much for the general good. Kaiser fired off an article that was printed in the *Washington Post.* In it he ticked off a short list of achievements culled from his 1936 classmates alone: Dyke Brown, one of the founders and first vice presidents of the Ford Foundation; Carleton Chapman, dean of the Dartmouth medical school and vice president of the Commonwealth Fund; Gordon Craig, one of the most productive and influential historians of modern Germany; Robert Ebert, dean of the Harvard medical school; Elvis Stahr, president of West Virginia University, then Secretary of the Army under John F. Kennedy, then president of Indiana University, and finally president of the Audubon

Society; Murat Williams, ambassador to El Salvador; and Walt Rostow, a respected economist and Lyndon Johnson's national security advisor. Kaiser also mentioned a few prominent scholars from other years: NATO commander Bernard Rogers; CIA director Stansfield Turner; *Foreign Policy* editor Charles Maynes (1960); *Time* editor-in-chief Hedley Donovan; *New York Times* editorial page editor John Oakes; plus the several who became U.S. senators or state governors. Kaiser might well have added his name to the list; his distinguished career had included service in the Federal Reserve System, in the U.S. Department of Labor, and in the Department of State. In addition, he had served as U.S. Minister to Great Britain and as Ambassador to Senegal, Mauritania, Hungary, and Austria.[6]

Despite the existence of obvious high achievers and valuable public servants among the 2,800 or so Americans who have been Rhodes Scholars, the program has had many critics. In dozens of magazine and newspaper articles over the past nine decades, various journalists and other observers have repeated a constant theme: that American Rhodes Scholars are not living up to Cecil Rhodes' expectations for leadership and public service.

Again and again in *The American Oxonian* through the first half of the century, Frank Aydelotte's defenses of Rhodes Scholars were mounted as responses to such criticisms. In 1927, for example, Aydelotte admitted that one unnamed, eminent critic was spreading the word that Rhodes Scholars were, by and large, "a quite ineffectual lot."[7] In 1936 Aydelotte reacted to charges that former scholars "were not ruling the state or the world of business" and were failing "to play their part in the great world."[8]

From 1904 to the present, the program's critics have had two main themes: first, that too many scholars were content with comfortable, safe jobs in academe, in law, and in business; second, that too few had careers in government or other fields where public service was the number-one goal. In 1938 journalist Milton Mackaye contributed an article entitled "What Happens to Our Rhodes Scholars?" to *Scribner's Magazine.* He sought to answer the question, "Do they become leaders in American life or fall into obscurity?" His answer was that they landed somewhere between those two extremes. Mackaye's highest praise for scholars as a group was distinctly muted:

> The fact is that the boys sent over to Oxford with their expenses paid have done reasonably well for themselves. Few of them are rich and few of them are internationally famous, but they probably have given a better accounting of their talent than an equal number of men chosen at ran-

dom from the alumni lists of Harvard or Yale. They pay their bills, they have substantial reputations in their home cities, and more than a hundred of them are represented in *Who's Who.* This volume, to be sure, has its weaknesses as a guidebook of success, but the roll call is significant enough in its way.[9]

Mackaye then discusses the biggest disappointment in the scholars:

One thing is obvious after thirty-odd years: In America the Scholarships have failed to produce national political leaders; the policy-making influence of Rhodes Scholars *en masse* is considerably less than that of, say, the Modern Woodmen of the World ...

No member of the Cabinet has ever been a Rhodes Scholar. No member of the Senate has ever been a Rhodes Scholar ... A sprinkling of men have served in state legislatures, but on the whole the political careers of the Oxonians have not advanced much since the era when it was customary at the annual Rhodes dinner in New York to toast wryly the mayor of Hohokus, New Jersey, as their one American statesman.[10]

Mackaye partially excuses Rhodes Scholars from this failure, noting that Cecil Rhodes was ignorant of American politics. In the United States, unlike Britain, a small caste of Oxbridge-educated gentlemen could not expect automatically to rise to the top in government.

Finally, Mackaye points out that Cecil Rhodes would have been profoundly disappointed to find that 40 percent of his scholars returned to the United States to pursue academic careers. Mackaye observes that Rhodes had contempt for the professorial mentality; in his will Rhodes said of the dons at Oriel, "the college authorities live secluded from the world and so are like children." Schoolteachers, in short, were not the kind of national leaders he had in mind.

One could cite dozens of other examples of such criticisms from over the decades. The gist of these is not that Rhodes Scholars were failures, but rather that these "supermen" who vowed to take leadership positions and serve the public good turned out to be mostly unexceptional. During a Rhodes Scholar reunion in Oxford in 1953 the *Daily Mail* ran the headline, "He [Cecil Rhodes] Wanted Giants – But He Got Solid Citizens."[11]

One of the most vitriolic attacks on Rhodes Scholars appeared in *Spy* magazine in 1988. It was written by Andrew Sullivan, an expatriate Briton who later became editor of *The New Republic.* Ironically, Sullivan had first gone to the United States on a Harkness Fellowship, one of many scholarships spawned in emulation of the Rhodes program. The title of his article reveals the thrust of his charges: "All Rhodes Lead Nowhere in Particular." He begins by describing a "typical" scholar:

At Oxford undergraduates soon learn to identify them. The strangers are friendly in an earnest, Dale Carnegie way but seem somehow oddly lonely, misfits by virtue of their bland eugenic perfection. Big, benign, boring: they stand apart. Those warm, nervous eyes, wincing ever so slightly as they dip toward another draft of warm English beer before looking up again, feet braced and head thrown back now to take in the clipped greensward and sixteenth-century towers of Oxford – *Oxford!* – those precisely engineered pectoral muscles straining against the under-sized tweed jacket; the furled copy of the *International Herald Tribune*; the bad haircut; the single fluid action of lowering the backpack and launch-ing the conversational opener about the U.S. electoral college...you see all this and you know: *Rhodes scholar.* You also know the chances are good that your Rhodes scholar is failing his coursework, hasn't had sex in six months and is afraid, quite sensibly, that this will be the high point of his life.[12]

Despite their awkwardness in Oxford, do Rhodes Scholars go on to become high achievers? Sullivan's pithy assessment:

> *Rhodes scholar.* The phrase has a weight to it, a pleasant, dignified heft that bespeaks accomplishment and promises greatness. Rhodes scholars are our titled nobility ... But the sad truth is that as a rule, Rhodies possess none of the charms of the aristocracy and all of the debilities: feckless-ness, excessive concern that peasants be aware of their achievement, and a certain hemophilia of character. Rhodes scholars are the apotheosis of the hustling apple-polisher, the triumph of the résumé-obsessed goody-goody, the epitome of the blue-chip nincompoop.[13]

They are, according to Sullivan, "high-profile losers." The "grim facts" show that the quality of scholars is declining. The old aphorism about Rhodies, that they are people with a great future behind them, is evident by their career paths – or so says Sullivan. Of the 1,900 or so living American scholars, he notes, about 250 fill middle-rank administrative and professorial positions in middle-rank state colleges and universities. Another 260, he says, "have ended up as lawyers, an oppressive fraction of them in Washington." Sullivan continues:

> On their way to lucrative white-shoe practices, a large number of Rhodies become special assistants to various establishment dignitaries, jobs that require maximum toadying and minimum risk – the ideal Rhodes scholar combination. Speech writers to major politicians, aides to CEOs – the important thing is to boost, boost, boost the résumé without ever committing to a particular line of endeavor. Rhodes scholars are to jobs what Don Juans are to women ...
>
> [Rhodes Scholars have] jobs where bland, mainstream intelligence is welcome; jobs that reward the very best of the second-rate, those adept at nattering away at the country's problems, prescribing solutions of soul-less reasonableness. Dean Rusk, who presided over the escalation of the

American involvement in Vietnam – a classic case of think-tank reasonableness holding steadfast in the face of reality – was a Rhodes scholar. Bill Clinton, governor of Arkansas and former Rhodes scholar, was given the prime-time nomination speech at this summer's Democratic National Convention in Atlanta; his tortuously reasonable, utterly passionless and absurdly long speech bombed, and Clinton left the stage to the only boos heard that week. Rhodes scholar Carl Albert was one of the weakest, least dynamic Speakers in the history of the House of Representatives...[14]

As is obvious, Sullivan lays his charges on with a sledgehammer. This is in part because *Spy* readers expect outrageous satire. Nevertheless, his statistics and analyses in many ways do hit their target. Several other critics, including some Rhodes Scholars themselves, had already made similar arguments – albeit without Sullivan's trenchant sarcasm.

Many Rhodes Scholars were outraged by the *Spy* article and considered rebutting it in *The American Oxonian*. However, they decided that such a response would only bring more publicity to the charges.[15] In strictly off-the-record interviews, several scholars asserted that Sullivan's animus resulted from purely personal grudges that he held against a few scholars. By going overboard in his clever witticisms, Sullivan weakens his case. Moreover, history has disproved the prediction that he made in his final paragraph:

> ... the Oval Office will probably never be occupied by a Rhodes scholar. How come? Because no other Rhodie has ever done it, so it must not be a thing Rhodes scholars do; because the presidency is not appointive; because it's a job with a huge amount of real responsibility; because a president can't just write editorials or position papers or head up committees – he or she has to *decide things*; because if you were president, you could never hope to put anything better on your résumé; and because that, to a Rhodes scholar, is tantamount to death.[16]

What about these allegations? The best way to address them is to survey achievements in some of the fields where scholars have been most active.

Education and Research

Education is the career field that has attracted the highest number of scholars. It is also the area in which scholars have had the greatest impact. In virtually every academic discipline, one can find Rhodes Scholars at or near the top of any short list of high achievers. Rhodes

Scholar historians provide some of the best examples. Five scholars have been elected President of the American Historical Association: Bernadotte E. Schmitt (1905), who became the first scholar to win a Pulitzer Prize, for his harsh evaluation of German war aims in his 1930 book *The Coming of the War 1914*; Crane Brinton, whose *The Anatomy of Revolution* (1938) remains a classic in comparative political history; John K. Fairbank, who almost single-handedly established the study of Chinese history in American universities; Gordon Craig, whose many books on modern German history have had an immense influence; and Robert Darnton, who has attracted a wide general readership with books like *The Forbidden Best-Sellers of Pre-Revolutionary France* (1995). Other Rhodes Scholar historians likewise have risen to the top in their particular areas: medievalists like Norman F. Cantor and George Cuttino (1936); French specialists like Arthur M. Wilson (1924) and Robert Paxton; Americanists like Daniel Boorstin and William J. Cronon (1976); and Russian experts like James Billington, Robert K. Massie, Nicholas Riasanovsky (1947), and Donald Treadgold (1947).

In the field of economics, the many scholars who could be cited include Walt Whitman Rostow, whose most famous publication remains his pathbreaking *The Stages of Economic Growth: A Non-Communist Manifesto* (1960); Kermit Gordon (1938), a member of John F. Kennedy's Council of Economic Advisors; William J. Barber, an authority on the history of economic thought; and George Goodman, better known to the American public as "Adam Smith" from his long-running PBS television series.

In the area of public-policy economic analysis, two of the most insightful writers of the last twenty years have been Lester Thurow and Robert Reich. The popularity of Thurow's books, especially *Zero-Sum Society* (1981), has led one observer to jest that he is "probably the most famous economist in America who has not been the host of a PBS television series."[17] Reich has become wealthy and influential from writing books like *The Next American Frontier* (1983) and *The Work of Nations: Preparing Ourselves for 21st-Century Capitalism* (1991). Because Thurow and Reich have aimed at shaping government policies and forming public opinion, rather than at appealing to fellow academics, some critics have accused them of being aggressive "policy hustlers" rather than original thinkers. Their response is that they prefer to have an impact in the real world rather than on dusty library shelves.

In most other fields in the humanities and social sciences, one can also find a sprinkling of Rhodes Scholars at the top. Among experts on classical Greece and Rome, one could mention Rhys Carpenter (1908), Richmond Lattimore (1929), William Arrowsmith (1948), and Michael Poliakoff (1975). Philosophers have included Brand Blanshard (1913) and Ronald Dworkin. In any list of influential sociologists currently active in the United States, one is sure to find Neil Smelser and John Gaventa (1971). Numerous Rhodes Scholars have excelled in literary criticism, perhaps the two most famous being Cleanth Brooks and Robert Penn Warren. Their New Criticism held sway for a half-century as the dominant mode of interpretation used in English departments around the United States. Paul Engle (1933) exercised a profound influence on two generations of American writers through the Writers' Workshop at the University of Iowa, which he headed from 1940 to 1967.

Among academic publishers and librarians, Rhodes Scholars also can be found at the zenith. From 1939 to 1959 John Crowe Ransom edited one of the most powerful organs in poetry and general literary criticism, *The Kenyon Review*. In addition, Ransom, Brooks, Warren and a slew of other Rhodes Scholars in the 1930s and 1940s served as editors or contributors to *The Southern Review*, a seminally important journal on southern literature and culture. Rhodes Scholar librarians have included the heads of libraries at several of the largest universities in the country as well as Chicago's Newberry Library (Stanley Pargellis, 1918) and the Library of Congress (Daniel Boorstin and James Billington). Publishers have included Frank Morley (1919), who helped to found Faber & Faber and later served as a vice president at Harcourt, Brace & Company; Joseph Brandt (1921), who directed the presses of the University of Oklahoma, Princeton University, and the University of Chicago, before assuming the presidency of Henry Holt & Company; Charles Bolté, executive secretary of the American Book Publishers Council and then a vice president at Viking; and John Fischer, editor-in-chief at Harper & Brothers.

Dozens of former scholars have also made significant contributions in medicine and science. Perhaps the most famous was Edwin Hubble. Working principally at the Mount Wilson and Mount Palomar observatories in California in the 1920s and 1930s, Hubble revolutionized astronomy. His observations and tabulations demonstrated that vast numbers of galaxies existed far beyond our own Milky Way. In 1931 Albert Einstein created headlines all over the world when he announced that he was changing his mind about the fixed size of the universe; Hubble had helped to convince him that a "big bang" at the beginning of time had led to an ever-expanding universe. (In the

1990s NASA's Hubble Space Telescope demonstrated that the universe was even older and larger than Hubble had imagined.)

Ever hungry for attention, Hubble won many awards during his lifetime. These included an honorary fellowship at his old Oxford college, the Queen's, and an honorary Oxford doctorate. Through intense campaigning he managed to get himself on the cover of *Time* and other magazines. His publicity agent fed journalists headlines like "Trouble, Trouble, Toil, and Hubble." His lobbying efforts and his genuine accomplishments, however, failed to win him the laurel he coveted most: a Nobel Prize. That disappointment resulted, in part, from a reluctance by some of the traditionalists on the Nobel selection committee to include astronomy in the category of physics.[18]

In medicine, the scholar who gained widest renown was Wilder Penfield (1914). He graduated from Princeton in 1913 and stayed there for an additional year as head football coach before winning his Rhodes Scholarship. Though Oxford's facilities lagged behind those of the best American universities in several areas of medical and scientific research, Penfield discovered that Oxford had one of the top neurologists, Sir Charles Sherrington. It was Sherrington's influence that led Penfield to specialize in that field. (In Oxford Penfield obtained a Second in his physiology B.A.; the typical Rhodes Scholar vacation travels plus his volunteer work in French hospitals during the war prevented a First.) After obtaining his M.D. at Johns Hopkins, Penfield became, in the eyes of many, the top neurosurgeon in the world. His many achievements included perfecting a surgical operation to curb severe epilepsy; mapping the various areas of the brain where different mental activities occurred; and applying an electrode to parts of the temporal lobes to trigger a patient's memories of the distant past. In the 1920s Penfield moved to Montreal, where he established a neurological institute and adopted Canadian citizenship. In 1944 Allied troops crossing the English Channel for D-Day were supplied with a seasickness remedy that he had concocted. By the time of his death in 1976, Penfield had received a wall full of honorary degrees and other awards – nearly everything but a Nobel Prize.[19]

Dozens of other Rhodes Scholar physicians and scientists have made noteworthy contributions. They have served as deans or directors of top medical schools and research institutes. Newcomb Chaney (1907) devised the carbon used in all American gas masks in the First World War.[20] Other chemists and physicists have worked on U.S. Antarctic expeditions and in the space industry – either for private corporations or for NASA. Robert Marston (1947) was dean of the medical school of the University of Mississippi and eventually

Director of the National Institutes of Health before spending ten years as president of the University of Florida. Gary Noble formerly was an Assistant Surgeon General and Director of HIV/AIDS programs at the Center for Disease Control in Atlanta. At present he is vice president of medical research at Direct Access Diagnostics, and he has helped to produce the first marketable home blood-collection kit for HIV testing. Lois Quam (1983) formerly served as Minnesota's health commissioner and as a member of the Clinton health-care task force. At present she is president of United Health Care, a private company. Some observers regard her as the nation's premier expert on rural health care.[21]

In addition to the dozens of Rhodes Scholars who have become deans of law schools, medical schools, schools of government, and the like, approximately sixty have become presidents of colleges and universities. In some cases these presidencies were not noteworthy and the institutions themselves were far from the upper echelons of academe. More than two dozen scholars, however, have headed some of the most visible and important academic institutions in the country. These have included such places as Harvard (Neil Rudenstine, 1956), the University of California (Charles J. Hitch, 1932), Purdue University (Frederick Hovde, 1933), the University of Virginia (Edgar Shannon, 1947), the University of Arkansas (J. William Fulbright), Reed College (Richard Scholz, 1904), the University of Rochester (Alan Valentine, 1922), Oberlin College (William Stevenson, 1922), and the United States Military Academy at West Point (Howard Graves, 1961). Some institutions have had more than one Rhodes Scholar president: for example, Swarthmore (Frank Aydelotte, John Nason [1928], and Courtney Smith [1938]), New York University (James Hester [1947] and John Brademas), and Pomona College (Wilson Lyon [1925] and David Alexander). Several Rhodes Scholars have become presidents of more than one college or university. In 1909 John Tigert (1904) became one of the youngest college presidents ever, when, at age twenty-seven, he was appointed head of Kentucky Wesleyan College; from 1921 to 1928 he was U.S. Commissioner of Education, and from 1928 to 1947 president of the University of Florida. A more recent example is Thomas Bartlett, who in the 1960s and 1970s served as president of the American University in Cairo, Colgate University, and the American Association of Universities, and in the 1980s and 1990s as chancellor of the state university systems in Alabama, Oregon, and New York.

Many of these college and university presidents had outstanding accomplishments. During the 1930s and 1940s Frank Aydelotte and

Alan Valentine often were classed with Harvard's James Bryant Conant and Chicago's Robert Maynard Hutchins as the chief spokesmen and reformers in American higher education.

Aydelotte in particular left an indelible impact on American universities, and he attributed his reforming zeal to his experiences in Oxford. From the time that he returned to the United States in 1907 to his death in 1956, he never ceased declaring that he aimed "to reprieve democracy from mediocrity." Aydelotte believed that academic excellence must be nurtured and not smothered by "mass" education. In an age when admission to college came to been seen as a birthright for all Americans, Aydelotte openly acknowledged that his number-one priority was to provide a challenging academic program for a minority, those students with ambition and keen intelligence. For him the Oxford tutorial system induced writing, reading, and thinking in ways unimaginable in the standard lecture hall American format.[22]

By the time Aydelotte became president of Swarthmore in 1921, he had settled on special honors programs as the way to reconcile equal opportunity with academic rigor. With apostolic zeal, he initiated a rigid curriculum reform – while silencing his campus critics with his triumphs as a fund-raiser as well. By 1925 Swarthmore's new honors program was in place. Above-average students were placed in small seminars and one-on-one tutorials; they were encouraged to pursue individual, cross-disciplinary research projects. As in Oxford, their final examinations were graded not by their tutors but by others. The goal was to instill these high achievers with confidence and ambition and prevent them from being slowed down and restricted in classes populated by "average" students.

Once his program was in place at Swarthmore, Aydelotte took it on the road. He became one of the most widely traveled public speakers on campuses around the country. In 1933 his leadership among Rhodes Scholars and his establishment of Swarthmore-style honors programs around the country won him a spot on the cover of *Time*.[23] Aydelotte also became known as a sort of "kingmaker" of college presidents.[24] He believed that the best way to promote academic excellence was to appoint Rhodes Scholars to every vacancy for college presidencies or deanships. Whenever he heard that a university was seeking a new executive or dean, he worked his private networks to ensure that Rhodes Scholars received serious consideration. Though no selection committee would ever admit it, it was widely believed that dozens of college presidents and deans owed their new jobs to his cloakroom lobbying.

By the time he left Swarthmore in 1940 to become director of the Institute for Advanced Study in Princeton, he had helped to establish honors programs on about one hundred campuses. But that figure is just a partial reflection of his infectious (and sometimes overbearing) influence. The concept of honors programs and individualized instruction on American campuses was not new with Aydelotte; a few universities had instituted experimental programs of this sort prior to his efforts. But his national prominence, his tireless campaigning, and the inspiration that he gave to hundreds of Rhodes Scholars who were professors and administrators around the country meant that his impact was wider than can be fully documented. Virtually all college campuses today offer a variety of honors programs and individual study options.

Some campuses go even further in emulating the Oxford/Cambridge system. For example, the "houses" in which most undergraduates live at Harvard and Yale emulate the Oxbridge colleges. Several faculty members live in or are closely associated with each house. One professor is the "master" of the house, and the others function as tutors. Over the decades many of these masters and tutors have been former Rhodes Scholars.

Dean Rusk provides another illustration of the Oxford influence. When he returned to the United States in 1934, there was a job waiting for him. Frank Aydelotte had intervened to get Rusk appointed assistant professor of government at Mills College in California. Within two years Rusk rose to become dean of the faculty, and he instituted a new course of study: an Oxford-style major in PPE.[25] In later decades several other American colleges likewise developed PPE programs.

To be sure, Frank Aydelotte was not single-handedly responsible for all of these developments. One must also recall that Rhodes Scholars were not the only Americans studying in Britain and bringing back ideas for educational improvements. Many Rhodes Scholars would have been inspired to push for academic excellence even without Aydelotte's prodding. In various writings and interviews, dozens have testified that their Oxford experience led them to initiate academic reforms – either on a large or small scale. Four good examples of this are Stringfellow Barr (1917), Scott Buchanan (1917), George Arthur ("Abe") Lincoln (1929), and Stansfield Turner.

Barr taught history at the University of Virginia from 1924 to 1937. There he edited *The Virginia Quarterly Review* and became perhaps the best-loved and also most-feared professor on campus. In his lectures he told students that they could sleep or read newspapers if they wished, and then he launched into such fiery orations that it was impossible to do anything but listen to him. He and his fellow faculty colleague Buchanan were dissatisfied with the traditional, unchallenging lecture format. In consultation with Robert Hutchins and Mortimer Adler (a professor at the University of Chicago and proponent of adult education), Barr and Buchanan devised a revolutionary curriculum. They aimed to educate students by putting them in small seminars and making them discuss "the Great Books of Western Civilization."[26]

In 1937 the trustees of St. John's College in Annapolis virtually gave Barr and Buchanan control of their declining, nearly bankrupt school. Barr became president and Buchanan the academic dean. Together they pushed through their new curriculum and placed their school in the national spotlight. Their Great Books program was controversial, but the charismatic, confident Barr and the disheveled, bookish Buchanan gloried in this "guerrilla" war against traditionalists. Barr and Buchanan left St. John's in 1946 and spent the rest of their lives propagating their educational ideas as well as becoming involved in international causes. Their espousal of a system of world government to ensure peace among nations got them into difficulties during the McCarthy era. Though Barr was an uncompromising educational reformer, he did have a sense of humor. His novel *Purely Academic or Professor Schneider's Revenge* (1958) is one of the great satires of higher education.

The Great Books curriculum initiated by Barr and Buchanan never spread to other campuses, except for St. John's sister campus established in Santa Fe, New Mexico in 1964. However, most educational experts agree that Barr and Buchanan helped to inspire many other campuses across the country to adopt at least an abbreviated version of the Great Books program. This is the core curriculum of general-knowledge courses that are required of college students nearly everywhere in the United States today.[27]

West Point graduate "Abe" Lincoln obtained his B.A. in PPE and spent the rest of his career in the army. He held a variety of positions, but he was most famous for his many years as a professor in the Department of Social Science at West Point – from 1937 to 1941 and 1947 to 1968. In 1948 he obtained special dispensation from the army and Congress so that he could avoid transfer to other postings and remain at West Point for the remainder of his career. Once he became head of his department, he ensured that six or more fellow Rhodes Scholars were always on the faculty with him.

This phalanx of Oxonians helped to transform the educational and moral ethos of the entire institution. Through the nineteenth and early twentieth centuries, the military academy had been primarily an engineering school. More than any other single individual, Lincoln refashioned it into an all-round, top-notch university. By the time he retired, the curriculum of the average student was two-thirds liberal arts (humanities, science, and math) and one-third applied science (primarily engineering). Under Lincoln's tutelage, the West Point debate team was usually ranked among the top ten in the nation.

Due in large part to Lincoln's efforts, the army came to agree that the nation would benefit if its future military officers had a broad academic background. Training in more specialized fields could come after graduation. Lincoln's careful supervision of the dozens of instructors who worked under him and his steadfast allegiance to the academy also helped to elevate the sense of duty and honor among all the students and faculty.[28] Lincoln died in 1975, but he remains a revered figure at West Point.

After obtaining his PPE degree in 1949, Stansfield Turner spent the following twenty years in a series of ever rising naval posts on board ships and in the Pentagon. He won a Bronze Star in Korea and commanded a missile frigate off the coast of Vietnam. In the late 1960s he served as executive assistant to the secretary of the navy in Lyndon Johnson's administration. In the mid-1970s he commanded the NATO forces in southern Europe. Prior to his appointment as CIA director by Jimmy Carter in 1977, however, Turner's chief claim to fame arose from his stint as commandant of the Naval War College, in Newport, Rhode Island, from 1972 to 1974. That institution offers advanced training to mid-career officers who are being groomed for top positions.

When Turner learned of his appointment in 1972, he ordered a complete overhaul of the curriculum even before he arrived in Newport. He decreed that naval officers must return to basics and become generalists. News of his educational theories made headlines across the country, as he announced that officers who wished to fight intelligently had to understand Thucydides's history of the Peloponnesian War. He replaced many of the lecture classes with seminars and debates – on topics like global military strategy, ethics, and contemporary Middle Eastern problems. Naval officers were encouraged to think in broad perspective, to write fast and clearly, and to articulate their views in lively discussions – in short, they were recreating Turner's Oxford tutorials of a quarter-century earlier.[29]

Turner is often credited with sparking a "Great Revival" that spread from the Naval War College to the Air War College in Montgomery, Alabama, to the Army War College, in Carlisle, Pennsylvania, and to the Army's various training programs at Fort Leavenworth, Kansas.

Officers in all the services are now expected to see education as a life-long experience. Many obtain advanced degrees – in history, international relations, politics, and related fields.[30]

One final area related to education in which hundreds of Rhodes Scholars have been active concerns the many private foundations and government programs that offer grants to universities, scholarships to students, and other means of support to teaching and research.

The Rhodes Scholarships were the first study-abroad academic program in the history of the world. Since their establishment, nearly every country in the world has, in some form or another, emulated them. The most famous and most important of these programs is the Fulbright Scholarships. In 1946 Senator J. William Fulbright sponsored the bill creating these awards. Even today nearly all the brochures and other materials for the program contain the senator's words from 1946, in which he declared that his Oxford experience was the key to making him realize the importance of foreign studies for future leaders of society.

Over the past fifty years the Fulbright program has grown exponentially. Dozens of other countries now contribute to the costs. Well over 200,000 scholarships have been awarded. The winners include Americans going abroad to teach or study and foreigners coming to the United States. In many ways Fulbright was accurate when he lightheartedly suggested that these Fulbright scholars were "grandchildren" of Cecil Rhodes. Some of these "grandchildren" have been Senator Daniel Patrick Moynihan, journalist George Will, poet Sylvia Plath, and novelist John Updike.

The list of other scholarships that were created, directly or indirectly, as a result of the success of the Rhodes Scholarships is much too long to give here. These programs have names like Henry, Davison, Choate, Maier, and AFS. Without too much exaggeration, one might say that virtually all of the study abroad programs offered by universities in the United States are byproducts of the pioneering Rhodes program.[31]

One the more famous programs spawned directly by the Rhodes example is that of the Marshall Scholarships. These were established by the British government in 1953 as a way of thanking the United States for its wartime help and for the Marshall Plan. Initially there were twelve Marshall Scholars each year; today there are forty. From their inception, the Marshalls included both men and women. The new program differed from the Rhodes in two significant ways. Marshall Scholars can attend any British university, not just Oxford. Moreover, the selection committees for the Marshall place a heavier stress on academic achievement – as opposed to the Rhodes emphasis on all-rounders. In recent years, however, the Marshall program has become more Rhodes-like, stating that it is seeking persons who also demonstrate leadership potential.

From 1953 to the present the Marshall and Rhodes programs have engaged in an informal rivalry – mostly friendly, although sometimes not so friendly. Nearly all Rhodes Scholars are willing to admit that, by and large, the Marshalls are superior if one looks just at grade point averages and other signs of academic achievement. Some Rhodes Scholars have said this candidly and admiringly. Others have said it with a touch of disdain. One recent Rhodes Scholar told us that the Marshalls are mere "nerds."

Most of the top American university seniors who hope to study in Britain apply for both a Rhodes and a Marshall; some win the first, some win the second, and some win both. The Marshall administrators (at the British Embassy in Washington, DC) have occasionally revealed their vexation when the "double" winners have, almost invariably, opted for the more famous Rhodes. Only one "double" winner has ever opted for the Marshall – much to the private displeasure of Rhodes administrators.

Several sources who wish to remain anonymous have related a story about Margaret Thatcher in the 1980s. The prime minister became irritated because Marshall Scholars never seemed to win the publicity that Rhodes Scholars did. Yet the Marshall Scholars received the same amount of scholarship money and had freedom to choose among dozens of British universities. She berated the staff at the Washington embassy. The British ambassador endeavored to soothe her and said, "But, Prime Minister, our scholars get better grades than the Rhodes Scholars." That was perhaps the worst thing he could have said to her. She retorted, "Don't give me bookworms and let all the good political types go to the Rhodes."

In more recent years, relations between the two programs have become much smoother. Several Marshall Scholars have cemented this *entente cordiale* by marrying Rhodes Scholars. In addition, it has become clear that not all Marshall Scholars are mere nerds. Indeed, a look at their careers demonstrates that the line between them and Rhodes Scholars is not so evident. Former Marshall Scholars include Duke University President Nannerl Keohane, Bill Clinton's Secretary of the Interior Bruce Babbitt, Pulitzer Prize winning authors Thomas Friedman and Daniel Yergin, Supreme Court Justice Stephen Breyer, Dolby Sound System founder Ray Dolby, and South Carolina Congressman John Spratt.[32]

Dozens of Rhodes Scholars have helped to establish or to administer the most important private foundations and government agencies related to education and research. As noted earlier, Dyke Brown was one of the chief architects of the Ford Foundation. Frank Aydelotte helped to organize the Commonwealth Fund (which brings British students to the United States). Along with fellow scholars Carroll Wilson (1908) and Henry Allen Moe (1919), Aydelotte also worked to establish the Guggenheim Foundation.[33] Moe spent most of his career as secretary and president of the Guggenheim Foundation before becoming the first chairman of the newly created National Endowment for the Humanities in 1966. Prior to his appointment as Secretary of State, Dean Rusk headed the Rockefeller Foundation for nearly a decade.

In all, perhaps a couple of hundred Rhodes Scholars have become deans, college presidents, foundation heads, or nationally recognized leaders in their specialized disciplines. That is, by nearly any measure, a sign of "success." But what of the other thousand or so Rhodes Scholars since 1904 who have become teachers or researchers and did not climb to such heights? Were they "successful?" This is a question that numerous observers have asked over the decades. Many Rhodes Scholars also have wondered if becoming an "average" faculty member at an "ordinary" high school or college is what they should be doing.

During the first half of the century, at any given time, several dozen scholars were elementary or high school teachers. Roughly half were in public schools and half were in prep schools. Places like Hotchkiss and Groton always had at least a couple of Rhodes Scholars on their staffs. The number of elementary and secondary school teachers among Rhodes Scholars has declined in recent decades, now amounting to no more than a dozen. Still today, however, several Rhodes Scholars are the headmasters of elite prep schools.

Many more scholars have settled into comfortable, tenured lives in the shady groves of colleges and universities. Over 450 of the scholars still at work today can be classified in education or research. Of these 450, perhaps fifty can be deemed national leaders in their fields – as college presidents, presidents of their professional associations, and so on. The other four hundred are assistant, associate or full professors in colleges and universities or research staffers in government or private organizations. Most of these four hundred publish books and articles in their fields; they teach their students as well as they can; they serve on local school boards, join Rotary clubs, and coach little league teams. In short, they are model citizens.

The same can be said for the fields of medicine and science. For every dean of a top medical school and award-winning surgeon or laboratory researcher, there are perhaps two or three who are "ordinary" physicians or staff members in private practices, in hospitals, and in the R&D offices of corporations.

Is that what Cecil Rhodes wanted? Rhodes officials and Rhodes Scholars have grappled with this question through the decades. David Alexander, Elliot F. Gerson, and Sir Anthony Kenny have offered the answer given most often over the years: Rhodes probably hoped for political leaders, but times have changed. There are ways in which a Rhodes Scholar can be a leader and bring about change in ways Cecil Rhodes never imagined.[34]

Some Rhodes Scholars have admitted that they are "frauds." James Griffin, for example, acknowledges that when he applied for a scholarship in 1954 he and several of his classmates inwardly knew that their hopes for quiet, though industrious, careers in academe were not what the program aimed for.[35]

David Howlett agrees. Like Griffin, Howlett is one of the handful of American Rhodes Scholars who have remained at Oxford for all or most of their careers. A specialist in medieval Latin documents, he does not feel in the least that he is a failure. Howlett maintains that his specialized publications serve to advance knowledge, and any improvements in our knowledge of the past help us to deal with current problems more wisely. In 1996 Howlett won a flurry of international attention with his announcement that he had determined the authorship of the great epic *Beowulf*.[36] Nevertheless, Howlett lightheartedly admits that "old Cecil would be turning in his grave if he knew what I was doing in my career."[37]

Mary Cleary Kiely (1981) returned from Oxford and took a job with a business corporation. Following that she worked for two years as an administrative assistant in the New York City Board of Education. That experience made her lose hope that any educational progress could ever come from the top. She went back to college to obtain her teaching credentials and then became a third grade teacher. This job made her so happy that her husband (a banker) was envious. Moreover, Kiely felt sure in her own mind that she was doing good for society – and thus living up to Cecil Rhodes' expectations. She realized that some Rhodes Scholars looked down on her. One Rhodes classmate even wrote to her, "Hear you're doing time in an elementary school."[38]

John Funari, a former dean of the Graduate School of Public and International Affairs at the University of Pittsburgh and for nearly a decade the editor of *The American Oxonian,* acknowledged that this attitude exists among many scholars. When selection committees interview candidates who propose to enter the field of education, they are more likely to give the nod to someone who says, "Twenty years from now I plan to be superintendent of schools in Philadelphia," rather than to someone whose goal is to remain a "mere" teacher in one of those schools. Christopher Brown confirms this, observing that selection committees welcome candidates proposing to become teachers, as long as these persons show the potential to become important leaders and innovators.[39]

Among college professors, many Rhodes Scholars have made solid contributions in their narrow fields. Rhodes Scholar authors and books include the following: Donald Sutherland (1953), *The Assize of Novel Disseisin;* Jonathan Culler (1966), *The Pursuit of Signs: Semiotics, Literature, and Deconstruction;* Darryl Gless (1968), *Dogmatic Mutability in Spenser's "Fairie Queene";* David Matthews Schaffer (1971), *Mandinko: The Ethnography of a West African Holy Land;* Michael Koziol (1973), *Gaseous Air Pollutants and Plant Metabolism;* and Lynn Enterline, *The Tears of Narcissus: Melancholia and Masculinity in Early Modern Writing.* Scholarly and worthy projects? Yes. The kinds of things Cecil Rhodes intended? No.

Dozens of other Rhodes Scholars, however, have become well known members of that dying breed: the public intellectual. These are people, both within and outside of academe, who combine sound scholarship and erudition with the ability to go beyond fellow specialists and shape public opinion and government policies. Scholars like Gordon Craig, Ronald Dworkin, George Steiner, Lester Thurow, and Randall Kennedy publish with university presses, hold prestigious academic posts, and yet also contribute frequently to periodicals like the *New Yorker* and the *New York Review of Books.* In 1993 one reviewer wrote the following about a new book by Dworkin:

> Dworkin ... is as thoughtful and creative a legal scholar as the American academy currently possesses; and his new book about abortion, *Life's Dominion* ... is as thoughtful and creative a scholarly treatment as the subject is likely to receive.[40]

The great majority of Rhodes Scholar academics have not received such praise. But many of these "average" teachers have touched the souls of thousands of students during their careers and received glowing testimonials at their retirements. On the other hand, a small minority of Rhodes Scholar academics have been, by most standards, professional and personal failures. One recent example is a scholar who spent nearly 40 years on the faculty of a rural, regional campus in one of the country's larger state university systems. Our own impressions of this individual were confirmed by one of his colleagues: "We could hardly believe this guy was a Rhodes Scholar. He never published, students disliked him, and he was a disaster as department chairman. Thank God he has retired."

Business, Law, and Other Professions

In the world of business, Rhodes Scholars have occupied virtually every level of every field. There has been at least one lumberjack, one disk jockey, and one gold prospector. Dozens have returned home from Oxford and taken up the family hog farms or cattle ranches. Others have become accountants, forest rangers, engineers, vocational counselors, and advertising executives. Some have been automobile salesmen, others have owned automobile dealerships, and a couple have become corporate vice presidents of the major American automobile manufacturers.

Several dozen scholars have had careers in the business or artistic sides of the entertainment industry. Kris Kristofferson is the only one to become a household name, but others have been important behind the scenes. A dozen or so have become screenwriters. Besides John Monk Saunders, Lawrence Allan Scott (1928) was the most famous. He wrote several Fred Astaire-Ginger Rogers films as well as others starring Katharine Hepburn. Hervey Cleckley (1924) was a psychiatrist, but one of his books became the basis of *Three Faces of Eve*, for which Joanne Woodward won an Academy Award in 1957. Eugene Burdick combined an academic job (professor of political science at Berkeley) with writing bestsellers that became Hollywood hits. His books include *The Ugly American* (1958, written with William J. Lederer) and *Fail-safe* (1962, written with W. Harvey Wheeler).

Sollace Mitchell (1976) has written television movies as well as screenplays for Claude Chabrol. Terence Malick (1966) directed two cult classics from the 1970s, *Badlands* and *Days of Heaven*. Malick then went into nearly two decades of seclusion and gained a reputation as the J.D. Salinger or Thomas Pynchon of film. When in 1997 he took up directing again, film aficionados showered his new movie, *The Thin Red Line*, with the kind of hoopla that might otherwise be reserved for the Second Coming.

Like most members from the class of 1939, John Jay was prevented from going to Britain by the war and opted not to go up to

Oxford afterwards. Nevertheless, he was considered a bonafide Rhodes Scholar, and in class notes over the next five decades he shared news about his career as one of the nation's top producers of documentary adventure films and travelogues.[41]

Bergen Evans (1928) became a radio star in the 1940s and an unlikely television celebrity in the 1950s. A professor of English at Northwestern University from 1932 to 1969, he specialized in lexicography and grammar. His witty, irreverent, and unfailingly knowledgeable comments on modern American usage made him America's number one arbiter in matters of word choice. Evans' many books included *The Natural History of Nonsense, Dictionary of Contemporary Usage,* and *Dictionary of Quotations.* His pseudo-English accent, his font of humorous anecdotes, and his bookish erudition made him a definite "character." On radio and television he hosted numerous different programs devoted to literature and language and also served as emcee on some early game shows. Behind the scenes, he was one of those who devised questions for "The $64,000 Question." His career was nearly ruined in 1957, when the public discovered that many of the show's contestants had been "coached" in advance. The show's producer, however, signed an affidavit swearing that Evans had not been a part of the sham. In 1959 Evans received a coveted Peabody Award for his work in the medium.[42]

In a slightly different area of entertainment, Jeff Shesol (1991) has rapidly become one of the top young syndicated cartoonists in the United States. His "Thatch" strip appears in one hundred and fifty newspapers across the country and has been hailed as the new "Doonesbury" for the twenty-something crowd. Shesol is also quickly establishing himself as a serious writer. His first book, *Mutual Contempt: Lyndon Johnson, Robert Kennedy, and the Feud that Defined a Decade* appeared in 1997.

On the administrative side of arts and entertainment, one could cite Frank Taplin (1937), who served as president of the Cleveland Orchestra and then president and CEO of the Metropolitan Opera. Stephen Stamas (1959) has held several prominent business posts, including a vice presidency at Exxon, while also serving as chairman of the New York Philharmonic. Dennis Stanfill (1950) rose to become chairman and CEO of Twentieth-Century Fox and later chairman of Metro-Goldwyn-Mayer. Frank Wells held the titles of president and CEO at Warner Brothers and later at Disney.

Nearly every field in the world of business has, at one time or another, had a Rhodes Scholar at or near its pinnacle. This short list will give some idea of the variety: Frederic Gamble (1920), president of the American Federation of Advertising Agencies; Carl Newton (1920), president of the Chesapeake & Ohio Railroad Company; William Vaughn (1925), chairman and CEO of Eastman Kodak; Malcolm MacIntyre (1929), president of Eastern Airlines and executive vice president of Martin Marietta; Harold Lumb (1933), vice president of law and corporate relations at Republic Steel; Dan McGurk (1949), president of the Computer Industry Association; Howard McKinley (1949), president of the Dubai Petroleum Company.

In the past couple of decades, the careers of Rhodes Scholars have reflected broad changes in trade and industry. A growing number of scholars have entered new or expanding areas like venture capitalism, the computer industry, and management consulting. The huge investment banking firm of Goldman Sachs, has included dozens of scholars over the past half century, but never as many as in the 1990s, when at any given moment at least a half dozen have been partners. McKinsey and Company is one of the country's largest and most aggressive management consulting firms, and since the 1980s its roster of partners has always included a dozen or more Rhodes Scholars.

In some cases, it is hard to see how Rhodes Scholar "captains of industry" are benefitting anyone but themselves. Among Rhodes Scholars, there is some occasional embarrassment on this topic. This has especially been true regarding McKinsey and Company. McKinsey sent recruiters to Oxford for the first time in 1985. Traditionally, the company had hired the top graduates from the Harvard Business School and a handful of other elite MBA programs. In 1985 the directors decided to branch out and increase the pool of likely candidates. What better recruiting ground than Oxford, where "the best men (and women) for the world's fight" were studying and preparing to enter the "real" world? The McKinsey team planned to interview Marshall and Fulbright Scholars, but their main catch would be the Rhodes Scholars. The Warden at that time, Dr. Robin Fletcher, permitted them to set up shop in Rhodes House – a decision that many Rhodes officials and scholars have since come to regret. About a half dozen Rhodes Scholars accepted jobs with the company. The starting salary of $60,000 was a definite attraction.[43]

It did not take long for McKinsey to become the infamous "M" word in Rhodes House, and its recruiters have never again held receptions there. Instead they have moved to the nearby Randolph Hotel. Over the past decade at least a couple of Rhodes Scholars have been hired each year – lured by starting salaries and signing bonuses that now exceed $100,000. McKinsey is both feared and respected for its work in advising corporations as they take over other companies or as they downsize to cut costs. This kind of activity might benefit the client companies (except for the employees who are downsized), but does it serve the public good in ways expected of Rhodes Scholars? That is a question asked by critics like Andrew Sullivan as well as many scholars themselves.

Several scholars who have become management consultants, investment bankers, and venture capitalists have defended their career choices by arguing that these careers have permitted them to earn enough money so that later they can quit business and enter public service. This argument is belied by the fact that at least half of all Rhodes Scholar businessmen/women have chosen to remain in their lucrative positions. Of course, this does not mean that they cannot benefit society by running efficient companies and, in their spare time, becoming involved in charities and community affairs. Stuart Swetland (1981) observes the following about several of his fellow scholars: they started out with idealism and a tremendous desire to change the world, were dazzled by the salaries offered by firms like McKinsey, intended to quit business as soon as they saved a sizable nestegg, and then in their thirties or forties realized they could not give up their comfortable lifestyles.[44]

One scholar who has candidly admitted this is Pat Haden. Nowadays he is a prosperous partner in the Los Angeles venture capital firm of Riordan, Lewis, and Haden. He is also a football commentator on Turner television and CBS radio. He has turned down other career opportunities, some of which could have taken him into public service, because he enjoys his business and sports jobs. He also likes having regular working hours that permit him to be at home at night with his four children. Finally, he admits that in his forties he has become more cynical about the world and less eager to devote all his energies to trying to improve it.[45] On Haden's behalf, one should add that he has coached three different little league teams and served on the boards of the University of Southern California, Boys Town, the Lifesavers Foundation, and the Los Angeles chapter of the Multiple Sclerosis Society.

One could cite several dozen other scholars who have successfully mixed business with public service or who have made personal fortunes and then quit business altogether. One of the most distinguished was Charles E. Saltzman (1925), who at varying times was a vice president of the New York Stock Exchange, and a partner in Goldman Sachs as well as other Wall Street investment firms. One of West Point's first Rhodes Scholars, Saltzman also had a distinguished military career: White House aide to Herbert Hoover, reentry into service in 1940 and eventual promotion to brigadier general. In between these jobs, he also worked as director of the American Zone in Austria, assistant secretary of state for Occupied Areas of Europe, and undersecretary of state for administration. The list of his decorations and awards would fill an entire page.

Other businessmen/public servants further demonstrate the diversity of Rhodes Scholars. Earl McGowin (1922) made a fortune in the lumber industry in Alabama, while at the same time serving for twenty years in his state legislature. Thanks to his lumber profits, he was able to establish several scholarship programs and donate funds for a new library at his old Oxford college, Pembroke. When George McGhee was at Oxford in the mid-1930s, he declared he would be a millionaire by the age of thirty. He kept that vow through good luck and hard work in the oil fields of Texas and Venezuela. He then spent most of the last three decades of his career in the army and the State Department. Among other positions, he served as U.S. ambassador to Turkey and West Germany.

McGhee's Oxford classmate John Templeton became perhaps the wealthiest Rhodes Scholar. Prior to his retirement in the early 1990s, he was regarded as one of the most astute gurus in the mutual fund business. Not content to manage his profitable Templeton Fund empire, he has remained active in philanthropy and education. In 1972 he created the annual Templeton Prize for Progress in Religion. He ensured that his yearly award was more lucrative than the Nobel Prizes, for he thought religion deserved more than any achievement in earthly sciences. Winners of his award have included Mother Teresa, Billy Graham, Paul Davies (an Australian mathematical physicist who has studied the relationship between science and religion), and Bill Bright (American evangelist and founder of Campus Crusade for Christ). The Templeton Foundation gives away millions of dollars each year for research, and it publishes books on religion, philosophy, and topics relating to spiritual health and happiness.

Since 1984 Templeton has contributed more than £7 million toward the upgrading of Oxford's Centre for Management Studies. In 1984 this Centre was transformed into Templeton College, which in 1995 finally acquired its charter as a fully recognized graduate college of the university. (Templeton was quick to stress that the name of the new college commemorated his parents, not himself.) In return for Templeton's benefactions, Queen Elizabeth II knighted him in 1987.[46]

One current example of a business entrepreneur who can now "afford" public service on a government salary is Ira Magaziner. For nearly two decades Magaziner earned up to $600 per hour advising Fortune 500 companies like Corning and General Electric. He was also hired by entire countries (Sweden, Ireland, Australia, Israel) to advise them on ways to energize their economies. Making a personal fortune for himself and helping corporations to please their stockholders was not enough, however. He turned to writing books about how U.S. political and business leaders could improve the lives of all citizens. One of his works, *Minding America's Business* (1982), was co-authored by fellow scholar Robert Reich.

When Magaziner's books failed to have the impact he desired, he decided to become more directly involved in the public sphere. He sold his private consulting firm, Telesis, in 1986, and established a private public policy institute. In 1993 and 1994 Magaziner became famous as the chief organizer of Bill Clinton's national health task force.

It is easy to see how other scholars have brought positive benefits to society through the very entrepreneurial endeavors that won them wealth and professional esteem. One recent example is John G. Simon (1984), chairman and CEO of UroMed, a dynamic young company that develops and markets products for the control of urological and gynecological disorders. .[47]

It is not surprising that a large number of American Rhodes Scholars have also become lawyers. Most attorneys are bright, good at working the "system," and articulate – some of the same qualities usually attributed to Rhodes Scholars. Given the fact that a large percentage of top college students in general opt for law school, it is perhaps natural that Rhodes Scholars share this tendency. On a per capita basis, the United States has a far larger number of lawyers, and lawsuits, than does any other country in the world.

About one-third of Rhodes Scholar attorneys have remained in private practice or in academic posts for most of their careers. Another third or so have spent most of their time as staff attorneys for private corporations. The remainder have devoted most of their careers to state or local government – as staff attorneys, judges, appointees of the party in power, and elected officials.

In response to critics who have complained that a well-paid job as a corporate attorney is not exactly public service, Rhodes Scholar lawyers have issued the same defenses offered by attorneys in general. The negative stereotypes of their profession, they maintain, should not blind one to the fact that most attorneys are honest and hard-working and help to ensure the smooth, orderly, and fair operation of U.S. government, society, and business.

Many Rhodes Scholar lawyers are also quick to point out that their profession is ideally suited to public service. Few other occupations provide the flexibility of being able to enter and reenter public life – secure in the knowledge that one can always return to private practice if one loses the next election or fails to get reappointed.

Despite the natural affinity of their profession to government, most Rhodes Scholar lawyers have never held public office. This nonpolitical majority would point out, however, that their profession as a whole contributes many pro bono hours to society at large each year – that is, free services to indigents, nonprofit organizations, and sundry public-interest causes. This is not the place for detailed discussion of the controversial topic of pro bono work. Suffice it to say that neither outside observers nor attorneys themselves have been able to agree to what level of pro bono activity constitutes an adequate amount of service to society.

One thing that does seem certain is that many attorneys (including some Rhodes Scholars) have not done enough for the public good. In 1965, as he neared the end of his career as a country lawyer, Axel Gravem (1918) candidly admitted, "I don't know, exactly, what my benefactor Cecil R. wanted me to accomplish, but whatever it was, I didn't do it."[48] Graven listed his life's achievements as getting an "undistinguished third" in his Oxford degree, helping to "lick the hell out of the Cantabs at tennis for three years," drinking his share of free beer at Vincent's Club, and paying off the mortgage on his house. With a bittersweet realization of the ordinariness of his life, George Tilley (1932) looked back on his law career some thirty years after Oxford:

> I sit around and fiddle with a few legal problems, none of which is apt to have a history-turning impact. I missed the boat by not getting into labor law and taxes, just pursuing a sort of fondness for what is quaintly called Common Law. I have published no texts or novels. In fact, let's face it, I haven't done much of distinction, run for any office, upheld any cause except justice, or tried to kill anybody except with kindness.[49]

One young Rhodes Scholar attorney (who will remain nameless) was interviewed in 1994 while in the midst of one of the country's biggest and bloodiest corporate takeover battles. This man's firm was fighting on behalf of a giant entertainment conglomerate against another entertainment conglomerate to see who could wrest control of yet a third entertainment conglomerate. When asked how this work was serving the public, he cited two ways: his CEO client was good at producing the kind of television shows and movies that

Americans wanted to see, and his client was good at earning profits for his stockholders. Realizing that these defenses might ring a little hollow, he quickly added that he planned eventually to leave his Manhattan firm and enter government. (As of this writing, that day has not yet come.)

Over the past twenty years many of the class notes in *The American Oxonian* have joked, sometimes uneasily, about the preponderance of attorneys. Bill Clinton's class of 1968 posted a record, when fifteen entered law school. Class secretary Robert Reich wryly admitted this was "a somewhat questionable distinction."[50] That record lasted only a few years. The class of 1972 was probably the most "legal" to the present date, with twenty-three lawyers.[51] In 1986 Linda Fletcher (1980) joked that she was proof "that not all Rhodes Scholars want to be lawyers when they grow up"; she was about to graduate from Harvard Medical School.[52] In 1991 Andrew Nussbaum, class of 1985 secretary, lightheartedly complained to his classmates, "Come on, people! In response to a request for opinions on the Iraqi War, and nominations for a Democratic presidential candidate, you send me only [news about] lawyers and babies."[53]

At times, the tone among Rhodes Scholars has been harsher. In 1983 Nicholas Kristof reported approvingly that the number of scholars turning to law was beginning to ebb. He also applauded those few young Rhodes Scholar attorneys who were bravely criticizing powerful law firms that did not donate sufficient time to pro bono activities.[54] In 1994 *The American Oxonian* published an article entitled "The Liberation of a Corporate Lawyer." The author, Duane Krohnke (1961), begins by stating, "What doth it profit a lawyer to make a bundle and lose his soul?"[55] Krohnke then proceeds to describe how he escaped the "billable-hour mindset" and became a pro bono attorney for aliens seeking asylum in the United States. Krohnke concludes by calling on all other Rhodes Scholars to take up the fight for human rights.

By and large, Rhodes Scholar attorneys have been "successful" as far as their standing in the profession goes. Few have been content to remain in small firms in small towns. But few Rhodes Scholars of any profession remain in small towns or "remote" states. The great majority reside on the east and west coasts, with the Washington, DC, New York City, and Boston areas being the most popular. Only a handful of former Rhodes Scholars of any profession currently reside in states like North Dakota, South Dakota, and Wyoming.

Those scholar attorneys who have stayed in private practice have tended to gravitate to the largest, most prestigious firms in the major

U.S. cities. Several blue-chip firms have been Rhodes Scholar "dens" for decades. Some that can usually count several Rhodes Scholars among their partners include Washington's Covington & Burling, Pittsburgh's Kirkpatrick & Lockhart, and Atlanta's Alston & Bird.

Despite the criticisms leveled against the legal profession, several dozen Rhodes Scholar attorneys clearly have met or exceeded any pro bono requirements during their careers. Approximately three dozen have devoted most of their careers to service as judges or public prosecutors – professions modestly remunerated when compared to private practice. One prominent example from the early scholars is John Kyle (1913). Over a span of forty-five years in his native Mississippi, he served as circuit judge, state senator, attorney general, and state supreme court justice.[56] The most famous scholar judges, of course, have been the three who have sat on the U.S. Supreme Court: John Marshall Harlan, Byron White, and David Souter (1961).

Several of Bill Clinton's lawyer classmates have distinguished themselves through their public service. As this book goes to press, Rick Stearns is a U.S. District Judge in Massachusetts. Alan Bersin is U.S. Attorney in the Southern District of California. Douglas Eakeley has been a national leader in promoting pro bono activities and for several years has headed the Legal Services Corporation, which provides aid to the indigent. Robert Reich held several federal posts in the 1970s and returned to Washington to serve as Clinton's Secretary of Labor. Tom Williamson left Washington's Covington & Burling and worked under Reich as chief solicitor in the Labor Department for the first three years of Clinton's presidency.

Many other scholar attorneys who have gone beyond the lucrative corridors of corporate law could be cited. Fowler Hamilton (1931) combined private practice in one of the country's most prestigious international law firms with distinguished government service. He served as U.S. assistant attorney general in the late 1930s, worked in the Board of Economic Warfare during the Second World War, and was appointed by John F. Kennedy as the first head of the Agency for International Development (AID).[57] A.B. Dick Howard (1958) has spent nearly his entire career on the faculty of the University of Virginia School of Law and is today recognized as one of the world's top constitutional experts. He was the chief author of the new Virginia state constitution that took effect in 1971. After the fall of Communism in the late 1980s and early 1990s, he helped write the new constitutions of Hungary, Poland, Bulgaria, Albania, Romania, and the Czech Republic.[58] Robert Edge has found a way to practice law while maintaining his passionate interest in music. For the past several years he has presided over the Atlanta Music Festival Association. As chair of the charitable Walter and Emilie Spivey Foundation, he sponsored a music series that coincided with the 1996 Olympics in Atlanta.[59] In October 1996 the city of Atlanta bestowed on him the W.H. Smith Lifetime Achievement Award for Business Leadership in the Arts. From 1973 to 1978 David Kendall (1966) worked as a staff counsel with the NAACP Legal Defense and Education Fund. In 1978 Mathew Valencic (1974) helped to establish HALT/Americans for Legal Reform, which has grown to include over 100,000 members and become a vocal lobbying group calling for equitable and efficient reforms of the legal system. Up to his death in a traffic accident in 1989, Valencic often found himself at loggerheads with lawyer-dominated state legislatures.[60] In 1995 attorney Peter Carfagna (1975) became co-owner of Cleveland radio station WMIH and gave it an all-Catholic format; "MIH" stands for Mary's Immaculate Heart.[61]

Journalism and Fiction

One of the few generalizations that hold true for nearly all Rhodes Scholars is that they are good talkers and writers. They have to be, in order to win their scholarships in the first place. It is not surprising, therefore, to see that a significant number of them have become journalists, broadcasters, novelists, and poets.

From the first half of the century, one could cite journalists Elmer Davis, Felix Morley, Beverly Smith (1920), Erwin Canham (1926), and Harlan Logan (1928). Davis was one of the most widely syndicated political commentators in newspapers, magazines, and radio. Morley edited the *Washington Post* from 1933 to 1940 and won a Pulitzer Prize in 1936 for his editorials. Smith worked for twenty years as Washington editor of the *Saturday Evening Post*, and Canham spent nearly half a century at the *Christian Science Monitor*, where he ended his career as editor- in-chief. Logan was the editor of *Scribner's* and later of *Look*.

During the past five decades, the *New York Times*, *Washington Post*, *Time*, and other major newspapers and magazines have always counted several scholars on their staffs. These have included three managing editors at *Time*, Hedley Donovan, Jason McManus, and Walter Isaacson; one managing editor of *U.S. News & World Report*, James Fallows; three editors of *Harper's*, John Fischer, Willie Morris, and Michael Kinsley. The latter probably holds some sort of record:

in addition to the top spot at *Harper's*, he has served as editor of *The New Republic* on two separate occasions, worked as "American Survey" editor of *The Economist*, and appeared weekly for several years as the house liberal on CNN's "Crossfire." In 1995 Washington-insider Kinsley astonished his fellow journalists by moving from the Capital to the "other" Washington. In Seattle he took on the editorship of Microsoft's experimental electronic magazine *Slate*.

Among women Rhodes Scholars, two thus far have gained national attention for their nonfiction books. Feminist champion Naomi Wolf has garnered both plaudits and derisive criticism for her string of bestsellers: *The Beauty Myth* (1992), *Fire with Fire* (1993), and *Promiscuities* (1997). Caroline Alexander has written books about exotic locales, such as *The Way to Xanadu* (1994), plus a study of black college athletes, *Battle's End: A Seminole Football Team Revisited* (1996).

Among those Rhodes Scholars who have become famous for their novels, short stories, and poems, several can be classified as literary "heavyweights." These include novelists Reynolds Price and John Edgar Wideman, novelist/poet Robert Penn Warren, and poets such as John Crowe Ransom, Robert Peter Tristram Coffin, Thomas McGrath (1939), Guy Davenport, and William Jay Smith (1947). Coffin won a Pulitzer prize for his poetry, but Warren holds the record in this regard: he won three Pulitzers, two for poetry and one for his novel *All the King's Men*. In 1968 Smith was appointed poetry consultant to the Library of Congress, and in 1986 Warren became the country's first poet laureate.

Of these writers, only Smith has frequently used Oxford in his works. Among other things, he has contributed several poems about Oxford to *The American Oxonian* over the years. When Guy Davenport was asked if Oxford had figured in any of his poems, he could recall only that it "may" have been mentioned in a couple of his early creations.[62]

Oxford appears prominently in only one of Reynolds Price's novels. Three of his books constitute a trilogy, as they trace the life of a professor of English at Duke University who studied John Milton in Oxford – all this like Price himself. The second book in the series, *The Source of Light* (1981), is set partly in Oxford. The protagonist, Hutchins Mayfield, finds himself one of the few students left in his college over one vacation. He can hear the dons, "surely brandied as Christmas peaches ... snoring in the chill."[63] Writing home, he laments:

Isn't this the first day of spring? I ask because I'm a shut-in here – the third straight day of rain, the air's solid water. I wonder how I'm breathing; gills would seem called for. And in fact there were long welts under my jaws when I looked just now – I'm evolving to last in a new world, I trust.

It's Easter vacation, six long weeks of it. After Easter I'll probably spend a week or so in Cumberland and Scotland ... Reading, reading – slow progress, wearing these deep-sea goggles.[64]

Through the first half of this century the Rhodes Scholar writer who was best known to the public at large was Christopher Morley. Along with his brothers Felix and Frank, "Kit" Morley ranked among the most anglophilic of all Rhodes Scholars. Through more than four decades after his return from Oxford in 1913, Morley proved himself a versatile and productive man of letters. He helped to found *The Saturday Review of Literature*, and he wrote or edited over forty books – novels, collected essays, and plays. He contributed countless reviews and articles to various magazines, and in his spare time he worked with a theater company in Hoboken, New Jersey. Morley's most popular work was *Kitty Foyle*, an atypically serious, tender love story about a working girl. Ginger Rogers won an Oscar when she played the title role in the 1940 film adaptation. Morley used Oxford as the setting for his novel *Kathleen*, and in his essays and other occasional pieces he often waxed nostalgic about merry old England. His literary style could best be characterized as whimsical archness. He was one of the creators of the Sherlock Holmes fan club known as the Baker Street Irregulars. In his entry for the British *Who's Who*, he listed his hobbies as "secondhand bookstores, whisky and plain water, swimming, and cooking." He compiled the eleventh edition of *Bartlett's Familiar Quotations*, at the end of one section he inserted his own quotation in Latin. Translated into English it says, "I've finished the job; for Christ's sake give me a drink."[65] A genuine "character," Morley became a popular radio and television pundit during his final years. In its obituary for Morley, the *New York Times* praised him but recognized that his fame was evanescent; the newspaper called him "one of the best minor writers of his time."[66]

Numerous other Rhodes Scholars have written novels or poems, but few have actually earned their living from it. Psychiatrist Stephen Bergman (1966), whose pen name is Samuel Shem, M.D., has written several novels and plays. His first work *The House of God* (1978), was a searing satire about a big-city hospital. It quickly became a cult classic among medical students around the country and inspired the television series *St. Elsewhere*. The hero of the novel, a former Rhodes Scholar, describes himself to a fellow intern in this way:

Me? I look great on paper. For three years after college I was on a
Rhodes Scholarship to England.
   Damn! You must be some ath-a-lete. What's your sport?
   Golf.
   You gotta be kiddin'. With those little white balls?
   Right. Oxford got fed up with the dumb Rhodes jocks, so they went in
more for brains my year. One guy's sport was bridge.[67]

Two particularly humorous novels based in Oxford stand out
among the writings of Rhodes Scholars – *The Great Pretender* by
James Atlas (1971) and *The Tormenting of Lafayette Jackson* by Andrew
Rosenheim (1977). Both writers poke fun at their surroundings and at
themselves.

Atlas works today on the staff of *The New Yorker* and writes biographies of literary figures like Delmore Schwartz and Saul Bellow. His
one effort at fiction, *The Great Pretender,* concerns Ben, a recent college graduate on fellowship in Oxford. He is not a Rhodes Scholar,
but he suffers through the same dreaded imposter complex. (How
did *I* get here? They must have made a mistake.) Shortly after arrival
in Britain, Ben meets Warren:

> Warren couldn't have been more than a year or two older than me, but
> he'd already perfected the manner of an Oxford don: the murmurous
> expostulations; the snuffling, throat-clearing stammer; the crisp emphasis
> of *actually* and *quite.*[68]

As did Atlas in real life, Ben resigns his scholarship and returns
home after one year.

Andrew Rosenheim is one of the handful of American Rhodes
Scholars who have made Oxford their home. Nowadays he lives on
Boar's Hill, which gives him the best view of the dreaming spires,
and he works at Oxford University Press as Director of Electronic
Publishing. His first novel, *The Tormenting of Lafayette Jackson,* is a
hilarious, thinly veiled recollection of the author's own days at Pembroke College. Though Rosenheim personally admired and liked
many of his Rhodes classmates, he lampoons some of them merci-
lessly in his book. The unnamed protagonist of the book is a keen
observer of all the "specimens" surrounding him. There is, for example, Sally Archimedes, "a Rhodes Scholar of fierce ambition and
voluminous thighs. She wanted badly to be a famous journalist and
worked during vacations as a 'stringer' for *Newsweek.*"[69] She enjoys a
hyperactive sex life and, in emulation of men, tells all her friends of
her conquests.
   Another character in the book is Charlie Bicker. He was:

... tall and brash and the most successful person I had ever met. He was not yet twenty-five but already in his second term in the New Hampshire state legislature ... This caused havoc with his tutorial schedule and extended his stay at Oxford by a year, but Bicker handled the resulting uncertainty, as he managed all mundane difficulties, with unflappable ease.

He had graduated from Princeton *summa cum laude* and reached Oxford on a Rhodes Scholarship. He had founded a successful newspaper in his New Hampshire hometown and in addition to his legislative duties worked as a peripatetic adviser to one of New Hampshire's two United States senators. He was, to boot, attractive to women ... Bicker, in short, had everything going for him.

... I liked him just the same. His self-assurance was accompanied by true modesty as well, and a willingness (rare in a Rhodes Scholar) to play second fiddle to a louder or more interesting set of strings. And Bicker's brashness brought with it a refreshing honesty... The Rhodes Scholars then at Oxford all seemed to want to be senators, and they acted accordingly in the manner they thought necessary for that role. Some were quite brilliant, some were astonishingly dull; all were accomplished in the dubious art of impressing their seniors and filling their peers with envious awe. They were always so tactful, bringing to the simplest act of friendship a diplomatic subtlety that I thought had expired with Dean Acheson. They remembered names, nicknames, alma maters, hometowns, birthdays, and, less openly, other peoples' failures; and they would greet the most casual acquaintance ... with the oiliness politicians exude as they turn from their chicken and peas to pump hands with their fund-raising dinnermates.[70]

Like many characters in the book, Bicker is a thinly veiled recreation of a real person. When Rosenheim's friend and classmate William Hunter first read the book he saw in a flash that *he* was Bicker – though it was in the Vermont legislature that Hunter sat while studying in Oxford.[71]

Government

Despite all the achievements of Rhodes Scholars in education, business, law, literature, and other professions, most Rhodes Scholars have realized that the type of person Cecil Rhodes especially had in mind was one who would pursue a full-time career in government. That field, Rhodes believed, was the one in which a man could effect broad change – presumably for the better. Yet the number of scholars in local, state, and federal government has remained at a steady 7 percent.

Rhodes officials and former scholars have addressed this issue in various ways. One response goes roughly along the lines, "Who cares what Rhodes wanted? Times have changed. If we stuck closely to what he desired, we would all be racist imperialists." Another line of defense is that society needs intelligent, honest lawyers, teachers, and businessmen. Most Rhodes Scholars are skillful and decent people. According to this argument, scholars can therefore be counted on to elevate the level of any profession they join.

Yet another approach is that of enumerating the Rhodes Scholars who have distinguished themselves in government service. About two hundred scholars have spent most of their working lives in government – the great majority of them at the federal level. In addition to the judges and public prosecutors, many have been career civil servants. They have worked in U.S. embassies and consulates around the world and in every domestic government agency. Most of them have had solid, but undistinguished, careers.

Perhaps forty or so can be said to have had a significant, national impact in their particular areas. One such person was Stanley Hornbeck (1904). From the presidency of Woodrow Wilson through that of Franklin Delano Roosevelt, Hornbeck was the principal China expert in the Department of State, serving as chief of the Division of Far Eastern Affairs for ten years.[72] Another was Charles Mahaffie (1905), who was appointed chairman of the Interstate Commerce Commission in 1936 and again in 1949. Robert Hale (1910) served in Maine's House of Representatives from 1923 to 1930, his last two years as Speaker. Arthur Hayes (1955) served as Commissioner of the Food and Drug Administration in the early 1980s. Several scholars have served as big-city mayors, including Richard Lugar in Indianapolis, Kurt Schmoke in Baltimore, and Thomas Allen (1967) in Portland, Maine.

Three scholars have become state governors: David Boren in Oklahoma; Richard Celeste (1960) in Ohio, and Bill Clinton in Arkansas. Twelve scholars have been elected to the U.S. House of Representatives: Robert Hale, Charles Clason (1914), J. William Fulbright, Carl Albert, John Brademas, Elliott Levitas (1952), Paul Sarbanes, Larry Pressler (1964), Thomas Allen, Tom McMillen, Jim Cooper (1975), and Mel Reynolds (1975). Seven reached the Senate: Fulbright, Lugar, Sarbanes, Boren, Pressler, Bill Bradley, and Russell Feingold (1975). More than a dozen have been appointed ambassadors to various countries around the world. In 1961 Dean Rusk became the first of several scholars to rise to cabinet-level rank, when John F. Kennedy named him Secretary of State. One Rhodes Scholar, to date, has been elected President of the United States.

These individuals and a few others, however, have been the exceptions rather than the rule. Andrew Sullivan's piece in *Spy* was right on target when it said that most Rhodes Scholars who have entered government have preferred the relatively safe, unspectacular, but solid road of appointed bureaucratic office to the uncertain, rough-and-tumble world of elective politics. Over the past three-quarters of a century Frank Aydelotte, Rhodes House wardens, Rhodes Trustees, and many scholars themselves have also admitted this.[73]

There is much evidence to show that many scholars do not believe their own words when they say that one can "fight the world's fight" in many kinds of careers besides government and politics. After Dean Rusk was appointed Secretary of State in 1961, *The American Oxonian* jubilantly noted that his new job had "deep meaning for Rhodes Scholars everywhere."[74] Rarely, if ever, had the magazine celebrated the accomplishments of a teacher, lawyer, or businessman in such solemn fashion. When Bill Clinton was elected President in 1992, the vast majority of Rhodes Scholars breathed a long, collective sigh of relief. Finally, one of their own had made it to the top. Of course, *The American Oxonian* devoted much space to the event. For the first time in its history, the magazine published a cartoon. Jeff Shesol's humorous sketch pokes fun at Clinton and at the many scholars who hoped to win jobs in the White House. Again, the magazine has never celebrated so lavishly the success of any non-politician scholar.

At the opening session of the Rhodes Scholar reunion at Georgetown in 1993, the hall was filled with about nine hundred scholars plus their spouses. Several Rhodes Scholar "dignitaries" who were present were singled out and asked to stand. They were not the university presidents, the AIDS researchers, or the award-winning writers. Rather, they were the Senators and White House staffers.

Special Achievements

Another way of measuring the accomplishments of Rhodes Scholars is to survey the awards they have won as well as the other ways they have received special notice. No U.S. scholar thus far has won a Nobel Prize, though Australia's Sir Howard Florey (1921) shared the award for physiology and medicine in 1945. U.S. scholars, however, have picked up twelve Pulitzer Prizes thus far: four in journalism (by Felix Morley, Robert Lasch [1928], Edwin Yoder, and Nicholas Kristof); four in literature (one by Robert Peter Tristram Coffin and three by Robert Penn Warren); and four in history and biography (by Bernadotte Schmitt, Daniel Boorstin, Robert K. Massie, and

Lawrence Henry Gipson). Six scholars have won the lucrative MacArthur Foundation Fellowships; these so-called "genius" awards have gone to poets Robert Penn Warren and Guy Davenport, historians Robert Darnton and William Cronon, physicist Frank von Hippel (1959), and sociologist John Gaventa.

Rhodes Scholars can also be found in less weighty categories of awards and achievements. For several years in the 1940s Arthur Chenoweth (1907) served as board member and, eventually, as president of the Miss America Pageant.[75] In 1955 two Rhodes Scholars won fame on television. Frank Swain (1913), then a judge in the Superior Court of Los Angeles, won the $10,000 jackpot on Groucho Marx's "You Bet Your Life."[76] Eddie Eagan, former Olympic champion and at that time the head of the U.S. Olympic Finance Committee, coached psychologist Dr. Joyce Brothers and shared her glory when she won the "$64,000 Question" in the category of boxing.[77]

When the popular PBS television program "Wall $treet Week with Louis Rukeyser" decided in the 1980s to establish a "Hall of Fame" to honor some of the experts who had appeared on the show, John Templeton was one of the first to be inducted. Kris Kristofferson is a member of the Country Music Hall of Fame, and in 1995 he was named the first winner in the annual Roger Miller Songwriter Award.[78] Joseph Torsella (1986) garnered his fifteen minutes of glory in 1995, when he resigned his post as a deputy mayor of Philadelphia in order to market his new invention, a spaghetti smock. The *New York Times* headlined its story on Torsella with the query: "For This He Needed to Become a Rhodes Scholar?"[79] In 1996 *Swing* magazine named Rhodes Scholar cartoonist Jeff Shesol in its list of "30 Most Powerful Twentysomethings in America." (Others on the list included actress Alicia Silverstone, talk show host Ricki Lake, rap singer Snoop Doggy Dog, and Netscape cofounder Marc Andreessen.)[80] For the past several years Harvard professor and national security expert Joseph Nye has been included in the Teaching Company's All-American "Dream Team" of great university lecturers; he and a small number of other academics can be heard and seen on videotapes and cassettes sold across the country.

Rhodes Scholars can be found in most national listings of "first this," or "greatest that." Pete Dawkins, for example, not only won the Heisman Trophy in football and a Rhodes Scholarship, but, at age forty-one, became the youngest person ever appointed brigadier general in the U.S. Army. In 1990 the Capitol Hill press corps selected Senators Richard Lugar and Paul Sarbanes for the elite group of "20 Smartest Members of Congress." Lugar was praised for actually writing his own books; Sarbanes was judged perhaps the wisest member of the Senate.[81] (On the other hand, during his three terms in the Senate, Rhodes Scholar Larry Pressler was invariably denigrated as one of the true lightweights in that body – "Senator Clueless" or "Forrest Gump," according to some critics. Even fellow Republicans like Bob Dole occasionally made jests at his expense.)[82]

When the respected, best-selling author David Halberstam was asked in 1984 to pick the number one journalist from the baby boomer generation, he unhesitatingly named Rhodes Scholar James Fallows.[83] In 1995 *Newsweek* devoted nearly an entire issue to those Americans rising to the top in America's emerging meritocracy. Those listed in the magazine's "Overclass 100" included Rhodes Scholars Kurt Schmoke, George Stephanopoulos (1984), Franklin Raines, Robert Reich, Strobe Talbott, and Walter Isaacson.[84] On several occasions over the years, *Time* has named "future" leaders of America. There have always been some Rhodes Scholars in these exclusive lists: Bill Clinton, Bill Bradley, and Lester Thurow in the early 1980s; Harvard Law School's Randall Kennedy, Clinton White House staffer Nancy-Ann Min (1979), and writer Naomi Wolf in the 1990s.[85]

In short, one can conclude that the great majority of Rhodes Scholars have had solid, respectable careers. Few of them have "changed the world," but most of them have been a credit to their professions, their families, and their communities. As a group, they have achieved success – on a local, and sometimes a national, level.

NOTES

1. A paragraph or so on each scholar can be found in the *Register of Rhodes Scholars* published by Rhodes House in 1981 and updated in 1996.
2. *TAO*, 5 (1918): 107.
3. *TAO*, 15 (1928): 182.
4. *TAO*, 19 (1932): 260-61.
5. Interviews with Kenny, 38 July 1993; Alexander, 23 May 1995; and Gerson, 10 October 1997. When Alexander gave up the secretaryship early in 1998, he became the new editor of *The American Oxonian*. Kenny is due to retire as warden in August 1999. In April 1998, the Rhodes Trustees announced that his successor will be Dr. John Rowett, a historian at Brasenose College.
6. *Washington Post*, 18 October 1992, C5.
7. *TAO*, 14 (1927): 32.
8. *TAO*, 23 (1936): 68.
9. *Scribner's Magazine*, January 1938, 9.
10. *Ibid.*, 10.
11. *Oxford Today*, Trinity issue, 1993, 7.
12. Andrew Sullivan, "All Rhodes Lead Nowhere in Particular," *Spy*, October 1988, 108-09.
13. Ibid., 108.
14. Ibid., 110.
15. John Funari interview, 11 October 1993.
16. Sullivan,"All Rhodes," 114.
17. Charles C. Mann, "The Man with All the Answers," *The Atlantic Monthly*, January 1990, 45.
18. Christianson, *Edwin Hubble*, 210, 317, and passim.
19. *TAO*, 40 (1953): 89; 45 (1958): 170; 63 (1976): 343-44.
20. *TAO*, 9 (1922): 67.
21. *Minneapolis Star Tribune*, 9 January 1995, 11A.
22. Blanshard, *Aydelotte*, chaps. 9-14; *TAO*, 38 (1951): 1-23.
23. *Time*, 5 June 1933.
24. Blanshard, *Aydelotte*, 135.
25. Rusk, *As I Saw It*, 84-85.
26. *TAO*, 25 (1938): 12-14; 55 (1968): 276-80; 69 (1982): 123- 26.
27. *The Capital* (Washington, DC), 12 April 1996, C1; *Washington Post*, 5 September 1996, M1; *TAO*, 84 (1997): 3-17.
28. *TAO*, 35 (1948): 249; 48 (1961): 199; 49 (1962): 179-85.
29. Turner interview, 31 March 1994.
30. *U.S. News & World Report*, 18 April 1988, 33ff.; *Washington Post*, 28 April 1991, C2; *Atlantic Monthly*, September 1996, 75-90.
31. Donna L. Bunce, "From Scholarship to Leadership: Rhodes Scholars and International Exchange Programs," unpublished paper, St. Bonaventure University, 1994.
32. Wayne W. Plasha, "The Marshall Scholarship Selection Process: Substantive Bias and Institutional Reform," unpublished paper, 1992; *TAO*, 81 (1994): 13-19.
33. Blanshard, *Aydelotte*, 245; *TAO*, 12 (1925): 53-54, 160.
34. Interviews with Kenny, 28 July 1993; Alexander, 23 May 1995; and Gerson, 10 October 1997.
35. Griffin interview, 27 July 1993.

36. *Sunday Times*, 13 October 1996, Home News section.
37. Howlett interview, 12 August 1993.
38. Cleary Kiely interview, 6 July 1994. Like several other women Rhodes Scholars, Cleary Kiely has interrupted her career to raise a family and accommodate her husband's job requirements. In 1996 she left teaching and moved to Paris, where her spouse accepted a position with the Banque Nationale de Paris.
39. Interviews with Funari, 11 October 1993, and Brown, 26 June 1997.
40. Stephen J. Carter in the *New Yorker*, 9 August 1993, 86.
41. For example, *TAO*, 42 (1955): 223.
42. *TAO*, 65 (1978): 185-86.
43. *TAO*, 73 (1986): 93-94.
44. Swetland interview, 20 February 1996.
45. Haden interview, 13 May 1994; *Los Angeles Times*, 10 December 1992, C3.
46. Templeton interview, 2 August 1994; *Oxford Today*, Trinity Issue, 1995, 40.
47. Simon interview, 11 April 1996; *PR Newswire*, 25 July 1996.
48. *TAO*, 52 (1965): 138.
49. *TAO*, 53 (1966): 214.
50. *TAO*, 60 (1973): 170.
51. *TAO*, 67 (1990): 192.
52. *TAO*, 73 (1986): 63-64.
53. *TAO*, 78 (1991): 368.
54. *TAO*, 70 (1983): 198-99.
55. *TAO*, 81 (1994): 146.
56. *TAO*, 52 (1965): 147.
57. *TAO*, 71 (1984): 243-46.
58. *TAO*: 68 (1981): 147; 83 (1996): 138.
59. Edge interview, 9 July 1996; *Atlanta Journal and Constitution*, 11 April 1995, 8E.
60. *TAO*, 71 (1984): 90; *San Diego Union Tribune*, 1 May 1984, B3.
61. *Phoenix Gazette*, 29 April 1995, B5.
62. Davenport, letter to authors, 30 June 1995.
63. Reynolds Price, *The Source of Light* (New York, 1981), 312.
64. Ibid., 316.
65. Mark Wallach and Jon Bracker, *Christopher Morley* (Boston, 1976), 14.
66. *NYT Book Review*, 14 April 1957, 2. Also see *Saturday Review*, 13 April 1957, 22; and *TAO*, 44 (1957): 158-63; 50 (1963): 101.
67. Samuel Shem, *The House of God* (New York, 1978), 31-32.
68. James Atlas, *The Great Pretender* (New York, 1986), 199.
69. Andrew Rosenheim, *The Tormenting of Lafayette Jackson* (Boston, 1988), 8.
70. Ibid., 75-76.
71. Hunter interview, 8 August 1996.
72. *TAO*, 54 (1967): 103-5; Shizhang Hu, *Stanley K. Hornbeck and the Open Door Policy, 1919-1937* (Westport, CT, 1995).
73. *TAO*, 8 (1921): 35; 11 (1924): 56-57; 23 (1936): 113; 60 (1973): 71; 71 (1984): 7.
74. *TAO*, 48 (1961): 1.
75. *TAO*, 37 (1950): 141.
76. *TAO*, 43 (1956): 187.
77. *TAO*, 43 (1956): 200.
78. *The Record*, 26 August 1995, L1.
79. *NYT*, 19 November 1995, F9.
80. *Austin American-Statesman*, 19 January 1996, F1.

81. *Roll Call*, 5 March 1990.
82. *Time*, 12 June 1995, 42-43; 19 August 1996, 30.
83. *Christian Science Monitor*, 12 May 1989, 13.
84. *Newsweek*, 31 July 1995.
85. *Time*, 5 December 1994, 48-75.

Chapter 15

THE OXFORD FACTOR

Winning a Rhodes Scholarship is one of the few things you can do at twenty-two they will chisel on your tombstone. No matter what else you do in life, that will be remembered.

Lester Thurow, class of 1960

Oxford has been a place of self-reflection for many of us. I think this is partially because ... many of us are able for the first time to "get off the train" which is moving quickly somewhere else – in New York, or Boston, or Washington, or San Francisco – to reconsider our place on that train. I think that this kind of reflection is hard to do unless it is possible to be outside ourselves for a little while.

Sarah Light, class of 1995

A Lasting Influence?

The previous chapter described the occupations and achievements of Rhodes Scholars. A related, and perhaps more important, issue is this: to what extent did the Rhodes Scholarships help to determine what the recipients accomplished in their lives? In other words, might J. William Fulbright, Byron White, Kris Kristofferson, and Naomi Wolf have ended up with the same jobs and awards if they had not gone to Oxford? In response to this question, several scholars have used the example of Bill Clinton and agreed that, with or without Oxford, he was determined and probably destined to become President. Is this true for Clinton as well as for the lives of other scholars?

There is no scientific means of measuring this question. Each person is shaped by every experience he or she undergoes – whether this be the birth of a child, a trip to Disneyland, years spent in a job, weddings and funerals, or residence in Oxford as a Rhodes Scholar.

Few individuals can select one incident or period in their lives and say that it was *the* big turning point for them personally or profes-

Notes for this chapter can be found on page 340.

sionally. The same goes for Rhodes Scholars. When asked how important the Oxford experience was for them, only a handful have said it transformed their lives in dramatic ways that could not have occurred otherwise. This fairly small number tend to have two things in common: in Oxford they studied in the areas for which Oxford is especially renowned; and after Oxford they pursued careers in academe. They include philosophers like Ronald Dworkin and James Griffin and medievalist David Howlett. These three individuals have rhapsodized about what it was like to study in Oxford in the 1950s and 1960s. In those decades Oxford was still the center of the universe in fields like philosophy, history, and law, with luminaries like H.L.A. Hart, J.L. Austin, Gilbert Ryle, Isaiah Berlin, and A.J.P. Taylor. Not coincidentally, Griffin, Dworkin, and Howlett today are members of the Oxford faculty.[1]

Only a few non-academics have reported that their coursework in Oxford had as great an impact on them. One of these is Stansfield Turner, who says that his challenging tutorials made him think and write on a level far higher than otherwise would have been the case.[2] As noted earlier, Oxford also inspired him to initiate his educational reforms at the Naval War College.

Many Rhodes Scholars cite non-academic ways in which the experience changed their lives. Dozens met their future spouses in Oxford. Since the entry of women into the program in 1977 there have been several cases of Rhodes Scholars marrying other Rhodes Scholars. Getting married is a major event in one's life, but it is not one of the major goals of the scholarship program. A person is just as likely to meet his or her future spouse in an elevator or a supermarket checkout line.

Some scholars report that the scholarships changed their career paths somewhat accidentally. Richard Celeste and George Stephanopoulos are thankful for Oxford because it kept them from going to law school; neither of them wanted to be lawyers, but without Oxford they might have followed that route in preparation for careers in government.[3] Oxford had the reverse impact on James Woolsey and Robert Edge. When they arrived there in the 1960s each aspired to a career in academe: Woolsey in history, and Edge in English literature or music. Both men loved Oxford but found that they were unsuited to a monkish academic life filled with unending reading lists. Upon returning to the United States, each entered law school.[4] Erwin Fleissner planned to become a philosopher when he arrived in Oxford in 1957. However, he found his tutor so unappealing and unchallenging that he turned instead to a career in medical research.[5]

Stuart Swetland's plans also were "derailed" by Oxford. When the Annapolis graduate arrived there in 1981, he assumed that he would return home to spend the rest of his life in the military. He did serve in the Persian Gulf War in 1991, but in Oxford he had been able to explore his inner thoughts more deeply than ever before. While reading PPE he converted from Lutheranism to Roman Catholicism. After the Gulf War he obtained permission to cut short his military service and enter a Catholic seminary. Today he works as a parish priest.[6]

Sometimes it is only years later that a scholar realizes how important Oxford was. *Time*'s Walter Isaacson, for example, studied PPE in Oxford "just for the fun of it." Subsequently, "both as a journalist and biographer, I've been surprised how often all the glories of Locke-Berkeley-Hume-Kant turned out to be not only interesting but useful."[7] This became especially clear in the early 1990s, when he was writing his magisterial biography of Henry Kissinger, who was himself an ardent student of Kant.

Bernard Rogers loved Oxford and returned there often in the decades after his student days in the late 1940s. It was only in the last phase of his career, however, that he realized how important his humanistic training in PPE had been for his life in the army. From 1979 to 1987 he served as NATO's Supreme Allied Commander in Europe. That job required wide knowledge about the culture and history of many countries plus acute skills in logic and communication. For the first time, Rogers felt that he was putting his Oxford training to good use. While serving as Supreme Commander he visited his old Oxford college (University) often. In 1983 he received an honor that pleased him perhaps more than any other: he and Robert Penn Warren were among the five people awarded honorary doctorates during a general Rhodes Scholar reunion in Oxford.[8]

When asked how the Oxford experience was important for them, the most common answer that scholars give is that it "broadened" them culturally and intellectually. For the great majority, it was their first time living abroad and their first opportunity to travel widely. Bill Bradley is a perfect illustration of this. When asked about Oxford, he has responded:

> My experiences as a Rhodes Scholar had a profound effect on me. The time I spent at Oxford allowed me to grow, both academically and personally ... I developed a new perspective on the United States – its traditions, culture, institutions, and people – by viewing it from the outside. Being in Oxford gave me a new frame for understanding the world and my role in it.[9]

Bradley is quick to add, however, that "other experiences have also played a contributing role" in shaping his views.

The second most common answer that scholars give, when asked how Oxford was important for them, is that it was a sort of intellectual vacation or respite from the pressures of home. As noted throughout this book, Rhodes Scholars since the beginning have devoted much of their energy to socializing and traveling. This was especially true for those scholars who were not intending to pursue careers in academe. Future lawyers, physicians, politicians, and the like realized that their Oxford degrees would not be particularly important for their later careers. Dean Rusk, Hedley Donovan, Bill Bradley, Bill Clinton, and Pat Haden are just a few of the many who have said that Oxford gave them one brief period in their lives when they could step off the fast track. As undergraduates in the United States, they felt driven to excel in academics, sports, and other activities. They would resume this hyperkinetic, high-pressure lifestyle after Oxford, when they resumed their ambitious climbs to success in their chosen fields.

Years later many fondly recalled that Oxford represented the only time in their lives when they had time for wide reading and thoughtful introspection.[10] Robert Reich, for example, has said that as an undergraduate at Dartmouth he ran around like a headless chicken; in Oxford he could "contemplate, assess, read, explore."[11] James Billington recalls that time seemed to slow down in Oxford. In the more relaxed atmosphere he found time to peruse all the classics of Russian literature for which he had no time back home. It should be noted, however, that the ambitious Billington also found time to complete his D.Phil. in Russian history. For George Stephanopoulos Oxford also represented a break from the norm. Prior to going to Oxford he had already worked on the staff of one U.S. Congressman and knew that he would return to the political arena afterward. Therefore in Oxford he chose to do something entirely unrelated to his career: he obtained a M.St. degree in theology.[12] (Often called a "choir boy," Stephanopoulos is the son and grandson of Greek Orthodox priests.)

The Rhodes system itself fosters this type of experience. Again and again during his long tenure as Warden of Rhodes House, E.T. Williams told scholars that they should "waste" their time in Oxford.[13] By this he meant taking time to think deep thoughts, reading books not directly related to one's career, traveling, and participating in lively discussions. Many of the former scholars who serve on selection committees tell the newly selected scholars the same thing. One journalist has said that the Rhodes system encourages "bars over the books."[14] Jacob Weisberg candidly acknowledges that for most Rhodes Scholars "the dominant academic message is: Relax."[15]

Some skeptics might scoff that the Rhodes Scholarships therefore have been nothing more than an extended vacation for pampered young men and women who were already destined for professional success. In short, does the endowment created by the imperialist Rhodes at the expense of millions of black Africans simply enable a lot of mostly white, mostly middle-class, mostly male young Americans to have an extended holiday?

Certainly, that has been the case for some scholars. On the other hand, many scholars have successfully mixed hard academic work in Oxford with their social life and travels. Moreover, several psychologists and other social scientists have concluded that such a "vacation" or temporary diversion from one's career path is often important for later success. Statistical studies of thousands of people who have achieved significant success in government, business, and other fields indicate that a high percentage of them had such an "incubation" period as young adults. This brief detour afforded them a time for reflection and exploration that would prove valuable in their later lives. One expert who has written extensively about the importance of such a "vacation" or "moratorium" is the late Erik Erikson. In his famous psychobiography of Martin Luther, Erikson claims to see such a phenomenon not only in Luther (with his years in a monastery prior to initiating the Protestant Reformation), but also in such diverse figures as Jesus (forty days in the desert), Charles Darwin (whose first choice of career had been medicine), and George Bernard Shaw (a business trainee before turning to literature).[16]

Cecil Rhodes himself may have enjoyed such a moratorium. Biographer Robert Rotberg suggests that Rhodes' trips back to the relatively quiet, slower-paced life in Oxford provided the ambitious young man with just the sort of environment he needed to chart his later career as an entrepreneur, explorer, and politician.[17] How appropriate, therefore, that his scholarships have been important in providing the same sort of introspective respite to all the young men and women who have received them.

A Ticket to Success?

One of the most common assumptions about Rhodes Scholars is that, once they return home, they have a guaranteed ticket to success. Having "Rhodes Scholar" on one's résumé and mentioning it casually in a job interview are thought, by many observers, to ensure wealth, fame, and power. The previous chapter's discussion of scholars' careers should dispel much of this stereotype. Most scholars have had solid, but not spectacular, careers. For those who have risen to the top, however, can one conclude that their Rhodes Scholarships were essential in the path to success?

In 1993 Rhodes House Warden Anthony Kenny reported the findings of a survey conducted among all living Rhodes Scholars. Among American scholars, 28 percent said the awards had been "very important" in landing them the jobs they sought. Another 34 percent said the scholarships were of "some" help. Those reporting that the scholarships were of little or no relevance to their professional advancement amounted to 38 percent.[18]

There are virtually no recorded examples of a person obtaining any job or promotion solely because he or she was a Rhodes Scholar. But having "Rhodes Scholar" on one's résumé does add luster to the credentials of a job applicant. In interview after interview, scholars have readily acknowledged this. The scholarship, they say, indicates that one is bright and ambitious. Because of the criteria for winning the award include a concern for one's fellow human beings, the scholarship also gives some indication of honesty and compassion.

John Brademas summarized this attitude when he said that a Rhodes Scholarship serves as a sort of Good Housekeeping Seal of Approval.[19] Kurt Schmoke agrees that the scholarship on one's résumé provides a "presumption of competence."[20] Randall Kennedy has said that a Rhodes Scholarship is an "all-purpose calling card."[21]

In short, the award opens doors and often gets one to the interview stage. But almost never has the scholarship in and of itself won a job for anyone. In fact, the attempt to use it to win jobs has sometimes backfired. John Funari recalled one such instance. In the early 1960s Funari was an executive assistant to Fowler Hamilton, the director of the federal government's Agency for International Development. One day the two of them interviewed a job candidate who, like them, was a former Rhodes Scholar. During the interview the candidate pointedly stressed his scholarship – and thus his special bond with Hamilton and Funari. The latter two considered this the height of "bad form," and the man never got the job.[22]

David Halberstam has provided one of the most perceptive, and unflattering, descriptions of the "résumé value" of the Rhodes Scholarships. In his classic book *The Best and the Brightest*, he describes how a combination of hubris, naiveté, and brashness dominated some of the keenest minds in the federal government in the 1950s and 1960s. The result was that gifted men like Robert S. McNamara, Dean Rusk, and Walt Rostow dragged the United States into the Vietnam quagmire. Rusk and Rostow were two of the most prominent Rhodes Scholars in the Kennedy and Johnson administrations. Halberstam concludes:

> In a nation so large and so diverse there are few ways of quantifying intelligence or success or ability, so those few that exist are immediately magnified, titles become particularly important; all Rhodes scholars become brilliant, as all ex-Marines are tough. To make it in America, to rise, there has to be some sort of propellant; sheer talent helps, but except in very rare instances, talent is not enough. Money helps, family ties and connections help; for someone without these the way to the power elite can seem too far, too hopeless to challenge. The connection is often a Rhodes scholarship. It is a booster shot that young men are not unaware of, that will make the rest of their lives a good deal easier. Doors will open more readily, invitations will arrive, the phone will ring (thus one young applicant brought before the Rhodes committee was asked at the end of his interview what he would choose for the epitaph on his tombstone. He quickly answered, "Rhodes scholar," and got his grant).[23]

Along the same lines, Michael Kinsley has stated that the Rhodes Scholarship "is a credential in a credential-obsessed society."[24] The result, he says, is that it has a self-fulfilling character, choosing those who are embarked for success and giving them an extra boost.

Many scholars, however, point to factors other than the Rhodes Scholarship as being more important for their careers. Andrew Nussbaum provides one example. In the early 1991 and 1992 he worked as a law clerk for Ruth Bader Ginsburg in the U.S. Court of Appeals in Washington, DC and then Justice Antonin Scalia in the Supreme Court. Today he works in a major law firm in New York City. When asked what was most important in getting him these jobs, he admits that the Rhodes Scholarship looked nice on his record. But far more important was what he had accomplished immediately after Oxford: doing well in the University of Chicago Law School and editing the law review there.[25]

Most Rhodes Scholar academics tell similar stories. Political scientist Daniel Stid (1987) believes that the scholarship helped him get his first teaching job, but that it was no more important than some other award or accomplishment might have looked on his record.[26] Poet and English professor Guy Davenport would agree. He has asserted that "a Rhodes Scholarship in academe means nothing," or at least no more than any other kind of prize or activity.[27]

Numerous Rhodes Scholar academics in such fields as History and English have announced in recent years that they have failed to win teaching positions or that their applications for tenure have been rejected.[28] When John Brademas was appointed president of New York University in 1980, one of the first things he did was dismiss the controversial Dean of the Faculty of Arts and Sciences; the latter was fellow Rhodes Scholar Norman F. Cantor.[29] (Cantor, however, retained his tenured position as professor of history.)

Outside of academe there are also many examples of Rhodes Scholarships not being an automatic ticket to success. When James Himes arrived home from Oxford in 1990, he expected to have no trouble landing a government job in Washington. He wanted to work in the State Department or some other agency dealing with Latin America. He spoke fluent Spanish and had spent much of his childhood in Latin America, where his father worked for the Ford Foundation. That background, plus his Rhodes Scholarship and Oxford M.Phil. in Latin American Studies, seemed to guarantee immediate access to the halls of power. After several weeks of tireless pavement pounding in the Capital, he gave up. He eventually landed a job as an investment banker with Goldman Sachs in New York City; he got his entry to that job through his former roommate at Harvard, not through any Rhodes connections. At Goldman Sachs his Oxford degree won him no benefits. He started out at the very lowest level, doing lots of proofreading and photocopying for more senior employees.[30]

A Rhodes Network?

Despite the examples of Himes and others like him, many Americans have assumed that an "old boy network" exists among Rhodes Scholars. Numerous magazine and newspaper articles over the years have echoed this view, comparing Rhodes Scholars to the alumni networks of Harvard, Oxford, Cambridge, and other elite institutions.[31] In January 1993, shortly before Clinton's first inauguration, C-SPAN aired twelve hours of programming on Rhodes Scholars. Dozens of current and former scholars were interviewed. Again and again the C-SPAN reporters asked the same three questions of each person: How did you come to apply for the scholarship? What was Oxford like? What about the Rhodes Scholar network or club in the United States?

When asked about this "network" on television or in the interviews conducted for this book, the great majority of scholars deny that it has ever had any significance in their own careers or say that it is mostly a loose, informal network of mere friends. Several have admitted that when they were applying for jobs, research grants, or other such things, they telephoned Rhodes Scholar friends who were in a position to aid them. But they also sought help from people in all their other "networks": friends from college or graduate school, neighbors from childhood, coworkers from current or past jobs, and so on.

Many scholars agree, however, that there is one area in which a strong Oxford network does seem to operate: government. Is this correct? The two most famous cases in which a Rhodes Scholar "old boy club" supposedly has existed are the presidential administrations of John F. Kennedy and Bill Clinton.

Shortly after Kennedy took office, former Rhodes Scholar Robert K. Massie contributed an article for the Sunday *New York Times Magazine*. It was entitled "Many Rhodes to Washington." Massie admitted that the President, a Harvard graduate, had appointed many alumni from his alma mater. With an obvious touch of pride, however, Massie added that Kennedy "has obviously been attracted to the qualities that are demanded of, and mark, most Rhodes scholars."[32] During one memorable luncheon at the Cosmos Club in Washington in the early 1960s, guest speaker Dean Rusk, then the Secretary of State, half-humourously observed about the Kennedy White House that "Harvard gets all the credit, but Oxford does all the work."[33] Many magazine and newspaper articles of the period spread the word that Rhodes Scholars seemed to be all over in Washington. In a 1964 article in *Harper's*, the former head of the Rhodes Trustees, Lord Elton, observed that "in the Kennedy Administration the constellation of Rhodes Scholars was almost startling."[34]

How many scholars did work in the Kennedy administration? Most observers, when pressed for a number, have said about a dozen.[35] Our own tabulation produced the figure of twenty-five. Is this a "startling" constellation? In general, if one says "White House" or "presidential administration," one means those who, directly or indirectly, are chosen by and are responsible to the President. This would include White House aides, Cabinet members and their top assistants, ambassadors, and a few other categories of public servants. Excluded are members of Congress, career civil servants, military officers, federal judges, and so on. A president's "administration" might be said to consist of about five hundred people. Given that, it is difficult to conclude that Kennedy's White House was overrun with Oxford graduates.

To be sure, the Rhodes Scholars who worked for Kennedy filled some important posts. In the State Department, they included Dean Rusk plus his assistant secretaries Harlan Cleveland (1938) and George McGhee (the latter until he was named Ambassador to West Germany in 1963) plus Walt Rostow, the chair of the Policy Planning Council. One should also cite Nicholas Katzenbach – at first Assistant and then later Deputy Attorney General (and finally Attorney General under Johnson); Byron White, Deputy Attorney General and then Justice of the Supreme Court; Charles J. Hitch, Assistant Secretary of Defense; Alain Enthoven (1952), Deputy Assistant Secretary of Defense; Elvis Stahr, Secretary of the Army; Kermit Gordon, a member of the Council of Economic Advisers and later the Budget Director; and Philip Kaiser, ambassador to Senegal and Mauritania. One could name about a dozen others.[36]

Did these men get their jobs because they were Rhodes Scholars? Almost certainly not. They came to Kennedy's attention because of their intelligence and wide-ranging experience in government and business. It should also be stressed that Kennedy allowed trusted assistants to do most of the hiring in "his" administration. In the State Department, venerable New Dealer Chester Bowles led the talent search. In the White House itself, Kennedy's brother-in-law Sergent Shriver did most of the searching and interviewing.[37]

Of course, having "Rhodes Scholar" on their résumés may have helped some of those hired – as would any mark of achievement. All of Kennedy's close associates and biographers agree that he liked to surround himself with bright, energetic men. What counted most was effectiveness. George McGhee recalls that Kennedy wanted results: "If you didn't get your job done, you were never given another one."[38] Elvis Stahr and Philip Kaiser have insisted that "Rhodes Scholar" was never mentioned at any time during their trips to the White House.[39] When asked whether a Rhodes network helped win him his appointment, Nicholas Katzenbach unhesitatingly replied, "Absolutely not!"[40] Walt Rostow maintains that the President simply wanted "the best men available."[41] Some of these happened to be Rhodes Scholars. Others were Harvard professors, old navy buddies, prep school chums, former roommates, venerable Washington insiders, or members of the Kennedy family.

Those pundits who stress the Oxford factor in the Kennedy administration should recall that the President vetoed the "obvious" choice for Secretary of State, Rhodes Scholar J. William Fulbright. Instead he chose Dean Rusk, whom he had met only a few days previously. Rusk got the nod because of his stellar track record in the public and private sectors over the previous quarter of a century, not because he was a Rhodes Scholar. He had served in the army from 1940 to 1946, rising to colonel and a job in the Operations Division of the General Staff. From 1946 to 1951 he had held various positions in the War Department and the State Department, including supervision of the United Nations desk and working as Assistant Secretary for Far Eastern Affairs. From 1952 until the Kennedy appointment he headed the Rockefeller Foundation.

What about the Clinton administration? During the 1992 campaign and through Clinton's first year in office the American and British press carried scores of stories on Clinton's Rhodes network. *Newsweek* trumpeted the emergence of "Clinton's Rhodes Brain Trust" and said he turned for help to his "Oxford brotherhood."[42] *U.S. News & World Report* pointed to the important "Rhodes Factor" in the new administration.[43] *Fortune* declared that Clinton's electoral victory made him the "Rhodes Poster Boy."[44] The *Washington Post* claimed that Clinton was leading "an army of fellow Rhodies ... poised to take over the world."[45] In Britain, the *Sunday Times* estimated that as many as twenty-five Rhodes Scholars "surrounded" Clinton in the White House,[46] while the *Sunday Telegraph* concluded that the new administration would be a "Rhodes operation."[47]

Writing in *The Nation* in December 1992, Christopher Hitchens predicted that one would not be able to count very many "genial, unpolished, small-town Arkansans in the new phalanx of power." That was because Clinton reached the top with the help of "the Rhodes alumni, a group to which he remains steadfastly loyal."[48] In March 1993 former scholar Douglas Jehl wrote a piece entitled "Rhodes to Rhodes" in the *New York Times*. It described the flood of Rhodes Scholars winning White House appointments. Jehl quoted Senator John Chafee, Republican of Rhode Island, who remarked that "they seem to be everywhere." Chafee had just come from a confirmation hearing in which he found himself staring at a table lined with Rhodes Scholars.[49]

How many Rhodes Scholars have joined the Clinton administration? As with the case of John F. Kennedy, one confronts the difficulty of defining precisely what one means by "White House" or "administration." Certainly one would include, among former and current Clinton staff members, the advisers George Stephanopoulos, Ira Magaziner, and Bruce Reed, as well as CIA director James Woolsey, Secretary of Labor Robert Reich, Deputy Secretary of State Strobe Talbott, and White House deputy chief of staff Sylvia Mathews (1987). But does the Clinton administration include Alison Muscatine, a speechwriter for Hillary Rodham Clinton? Or Kevin Thurm (1984), chief of staff for Donna Shalala in the Department of Health and Human Services? Or Daniel Porterfield (1984), a speechwriter for Shalala? Or Robert Rotberg, a member of the advisory board of the National Endowment for the Humanities? Or Walter Slocombe (1963), Under Secretary of Defense for Policy? Or Patrick Shea (1970), Director of the U.S. Bureau of Land Management? Or Tom McMillen, co-chair (until mid-1996) of the President's Council on Physical Fitness? If one takes a broad view of "administration," the number of Rhodes Scholars who have served Clinton amounts to perhaps fifty or so.

Does this mean that his presidency has been a "Rhodes operation"? No, for several reasons. First, these few dozen comprise only a small percentage of the full administration. Second, if one looks at the Rhodes Scholars Clinton knew in Oxford in the late 1960s, one sees that only a handful received presidential appointments of any sort. In addition to Reich and Talbott, these have included presidential adviser Ira Magaziner, U.S. District Judge Rick Stearns, Chair of the Legal Services Corporation Douglas Eakeley, U.S. Department of Labor solicitor Tom Williamson, and U.S. Attorney Alan Bersin. Several other Oxford friends campaigned for Clinton in 1992 and again in 1996; either they did not want government jobs after the elections or, if they asked, they did not receive.

The issues of *The American Oxonian* in 1993 amounted to a virtual Clinton lovefest. William Jay Smith contributed a poem called "The Man from Hope."[50] In the notes for the class of 1968, Robert Reich (remaining class secretary while also assuming his job as Secretary of Labor) reported in his best tongue-in-cheek fashion, "Bill Clinton writes that Chelsea's ballet skills have reached a new level of perfection, and that Hillary remains busy. Bill notes that in early November he was elected President of the United States." The elfin Reich also offered some advice to the new leader of the free world: "Be skeptical of any economic advice you receive from short people."[51] The class of 1951 reported that twenty-eight of them voted for Clinton, with only two for Bush and none for Perot; four years earlier a majority of the class had voted for Bush.[52] Thomas Blackburn, class of 1954 secretary, cheerfully proclaimed that "Rhodomania" was sweeping the Capitol and confessed he could not "help feeling excited and hopeful that a Scholar has made it to the White House."[53]

Jeff Shesol, who was studying at Clinton's alma mater, University College, at the time of the 1992 election, drew a humorous cartoon about the torrent of Rhodes Scholars who would be clamoring to join the new administration. Shesol was prophetic, for scores of scholars did actively seek appointments or make it known that they "might" consider an offer.[54] Myriad FOBs (Friends of Bill) from Arkansas, Georgetown, and Yale also faxed in their résumés. Yet only a small percentage from any of these Clinton "networks" obtained positions of some sort.

For all the hoopla about Clinton's victory and what it meant for Rhodes Scholars, perhaps the most amazing thing is that so few, rather than so many, landed top Washington jobs. Moreover, regarding those scholars who did get the call from Clinton, there is much to show that their having been Rhodes Scholars was not the determining factor. To be sure, Clinton had come to know and like Talbott, Reich, and Magaziner in Oxford. He had kept in close touch with Talbott and Reich through the 1970s and 1980s. During those decades Talbott had risen to become *Time*'s reigning expert on the Soviet Union and national security affairs. Reich gained wealth and prominence as a Harvard lecturer and author of several best-selling books on what ailed the U.S. economy. Without these impressive credentials, neither would have received presidential appointments.

The case of Magaziner is more unusual. He completely lost contact with Clinton for more than fifteen years after Oxford. In the mid-1980s he got to know Hillary Rodham; both of them worked on the privately funded Committee on Skills in the American Work Force as well as on a number of other public and private task forces studying issues relating to the economy and education. When Magaziner and Rodham first met they realized they had two things in common: their joint appearance in *Life* magazine's 1969 article on student leaders and their connection to Bill Clinton. From that time on, Magaziner maintained steady contacts with both Rodham and Clinton.

When questioned about his relationship with the President, Magaziner maintains that the subject of Rhodes Scholarships has never come up – except in a couple of purely incidental ways, such as the President's trip to Oxford in 1994 for an honorary degree. It was Magaziner's keen mind and zeal for public service that led Clinton to pick him for his staff. Moreover, Magaziner says that he and other Rhodes Scholars in the White House have never sat around and said anything like, "Wow, we now have a chance to fulfill Cecil Rhodes' dream about making a difference in the world."[55]

George Stephanopoulos, Bruce Reed, James Woolsey, and others selected by the President have echoed the same sentiments. Winning a Rhodes Scholarship looked good on their résumés – as did their other awards. The President chose them, however, because of their solid record of accomplishment rather than because of any academic degrees they possessed. In the case of Stephanopoulos, it was a case of him choosing Clinton as much as Clinton choosing him. By the time he was thirty years old, Stephanopoulos was already a seasoned Capitol Hill insider. He had worked as an assistant to Democratic Representative Edward Feighan of Ohio in the early 1980s. In 1988 he served as Communications Director in the doomed presidential campaign of Michael Dukakis. Following that he became executive assistant to House Majority Leader Richard Gephart.

Early in 1992 Stephanopoulos began to search for a Democratic presidential candidate whose ideas he could support and who seemed to have the right instincts about winning. At about the same time two candidates tried to woo him; they were Nebraska Senator Bob Kerrey and Bill Clinton. Clinton wanted Stephanopoulos for his experience both in Congress and in the Dukakis campaign; Stephanopoulos would be able to tell Clinton all that had gone wrong in 1988 so that the Democratic candidate could do the opposite in 1992. When they agreed to join forces, the subject of Oxford never came up.[56]

Clinton picked Woolsey in 1992 because the latter was one of the most respected national security experts and Washington insiders. Woolsey had been working full- or part-time for every President, Democrat and Republican, since the time of Jimmy Carter – as undersecretary of the navy, disarmament treaty negotiator, and foreign policy adviser. At the moment when Clinton chose him as the new CIA director, Woolsey was not even sure that the President knew he was a former scholar; at any rate, the topic never arose.[57]

The same kind of story applies to Bruce Reed. From 1986 to 1988 he had actually worked on the campaign staff of the then Senator Al Gore. Only in 1990 did Reed come to know Clinton well. In that year Reed became policy director of the Democratic Leadership Council, a group of centrist Democrats that Clinton had helped to found. During the 1992 campaign Reed served candidate Clinton as a sort of jack-of-all-trades adviser and speechwriter. Through the first Clinton administration, Reed's influence was felt in health policy issues and other domestic affairs. As plans for the 1996 election were formulated, Reed concentrated on pulling Clinton back to the political center and devising a list of issues that would attract popular support. He played a central role in plotting Clinton's successful reelection campaign.

In short, Clinton sought people who could serve him well; if they happened to be former Rhodes Scholars, that was fine, but of minor importance. Moreover, several of the Rhodes Scholars who did join his team had less than happy tenures in office. It was widely known that Clinton's good friend Reich was "out of the loop" on many issues relating to the economy and employment. The Secretary of Labor wanted to invest heavily in education, in job retraining programs, and other economic infrastructure programs designed to help the working poor and middle class. What Reich discovered was that he faced an unbeatable coalition of foes: Republicans and moderate Democrats bent on balancing the budget plus Federal Reserve Chairman Alan Greenspan, who worried about interest rates rising due to any new government spending.

Within months of leaving Washington at the end of Clinton's first term, Reich chronicled his experiences in his book *Locked in the Cabinet.* Knowing that he was a dangerous liberal in the eyes of Wall Street, Reich imagined that Greenspan considered him a "Bolshevik dwarf."[58] Full of wry anecdotes, gossipy insider stories, and thoughtful ruminations on government and society, the book offers a candid, though cordial, portrait of Bill and Hillary Clinton. From the start of his job as Secretary of Labor, Reich worried that his friend Bill's desire to please all sides might doom any efforts to put his own policies into practice.[59] Reich's official reasons for returning to Massachusetts and a professorship at Brandeis University were that he hated the backstabbing atmosphere of Washington and wanted to spend more time with his wife and children. Clearly, however, he also left because of disappointment at what he had been unable to accomplish.

James Woolsey abruptly resigned from the CIA in December 1994. He was held accountable when scandals like that of Aldrich Ames, arrested for selling secrets to the Russians, erupted during his tenure. He also had failed to build up morale and bring more efficiency to the beleaguered agency. Moreover, his prickly defense of his agency alienated several members of Congress. What was worse, he and Clinton never developed a close personal rapport. Political observers pointedly noted that Woolsey was not among the inner circle to whom the President turned first for advice on foreign policy. Clearly peeved about his treatment in the Clinton administration, Woolsey announced in the fall of 1996 that he would be voting for Bob Dole.[60]

After the failure of the President's health-care reform package in 1994, Ira Magaziner's White House star plummeted. Journalists and congressional opponents almost seemed to compete for the most colorful epithets they could hurl at him: "quixotic," "Uriah Heepish," "a policy monk," "a laughingstock," and "the worst politician in the country."[61] Chastened but doggedly determined to serve his friend the President, Magaziner survived into the second administration. He retained the lofty title of Senior Policy Adviser, working chiefly on matters regarding the Internet, but he sank into near invisibility. The President's staff kept him from having any significant personal contacts with members of Congress, the press, or foreign governments.[62] In other words, neither Magaziner's status as a Rhodes Scholar or a clever business consultant prevented Clinton from relegating him to the back corridors.

Like Robert Reich, George Stephanopoulos decided to leave the White House at the end of the first term. Though he was still a close personal adviser to the President, his influence and access to the Oval Office had waned. That was due in part to his disastrous stint as White House Communications Director early in Clinton's presidency. It also resulted from the fact that Stephanopoulos was known as a liberal, in an administration that was increasingly veering back toward the center. He left government on friendly terms with Clinton, and there is no reason to doubt him when he said that he was simply burned out. The offer of a professorship at Columbia University, a book contract worth nearly three million dollars, generous fees for his lectures, and regular television appearances as a political commentator no doubt helped to persuade him to depart. In January 1998, when the public learned of White House intern Monica Lewinsky's claims of a sexual affair with Bill Clinton, Stephanopoulos' observations on various television and radio programs were remarkable for their dispassionate analysis – rather than their fervent support of the President. Privately, the White House was said to be furious that Stephanopoulos even brought words like "impeachment" into the discussion.[63]

Whereas at least a dozen Rhodes Scholar appointees have left the Clinton administration – willingly or otherwise – other former scholars have come on board. One of the most prominent is Franklin Raines. After Clinton won the November 1992 election, Raines joined the transition team and supervised matters dealing with economic policies and federal agencies. Shortly thereafter, he accepted the post of Vice Chairman of the Federal National Mortgage Association (Fannie Mae). In September 1996 Congress approved his appointment as Director of the Office of Management and the Budget (OMB).

Did he get these jobs because he was a Rhodes Scholar? No. Like that of many others in the Clinton administration, Raines' career has interwoven high-paying work in the private sector with stints in government service. During the 1980s Raines amassed a personal fortune as a partner in the Lazard, Freres & Co. investment banking firm. Prior to that he worked in the OMB during the Carter administration. Raines and Clinton had never met in Oxford – Raines arrived in 1971, by which time Clinton was in Yale Law School. The two men were drawn to each other because they were both centrists in economic policy. Moreover, when Raines won his promotion to head the OMB, *Time* asserted that he got the job partly through the lobbying of Vice President Al Gore. Raines was, according to the magazine, one of several Gore "groupies" rising to prominence in the Clinton White House.[64]

By the end of the first Clinton administration political commentators had stopped talking about any sort of Rhodes network dominating the White House. In part this was because astute observers came to realize that Rhodes Scholars were merely one of several networks from which the President drew friends and supporters. In his book *The President We Deserve*, Martin Walker carefully delineates seven primary Clinton "networks": Arkansas, Georgetown, Rhodes Scholars, Yale, the Legal Services Corporation, the Children's Defense Fund, state governors, the Democratic Leadership Council, and the Renaissance Group (the policy wonks and celebrities who convene annually during the New Year's holidays at Hilton Head, South Carolina).[65] Several of Clinton's closest friends and associates are members of two or more of these groups, which compounds the difficulty of seeing Rhodes Scholars or any other network as having a predominant influence. Reich and Talbott, for example, had attended Yale as well as Oxford. Should one count them as part of the Yale network or the Rhodes network – or both, or neither? By the end of the first administration, it was also becoming evident that Clinton was relying increasingly on political and economic experts whom he barely knew or had not known at all before he became President. These included Treasury Secretary Robert Rubin and Chiefs of Staff Leon Panetta and Erskine Bowles.

There is yet another reason why the whole notion of Clinton favoring a Rhodes network makes no sense. If a fair number of Rhodes Scholars have risen to prominence in the Clinton White House, this results from the same reason why some were highly visible under Kennedy, Johnson, and Carter: namely, the fact that most Rhodes Scholars are Democrats. Only three of the twelve scholars elected to Congress thus far have been Republicans (Hale, Clason, and Pressler), along with only two of the seven elected to the Senate

(Lugar and Pressler). These figures exaggerate the Democratic tilt among scholars as a whole, though it is difficult to gauge the extent. There has never been a survey among scholars asking for party affiliation. However, the class notes in *The American Oxonian* from its first issue in 1914 to the present along with other evidence reveal a steady pattern. Over the decades, roughly two-thirds have tended to identify themselves as Democrats.

Why this political tilt? When Republican Richard Lugar was asked this question, he acknowledged that it existed but smiled and shrugged his shoulders.[66] Lugar's good friend, Democrat Paul Sarbanes, professed surprise when he was told that most scholars have been Democrats.[67] Democrat John Brademas ebulliently declared that most scholars are smart and therefore are Democrats![68] Attorney Donald Rivkin (1949), a longtime supporter of Democratic candidates, surmised that wealthy young Republican boys and girls do not need to go to Oxford; therefore most of the applicants for the scholarships come from middle and working-class families, which tend to be Democrat.[69] Several other scholars have said that the great majority of Rhodes Scholars tend to believe in the power of ideas, in the beneficial power of government and other public agencies, and in the utility of careers in public service. These are precisely the same attitudes that are usually more associated with Democrats than with Republicans.

This is not to say that the Rhodes Scholarship program can be considered a wing of the Democratic National Party. Most scholars, whether Democrat or Republican, steer toward the safe center. Indeed, one of the criticisms of the program is that it tends to select career-oriented, non-controversial candidates who can please any selection committee. This point was made by Andrew Sullivan in his *Spy* article, but scholars like Michael Kinsley and Jacob Weisberg have agreed. As Randy Berholtz (1985) has said, there are few iconoclasts or political rebels who apply for the scholarships, and even fewer who get the nod from the selection committees.[70]

Numerous scholars have worked in Republican presidential administrations. Some top Reagan appointees included Richard Haass (1973) at various bureaus in the State Department; and Roger Porter (1969), a deputy assistant to the President and Director of the Office of Policy Development; and Scott Thompson, an assistant to the Secretary of Defense. One could go on to enumerate other scholars who worked for Reagan as well as for other Republican presidents.

There are even a few scholars who could be labeled extreme rightwingers. In 1972 Bradford Trenham (1921) exploded in anger as the Watergate affair began to envelope his friend Richard Nixon. In *The American Oxonian*'s class notes he argued that Nixon would, in the end, "come out on top." Trenham maintained that the country would be better served with investigations into some other questions:

1. Did the Democrats deliberately sabotage the Hoover administration …?
2. Did Roosevelt plan the Pearl Harbor attack to infuriate the American people and get us into W.W. II (many generals think so)?
3. Why was Roosevelt sent to Yalta, to sell out to Stalin, when he was dying?
4. Why was Chiang Kai Shek dumped so the Communists could take over China?
5. Why was MacArthur stopped at the Yalu just when we had a chance to wreck Chinese Communism?
6. Why did the Kennedy Kids make such a mess of the Bay of Pigs?
7. Why didn't Teddy Boy try to save that girl's life?[71]

During the 1980s Mary Norton McConnell (1977) came to be called the Republican Party's "whiz kid" in Washington. She worked for Congressman Jack Kemp and then became a speech writer for Defense Secretary Caspar Weinberger. Nowadays, despite the election of fellow scholar Bill Clinton, Norton McConnell freely acknowledges that she remains a "paleo- conservative."[72]

The assumption that Rhodes Scholars have somehow had an unusual amount of influence on the Clinton administration is further belied by the fact that three of the politicians who caused the President the most headaches during his first administration were Democrats as well as former scholars. Representative Jim Cooper contributed to the defeat of the Clinton health care plan by proposing a less-comprehensive plan of his own – often dubbed "Clinton lite." In the end, neither Clinton's nor Cooper's schemes got through Congress. Senators Bill Bradley and David Boren sparred with Clinton on numerous foreign and domestic policy issues. In the fall of 1994, shortly before he left the Senate to assume the presidency of the University of Oklahoma, Boren fired a parting shot at the President. For the good of the party and of the country, Boren called for Clinton not to seek a second term.[73] During much of 1994 and 1995, Washington was abuzz with speculation that Bradley might mount an Independent Party challenge to Clinton for the presidency in 1996.

A Conspiracy?

From all of the above, it should be clear that even in politics there has been no Rhodes Scholar "old boy network." It is important to stress this, because since the inception of the program some die-hard critics of the program have assumed that the scholars are part of some sort of closed brotherhood or conspiracy.

When Cecil Rhodes' will was published in 1902, some Irish-Americans feared that the scholarships were designed to inculcate Anglophile sentiments into American business and political leaders. The result would be continued discrimination against the Irish in both the Old and New Worlds. In the 1930s and 1940s, the leading anti-Rhodes Scholar crusader was Colonel Robert R. McCormick, publisher of the *Chicago Tribune.* McCormick also hated Franklin Delano Roosevelt, to the extent that the *Tribune* opposed virtually every domestic and foreign policy that Roosevelt advocated. A rabid isolationist, McCormick believed that pro-England scholars were plotting to drag the United States into another foreign conflict. The eventual eruption of the Second World War seemed to confirm his worst fears. In a 1943 editorial, the *Tribune* proclaimed that "no Rhodes Scholar can escape the suspicion of being consciously or unconsciously an alien agent." Because of this "Oxford Conspiracy," the paper stated that all scholars should register their names with local government authorities. In addition, the *Tribune* suggested that all those who turned their backs on wholesome American education and went abroad to study must likewise be suspected of treason.[74]

Rhodes Scholars themselves shrugged off these charges and even laughed about them. Some bragged about being on McCormick's list of enemies. Most mainstream newspapers and magazines, including the other major dailies in Chicago, viewed McCormick's vituperative comments as either amusing drivel or irresponsible rantings.[75]

During the Cold War Era, rightwing conspiracy theorists concocted yet another charge against Rhodes Scholars. With slight variations from one person or group to another, this accusation holds that Rhodes Scholars are part of a vast conspiracy to overthrow the United States. Brainwashed by welfare-state socialism and pacifist internationalism as a result of their studies in Oxford, Rhodes Scholars have returned to the United States determined to establish socialism (or Bolshevism) and place the United States under one world government. This will be "the new world order." Rhodes Scholars, according to this theory, have many allies: numerous mainstream Democrat and Republican politicians (including Richard Nixon,

Henry Kissinger, and George Bush!), the United Nations, prominent Jewish financiers, Yale's Skull & Bones Society, the Trilateral Commission, and the Council on Foreign Relations, among others.[76]

Most of the leading exponents of this conspiracy theory are little known to the general public, but they have thousands of devoted, fanatical fellow-believers. From the late 1940s to the present day they have churned out thousands of books and newsletters claiming to provide incontrovertible proof of their charges. Two of the most famous books are Rose L. Martin's *Fabian Freeway: High Road to Socialism in the U.S.A.* (1968) and Gary Allen's *None Dare Call it Conspiracy* (1971). One of the more influential of the periodicals espousing these views is the aptly titled *Steamshovel.*

Though most Americans know nothing of these publications, everyone is now familiar with the militia-type groups sprouting up across the nation. The literature published by many of these groups includes the charges against Rhodes Scholars. This conspiracy theory reached mass audience, bestseller status in 1992 with the publication of Pat Robertson's book *The New World Order.* Therein one can find one of the most comprehensive elaborations of the conspiracy theory.

There is not room here to address these conspiracy charges in any detail. Nor would refutation of them serve any purpose, for most conspiracy theorists refuse to change their views or accept evidence with an open mind. It will suffice here to say that the evidence for Rhodes Scholars belonging to any formal network or conspiracy of any kind is preposterous.

It is true that most Rhodes Scholars tend to be internationalists, in the sense that they favor good relations with the rest of the world. Most scholars have supported the League of Nations and the United Nations. Many have been active in organizations like the Carnegie Endowment for International Peace, the Council on Foreign Relations, and the World Peace Foundation. But these are groups open to public scrutiny, not secret conspiracies. Moreover, it is not surprising that most Rhodes Scholars are not isolationists. An isolationist probably would not apply to study abroad in the first place.

Anyone attending the North American Rhodes Scholar reunion at Georgetown in 1993 could have perceived immediately that this was no close-knit group of conspirators. All of the nine hundred or so scholars in attendance wore large sandwich signs over their shoulders, so that their names were displayed in bold letters on both front and back. If this was a tightly-knit brotherhood, they would have been able to recognize each other without such props. Moreover, secret cabals generally do not advertise their operations. The Rhodes reunion, however, sought all the publicity it could get. The *Washington Times* described the reunion as "academia's Hell's Angels" sweeping into town.[77]

Moreover, it they are part of a conspiracy, it is an awfully sluggish, ill-organized one. The conveners of the 1993 reunion repeatedly mentioned that this was the fourth such general meeting in the United States – the earlier ones being in 1933 (at Swarthmore), 1947 (at Princeton), and 1965 (again at Swarthmore). Actually, the Georgetown affair was the fifth. Research for this book turned up a sparsely-attended general reunion in 1911 at Mackinac Island.[78] It is clear that American Rhodes Scholars do not meet very often and do not keep elaborate files on their operations.

The fact that many of them feel no special bond with all their fellow scholars was demonstrated in spectacular fashion by Daniel Boorstin. While studying in Oxford in the 1930s Boorstin and several of his classmates dabbled in leftish politics; several scholars of that era even joined the Communist Party. By the 1940s, however, Boorstin himself had become a hardline conservative. In 1950 Boorstin was called to testify before the House Un-American Activities Committee. He obligingly named names and included his fellow scholar Richard Goodwin (1934) among those who were, or had been, members of the Communist Party. Boorstin agreed that Communists should not be allowed to teach in the United States. As a result, later that year Goodwin was denied tenure in the economics department at Harvard. Ousted from his job in Cambridge, Massachusetts, Goodwin went on to a distinguished career at Cambridge in England. But neither he nor several of his classmates ever completely forgave Boorstin.[79]

Even a casual glance through recent issues of the "conspiracy's" chief organ, *The American Oxonian*, reveals that it continues to be a relatively tame publication and not the product of a close-knit band of revolutionaries. The first issue of 1997 includes a section on "books every American ought to have read." The magazine's editor, James O'Toole, had written to sixty scholars, asking each to submit the names of ten books. Only 17 scholars responded. The great majority of the books selected were standard classics: the Bible, Shakespeare, Homer, Melville, Tocqueville's *Democracy in America*, *The Federalist*, and so on. There was no mention of Karl Marx or other "subversive" authors.

Still today class secretaries plead with their fellow scholars for bits of news for the annual class notes. Most of the news submitted has to do with the mundane issues of youth (having babies, finding jobs) and old age (illness, retirement travels, hobbies). Hardly the stuff of insidious conspiracy.

The same issue of *The American Oxonian* that discussed great books also contained a review of George Steiner's most recent volume, *No Passion Spent: Essays 1978-1995*. The essays in this book cover a broad range of topics concerning literature and American culture. In his review of the book, Brian McHale (1974) acknowledges Steiner's "characteristic erudition and virtuosity" and admits that in some ways the book is "a tour-de-force of historical imagination." Yet McHale accuses Steiner of "willful amnesia" in some of his judgments about literature. Even more strongly, McHale asserts that Steiner's dismissal of American culture as largely empty or derivative reveals Steiner's "blind-spots" that are "many and dark." Though the book offers many fresh and insightful interpretations, McHale concludes that Steiner is "arrogant, irritating, occasionally sententious, often perverse or just plain wrong."[80]

So much for the Rhodes brotherhood or network.

NOTES

1. Interviews with Griffin, 27 July 1993; Dworkin, 19 November 1993; and Howlett, 12 August 1993.
2. Turner interview, 31 March 1994.
3. Interviews with Celeste, 11 January 1994, and Stephanopoulos, 1 April 1995.
4. Interviews with Woolsey, 9 June 1994, and Edge, 9 July 1996.
5. Fleissner interview, 29 December 1993.
6. Swetland interview, 20 February 1996.
7. Isaacson, letter to authors, 10 December 1993.
8. Rogers interview, 19 April 1994.
9. Bradley, letter to Donna Bunce, 25 March 1994.
10. *TAO*, 57 (1970): 537; 64 (1977): 217; 72 (1985): 171; 74 (1987): 156; 80 (1993): 15.
11. *TAO*, 65 (1978): 135.
12. Stephanopoulos interview, 1 April 1995.
13. *TAO*, 64 (1977): 2.
14. Topping, "Best Men," 8.
15. Weisberg, "Clinton at Oxford," 177.
16. Erik Erikson, *Young Man Luther: A Study in Psychoanalysis and History* (London, 1958), 40-45, 94-96.
17. Rotberg, *The Founder*, 98-99, 106-7.
18. *TAO*, 80 (1993): 238.

19. Brademas interview, 28 December 1993.
20. Schmoke interview, 2 August 1994.
21. *TAO* ,66 (1979): 251.
22. Funari interview, 11 October 1993.
23. David Halberstam, *The Best and the Brightest* (New York, 1972), 316.
24. *Washington Post*, 1 July 1983, D1.
25. Nussbaum interview, 27 December 1993.
26. Stid interview, 28 March 1995.
27. Davenport, letter to authors, 30 June 1995.
28. *TAO*, 65 (1978): 302; 70 (1983): 69, 241; 74 (1987): 64; 78 (1991): 85.
29. Brademas interview, 28 December 1993.
30. Himes interview, 31 December 1993.
31. For example, "The Good Network Guide," *The Economist*, 26 December 1992-8 January 1993, 20-24.
32. *NYT Magazine*, 16 April 1961, 54.
33. *TAO*, 52 (1965): 111-12.
34. Elton, "An Englishman's Audit," 104.
35. For example, Hitchens, *Blood, Class, and Nostalgia*, 303; *Newsweek*, 4 May 1992, 27.
36. See Carole J. Coveney, "Oxford to Camelot: The Rhodes Scholars of the Kennedy Administration," unpublished paper, St. Bonaventure University, 1994. Class notes in *TAO* throughout the early 1960s also give details on scholars working for the Kennedy administration.
37. Rostow interview, 14 April 1994.
38. McGhee interview with Carole J. Coveney, 13 April 1994.
39. Interviews with Kaiser, 9 April 1994, and Stahr 11 October 1995.
40. Katzenbach interview, 30 March 1994.
41. Rostow interview, 14 April 1994.
42. *Newsweek*, 4 May 1992, 27; 19 April 1993, 26.
43. *U.S. News & World Report*, 14 December 1992, 18.
44. *Fortune*, 8 February 1993, 16.
45. *Washington Post*, 7 January 1993, C1.
46. *Sunday Times*, 27 February 1994, sec. 4, 6.
47. *Sunday Telegraph*, 21 March 1993, 22.
48. *The Nation*, 14 December 1992, 726.
49. *NYT*, 21 March 1993, E2.
50. *TAO*, 80 (1993): 2-3.
51. *TAO*, 80 (1993): 83-87.
52. *TAO*, 80 (1993): 175.
53. *TAO*, 80 (1993): 175.
54. *TAO*, 80 (1993): 4-5.
55. Magaziner interview, 8 June 1994.
56. Stephanopoulos interview, 1 April 1995; C-SPAN, "Oxford/American Connection."
57. Woolsey interview, 9 June 1994.
58. Reich, *Locked in the Cabinet*, 82.
59. Ibid., 7, 9, 17, 72, and passim.
60. *NYT*, 29 December 1994, A1; 28 October 1996, A1.
61. Jacob Weisberg, "Dies Ira: A Short History of Mr. Magaziner," *The New Republic*, 24 January 1994, 18-25.
62. *Providence Journal-Bulletin*, 21 January 1996, D7.

63. CNN special, 28 January 1998; ABC Good Morning America, 28 January 1998; *Washington Post,* 29 January 1998, B1; Larry King Live, 2 February 1998.
64. *Time,* 2 September 1996, 36.
65. Walker, *The President We Deserve,* 5-9.
66. Lugar interview, 11 June 1993.
67. Sarbanes interview, 8 June 1994.
68. Brademas interview, 28 December 1993.
69. Rivkin interview, 27 December 1993.
70. Berholtz interview, 14 February 1995.
71. *TAO,* 59 (1972): 67-68.
72. *TAO,* 70 (1983): 243-44; Norton McConnell interview, 12 June 1996.
73. *NYT,* 17 November 1994, A23.
74. Reprinted in *TAO,* 30 (1943): 190-94.
75. *TAO,* 31 (1944): 32-39; 36 (1949): 195; 39 (1952): 119. Also see Jerome E. Edwards, *The Foreign Policy of Col. McCormick's Tribune, 1929-1941* (Reno, Nevada, 1971) and Richard Norton Smith, *The Colonel: The Life and Legend of Robert R. McCormick* (New York, 1997).
76. Bill Stephens, "Conspiracy Theorists' Views on the Council on Foreign Relations and the Trilateral Commission," unpublished paper, St. Bonaventure University, 1994.
77. *Washington Times,* 11 June 1993, E1.
78. *The Alumni Magazine,* 4 (August 1911): 2-3; 4 (November 1911): 1.
79. *TAO,* 65 (1978): 7-15; 84 (1997): 215.
80. *TAO* 84 (1997): 39-44.

→Chapter 16←

THE RHODES AHEAD

Not all Rhodes Scholars are anything. Some are successes, some are failures, some are straightforward, some are devious, some are good, some
are in jail.

Stansfield Turner, interview with authors

In his three and one-half years at the University of Nebraska, Jeremy has
completed approximately 250 credit hours while maintaining a 4.0
G.P.A.; he is on course to graduate with six majors and four minors. He
is a 1993 Presidential Scholar and a World Herald Honors Scholar. He is
president of the Honors Program Student Board, vice-president of the
Residence Hall Association, and cofounder of the Allies group, an organization of straight students for gay rights. As vice-chair of the Nebraska
delegation to the 1996 General Conference of the United Methodist
Church, he authored three successful amendments to the church's law-
book, including one rewriting the church's position on science and technology. Jeremy belongs to the marching, concert, and jazz lab bands, as
well as to the University Singers, the oratorio chorus, and the glee club.
He enjoys piano and organ, hiking and running, and travel.

Entry for Jeremy Vetter, class of 1997, American Rhodes Scholar Newsletter

Transformations and Continuities

If Cecil Rhodes could return to life, he would be struck by the many
changes in the University of Oxford and in the scholarship program
that bears his name. The biggest transformation for the university
lies in its growth. The student population of nearly fifteen thousand
is several times that of 1900. Moreover, the colleges no longer shut
down during the long summer vacations. To boost revenues, they
keep their rooms filled with conferences for business executives and
academic programs for foreign students.

Rhodes would also be struck by how the central university administration has gained enormous power at the expense of the thirty-
nine colleges. The growth of the central authority resulted from the

need to support the huge costs of scientific laboratories, from regulations calling for a main office to oversee disbursement of government financial support, and from the establishment of a coordinated, ongoing fund-raising operation.

Rhodes would also be struck by the unending string of curriculum alterations. Approximately one-third of Oxford's students today are studying for advanced degrees, none of which existed in 1900. Oxford's vaunted undergraduate tutorial continues to function splendidly for the majority of undergraduates, and the university has retained its traditional eminence in areas like classics, history, literature, and philosophy. But students in those fields now must share equal space with those reading in the "new" disciplines of sociology, political science, physics, psychology, biology, engineering, and the like. Two of the most recent major additions to Oxford's academic slate are business and American studies.

Templeton College offers continuing education classes for business executives as well as graduate degree programs in industrial relations. To satisfy the needs of those students who want full-fledged undergraduate or graduate degrees in business, the university is instituting a panoply of new degree programs. In the fall of 1996 the first students were admitted into Oxford's MBA program. Many of the faculty who supervise the undergraduate and graduate students in various business-oriented programs are members of the School of Management Studies that was established in 1992. In 1996 a Syrian-born businessman and philanthropist named Wafic Rida Said pledged £20 million for the construction of a building to house a new business school.

This rush to pull Oxford into the twentieth century before the century ends has been too much for many dons in the older disciplines. One don sniffed that having a business institute in Oxford was "a distinctly discomforting arrangement." Another called management studies "a phony academic subject, a shallow contemporary shibboleth promoting a noxious cant."[1] In November 1996 the university's Congregation (often called the "parliament of dons") vetoed the first site chosen for Said's new structure. Nonetheless, most of the faculty and students in Oxford accept business studies as a necessary element in the makeup of a great university in the contemporary world. A different location for the building was selected, and the School for Management Studies will take up residence there before the end of the decade.[2]

Whereas in the early 1900s American history and culture were denigrated as too insignificant to merit detailed study, Oxford today is devoting increasing amounts of time to the study of the United States. Most of the colleges have two or more history and literature dons who specialize in American topics. Over 8 percent of all the dons in Oxford now actually are Americans.

Increased attention to the United States is justified academically and also financially. American undergraduate and graduate students now number about one thousand in Oxford during the regular academic terms and more than two thousand each summer. These Americans bring hard cash to Oxford, and many of them later become generous benefactors. Two Oxford Colleges now bear the names of Americans. In addition to Templeton College there is Kellogg College. In 1994 the foundation created by the breakfast cereal baron donated funds for the expansion of what was formerly called Rewley House (which specializes in continuing education and summer programs.) In the 1990s two former Rhodes Scholars – John Morrison (1955) and Stephen Stamas – served as chairs of Oxford's Annual Fund in the United States.[3]

The university's ties to the United States will become even more evident with the completion of the new Oxford Institute for American Studies. This new entity will serve as a research center and library. Construction is scheduled to begin in 1998 on grounds adjacent to Mansfield College. The Rhodes Trust has donated more than £4 million toward the total cost of the project.[4]

In short, Oxford has retained its dreaming spires , its eccentricities, its tutorials, and other traditional features while also adapting to the new. By 1997 the university as a whole and most of the colleges had even developed their own home pages on the World Wide Web.[5]

Rhodes Scholars also have changed. Initially there were fifty-seven per year; the number now is eighty-five, with several from countries that did not exist at the time of Rhodes' will. As of 1998 the constituencies and their allotment of scholars were: United States (32), Canada (11), Australia (9), South Africa (9), Germany (4), India (4), New Zealand (3), Commonwealth Caribbean (2), Zimbabwe (2), and one apiece for Bermuda, Hong Kong, Jamaica, Kenya, Malaysia, Pakistan, Singapore, Uganda, and Zambia. The scholars themselves have also changed in ways that would startle the founder. More than a third in any given year are non-white, and about half are women. In 1995 the Rhodes Trust announced that married persons could also apply. The first married candidate to be awarded a scholarship was Jennifer DeVoe (1996).

The experience of the scholars in Oxford has also evolved over the past century.Robert Edge, the current President of the Association of American Rhodes Scholars, has echoed the opinion of many former scholars by lamenting that the Oxford experience for today's Rhodes Scholars is probably not as special as it was for earlier generations. One reason for this is that Oxford itself has lost some of its aura. It no longer towers above American universities as it seemed to do a hundred years ago. Indeed, the race to compete against universities in the United States and elsewhere has led some doomsayers to declare that Oxford is in danger of losing its status as a world-class university. A dozen or more American institutions now have endowments larger than that of all Oxford's colleges combined. Even within Britain, Oxford's position has weakened. In past decades, Oxford and Cambridge were recognized as far superior to all other universities – with the London School of Economics and other divisions of the University of London distant runners-up. The rapid proliferation of new universities throughout the country (now standing at about one hundred) and the increasing competition for government and private funding have meant that Oxford must work hard to remain merely the first among equals. In 1993 Oxford suffered a terrible humiliation when the British government's Higher Education Funding Council rated Cambridge the number one research institution in the country. Oxford rejoiced when it regained the top spot in 1996. Nonetheless, all members of the British scholarly community now acknowledge that for numerous fields of research the universities in places such as Warwick, York, Bath, and Manchester are equal or superior to Oxford and Cambridge.[6]

Rhodes House Warden Anthony Kenny has mentioned a related consideration: Britain has declined as a world power throughout this century. The country has witnessed a drop in military and diplomatic clout, the disappearance of the Empire, and a host of humiliating social and economic problems at home. The resulting malaise among the people became well known in the early 1990s when a survey of British citizens indicated that 50 percent would, if given the opportunity, emigrate to another country. Kenny admits that the rise of other universities around the world and Britain's relative (if not absolute) decline has taken a bit of the luster away from coming to Oxford. For Americans this has had an unfortunate consequence. Along with former American Secretary David Alexander and several rank-and-file scholars, Kenny has admitted that some Americans who have won Rhodes Scholarships have been disappointed to learn that they would actually have to go to Oxford. Selection committees throughout the United States are now warned regularly to reject these "trophy hunters," who want the scholarship simply because of its résumé value. Committees are instructed to make sure that each winner exhibits a sincere desire to study in Oxford.[7]

Many scholars must have winced when they read the *Sunday Telegraph*'s 1993 article on Stan McGee (1992). The newspaper's reporter, Helena de Bertodano, interviewed McGee in his room at Hertford College. She noted that McGee was from a small southern town, that he played the saxophone, that he was a Democrat, and that he wore his short hair cropped back. McGee admitted that "the comparisons with Clinton are obvious ... And I make no bones about it. I'd be lying if I said I hadn't dreamt of becoming President." Above McGee's bed was a world map with thumb tacks stuck into those places he had "conquered." McGee said that a Rhodes Scholarship was important as "an entree into the power elite ... It is the be-all and end-all of academia in the US." Though he said he had a sincere interest in being in Oxford, the article left the clear impression that the scholarship was more important as a trophy bagged for the mantle piece.[8]

Numerous older scholars have pointed out yet other reasons why the experience might be less meaningful today. Most current scholars pursue graduate degrees, which means that they bypass the undergraduate tutorials. As a result, the Americans mix even less with British students than they did formerly. The fact that some scholars live with their spouses in Oxford further means that they are isolated from the communal residence hall life that Cecil Rhodes considered so important for the program. In addition, television, the Internet, and other rapid means of communication provide Americans with considerably more knowledge about Britain than their predecessors had prior to arrival there. The proliferation of study-abroad programs for American undergraduates and the relative cheapness of air travel also mean that many new Rhodes Scholars have already traveled abroad extensively. Hence there are fewer rustics like Dean Rusk, for whom the Oxford experience opened heretofore undreamt adventures. Moreover, air travel makes it possible for today's scholars to return home once or twice each year during vacations. Scholars of earlier generations were away from home for the entire two or three years. The result of all these factors is that living in Britain is a less-foreign, less-intense experience for most scholars. This does not necessarily mean, however, that it is less enjoyable or less important for them.

Despite the many changes in Oxford and in the makeup of Rhodes Scholars, there are numerous remarkable continuities. Oxford's many new building projects have led some observers to call it the "city of dreaming cranes," and yet the magnificent, centuries-old quads, dining halls, and chapels continue to enchant most students and visitors. Though Cecil Rhodes would be shocked to see that his "boys" often are married, non-white, and – indeed – not boys at all, he would undoubtedly be happy to find that the criteria he established are still those used by selection committees. The ideal Rhodes Scholar is intelligent, physically vigorous, displays leadership potential and good character, and desires in some way to serve the public good.

Another remarkably stable feature of the program concerns how the scholars adapt – or fail to adapt – to life in Oxford. Still today many Americans complain about the rain and the soggy vegetables. They also bemoan the fact that the Bodleian Library's drive to computerize its catalogs is woefully behind American standards. Moreover, it is still impossible to check books out of the Bodleian, though students can borrow books from the smaller college libraries.

Rhodes Scholars and other Americans in Oxford today no longer shiver in their rooms or make long treks to latrines at the other end of college. Most student rooms today have central heating or individual electric heaters, and each building possesses its own ample supply of bathroom facilities – though some Americans are disappointed to find that the older buildings tend to have bathtubs rather than showers. In the 1990s Americans are also dismayed that few student rooms are equipped for telephones or computer hookups.

Knowing that Americans prefer all the "modern conveniences," the colleges often place them in the newest residence halls. To the consternation of college officials, even this does not please some of them. Many Rhodes, Marshall, Fulbright, and other scholars want it both ways – having the charm of a five-hundred-year old room plus all the gadgets of a modern building. More than one Rhodes Scholar has told us that he did not like being assigned a room in a new residence hall that looked like a Holiday Inn.

Another striking continuity in the program is that from 1904 to the present a vocal minority of Rhodes Scholars – perhaps 15 or 20 percent – simply have not been able to get along well with most British dons and students. Despite all the social leveling that has occurred in Oxford since the Second World War, many Americans have complained about intellectual arrogance and snobbishness. One Rhodes Scholar from the 1970s told us he hated the English and disliked more than he liked in his daily life in Oxford. He was glad to have won the award, however, because of the friends he made among fellow scholars and because the experience broadened his horizons. He did not wish to speak on the record, however, because he did not want to appear like "an ungrateful jerk."

Mike Lanese, on the other hand, had no such reservations. After he moved into Worcester College in 1986, he and another scholar promptly agreed, "The worst thing about being a Rhodes Scholar is going to Oxford." He conceded that it was a great university, but he detested the climate, the people, and the food.[9]

Another who has spoken on the record about his less-than-happy experiences is George Stephanopoulos. He found many dons and students to be anti-American and cold – rather than merely shy and reserved. He was miffed when he called out to British classmates on the streets, only to be met by their blank stares. He and some American friends came to call this the "bird in the tree" syndrome, because when English people spotted Americans approaching, their typical response was to avoid eye contact and focus on a bird in a tree. Stephanopoulos also took offense at a college theatrical skit that featured an awkward American character who wore a football jersey and kept repeating, "Hi there, Hi there!" He concluded that "Oxford forces you to choose – either you are American, or you turn your back on America." Stephanopoulos did, nonetheless, enjoy being a Rhodes Scholar. But what he liked tended to be things other than the Oxford experience itself: the opportunity to travel widely, the time to read extensively, and the making of new friends (chiefly American, not British).[10]

Over the past half dozen years or so *The American Oxonian* has published several articles by current Rhodes Scholars who complain of the same sorts of treatment. John Cloud (1993), for example, described a formal gathering that took place soon after he arrived at Brasenose College. He found himself standing next to a mathematics don, who had "an appropriate measure of Senior Common Room *gravitas*." When the don asked where he was from, Cloud responded, "Arkansas ... Home of the President." "Yes, well, right," the don muttered, adding, "I would have expected you to be a bit broader." Cloud took this gratuitous reference to Bill Clinton's ample girth to be only one in a long string of insults, slights, and inconveniences to be endured in Oxford.[11]

Rhodes Scholars have not been alone in uttering such complaints. Rosa Ehrenreich created a minor stir in 1994 with her book *A Garden of Paper Flowers: An American at Oxford.* It is the thinly fictionalized story of a Marshall Scholar's first year in Britain. It was a bestseller in Oxford, as students and dons rushed to see if they were among those skewered in its pages. The book is an encyclopedia of all the standard complaints that many Americans have had while studying there. Several Rhodes Scholars, to their amusement or unease, found themselves ridiculed. Sir Anthony Kenny admitted that some of Ehrenreich's criticisms were well founded, but he concluded that for the most part the work represented "juvenile homesickness." One politics don who recognized himself in the book threatened to sue Ehrenreich for libel. Another don reviewed the book in the *Times Literary Supplement* and called its author "naive, insular, arrogant, and uncomprehending."[12] One might expect such reactions from the Oxford establishment, but most Rhodes Scholars and other Americans also agreed that Ehrenreich's jeremiad went overboard.

We asked several of our Oxford friends what they thought about the above criticisms issued by Americans. Regarding the "bird in the tree," they conceded that *some* Americans might get that impression of *some* English people. But they insisted that the British deportment was not unfriendliness but the traditional old reserve. As a general rule, Britons simply do not call out to others while walking along the street.

When asked if there is some snobbishness and arrogance in Oxford, these same people agreed that some Oxford dons and students do possess these characteristics. But these individuals behave churlishly to nearly everyone, not just to Americans. Furthermore, an impartial observer should be able to see that most Oxford dons and students are friendly and, since the Second World War, from middle-class, rather than aristocratic or wealthy, backgrounds. Finally, our friends in Oxford point out that perhaps just as much snobbishness and arrogance can be found in numerous American prep schools and Ivy League campuses.

Regarding the Brasenose don's opening remark about people from Arkansas being "broad," several persons in Oxford conjectured that the Rhodes Scholar may simply have misread the don's intent. Oxford remains famous as a place of conversation, of banter, of witty jibes. The don merely may have been inviting the young American to join in this game of irreverent give-and-take. Perhaps, like Beerbohm's doltish Abimelech V. Oover, this American and numerous others "just don't get it."

While the complaints about Oxford have gained the most public attention, one must remember that the complainers are a distinct, though vocal, minority. One scholar has said that the "current crop" of those filling pages in *The American Oxonian* with polemics against Oxford are "a bunch of whiners." Another former scholar dismissed some of the discontented younger ones as "immature smart alecks." Well over 90 percent of the scholars interviewed for this book eagerly concurred that they enjoyed living and studying in Oxford;

there were some minor annoyances, they admitted, but one can expect to encounter some problems living anywhere on earth.

In 1992 Sir Anthony Kenny conducted a survey of all Rhodes Scholars. His findings corroborate the anecdotal evidence. Scholars ranked their answers from 1 (very good) to 5 (very bad). When asked to evaluate their overall personal experiences in Oxford 92 percent of Americans said "very good" or "good." Only 1 percent said "very bad." Regarding their academic experience, 79 percent placed it at "very good" or "good," and only 7 percent put it in the bottom two levels. In answer to the question, "Would you with hindsight make the same choice of accepting a Rhodes Scholarship?" 87 percent responded "definitely yes." Kenny conceded, however, that this last figure was down from the 98 percent recorded in a survey of the 1920s.[13] Most American universities would be thrilled if 87 percent of their alumni said they would definitely go there if they could do it all over; the national average is roughly 60 percent.

Generalizations

Is it possible to offer any valid generalizations about Rhodes Scholars? The previous two chapters demonstrate that this is impossible in terms of their careers, achievements, political views, and so on. What about personality and character? When Rhodes Scholars themselves are asked to describe other Rhodes Scholars they have given a variety of answers. The only common characteristics that they have hit upon are the following: Rhodes Scholars, as a group, are intelligent, decent persons who are good conversationalists.

Even these characteristics are not applicable to 100 percent of them. Most scholars, indeed, are decent, upstanding citizens. Stansfield Turner was correct, however, when he noted that some have ended up in jail. At least two scholars have served prison terms since the 1980s. In 1983 Harold Griffin (1969) pleaded guilty to helping investors avoid paying taxes by hiding their profits. A U.S. district court judge in Los Angeles sentenced him to six months in prison, along with five years of probation, 300 hours of community service, and a $5,000 fine.[14]

Much more notorious is the case of Mel Reynolds (1975). Reynolds won his Rhodes Scholarship in large part because his selection committee considered him a "bootstrapper," someone who had overcome numerous handicaps. Reynolds had been born to a poor, black sharecropping family in Mississippi and had spent his youth in

Chicago's tough West Side. He had graduated from the University of Illinois and started law school at Harvard before heading for Oxford. In Britain he was well liked by some fellow scholars but suspected by others of being an outright fraud. The latter proved, in the long run, to be closer to the truth. In Oxford Reynolds read for a B.A. in jurisprudence. When the time came for his final examinations, he showed up with an arm in a sling. He claimed to have hurt it while playing basketball and announced that he would be unable to write the long essays required for a degree. Several other scholars could barely conceal their doubts about this supposed accident, as it seemed to confirm their suspicions. Reynolds did not sit for the exams, but afterwards he claimed he returned to Oxford the following year to take them. Rhodes House Warden Sir Edgar Williams later recalled that he had not considered Reynolds "academically remarkable." Furthermore, the Warden recollected that Reynolds had showed "the deepest reluctance to face his examiners." Williams also acknowledged that he possessed no evidence of Reynolds actually obtaining a degree.[15] We perused several years worth of the *Oxford University Calendar*, which lists all degree recipients, and could not find Reynolds' name.

Yet for over fifteen years after his return from Oxford Reynolds did claim to have received his degree. In the *Congressional Directory* and various other reference works, Reynolds listed his Oxford degree variously as a B.A., an M.A., a J.D., and an LL.B. As far as can be determined, he obtained none of these in Oxford; indeed, Oxford does not even grant a J.D. or LL.B.

Reynolds won a seat in the U.S. House of Representatives from the district representing the south side of Chicago. His easy reelection in 1994 seemed to augur a continual ascent in his political career, but the edifice crumbled shortly thereafter. In 1995 he resigned his seat in Congress and took up residence in a penitentiary. He was convicted of having sex with an underage campaign worker and of obstruction of justice. That scandal was followed by news of other problems: unpaid debts, the writing of bad checks, and campaign finance violations.

The personality flaws of other Rhodes Scholars are far less flagrant. Most of the scholars interviewed for this book agree that each class of thirty-two possesses a couple who are boorish know-it-alls. We encountered several of them. One scholar loudly slammed his phone down when we called to try to arrange an interview. Another one asked whether we ourselves were Rhodes Scholars or, at the very least, graduates of Oxford University. When we answered "no" on both counts, he imperiously declared that we were totally incapable and lacking in the necessary credentials for writing a book on Rhodes Scholars. He suggested that we read one of his books for lessons on proper research and writing. (The latter scholar was one of the oldest still alive and has since passed away. We attributed his lack of grace to the fact that he dated from an era when wearing tweeds and coming from the "right college" and "right family" meant more than they do today.) Such characters are minor exceptions to the standards of courtesy and candor that we experienced in dealing with Rhodes Scholars and officials during work on this project.

While he was still the editor of *The American Oxonian*, and thus in a good position to know, John Funari added another generalization about Rhodes Scholars: nearly all have an impostor complex.[16] At the moment they win the award, they worry about being worthy of it, and afterwards they often wonder if they are doing enough to "fight the world's fight." The "impostor complex" is another way of expressing the jibe about Rhodes Scholars having a good future "behind" them. When other scholars have been asked, however, about this complex, their responses have varied widely. Some have agreed with Funari. Others have denied that it is an issue at all, except perhaps in a tiny minority. Yet others have agreed that it is a "modest" factor in a larger number of scholars but that it causes extreme anguish for only a few. Finally, some scholars have maintained that the expectation of "fighting the world's fight" serves as a positive incentive to do good rather than a negative problem that brings psychological distress.

Many share the feeling of Christopher Brown, who was filled with a heightened confidence in his ability to do great things after he returned from Oxford in 1994.[17] But others would agree with Jennifer Bradley. In 1994, as she prepared to leave Oxford and enter a career, she was consumed with self-doubts and feared that everyone was looking at her and saying, "You're a Rhodes Scholar for heaven's sake. You cannot fail."[18]

A Rhodes Scholarship is not a ticket to professional success in one's career; nor is it a guarantee of personal happiness. From 1904 to the present day, virtually every year's class of Americans has witnessed its share of personal disasters. These include persons who dropped out of Oxford after just one or two terms, others who have nervous breakdowns while in Oxford, and others who led unhappy lives upon return to the United States. In the latter category, one can place those who have become alcoholics or drug abusers, those who have run through strings of broken marriages, and those who committed suicide.

The suicides – about three dozen – have been a particularly troubling element throughout the history of the program. As in the case of anyone who takes his or her own life, it is impossible for another person to get into the mind of the deceased to see exactly what triggered the action. In a few of the cases, the persons were suffering from serious illnesses that probably led them to terminate their lives. Might the "impostor complex" have been a factor in the other cases? And if it was, did Oxford instill it, or would the person have derived the same feelings from other sources? In the case of Denny Hansen, we know that his homosexuality and disappointments in his professional career played some role. In the case of Frank Aller, Vietnam and the draft certainly were a part.

Two recent suicides that have sent shocks through the ranks of Rhodes Scholars have been those of Holly Wyatt-Walker (1989) and Reza Gandjei. Wyatt (as she was known prior to marriage) struck all friends as a bubbly, determined, high achiever. She started college at the University of Southern California while still completing high school. In college she had two majors plus a minor concentration and graduated with a nearly perfect 3.97 average. On the side, she taught herself Italian and counseled inner-city youths. To top it off, she put herself through college by working long hours as a waitress. When she applied for a Rhodes Scholarship, she said she aspired to be an arms-control expert. When the *New York Times* ran its article on the new Rhodes Scholars chosen for 1989, she was the one spotlighted as the most remarkable. Her time in Oxford seemed equally hectic and productive. She studied international relations, rowed for her college crew, and played point guard on the Oxford women's basketball team. She obtained an Oxford D.Phil. and then went to work for McKinsey & Co. in the United States. At the time of her suicide in 1995 she was twenty-seven years old, happily married, popular, and well on the road to professional success.

Gandjei had been born in Syria, moved to Britain with his family when he was four, and then moved with them again to the United States when he was sixteen. By the time he won his Rhodes Scholarship for the class of 1990 he had graduated from Berkeley and begun medical school at Harvard. Everyone seemed to agree that the effervescent, charismatic young man was the brightest star among his Rhodes class. He turned down a Marshall Scholarship and with his Rhodes money he seemed happy studying PPE at Balliol, where he obtained a First. He applied for a third scholarship year and spent it doing an M.Phil. thesis in philosophy at Cambridge. His thesis won the highest marks of the year. In his "spare" time he rowed crew, jogged, and became an expert photographer. Upon return to the United States he completed medical school at Harvard and took up a residency with the University of California at San Francisco. He never completed that residency. He was thirty years old when he committed suicide in February 1997.

The deaths of Wyatt-Walker and Gandjei, both well liked and gregarious, stunned all who knew them. Did Oxford contribute in any way to their tragic ends? In the case of Wyatt-Walker, it was evident at the University of Southern California and at Oxford that she was a perfectionist who rarely felt her work was good enough. The high-pressure job she took with McKinsey gave her more reasons to fear she was not measuring up to expectations. Thus she did have the impostor syndrome. Oxford did not instill it, but Oxford also did not give her the self-confidence needed to overcome it.[19]

The case of Gandjei was similar. Despite his outward good cheer and brashness, he had been filled with self doubts since childhood. Throughout his early years in Britain he was taunted by schoolmates because of he was pudgy and dark skinned. By the time he reached Oxford, he was trim and in top physical shape. Only after his death did friends realize that his mania for long jogs in Oxford may have resulted from his fear of ever becoming pudgy again. In Oxford Gandjei found the courage to reveal to some friends that he was gay. He had difficulty in accepting that fact, and some scholars sensed his anxieties about being rejected. During the last year of his life, he became paranoid, withdrew from friends, and became addicted to crystal methamphetamine. As with Wyatt-Walker, it is impossible to link Oxford directly to Gandjei's death. But the high expectations that society often imposes on a Rhodes Scholar may have increased his insecurity. The open admission that he was gay may also, for Gandjei as for other homosexuals, have been difficult to reconcile with being a Rhodes Scholar.[20]

Perhaps the best way to view most of the Rhodes Scholars who have had psychological problems or who have committed suicide is to see them as "Type A" personalities. Psychologists use this term to describe some highly gifted, compulsive individuals who never seem satisfied with what they have done. For these kinds of people, the Rhodes Scholarship does not instill confidence but rather the opposite. An noted earlier, British literary critic Cyril Connolly provided another way of viewing these types of persons. He once wrote, "Whom the gods wish to destroy they first call promising." That could apply to numerous Rhodes Scholars as well as to many others, including Connolly himself. When Connolly died in 1974, nearly all his obituaries echoed the same thoughts: Connolly was prey to long periods of sloth and depression, brought about in part because his output never matched what everyone thought to be his potential. In short, for Rhodes Scholars and others, being anointed the world's best and brightest widens the gap between who they are and who they think they should be.

And who should they be? Certainly not the Rhodes Scholars of the popular imagination. All too often, Rhodes Scholars are portrayed as either of two extremes: super geniuses or washed-up "has beens." One the one hand, being called a Rhodes Scholar can be a compliment. If one wants to ridicule a person who does not seem too bright or capable, the cliché often used is, "He (or she) is no Rhodes Scholar." In movies and television, a Rhodes Scholar is often used as a symbol of all around excellence. For example, in one episode of the popular television series "ER," George Clooney's character wanted to convince others that for once in his life he was interested in a woman for reasons other than her body. The solution: tell them (falsely) that she was a Rhodes Scholar.

On the other hand, calling someone a Rhodes Scholar has sometimes been used as an insult. In several speeches given when he was President, Ronald Reagan used the phrase "I'm no Rhodes Scholar." What he wished to imply was that he was not an elitist intellectual but rather an ordinary American. George Bush endeavored to make the same point in the 1992 election campaign, with his many references to the fact that he had not gone to Oxford.

If one looks at novels and plays, one finds that Rhodes Scholars generally get rough treatment. Randall Jarrell's 1954 novel *Pictures from an Institution* remains one of the great satires of academe. The new president of the fictional Benton College, Dwight Robbins, is one of the "Select Few" of the world, a good talker, a phony who manages to impress most people – in short, a Rhodes Scholar. He himself does not have a Ph.D.; nor do the several Rhodes Scholars that he adds to the faculty.

The year 1954 also marked the debut of William Inge's play *Bus Stop*. One of its characters is Dr. Lyman, a Rhodes Scholar who became a college professor. By the time of the action in the play, Lyman has quit his job, disillusioned because his Rhodes Scholarship had not brought him anything greater in life. He is a mournful, seedy wanderer who hopelessly flirts with young girls.

In response to the question, "Who are Rhodes Scholars?" Walter Isaacson has given an answer quoted by several authors:

> You share this dirty little secret with other Rhodes Scholars, which you know and they know but no one else knows: that it doesn't really mean much at all.[21]

When asked what he meant by this, Isaacson explained that he was not referring to the scholarship itself or to the experience of living in Oxford. He is happy to have won the award, and he enjoyed his studies in Britain. What he was referring to is society's exaggerated opinions of Rhodes Scholars. Isaacson said that Rhodes Scholars themselves know that winning the scholarship does not mean that they are smart or that they will revolutionize the world. The real geniuses, he noted, were the Marshall Scholars. (In saying this, Isaacson reflected the view of most Rhodes Scholars and most Oxford dons.) Instead, Isaacson went on, Rhodes Scholars in general were fairly intelligent, well-rounded, honest people who could be counted on to be upstanding citizens.[22]

Isaacson was too modest. The fact that many Rhodes Scholars also win (and turn down) Marshall, Fulbright, and other scholarships indicates the kind of academic ability required make the final cut. But he was right in indicating that most Rhodes Scholars are not some combination of Albert Einstein and Indiana Jones who will transform science, government, and education while also bringing permanent peace to the world. The great majority of Rhodes Scholars are well adjusted enough to know that they do not fit that mold. As a result, they do not end up in either of the stereotypical extremes: obnoxious braggadocio or self-loathing failure.

If Rhodes Scholars as a whole perform at a less brilliant level than do Marshall Scholars in Oxford, this results in part from the very success of the Rhodes program. A higher percentage of Marshalls tend to go on to careers in academe and research, whereas Rhodes Scholars are more evenly scattered through the full range of professional occupations. Since Rhodes Scholars are expected to be all-rounders, this means that many of them devote much of their time in Oxford to pursuits besides merely their course work. Moreover, the very fame of the Rhodes Scholarships leads some of them to conclude that merely winning the award is more important than their exam scores in Oxford. The result is that they tend to coast a little while in Britain, for they know the treadmill awaits them upon their return to the United States. As mentioned in the previous chapter, the more relaxed pace of their lives in Oxford provides many of them with an important opportunity for reading and self-reflexion.

What would Cecil Rhodes think of the accomplishments of his U.S. scholars? He might be disappointed that they had not acted more in union, as a hearty band of brothers filled with ideas and enthusiasm bestowed on them in the hallowed halls of Oxford. He might be dismayed that not more of them had chosen to fight the world's fight from the most "obvious" careers: as politicians and statesmen. He might be disheartened to discover that there was no obvious way in which Rhodes Scholars, as a group, had made the world a better place.

Yet one must recall that Rhodes was, with all his flaws, a resourceful visionary. We today might not share his same vision of Anglo-Saxon males leading the world to peace and prosperity. But Rhodes was flexible and recognized that his own personal life was not a model for his scholars. He consciously selected criteria that did not obviously describe himself. Moreover, as a dynamic mover and shaker in the fields of business and government, he recognized that what was suitable for today might not be suitable for tomorrow. By extension, therefore, Rhodes would probably acknowledge that the ways in which one leads a good, productive life have changed. In short, there is every reason to believe that he would be at least moderately pleased.

Those of us today who view the program can be even more positive. Rhodes Scholars as an organized group have not elevated the world to a new, higher level of existence. But as individuals many of them have had a significant, beneficial impact on society in general or on their chosen spheres of endeavor. The Rhodes Scholarships and the scores of study-abroad programs that they helped to spawn certainly have, in immeasurable ways, fostered better international relations. To the extent that the Oxford experience has helped to promote these careers and activities, we can be grateful for the bequest that Cecil Rhodes left to the world.

NOTES

1. *Macleans,* 18 November 1996, 43; *TAO,* 84(1997): 129-30.
2. *Oxford University Gazette,* 25 July 1996, 1; *The Guardian,* 6 August 1996, 3; (Oxford) *Development News,* December 1996, 3.
3. *Independent,* 29 June 1994, 4; *Oxford Today,* Michaelmas Issue, 1996, 53; (Oxford) *Development News,* June 1997, 6.
4. (Oxford) *Development News,* June 1997, 1; Warden's Christmas letter, December 1997, 2.
5. See http://www.ox.ac.uk/.
6. *Chronicle of Higher Education,* 20 January 1993, A47; 23 November 1994, A37; 19 April 1996, A56; 28 February 1997, A48. Also see: *The Guardian,* 20 December 1996, 6; *Sunday Times,* 2 February 1997, sec. 4, 5.
7. Interviews with Kenny, 28 July 1993, and Alexander, 23 May 1995; Warden's Christmas letter, December 1996, 8-9.
8. *Sunday Telegraph,* 21 March 1993, International sec., 22.
9. *OSU Quest,* Winter 1988, 10.
10. *The New Republic,* 5 July 1993, 43; *Sunday Times,* 27 February 1994, sec. 4, 6; Stephanopoulos interview, 1 April 1995.
11. *TAO,* 81 (1994): 267.
12. *TLS,* 14 October 1994, 33.
13. Kenny speech in Georgetown, 11 June 1993. The authors wish to thank Sir Anthony for providing a copy of the survey results.
14. United Press International, 15 September 1983.
15. *Chicago Tribune,* 7 May 1995, 1.
16. Funari interview, 11 October 1993.
17. Brown interview, 26 June 1997.
18. *TAO,* 81 (1994): 143.
19. *Los Angeles Times,* 12 December 1988, Metro sec., 3; *TAO,* 83 (1996): 109-12.
20. *TAO,* 84 (1997): 226-30.
21. Topping, "Best Men," 7.
22. Isaacson, letter to authors, 17 July 1995.

APPENDIX

*U.S. Rhodes Scholars, 1904-1998**

1904

Stanley Royal Ashby
George Emerson Barnes
Ralph Hervey Bevan
Ralph Eugene Blodgett
C.F. Tucker Brooke
Robert Preston Brooks
Julius Arthur Brown
Charles Whiteley Bush
Neil Carothers
Raymond Huntington Coon
William Clark Crittenden
Harvey Bruce Densmore
William Alexander Fleet
Francis Howard Fobes
Lawrence Henry Gipson
George Earl Hamilton
Robert Llewellyn Henry
Henry Hinds
Stanley Kuhl Hornbeck
Baltzar Hans Jacobson
Joel Marcus Johanson
William Leamon Kendall
Paul Kieffer
James Holtzclaw Kirkpatrick
Harold Guy Merriam
Earle Walter Murray
Paul Nixon
David Richard Porter

Benjamin Marsden Price
Amasa Kingsley Read
Thomas Ellis Robins
Richard Frederick Scholz
Warren Ellis Schutt
John Calvin Sherburne
Willard Learoyd Sperry
Clark Tandy
John James Tigert
William Henry Verner
George Clark Vincent
Benjamin Bruce Wallace
Joseph Garfield Walleser
James Homer Winston
Paul Murray Young

1905

Cary Rudolph Alburn
Leigh Alexander
Edward McPherson Armstrong
Frank Aydelotte
Thomas Sydney Bell
William Henry Branham
Frederick William Buchholz
Leonard Wolsey Cronkhite
Samuel Ely Eliot
Newton Edward Ensign
Ebb James Ford
Carol Howe Foster

---

* Numerous women have changed their names upon marriage. This listing gives all
  names as they appeared when the scholarships were awarded.

Roy Kenneth Hack
Harris Hazleton Holt
Henry Richards Isaacs
Edwin Russell Lloyd
Charles Delahunt Mahaffie
Ralph Conover Many
Arthur Henry Marsh
Henry Sewall Mitchell
Frank Martin Mohler
Hugh Anderson Moran
Raymond Clinton Platt
Lewellyn Gordon Railsback
Athol Ewart Rollins
John Newton Schaeffer
Bernadotte Everly Schmitt
Harold Williams Soule
Harry Peyton Steger
Albert Mason Stevens
William W. Thayer
Eugene Sumter Towles
Henry Trantham
Beverley Dandridge Tucker
Jacob Van der Zee
Thomas Henry Wade
George Andrews Whiteley
Ralph Claude Willard

1906

There were no U.S. Rhodes Scholars appointed for this year.

1907

Dudley Babcock Anderson
Warren Ortman Ault
Richard Capel Beckett
Berkeley Blackman
Shirl Hyde Blalock
Newcomb Kinney Chaney
Arthur Shamberger Chenoweth
John Sherman Custer
Henry Markley Gass
Farnham Pond Griffiths
Clarence Henry Haring
Robert William Hartley
Donald Grant Herring
Lawrence Cameron Hull, Jr.
George Hurley

Joseph Hoyt Jackson
Alfred Proctor James
Wayne Clark Jordan
Charles Alexander Keith
Earl Kilburn Kline
Benjamin Rice Lacy, Jr.
Alain LeRoy Locke
John Roy McLane
Wilson Plumer Mills
McKenn Fitch Morrow
George Whitefield Norvell
Samuel Mayo Rinaker
Arthur Leonidas St. Clair
Albert Godfrey Sanders
Robert Maxwell Scoon
Robert Parvin Strickler
James R. Thomas
Ben Tomlinson
Guy Richard Vowles
Wilson Dallam Wallis
Everett Franklin Warrington
Allen Brown West
Albert Kitchel Whallon
Addison White
Cyrus French Wicker
Charles Chase Wilson
Edward Jones Winans
Shirley Townshend Wing
Jay Walter Woodrow
Millard Fillmore Woodrow

1908

Willard Titus Barbour
Robert Edwin Blake
Matthew Alec Brown
Robert Wilbur Burgess
Walter Stanley Campbell
Rhys Carpenter
Herbert Green Cochran
George Henry Curtis
William Strong Cushing
Charles Wendell David
Lucius Arnold Frye
Morrison Beall Giffen
Thomas Porter Hardman
Frank Ezekiel Holman
Grover Cleveland Huckaby

John Lee Hydrick
Wistar Wayman Johnson
Ballard Freese Keith
Earle Hesse Kennard
Frank Chellis Light
Edmond Earl Lincoln
Theodore Trimmier McCarley
Thomas J.A. McClernan
Arthur Bond Meservey
Frederic Dan Metzger
William Burt Millen
Grover Cleveland Morris
Thomas Jefferson Mosley
James M.D. Olmsted
Claude Albert Pifer
Francis Marmaduke Potter
George Ellsworth Putnam
Oscar Ripley Rand
Albert Graham Reid
Frank Alfonso Reid
Jael Jackson Rodgers
Richard Schellens
James Huntly Sinclair
Joseph Earl Smith
Clarence Arthur Spaulding
William Tennent Stockton
Winchester Stuart
William Scott Unsworth
Henry L.J. Williams
Carroll Atwood Wilson

1909

There were no U.S. Rhodes Scholars appointed for this year.

1910

William John Bland
James Insley Boyce
Charles Simonton Brice
Frank Baker Bristow
Henry Chase Brownell
Hugh McLellan Bryan
Walter Speight Bryan
Toney Taylor Crooks
Clayton Edward Crosland
Elmer Holmes Davis
Richard Lester Disney

Edward Henry Eckel
Albert Russell Ellingwood
Leonard Eugene Farley
William Monroe Gaddy
Robert Hale
William Shacklett Hamilton
Joseph Barlow Harrison
Ralph V.L. Hartley
Milton J. Hoffman
Earnest Albert Hooton
Edwin Powell Hubble
Elmer Davenport Keith
Alexander Peebles Kelso
Ray Loomis Lange
Roger Sherman Loomis
Cecil Kenyon Lyans
McDougal Kenneth McLean
Christopher Morley
Claud Dalton Nelson
Archie Huston Ormond
William Francis Raney
John Crowe Ransom
Edward Noel Roberts
Whitney Hart Shepardson
Herbert Rowell Stolz
William Alexander Stuart
Howard Alfred Taber
Joseph Tetlie
William L.G. Williams
Stanley Mayhew Wilton
Joseph Washburn Worthen
Charles Franklyn Zeek
William Alexander Ziegler

1911

Ernest Tolbert Adams
Allen Barnett
Hubert Kingsley Beard
Cedric Harding Beebe
Francis Foulke Beirne
Irvine Furman Belser
Maurice Cary Blake
Vincent Kingwell Butler
Vest Davis
Samuel Arthur Devan
McPherrin Hatfield Donaldson
Horace Bidwell English

Esper Wayne Fitz
Ludwig Sherman Gerlough
Van Wagenen Gilson
William Chase Greene
Henry Alvin Gunderson
Carl Haessler
John David Hayes
Roy Helm
Harold Brooks Hering
Harris Gary Hudson
Warren Clifford Johnson
Karl Karsten
Edward Eugene Kern
Jakob A.O. Larsen
Solomon Lester Levy
Walter Clay Lowdermilk
Elias Lyman
Thomas Means
Edwin Warren Moise
James Insley Osborne
Harold Scott Quigley
John Andrew Rice
William McMillan Rogers
Franklin Ferriss Russell
John LeRoy Shipley
Matthew Glenn Smith
Charles Benjamin Swartz
Quitman Underwood Thompson
Edgar Turlington
William Claude Vogt
James Keir Watkins
Philip Wright Whitcomb
Carroll Hill Wooddy
Stanley Yates

1912

*There were no U.S. Rhodes Scholars
appointed for this year.*

1913

Walter Carl Barnes
Brand Blanshard
Wayne Cook Bosworth
Henry Reginald Bowler
Philip Henry Brodie
Homer Lindsey Bruce
Henry Van Anda Bruchholz

Floyd Sherman Bryant
Oliver Cromwell Carmichael
Laurence Alden Crosby
Weldon Frank Crossland
Wilburt Cornell Davison
Arthur Brittan Doe
Terry Colley Durham
Ralph Baxter Foster
Frank Hoyt Gailor
George Hussey Gifford
Valentine Britton Havens
Thomas Hawkins Jones
James Noel Keys
William Kyle
Lincoln Sydnor Laffitte
Preston Lockwood
Robert Valentine Merrill
Emory Hamilton Niles
George Bernard Noble
Francis Lester Patton
John Robertson Paul
Edward Forrest Porter
Levi Arnold Post
Lawrence Howard Riggs
Richard Harvey Simpson
Fred Manning Smith
Conrad Edwin Snow
George Frederick Spaulding
Frederick Dorsey Stephens
William Warren Stratton
George Wilfred Stumberg
Frank Graham Swain
Norman Stephen Taber
Hatton Dunnica Towson
George Van Stantvoord
Paul Graves Williams

1914

William Hendrick Arnold, Jr.
Carleton Goldstone Bowden
Morrison Comegys Boyd
Bennet Harvie Branscomb
Clarence Austin Castle
Charles Russell Clason
William Coburn Cook
Clyde Eagleton
Alexander Green Fite

William Willard Flint
Cyrus Stokes Gentry
John Lyles Glenn, Jr.
Robert Kent Gooch
Paul Francis Good
Charles Harold Gray
Charles Francis Hawkins
Howard Stevens Hilley
Emile Frederic Holman
Benjamin Clark Holtzclaw
Paul Thomas Homan
Paul Edgar Hubbell
Everett Banfield Jackson
Walter Clarence Jepson
Richard Ridgely Lytle
Milo Leo March
Thomas Franklin Mayo
Baxter Merrill Mow
David Theodore Nelson
Scott Hurtt Paradise
Wilder Graves Penfield
William Prickett
John Vickers Ray
Frederick William Rogers
Stanley Israel Rypins
James Hamilton St. John
William Webster Sant
Seymour Sereno Sharp
Lucius Rogers Shero
Gilchrist Baker Stockton
William Matthew Sullivan
Moyer Delwyn Thomas
Robert Hamilton Warren
Carl Jefferson Weber
Philip Prentiss Werlein
James Herbert Wilson
Edward Pinckney Woodruff
Hessel Edward Yntema

1915

There were no U.S. Rhodes Scholars appointed for this year.

1916

Luton Ackerson
George Wayne Anderson, Jr.
Joseph Bartlett Armstrong

Alexander Kirkland Barton
Miner Searle Bates
John Howard Binns
James Howard Bishop
William Russell Burwell
Eugene Parker Chase
Robert P.T. Coffin
Chester Verne Easum
Lawrence William Faucett
William Luther Finger
Raymond Leonard Grismer
Latimer Johns
Spurgeon Milton Keeny
Paul Banwell Means
Douglas Phillips Miller
Lewis Rex Miller
Vernon Nash
Elbert Benjamin Naugle
Parker Newhall
William Armour Pearl
Samuel Van Orden Prichard
Roy M.D. Richardson
Wyatt Rushton
Norman Dunsbee Scott
Fred Tredwell Smith
Robert Montgomery Stephenson
Reuben Thornton Taylor
Frederick Gale Tryon
George Stevens Whitehead

1917

David Muir Amacker
Roscoe Ashworth
Charles Rutherford Bagley
Frank Stringfellow Barr
Scott Milross Buchanan
Alexander Coldough Dick
Richard William Dunlap
Thomas H. Edsall
George Adlai Feather
Ernest Stacey Griffith
LaPenne J. Guenveur
Rexford Brammer Hersey
Clark Hopkins
Benjamin Mayham Hulley
Joseph Clyde Little
Marvin Manley Monroe

Felix Muskett Morley
John Ohleyer Moseley
Harold Delmar Natestad
Edward Abbe Niles
Thomas Kenneth Penniman
Ordean Rockey
Daniel Parkhurst Spalding
Neal Tuttle
Elmer Hoover Van Fleet
Arthur Preston Whitaker
Horace North Wilcox
John Milton Williams

1918

Raymond Wesley Anderson
John Rea Bacher
Bryton Barron
Raymond Peter Brandt
Ralph Moore Carson
Francis Bayard Carter
John Archibald V. Davies
Joseph David Doty
Clifford Judkins Durr
Bryan England
Elwyn Evans
Axel Berg Gravem
Julian Lamar Hagen
Virgil Melvin Hancher
Robert Lee Humber
Philip Harold Jones
Davidson Rankin McBride
Franklin Pierce McGowan
Thomas Oscar McLaughlin
Thomas Myers Palmer
Stanley Pargellis
Donovan MacNeely Richardson
Walter Edward Sandelius
John Monk Saunders
Samuel Stephenson Smith
Eugene Hendrix Stevenson
Clarence Kirshman Streit
William Benjamin Stubbs
James Alfred Tong
George Findlay Willison
Ralph Timothy Wilson

1919

Ernest Roscoe Baltzell
Boardman Marsh Bosworth
Crane Brinton
Ford Keeler Brown
Leroy James Burlingame
Charles Willard Carter, Jr.
John Murdoch Clarke
Herbert Eugene Clefton
Paul Robinson Coleman-Norton
Philip Dyer Crockett
Arthur Kyle Davis, Jr.
William Ray Dennes
William Yandell Elliott
Frank Cudworth Flint
Marshall Nairne Fulton
Harold Sanford Glendening
Robert Patrick Hamilton
Frank Walker Harrold
Maxwell Haines Herriott
Louis Meredith Jiggits
Shelby Thomas McCloy
John Griffith Madden
Edward Sagendorph Mason
Francis Pickens Miller
Clark Leslie Mock
Henry Allen Moe
Frank Vigor Morley
Chester Arthur Osler
Calvin Jennings Overmyer
Ira Chambers Powers
Alfred Irvin Reese
Walter Elmer Sikes
George Ginger Thomas
William Dwight Whitney
Theodore Stanley Wilder
Charles Weston Williams

1920

Radcliffe Harold Beckwith
Charles Bryant Coolidge
Franzo Hazlett Crawford
John Henry Davis
Oscar Fulton Davisson, Jr.
James Quayle Dealey
William Coleman Frierson
Frederic Russell Gamble

Milan Wayne Garrett
William Paul Hamilton
John Marshall Harlan
William Collar Holbrook
Wilbur Jennings Holleman
Arthur Lee Kinsolving
Ralph Ellerbeck Lewis
Ernest Kidder Lindley
Norman Mather Littell
John Valentine Lovitt
Albert Lincoln McMillan
Arthur Prichard Moor
Edwin Fountain Moseley
Carl Elbridge Newton
John Howard Powers
Beverly Waugh Smith, Jr.
Robert Aura Smith
Corydon Perry Spruill
Alexander Buel Trowbridge, Jr.
Alexander Seymour Van
Santvoord
Arthur Vidrine
Franklin Dickerson Walker
Samuel Walter Washington

1921

Williams Forbes Adams
William Bryan Bolich
Joseph August Brandt
Charles Marvin Chatfield
James Saxon Childers
James Morris Christensen
Kenneth Carey Cole
Henry Harrison Cooke
Edward Dubuisson
Corwin D. Edwards
Clyde Emery
James Alexander Farmer
Robert Michael Field, Jr.
Edwin Douglas Ford, Jr.
Herbert Giddens Ford
Mowat Gjems Fraser
John Farquhar Fulton
Lloyd Haberly
Robert Graham Heiner
John Vernon Hopkins
Joseph Tomlinson Hunt

Albert Charles Jacobs
Sinclair Kerby-Miller
Marshall Mason Knappen
Frederick William Layman
Frank Kirby Mitchell
Joseph Edwards Norwood
Willis Dwight Nutting
Russell Holt Peters
Richard Scofield
Murray Fontaine Skinker
Newton Bradford Trenham
Christopher Longstreth Ward, Jr.

1922

Montgomery Drummond
Anderson
Richard Hindry Barker
Charles Caldwell Bowie
Thomas Parmelee Brockway
Bertrand Harris Bronson
William D.P. Carey
John Porter Carleton
Earl Meadow Dunbar
Edward P.F. Eagan
Paul Theodore Ellsworth
Fitzgerald Flournoy
Malcolm Fooshee
Albert Frank Gollnick
William Chace Greene
Ford Poulton Hall
Everett Way Highsmith
Allen Sheppard Johnson
Lawrence Keville Larson
Walter H.D. Lester
Earl Mason McGowin
William Percy Maddox
William Joseph Maier, Jr.
William Hugh Peal
Charles Wooten Pipkin
James Alexander Ross, Jr.
Daniel Heckert Sanders
Royall Henderson Snow
Woodson Spurlock
William Edwards Stevenson
Charles Wright Thomas
Alexander Thomson
Alan Valentine

1923

Ned Bliss Allen
Troyer Steele Anderson
Benjamin May Baker, Jr.
William Maxwell Blackburn
Leslie M. Bruce
Philip Wallenstein Buck
Robert Emmett Burk
Arthur Keeler Burt
Eldridge Houston Campbell, Jr.
George Gray Carter
Francis de Leisseline Fergusson
Edwin Medbery Fitch
Edward Billings Ham
Francis Herkomer Herrick
Ralph Ernest Huston
William Strother Hynes
Raymond Harvey Jack
George Vincent Kidder
Russell Krauss
Thomas Covington MacEachin
Francis Otto Matthiessen
Alpheus Hyatt Mayor
Edwin Mims, Jr.
Robert Logan Nugent
Sherrow Glenn Parker
Walden Pell II.
Haven Palmer Perkins
James McDowell Richards
Robert Driscoll Shea
Edward Trudeau Thomas
John Andrew Wilson
Jackson Thornwell Witherspoon

1924

Charles David Abbott
Joseph Dexter Bennett
Hugh Bradley
Carter Marshall Braxton
Robert Bigham Brode
William Walton Butterworth
Raymond Giddens Carey
Paul Christopherson
Hervey Milton Cleckley
Wilton Donald Cole
Harold Hess Davis
John Philip Dawson

Florien Preston Gass
Walser Sly Greathouse
Robert Lee Guthrie
Paul Atkins Harwood
Robert Lee Hyatt, Jr.
Otis Hamilton Lee
John Lisgar Merrill
Wallace Edward Robertson
William Arthur Roseborough
Oris Edward Sandusky
Felix Ira Shaffner
Sullivan Thorne Sparkman
Donald Alfred Stauffer
Carl Walther Strom
Mack Buckley Swearingen
Sheldon Tefft
Gamber Frederick Tegtmeyer
Earl Russell Thoenen
Israel Treiman
Frederick Thomas Wagner
Arthur McCandless Wilson
Thomas James Wilson

1925

Frank Davis Ashburn
Robert Lee Baker
Arthur Doerr Bond
Reuben August Borsch
Neil Louis Crone
Edward Francis D'Arms
James William Fulbright
Franklin Dingwall Gray
Mason Hammond
John L.J. Hart
Paul Swain Havens
Clinton Newton Howard
Ralph Merle Hower
Francis Rarick Johnson
Lawrence Brock Leighton
Elijah Wilson Lyon
James Hervey Macomber, Jr.
John Whipple Olmsted
Arthur Worthington Packard
Owen Brooke Rhoads
Philip Blair Rice
Joseph Wilfred Sagmaster
Charles Eskridge Saltzman

Robert Shields Sams
William Terrell Sledge
Douglas Van Steere
Robert Jemison Van De Graaff
William Scott Vaughn
Coleman Carter Walker
John Deans Westermann
Standish Weston
John C.R. Whiteley

1926

Edgar Elliot Beaty
Ernest Russel Boller
Robert R. R. Brooks
Walter Lindsey Brown
Erwin Dain Canham
Gordon Keith Chalmers
John Waddell Chase
William Johnston Cocke
Reginald Lansing Cook
Clayton Bion Craig
Roscoe Cross
Robert Newton Cunningham
Robert Franklin Davidson
Caleb Frank Gates
Paul Kirby Hennessy
Theodore Carswell Hume
John Morris Legendre
William Ezna Lingelbach, Jr.
Edward George Lowry, Jr.
Edmund Robert McGill
George Sinclair Mitchell
Milton Charles Nahm
William Ichabod Nichols
John Burdon Ocheltree
Joseph W. Ogle
Nathan Kuhns Parker
George Roberts Pfann
George Taylor Ross
Cornelius Alfred Tilghman
Carlton Beebe Wicart
Gordon Coleman Woodbury
Harold Charles Wyman
Karl Egbert Young

1927

Edgar Holt Ailes
Robert Henry Baugh
Edmund Olaf Belsheim
Wallace Cable Brown
Jefferson DeMent Burrus, Jr.
Dean Alexander Clark
Andrew Vincent Corry
Hugh B. Cox
Woodford Agee Heflin
Robert Frederick Heilbron
Charles Horowitz
Paul Clark Kimball
Alfons Ludwig Korn
Samuel Adams McCain
Myres Smith McDougal
Furman Gordon McLarty
Edward Otis Mather
Ben R. Miller
John Edmonds Mock
Hudson Moore, Jr.
Brewster Bowen Morgan
Charles S. Parker, Jr.
Robert Beatty Patrick
Allen Williams Post
Edwin Macdougall Rhea
Samuel Henry Sabin
Frederic John Siebert
DeWitt Hendee Smith
William Mode Spackman
Charles Eugene Springer
Joseph Morgan Stokes
John E. F. Wood
Herbert Brookhart Woodman

1928

Robert Farnham Baker
William Arthur Breyfogle
Thomas Warren Childs
William Everett Derryberry
Bergen Evans
Larkin Hundley Farinholt
Lucien Pinckard Giddens
Charles Lucian Gleaves
Eugene William Goodwillie
Richard Crocker Gurney
Thomas Jefferson Hamilton, Jr.

William Clark Helmbold
Hebbel Edward Hoff
Champness T.S. Keep
Clyde K.M. Kluckhohn
Robert Lasch
William Murray Lockwood
Harlan DeBaun Logan
John Justin McDonough
Andrew Douglas McHendrie
Holbrook Mann MacNeille
William Nash
John William Nason
Alfred J. Orselli
Paul Eugene Pfuetze
Allen Walker Read
Arthur Clendenin Robertson
Theodore Cedric Ruch
Lawrence A.L. Scott, Jr.
Abbot Emerson Smith
Robert Penn Warren
Walter B.C. Watkins
Dixon Wector

1929

Frederick Mather Anderson
Armistead Lloyd Boothe
Cleanth Brooks
Royal Calvin Bryant
Robert E. Burns
Edwin Readle Casady
Aubrey Marion Cates, Jr.
Albert Charles Cornsweet
John King Fairbank
Rudolph Maximilian Goepp, Jr.
Manasses Jacob Grove
Robert Zachariah Hickman
Robert Emmett Houston, Jr.
Frederick Lawson Hovde
Daniel Edward Hudgins
Richard Kendall Irons
Farnsworth Leroy Jennings
Richmond Lattimore
George Arthur Lincoln
Savoie Lottinville
Robert Earle McGee
Thomas Arnold McGovern
William Winters McQuilkin

Malcolm Ames MacIntyre
Charles Frederick Malam
Richard Davis Mallery
Albert Alexander Murphree
Matti Hugo Pakkala
Paul Davis Schettler
Carl Bernhardt Spaeth
Dana Merrill Swan
Samuel Roger Tyler, Jr.
George Thomas Washington

1930

Frank Marshall Adamson
Calvin Smith Brown
George Springer Craft
George Hedwig Deiter
Paul Louis DeVos
Francis Rahr Duborg
Robert Eikel
Franklin Brewster Folsom
Grady Craven Frank
James Lambert Gibson
Donald Westey Gladney, Jr.
Maure L. Goldschmidt
George Losie Huber
George Clarence Kent
Samuel Kenneth Kurtz
Emory Kemton Lindquist
George John Miller
John Davisson Phillips
William Poole
Earl Hampton Pritchard
Irvin Rudolph Schimmelpfennig
John Paul Scott
Arthur Fleming Scotten
Allan Seager
Charles Gordon Siefkin
Dorr Covell Skeels
Lewis A. Smith
Robert Sydney Smith
James Alexander Spruill, Jr.
Robert E. Van Meter
Leland Alfred Watson
William Whipple

1931

Carl Bert Albert
Charles Hartwell Bonesteel III
Julius Byles
George Alfred Carlson
Francis Fleming Coleman
Alexander Barrow Daspit
Benjamin Cushing Duniway
Austin Faricy
David Marvin French
Patrick Armistead Gibson
Glenn Donald Gosling
Milo Fowler Hamilton
Dudley Lee Harley
Alfred Hayes
Joseph Cameron Hickingbotham, Jr.
Grenville Ross Holden
George Chandler Holt
Robert Franklin Jackson
Milton Preston Jarnagin III
Robert Eugene Johnson
Van Loran Johnson
William Thomas Jones
William Koren, Jr.
Charles Maxwell Lancaster
John Butlin Martin, Jr.
Edward Minter Parker
James Parker Pettegrove
John Charles Pirie
Lawrence Hugh Rogers
Dean Rusk
Morris Frank Shaffer
Ferdinand Fairfax Stone
Byron Kightly Trippet

1932

Carl Barnett Allendoerfer
Atherton Bean
Samuel Hutchison Beer
Thomas Lynn Beyer
Roger Derby Black, Jr.
Robert Minge Brown
Clayton Lee Burwell
Richard Norman Clark, Jr.
Burnet Maduro Davis
Jules Richard DeLaunay
Edward Francis Drake

Frederick Arthur Ficken
Joseph Harold Fitzgerald
Albert Henry Garretson
Albert Price Heusner
Charles Johnston Hitch
Willmoore Kendall
Lewis Arthur Larson
Turner Hudson McBaine
James McCormack, Jr.
Critchell Parsons
Harold Payson, Jr.
John White Pendleton
Spencer Drummond Pollard
Don Krasher Price
Howland Hill Sargeant
William Herbert Sweet
George Cook Tilley
James Miller Tunnell, Jr.
Houston Hutchinson Wasson
John Ashley Wells
David Carnahan Williams

1933

Frederic Tremaine Billings, Jr.
John Weeks Bodine
Arthur Albert Brown
Augustus Merrimon Cuninggim
John William Dowling
Arthur Butler Dugan
Wilson Homer Elkins
Paul Engle
John Fischer
Fenton A.S. Gentry
Ivan Alexander Getting
Lincoln Gordon
Edward Burns Gregg
Gregory Kemenyi Hartmann
Charlton J.K. Hinman
Samuel Shepard Jones
Joseph Burke Knapp
Clarence Pendleton Lee
Harold Crowson Lumb
William Allan McRae, Jr.
Thomas Corwin Mendenhall II
Rex Burns Pontius
Raymond Donald Pruitt
David St. Clair

Alden Kingsland Sibley
Don Douwe Stuurman
Charles Eugene Sunderlin
Lewis Harlow Van Dusen, Jr.
Frank Henry Verhoek
Owen Franklin Walker
Albert Jacob Weinrich
Alfred Ellis Wilhelmi
John Page Williams

1934

Samuel Thompson Adams
Robert Warren Barnett
Norman Ritner Beers
Daniel Joseph Boorstin
Eugene Theodore Booth, Jr.
Walter Alexander Chudson
Hugh Terry Cunningham
Hedley Williams Donovan
Charles Lyman Emrich, Jr.
Oscar Gass
Richard Murphey Goodwin
George Arthur Gordon
Chauncy Dennison Harris
Joseph Elmer Hawkins, Jr.
Robert Hayter
Edward D.H. Johnson
Harry Willmer Jones
Murray Delmar Kirkwood
Eugene Kenneth McClaskey
George Crews McGee
Robert H. Michelet
Robert Clarence Moore
John Bertram Oakes
Thornton Leigh Page
Robert Eugene Pflaumer
Herbert Chermside Pollock
Richard Bulger Schlatter
Wilfrid Stalker Sellars
Morgan Sibbett
Charles Robert Sleeth
John Marks Templeton
William Willeroy Wells

1935

Richard Brown Baker
Marshall Ballard, Jr.

Charles Arthur Bane
Herbert L. Brown, Jr.
John R. W. Carpenter
Royston Canon Clements
Horace Willard Davenport
Samuel Rhodes Dunlap
John Jenkins Espey
William Alfred Franta
Frederick Gillen
James Goodfriend
John Thomas Hays, Jr.
Marion Gordon Knox
Duncan Chaplin Lee
Willard Deming Lewis
Thomas Huston Macbride
William Harvey Maguigan
Milton F. Meissner
Herbert C.L. Merillat
Ray Miller
William Strake Mundy, Jr.
Henry Allison Page III
Sherman L. Pease
Carl Pfaffmann
William Lewis Sachse
Walter Hugo Stockmayer
Martin Wagner
Samuel Gardner Welles
Donald Niven Wheeler
Clayton Samuel White
James Gaston Williamson

1936

Henry Shull Arms
Rodney Montgomery Baine
Robert C. Barnard
Charles Greenleaf Bell
Franklin Moore (Dyke) Brown
Carleton Burke Chapman
William Mellard Connor
Frank W. Crabill
Gordon Alexander Craig
Dean Kneeland Crystal
George Peddy Cuttino
Robert Higgins Ebert
Francis Cope Evans
Guy Otto Farmer
Louis Earl Frechtling

Richard William Horner
Philip Mayer Kaiser
Thomas Francis Lambert, Jr.
Charles Bernard Lewis, Jr.
James Rodney Nelson
Deric O'Bryan
John Granville Rideout
Dwight Edwards Robinson
Walt Whitman Rostow
James Hinton Sledd
Carl Theodore Solberg
George Fredrick Somers
Emerson George Spies
Elvis J. Stahr, Jr.
Edgar William Timm
Alba Houghton Warren, Jr.
Murat Willis Williams

1937

Robert Shillingford Babcock
Dana Kavanagh Bailey
Stephen Kemp Bailey
Robert Caldwell Bates
Robert Carlyle Beyer
Wallace Sands Brooke
Norman Ralph Davidson
James L.N. Egan
Leslie Alan Falk
Wilson Farnsworth Fowle
James Richard Gardner
Robert Averill Harman
Cresson Henry Kearny
Penn Townsend Kimball II
James Ervin King
Horton Meyer Laude
Nelson Jordan Leonard
Bernard Andrew Monaghan
Guy Theodore Nunn
John J.E. Palmer
Thomas Lockwood Perry
George Piranian
William C.H. Prentice
Karl Rhorer Price
Edwin Lemoine Skinner, Jr.
Howard Kingsbury Smith
William Denham Sutcliffe
Frank E. Taplin

Sam John Van Hyning, Jr.
Richard Frye Watt
Bruce Stanton Waybur
Harvey Russell Wellman

1938

Ford Lewis Battles
Gerald Brown
William Caswell Carter
John Chalmers
James Harlan Cleveland
Robert Denoon Cumming
James Hector Currie
LeRoy William Earley
Harry Davis Flory, Jr.
Leigh Gerdine
Chadbourne Gilpatric
John Ford Golay
Kermit Gordon
Louis Julius Hector
Jerome Himelhoch
Peter Carl Hoch
Charles Frank Jelinek
George Fenwick Jones
Armistead Mason Lee
John Morter Luttrell
Leslie Grant McConell, Jr.
Russell West McDonald
William Shelley McEwan
Robert Mathew Muir
Jere Wescott Patterson
Courtney Craig Smith
Gilmore Stott
Frederick Ralph Suits
Benson E.L. Timmons
Edward Ronald Weismiller
Byron Raymond White
Marshall James Wolfe

1939

Morris Berthold Abram
Frederick Lyman Ballard, Jr.
Charles Finch Barber
Birdsall Newbury Carle
Charles Cummings Collingwood
Ernest Craige
DeVan Damon Daggett, Jr.

Edward Charles Freutel, Jr.
George Baucum Fulkerson
Edward Le Roy Hart
John Hopkins Heires
John Clarkson Jay
Tom Killefer
Martin Henry Kruskopf
Vernon Garvey Lippitt
Thomas Matthew McGrath
Lionel Wilfred McKenzie, Jr.
Thomas Roberts McMillen
Robert William MacVicar
Harry Hartwood Mitchell
Robert T.A. Molloy
Waldemar August Nielsen
Edward Joseph Pelz
Luke Harvey Poe, Jr.
Henry Lithgow Roberts
Archibald Bullock Roosevelt
Robert Vincent Rosa
Stanley Eugene Sprague
Murray Salisbury Stedman, Jr.
Donald Wayne Taylor
Jesse Eldon Thompson
Robert Lauren Tichenor

1940–1946

There were no U.S. Rhodes Scholars appointed for these years.

1947

William Bridewell Adams
Warren DeWitt Anderson
Timothy Breed Atkeson
Frank Rockwell Barnett
Roger Redmond Bate
Paul James Bohannan
Charles Guy Bolté
Lee Carrington Bradley
Jack Edward Brooks
Bille Chandler Carlson
Richard Leigh Chittim
Edmund Dews
James Bruce Engle
Peter Ward Fay
James Randlett Fowler
Gilbert Pierce Haight

James McNaughton Hester
J. Raymond Hinshaw
Thomas Lowe Hughes
Charles Harold Jepsen
George Hilton Jones
Amos Azariah Jordan
Nicholas deBelleville Katzenbach
Spencer LeVan Kimball
Wilfred Martin Kluss
Henry Bruce McClellan
Joseph Webb McKnight
Robert Quarles Marston
James F.L.S. Matthews
Charles John Merdinger
Peter Briggs Myers
Richard Henry Nolte
Robert Robinson Porter
Gordon Raisbeck
George Anthony Rebh
Nicholas Valentine Riasanovsky
Bernard William Rogers
Calvin Dwight Rollins
Edgar Finley Shannon
William Jay Smith
Frank Donovan Tatum
Robert Lawrence Taylor
Donald Warren Treadgold
Stansfield Turner
William Nelson Turpin
James Buckley Whitlatch
Frank H.J. Worland
Leslie Lawson Youngblood

1948

Curtis Cosmos Aller
William Ayres Arrowsmith
Frederick Lee Beaty
Arthur W.J. Becker
Jeremy Blanchet
Nathaniel Bernard Blumberg
Fred William Bornhauser
Gene Adam Brucker
Eugene Leonard Burdick
Neil Carothers
James Hamilton Clarke
Albert Jay Colton
Paul Mix Craven

Guy Mattison Davenport
Ralph Kirby Davidson
John Woolman Douglas
Walter Newell Elder
William Richard Emerson
James Robert Frolik
Reuben Herman Gross
Henry Paul Grosshans
Karl Gottlieb Harr
Donald Graham Henderson
John Quitman Hill
William Lowry Howard
Raymond Earl Jacobson
Hugh Rodney King
Malcolm McLane
John Theodore McNaughton
Gerald Mason McNiece
James Ross Macdonald
Gerald Marvin Meier
Henry Laurence Miller, Jr.
Ewell Edward Murphy, Jr.
Homer Kittrell Nicholson
Wesley Wentz Posvar
George Lauck Powell
Donald Herschel Rivkin
James Edgar Roper
David Samuel Shwayder
William Ellis Slesnick
Edson White Spencer
Elmer de Loss Sprague
Stephen Wayne Terry
Harry Andrew Watson
Roger Williams Wescott
Elmus Rogers Wicker
Truman Owen Woodruff

1949

Claude Taylor Anderson
William Joseph Barber
David Nickerson Barus
David Howland Bergamini
Robert James Brentano
Herbert Cahn
Richard Theron Carvolth
Mortimer Hardin Chambers
Barney S. Childs
Robert Wayne Clower

Walter Stanford Frank
Robert Lowell Johnston
Frank H.H. King
Robert Lawhead Kirkpatrick
Hugh Montgomery Long
Dan Lockwood McGurk
Howard A. M. McKinley
Thad Norton Marsh
Steven Muller
George Barber Munroe
George Winters Rogers
Martin Adrian Rush
Lewis Spencer Salter
William Reece Smith
Milton Albert Strain
Louis Herbert Sugg
Richard Standish Sylvester
Nelson Ferebee Taylor
Ross Stansbury Thackeray
James Jerome Walsh
Richard Arthur Wiley
Merrill Cranston Windsor, Jr.

1950

Douglas Elliott Ashford
Robert Lesh Baldwin
Robert Wauchope Bass
Herbert David Benington
James Hadley Billington
Stephen John Brademas
Jeffrey Bush
Don Duane Cadle
Charles Till Davis
Bertram Gale Dick
John Wallis Dickey
Francis Remington Drury
Marvin Bresler Durning
Joseph Anthony English
Thomas Paton Goodman
Charles Louis Hamilton
Herman Hardy Hamilton
John Buxton Lawson
Lawrence Carroll McQuade
Kirk Warren McVoy
Robert Kinloch Massie
G. Michael Morris
James Emory Price

Ralph Oliver Simmons
Eugene Bertram Skolnikoff
Sterling Eugene Soderlind
Richard Frank Srb
Dennis Carothers Stanfill
George Steiner
Paul Emery Thomas
Alan Mark Thornton
Philip Tyler Zabriskie

1951

William Dickson Barcus
Thomas Alva Bartlett
Aldon Duane Bell
Walter Clemons
Kalman Joseph Cohen
Frederick Ward Frey
John Henry Funari
Richard Newton Gardner
Prosser Gifford
Donald Leonard Glusker
Carl Thor Hanson
Robert J. Harris
John David Hemenway
Kenneth Keniston
Arthur Walton Litz
Eugene Charles Luschei
George Carl Mohr
John Lovell Moore
Lewis Seymour Mudge
Joseph James Murray
Seaborn Alton Newton
Robert Dean Pue
Richard Crauford Pugh
Andrew Cunningham Remson
John Hall Richards
Paul Everett Shay
Robert Earl Shepherd
David Stanley Staiger
James Mason Thompson
Linton Satterthwaite Thorn
Peter John Urnes
John Richard Walsh

1952

Michael Vander Laan Bennett
Staige Davis Blackford

John Ramsey Bronk
Howard Jerome Burnett
Hugh Allan Burns
William Daniel Carmichael
Alain Charles Enthoven
Richard Merrill Fink
George J.W. Goodman
Robert Willis Hellwarth
Thaddeus Goode Holt
Jonathan R.T Hughes
Jack Burton Justice
George Henry Kinter
Elliott Harris Levitas
Francis Dummer Logan
Robert Philip Moncreiff
Alan Andrew Nord
Richard Alfred Norris
Carter Curtis Revard
Alexander Valentinovich
Riasanovsky
Dennison Ivan Rusinow
John Rogers Searle
Carl Abraham Shiffman
Neil Joseph Smelser
James Leslie Steffensen
Charles Ross Wallis
Arthur Allen Wasserman
William Vandervoort Whitehead
Clyde Michael Williams
John Wallace Willoughby

1953

Robert Armstrong Anthony
Joseph Breckinridge Board
Robert Hamilton Boyer
Thomas Andrew Brown
Guido Calabresi
Hugh Cannon
William Richard Cantwell
Carmen Keith Conners
Edwin Parker Conquest
Walter Raleigh Coppedge
Ronald Myles Dworkin
Ernest Russell Eggers
Donald Allan Erickson
James Frederick Garner
Hugh Gaston Hall

Alan Karl Illig
Vincent Wendel Jones
Daniel Clyde Jordan
William Ezra McCulloh
Charles Peter MacVeagh
Raymond Charles Mjolsness
William Brown Patterson
Charles Albert Perlitz
Frederick Jackson Piotrow
Kenneth Edward Reich
Richard Jay Selig
Thomas Graves Smith
Stephen Stamas
Donald Wayne Sutherland
Albert Edgar Utton
Frank Godfrey Wells
John DeLane Wilson

1954

Ames Scribner Albro
John David Alexander
Ralph David Amado
Paul Barford Banham
John Chapman Bard
James John Barnes
Thomas Harold Blackburn
Brock Hendrickson Brower
Floyd McKee Cammack
Thomas Clayton
Milton Curtis Cummings
Simpson Bobo Dean
Raymond Jerome Dougherty
Montgomery Furth
Frank Ira Goodman
George Washington Hardy
Eliot Dexter Hawkins
Martin Alvord Kramer
Karl Allen Lamb
Jack Wayne Love
Richard Green Lugar
Mancur Lloyd Olson
James Covington Parham, Jr.
Robert Owen Paxton
Elmer Roy Pfefferkorn
Ronald Alexander Rebholz
Paul Spyros Sarbanes
Paul Douglas Sheats

Erling Raymond Skorpen
Dale Allen Vesser
William Webb White

1955

Diogenes Allen
Donald Jerome Bruckner
Stephen George Brush
John Samuel Davison
Jack Stanley Dennis
Walter Warren Eyer
H. Kenneth Fisher
Harvey Arlen Garn
James Patrick Griffin
John Lynden Hall
John Thomas Hamilton
Arthur Hull Hayes
James Bickford Hurlock
Rex Lindsay Jamison
Verdel Amos Kolve
Paul Ross Likins
Kenneth John Love
Martin Cyril McGuire
David Samuel Maxwell
William Bethel Minter
John Horton Morrison
Lee Donne Olvey
Edward Reynolds Price
Howard Schell Reilly
Hamilton Farrar Richardson
Jacquelin Taylor Robertson
John Winthrop Sears
Frank Arne Sieverts
Richard Edwin Stewart
William Gilbert Strang
Richard Sackett Thompson
Richard Henry Ullman

1956

B. Conn Anderson
Richard Henry Baker, Jr.
Robert Markham Ball
Davis Bernard Bobrow
Paul Richards Burgess
Paul Douglas Carter
Gary Brandt Christiansen
Olaf Grobel

Michael Peter Hammond
Oliver Davis Johns
Vincent Ronald Larson
Russell Keith McCormmach
William Weaks Morris
Frederick Glynn Myers
Van Doorn Ooms
William Carey Parker
Robert Alan Picken
Robert Burns Pirie
Neil Leon Rudenstine
John Richard Sadler
Albert Truman Schwartz
Edward Isaac Selig
Thomas Fairchild Sherman
Arthur Grant Siler
Donald Chester Sniegowski
Reginald Stanton
Richard Disbro Sylvester
Edward Milton Taylor
Clifford Fritz Thompson
Jess Brooks Woods
Edwin Milton Yoder

1957

David Watson Baad
George Webster Baer
Gordon Carl Bjork
Glen Warren Bowersock
William Bruce Cook
Clark Edward Cunningham
Charles Joseph DiBona
George Albert Drake
Erwin Joseph Fleissner
Thomas David Gelehrter
Antonio Marion Gotto
Erich Stephen Gruen
Roger Dennis Hansen
Donald Weldon Hanson
Harry Stewart Havens
Roy Mark Hofheinz
Theodore Lewis Houk
William Sterling Huff
Dale Arthur Johnson
John Edward Jordan
Dennis Vincent Moran
James Robert Murphy

Edward John Nell
Peter Standish Paine
Richard William Pfaff
Robert Irwin Rotberg
George Dann Sargent
Don Alan Smith
Michael MacCracken Stewart
George Bryson Thomas
John Gardner Wofford

1958

Roger Mendenhall Baty
Michael Alan Boyd
Robert D. Childres
Clifton Rance Cleaveland
Leslie Chant Dirks
Daniel Edward Feldman
Alexander Lees Fetter
Charles Kelleway Fish
John Vincent Fleming
James Douglas Gunton
Lawrence Maximilian Hartmann
David Michael Heilbron
Samuel C.O. Holt
A.E. Dick Howard
Roger Howell, Jr.
Stuart Davis Jordan
Gordon Rolfe Kepner
Jonathan Kozol
Kristoffer Kristofferson
Jason Donald McManus
Bruce Tein Marcus
Eugene Paul Nassar
Howard Ian Needler
Gary Rollin Noble
Joseph Samuel Nye
Melvin Lawrence Popofsky
Philip Christopher Ritterbush
Paul Rogness
John O. B. Sewall
Jackson Caflin Stromberg
Norman Edwards Terrell
Roger William Tompkins

1959

John Luster Brinkley
Ludwig Walter Bruch
Joseph Daryl Canfill
Peter Miller Dawkins
John Ludwig Deutsch
Paul Michael Dodyk
Benjamin Bernard Dunlap
David Alan Dunn
Michael Martin Fried
Michael James Gillette
William Harley Henry
Thomas English Hill
Bradley Clark Hosmer
Cuthbert Powell Hutton
Stanley Martin Kanarowski
Ronald James Lee
Robert Gould McKelvey
Richard Austin Merrill
Gerald Demuth Morgan
Bryce Eames Nelson
David Ainsworth Ontjes
John Naber Paden
Alan Reeve Parker
Anthony Preus
James Floyde Ray
Erik Sedman Ronhovde
Richard Edward Rubenstein
Aaron Lee Segal
Steven Michael Umin
Frank Neils Von Hippel
John Womack, Jr.
Roger Caleb Young

1960

Robert Frederick Ashman
David Mark Balabanian
Jonathan Dewey Blake
Ralph Clement Bryant
Richard Frank Celeste
Robert Choate Darnton
Hoyt Nolan Duggan
Robert Glenn Edge
Leslie Epstein
George Peter Giard, Jr.
John Southy Grinalds
Jack Ogilvie Horton

Howard James Kaslow
Langley Carleton Keyes
Julius Byron Levine
Charles Ellis Lister
John Blythe McLin
Charles William Maynes
Warren Andrus Miles
Robert Everard Montgomery, Jr.
Raymond Lindley Nichols
Matthew Nimetz
Edward Wardwell Pell
John Roy Price
Theodore Lee Rodrick
Daniel Martin Sachs
William Dennis Shaul
Lester Carl Thurow
Paul Bartlett Van Buren
Thomas Vargish
Theodore O.M. Wills
David Garrett Winter

1961

Lee Douglas Badgett
William Grandin Bardel
Larry Donald Budge
Benjamin Pfohl Campbell
Gary Erskin Cathcart
Floyde Dean Copeland
Brian Edward Daley
Dwight Lyman Eddins
David Samuel Eisenberg
Herman Harris Funkenstein
Michael Robert Gordon
Howard Dwayne Graves
William Morris Hartmann
Augustus Blagden Kinsolving
Duane Ward Krohnke
Melvin David Levine
Gilbert William Low
Michael Tucker McNevin
Paul Lindsay Miles
James Sayle Moose
Fred LaMont Morrison
David Norman Ness
Robert Thomas Orrill
Gaines Post
Herschel E. Post

Orin Ralph Raymond
Anthony Abraham Sholl
Henry Greyson Shue
David Hackett Souter
William Wallace Sterling
Richard Burleson Stewart
David Lawrence Wilkinson

1962

Rex Dee Adams
Robert Henry Baxter
Edward David Berman
Robert Harvey Bolton
David Anderson Brownlee
Jay Wayne Butler
John Undem Carlson
Winston John Churchill
Stephen John Dickinson
James Robert Doty
Louie Samuel Echols
James Joseph Fox
David Braden Frohnmayer
Nicholas James Gubser
Richard Ray Hallin
Jack Vernon Haney
Russell Hardin
Alan Keith Henrikson
Bishop Carleton Hunt
John Joseph Kirby
Robert Bruce Partridge
Richard David Portes
David Hartley Roe
David William Schindler
Judson Dean Sheridan
Michael Ralph Sherwood
Jeffrey Franklin Sicha
John Robert Sobotka
John Daniel Sullivan
Norton Fortune Tennille, Jr.
Stephen Vargish
William Leo Zeltonoga

1963

Paul Gustav Bamberg
David Odell Beim
David Lyle Boren
Josiah Bunting

Russell Higson Carpenter
Daniel Allan Carrell
Wayne Goldsworthy
William Edward Holland
Robert Edward Johnston
William Turnbull Kerr, Jr.
Richard Leo Klass
John Albert Knubel
William Walker Lewis
Robert Patrick McNeill
Philip Hartwell Martin
George Edward Peterson
Max Singleton Power
Joseph Levering Price
James Arthur Quitslund
John Hart Raaf
Michael Steven Rice
Joseph Howard Romig
Joseph Stanley Sanders
Mark Elwood Schantz
Walter Becker Slocombe
Robert Thomas Smythe
Andrew Peter Sundberg
Willard Scott Thompson
Sam Wilkins Westbrook III
John Edgar Wideman
Donald Joseph Wood
R. James Woolsey

1964

John Howard Bohstedt
Nicholas Frederick Bunnin
Lee Orin Coldren
Michael Blanchard Cook
Richard Melvyn Cooper
W. Bowman Cutter
Earl Thomas Davis
John Walter Erwin
Thomas Patrick Gerrity
Ross Frank Hamachek
Richard Harry Holmquist
Morton G. Kahan
Robert Thomas Kudrle
David John Lutzer
Morris Allen McCain
Bert Breon Mitchell
Robert Sims Munford

Richard Scott Noble
Guy W. H. Parkhurst
Larry Lee Pressler
Paul Moffatt Pressly
William Leigh Risser
Thomas Dudley Rowe, Jr.
Lee Waldo Saperstein
Michael Lewis Skolnik
Stephen Kendall Smith
James Gustave Speth
Carlton Ray Stoiber
Davis Taylor
Bruce Richard Thomas
Jon Norman Westling
Peter Hutchins Wood

1965

Danilo Nicholas Bach
Ronald Mann Bancroft
Bernard George Barisas
William Warren Bradley
Thomas Arthur Cotton
Richard Jeffrey Danzig
Victor Rodger Digilio
Brian Curtis Fay
Alan Joseph Gayer
John Joseph Gearen
Wayne Eugene Groves
Benjamin Walter Heineman, Jr.
Alva Bart Holaday
John Alexander Hottell
William Carroll Keach
Robert Hazard Knapp
John Timothy Londergan
Merle Steven McClung
Peter Neely McCormick
William Clement McGrew
James Morris Markham
Miles Morgan
Richard Dale Nehring
James Daniel O'Flaherty
John Bundy Ritch
Richard W. B. Ruffin
Robert Lewis Sansom
Michael Edward Smith
Richard Parry Sorensen
Robert Worthington Spearman

Thomas Burrowes Stoel
Timothy Arthur Vanderver

1966

Ralph Walter Bachman, Jr.
Stephen Joseph Bergman
Michael Buckley
Wesley Kanne Clark
William Mackey Clark
Richard Lawrence Cohen
Jonathan Dwight Culler
Stewart Early
Charles Webb Filson
William Preston Frerking
Curtis Alan Hessler
Gerald Paul Hillman
David Robert Howlett
Richard Anthony Joseph
David Evan Kendall
William David Knox
Philip Jeffry Le Cuyer
Terrence Frederick Malick
Richard Charles Marston
Michael Murray Martin
Stephen Roger Munzer
James Joseph O'Toole
Douglas Duane Paschall
Robert Hey Rawson, Jr.
Donald Harris Regan
John William Roper
James Edward Schindler
Michael Sam Teitelbaum
Richard Winyu Tsien
Robert Shelby Wagers
William Frank White
Douglas Thomas Yates

1967

Charles Stevenson Abbot
John Rowell Alexander
Thomas Hodge Allen
David Ruick Bock
Kenneth Steven Brecher
Edward Winslow Campion
William Clark Clendaniel
William Michael Duff
Barry Ian Forman

Michael Allan Fredrickson
David Carter Hardesty, Jr.
John Patton Harrod
Stephen Ballinger Hitchner
Warren Mamoru Iwasa
Ronald Stanley Katz
Mark Robert Killingsworth
Jerome Michael Kirchberg
Karl Arthur Marlantes
Stephen Alan Oxman
Richard Joseph Pedersen
Charles Peters
Kent de Mers Price
Robert Carter Randolph
Stephen Daniel Schaffran
Richard Louis Schaper
James Robert Sheller
Robert Earl Stillwell
Samuel Baker Stocking
Daniel Ireland Twomey
Harris Wagenseil
Thomas Reid Ward

1968

Frank William Aller
Alan Douglas Bersin
Dennis Cutler Blair
Thomas John Brewer
George Charles Butte
William Jefferson Clinton
James Ellis Crawford
Douglas Scott Eakeley
Robert Lawson Earl
William Alan Fletcher
Darryl James Gless
John Magyar Isaacson
Robbin St. Clair Johnson
Boisfeuillet Jones
Christopher Scott Key
Robert Parker Kimberly
Robert Davis McCallum, Jr.
Thomas George McFadden
Keith Cooper Marshall
Dell Howard Martin
Paul Merrel Parish
Walter Floyd Pratt, Jr.
Robert Bernard Reich

Thomas Leonard Reinecke
Frederic Nash Ris
David Alexander Samuels
David Arnold Satter
Michael Alan Shea
Daniel Edwin Singer
Richard Gaylore Stearns
Nelson Strobridge Talbott
Thomas Samuel Williamson, Jr.

1969

Walter James Amoss
Tyler Alexander Baker
Thomas Neville Bose
Charles Credille Calhoun
Randall Lee Caudill
Grant Fotheringham Crandall
Wayne Arthur Drugan
Harold Eugene Griffin
John Robert Higham
Mark Weston Janis
Hikaru Tsuruoka Kerns
Marc Edward Lackritz
William McCurine
Ira Charles Magaziner
Richard Glen Menaker
Steven John Michaud
Lawrence Allen Miller
Patrick Michael Norton
David Jonathan Okerson
Steven Bernard Pfeiffer
Randel Eugene Phillips
Michael Adrian Ponsor
Roger Blaine Porter
David Benson Roe
James Milton Roelofs
Paul Francis Saba
Pieter Meade Schenkkan
Erich Kurt Schork
Barth David Schwartz
Steven Ross Sturm
Howard Jackson Von Kaenel
Timothy Claude Weiskel

1970

Joseph Louis Badaracco
Scott Soper Barker
John Robert Boly
Bruce Ambler Boucher
Bruce Edward Cain
Richard Randolph Crocker
Heyward Harrell Dotson
Charles Robert Engles
James Mackenzie Fallows
Raymond John Gibbons
Eric C.T. Hanson
David Vern Hicks
Dennis James Hutchinson
Kent Marsteller Keith
George Randolph Keys
Maxwell Jonathan Mehlman
Wentworth Earl Miller
Robert Dean Neugebauer
David Sidney Painter
Gregory Anthony Petsko
David Michael Quammen
Eric Redman
Jeffrey Bruce Rudman
Charles Algernon Shanor
Patrick Arthur Shea
Stephen Douglas Smith
Richard Hughes Trainor
Carlos Christopher Trower
Paul Sears Viita
Stephen Louis Wilson
William Harlow Wolfe
William Augustus Wright

1971

James Robert Atlas
John Charles Baldwin
Thomas Michael Bello
Perry Justin Blackshear
Willie Clyde Bogan
Patrick Joseph Call
John Hugh Churchill
Jerome Davis
Stephen Carl Ferruolo
John Price Gaventa
Donald Jay Gogel
Larry Richard Grisham

Marvin Charles Henberg
Douglas Gene Hunt
David John Kuter
George Todd Ligler
John Carlton Luik
Thomas Wendell Merrill
John Peter Moussouris
Thomas Brown Neville
Thomas William O'Brien
John Martin Page, Jr.
Paul Anthony Rahe
Franklin Delano Raines
George Machado Rosa
Robert Allan Rosenfeld
Thomas Alexander Sancton
David Matthews Schaffer
Kurt Lidell Schmoke
Paul Lewis Shechtman
Richard Lewis Taylor
Alfred Michael Wurglitz

1972

Robert Darryl Banks
Thomas Francis Birmingham
Bruce Terry Bjerke
James McCarty Braden
Thomas Edgar Carbonneau
Daniel Gray Clodfelter
Keith Paty Ellison
Andrew Richard Embick
Steven Michael Fall
William Horace Farley
Timothy Pishon Gardner
Herve Gouraige
Paul Hess Haagen
Robert Theodore Haar
Richard Michael Harley
Gregory Alan Hicks
Lane Palmer Hughston
Gary Thomas Johnson
Stanley Seburn Jones
Michael G. Ezra Kinsley
Richard Theodore Koskella
Robert David Luskin
Samuel Pyeatt Menefee
Gerald Lewis Sauer
Nicholas John Spaeth

Jesse James Spikes
Harold Watkins Stanley
Timothy James Toohey
Byron Roscoe Trauger
Alan Lee Ver Planck
Leonard Lewis Wall
Jack Carl Zoeller

1973

Marshall Williams Bautz
Paul Jeffrey Blustein
John Mathews Bowers
Raymond Malcolm Burse
Michael Richard Cannon
Paul Edward Coggins
Eugene Joseph Dionne
Spencer Eth
John Riche Ettinger
Richard Nathan Haass
Chris Thompson Hendrickson
Phillip Lee Jackson
Peter John Kalis
Frank Graham Klotz
David Alexander Koplow
Michael John Koziol
Philip Ray Lindner
Timothy Townley Lupfer
Frederic Fairfield Manget
Mark Steven Peppler
John Misha Petkevich
James Zachary Pugash
Lyle Clift Rexer
Robert Brian Rice
Richard Alan Sauber
Burton David Sheppard
Ralph Harrison Smith
John Lloyd Tillman
Terence David Valenzuela
Michael David Waters
Mark Richard Williams
Wendell Lewis Willkie

1974

Nicholas William Allard
Thomas Archibald Barron
Theodore Eugene Burk

Maurice Joseph Burke
John David Carter
Charles Edward Coffey
David McMullin Fowler
Charles Edward Garvin
Elliot Francis Gerson
Bruns Holland Grayson
Brian Colvert Griffin
Malcolm Llewellyn Hunter, Jr.
Walter Seff Isaacson
David Lawther Johnson
Alex Arthur Kerr, Jr.
Albert Sidney Kyle
Brian Geoffrey McHale
Harold Brent McKnight
Charles Thomas McMillen
Robert Bertelson Mitchell, Jr.
James Stephen Moran
Michael Louis Oristaglio
John Michael O'Shea
Roy David Pea, Jr.
Kerry Kirwin Pierce
Leif Dov Rosenblatt
William Josephus Sims
James Austin Talcott
Mathew Thomas Valencic
Harry Randolph Weinburg
Erik Zeno Woody

1975

Kenneth Charles Brown
Peter Alphonso Carfagna
Clayton Magleby Christensen
Donald S. Collat
James Hayes Cooper
Eric Carl Dahl
Richard Henry Fallon
Russell Dana Feingold
George Chester Freeman
Joel Kramer Goldstein
Patrick Capper Haden
Griffith Rutherford Harsh
Paul Martin Hunt
James G. LeMoyne
Robert Leo Liberty
Michael G. McCaffery
Scott Milne Matheson

James Hart Merrell
William Stewart Pease
Christopher Lyons Peisch
Michael Baron Poliakoff
Melvin Jay Reynolds
Bernard Clayton Rolander
Carlisle Ford Runge
Larry Joseph Sabato
Michael Joseph Sandel
Andrew Wade Savitz
Flint Dore Schier
Craig Howard Seligman
Roger Darrell Sorrell
Timothy Lee Tabor
Emile LeRoy Wilson

1976

John Arthur Ausink
Samuel Andrew Banks
James Glynn Basker
Troyen A. S. Brennan
William Harvey Brundage
Ashton Baldwin Carter
William John Cronon
Danny Mac Davis
John Carroll Dupree
Mark Wayne Eisenbraun
Allen DeVaney Elster
Christopher Patrick Hall
Robert Steven Harrison
Paul Thomas Hasse
Steven Heywood Holtzman
David Allen Jensen
Hubert Philip Joswick
Charles Seth Landefeld
Peter Marvin Larson
James J. McGuire
Jefferson Allen McMahan
Mitchell Solace
Richard Morales
Keith Elliot Mostov
James Richard Murray
Steven Garth Nelson
George Braxton Newhouse
David Moisseiff Scobey
James Milton Steckleberg
Alfred Douglas Stone

Lawrence Paul Tu
Darrell Eugene Walker

1977

Maura Jean Abeln
James Eli Adams
Caroline Elizabeth Alexander
Daniel A. Barker
Catherine Lynn Burke
Nancy Lee Coiner
Diane Louise Coutu
Sarah Jane Deutsch
Laura Justine Garwin
Edgar Gentle
Gerrit Walter Gong
Sue Michelle Halpern
Douglas Earl Holmgren
William Armstrong Hunter
Clay Straus Jenkinson
Randall LeRoy Kennedy
Dennis Kloske
Daryl Koehn
William Leland Kynes
Daniel Lee Lips
Stephen Harold Lockhart
Richard Lewis McHenry
Alison Muscatine
Mary Cargill Norton
Robert Hoke Perkins
Suzanne R. Perles
Scott Joseph Rafferty
Andrew K. Rosenheim
Richard A. Stengel
Denise Ann Thal
Hubertus Jan Van Der Vaart
Milton Minoru Yasunaga

1978

Mark David Agrast
Jennifer Carol Barber
Kenneth Reid Beesley
Mark Andrew Bradley
Carter Jeffrey Brandon
Fred Ehrenkranz Cohen
Susan Eileen Duffey
Lynn Elizabeth Enterline
Eric Oliver Fornell

Mark Milton Foulon
Jeffrey Alan Greene
Barbara Anne Grewe
Mark Edmonde Haddad
Ann Marie Haight
Lonnie Dean Henley
Justin Severance Huscher
Ann Meredith John
Rachel Ellen Klevit
Eric Steven Lander
Oliver Emerson Miller
Ann Olivarius
Richard Watson Parker
Harry William Printz
Bruce Kalman Rubin
Susan Elizabeth Russ
Virginia Ann Seitz
Kim Ann Severson
Roald Bradley Severtson
Frederick Theodore Smith
Jane Elizabeth Stromseth
Doron Weber
Daniel Walter Williams III

1979

Frank Hedrock Allen
Kenneth Whittemore Banta
Pat McKinney Baskin
Daniel Hibbard Case
William Charles Crowley
James Arthur Der Derian
Glenn Alan Fine
Charles Daniel Goodgame
Paul Eliot Gootenberg
Helen Evarts Graham
Jennifer Ann Haverkamp
Elaine Carol Hefty
James Earl Hildreth
Michael Lynn Hoffman
Michael Jerome Hopkins
Jeffry Alan Jackson
Mary Victoria Kiechel
David Michael Lodge
Sara Matilthe Lord
Robert Keller Maloney
Deborah Joan Marvel
Ruth Sarah Mazo

Nancy-Ann Elizabeth Min
Jon Alan Peacock
Robin Uriel Russin
John Phillip Santos
Thomas A.C. Smith
Karen Leslie Stevenson
Nicholas Augustine Ulanov
Stefan Richard Underhill
Margaret Mary Vaillancourt

1980

William Carl Altman
Betsy L. Anderson
William Henry Bender
Gordon Crovitz
Steven A. Crown
Clark Kent Ervin
Ihor Orest Fedorowycz
Linda Lucille Fletcher
Ross Harold Frank
Susan Linda Goodkin
Adam Daniel Helfer
Andrea Lee Hollen
Ann K. Jorns
Susan Louise Karamanian
Mary Carolyn King
Ronald Derek Lee
David W. Levine
Robert J. L. London
Robert Allen Long, Jr.
Christopher D. Miller
Stephen Reeder Morillo
Barry James Nalebuff
Eli Nathans
Adam Ward Rome
Bror V. H. Saxberg
David Gilliam Schatz
Adam Leon Schulman
Mortimer Newlin Sellers
Athan James Shaka
Craig Hall Underwood
Ronald J. Van de Krol
Karon Sue Walker

1981

Kevin Guy Anderson
Susan G. Billington

Melissa Burch
Ila Leola Burdette
Craig A. Canine
Mary Elizabeth Cleary
David Llewellyn Dodds
Ramona Loret Doyle
Daniel L. Dreisbach
Wade Thompson Dyke
Daniel C. Esty
Nanette J. Fondas
Peter Glomset
Rebecca Nan Gray
Deborah Sue Jacobs
Edward A. Johnson
Michelle Denise Johnson
Karl N. Knapp
Nicholas D. Kristof
Clifford R. Larsen
John W. McLendon
Roger W. Mastalir
Ray Dean Mize
Robert Morstein-Marx
Mary G. Murphy
Mary Kathryn Peckham
R. Jahan Ramazani
Elizabeth Deirdre Sherwood
Peter S. Stamos
Christopher D. Suits
Stuart W. Swetland
Jessica Alix Teich

1982

Thomas Charles Berg
Susan Biemesderfer
Daniel Mark Bloomfield
John Arnold Board
Molly K. Brennan
James E. Butcher
Christopher J. Canfield
William Bradford Chism
David S. Fadok
Michael Fleming
Timothy John Galpin
Barton D. Gellman
Michael A. Gillette
Donald W. Hawthorne
Mark H. Helmericks

Frances Louise Kellner
Caleb Kimball King
Mark N. Kramer
Kathrin Day Lassila
Henriette Lazaridis
Jean McCollister
Nina Morishige
Anne G. Perkins
Ellen M. Pint
Bruce Nelson Reed
Douglas J. Tilton
Lawrence John Vale
Rick Waddell
Michele S. Warman
Heather A. Warren
Heather A. Wilson
Samuel D. Zurier

1983

Marshall Jones Bouldin IV
Wade B. Buchanan
Brenda L. Buttner
Charles R. Conn III
Patricia E. Connelly
David Duncombe
Christopher Eisgruber
Lawrence T. Ellis, Jr.
John Whitaker Fanestil
David C. Frederick
Geoffrey T. Gibbs
Timothy C. Gokey
Mark Gorenflo
Mark R. Hagerott
William Amos Halter
Robert Charles Hockett
Elizabeth Kirkland
Elizabeth E. Kiss
Richard Klingler
Marvin Krislov
Margaret O. Little
Mark Martins
Raymond Paretzky
Lois Quam
Jerri-Lynn Scofield
Claudena M. Skran
Richard F. Sommer
Arthur Dar Tai

Terrence Tehranian
Barbara J. Toman
Paul M. Vaaler
David Bruce Vitter

1984

Stephanie A. Dangel
Kenneth Davison
Maureen Emily Freed
Arthur Keith Green III
Brian R. Greene
Michael E. Hasselmo
Jonathan Hay
Christopher Hedrick
Storrs Townsend Hoen
Douglas D. Jehl
Craig G. Kennedy
Kelley H. Kirklin
Catherine Kissee-Sandoval
Carlton Long
John M. (Jay) MacLeod
Sean O. Mahoney
Robert Malley
Laurel McFarland
Hunter Monroe
Christopher Murray
David A. Noever
Jeannette M. Pitts
Daniel R. Porterfield
Katherine Ruth Richards
Steven D. Runholt
Sarah Sewall
John G. Simon
George Stephanopoulos
Judith Stoddart
Kevin L. Thurm
John C. Vlahoplus

1985

Michael R. Anderson
Randy John Berholtz
Lance D. Bultena
Steven M. Dunne
David L. Finegold
Paul Saveno Giordano
Robyn S. Hadley
Barbara Ann Harmon-Schamberger

Mark Kasevich
Stephen B. Kinnaird
Paul Kusserow
Mary Stella Larson
Robert W. Leland
Robert A. Madsen, Jr.
Matthew R. Martin
Peter Muller
Stuart Benjamin Munsch
Andrew J. Nussbaum
Jeffrey A. Rideout
Ronald J. Rinaldi
Ginger Rinkenberger
Leonard J. Schoppa, Jr.
Paul Schulz
Juan Sepulveda, Jr.
Jonathan Scott Shapiro
Ruth Renee Stone
Ronald J. Tenpas
Joel N. Thomas-Adams
Robert Vonderheide
Eric Otto Wear
Ursula S. Werner
Naomi R. Wolf

1986

Gregory D. Abowd
Lisa Ione Backus
Kenneth Bobroff
Richard O. Chapman
Susan J. Craighead
Ken Crouse
Teresa Doering
Beth Ellen Ebel
Barry Edelstein
William R. Handley
Maurice A. Jones
Jeffrey D. Julum
Michael A. Lanese
Vivian S. Lee
Michael McFaul
Jeffrey Scott McKinney
Gregg Meyer
Thomas B. Mueller
Elizabeth J. Murphy
Martha Oakley
Eric R. Olson

Victoria L. Phillips
Nadine Pinede
Elliott Ivan Portnoy
Susan E. Rice
Bonnie Saint John
Benjamin B. Sherwood
Heidi Elizabeth Tinsman
Joseph M. Torsella
Andrew J. Vliet
Virgil Wiebe
E. Wrenn Wooten

1987

Jocelyn H. Alexander
Michael S. Barr
Nina R. Bowen
Kenneth Brashier
D. Andrew Chin
Sarah H. Cleveland
James J. Collins
Elizabeth M. Cousens
Robert M. Dow, Jr.
Michael Gaffney
Atul A. Gawande
William H. Lipscomb
Andrew Z. Lopatin
Paul W. Ludwig
Sylvia M. Mathews
Kathleen L. McLaughlin
David H. Mehnert
Maria Weston Merritt
C. Damon Miguel Moore
Mark Ouweleen
Susan Pepin
Barbara Petzen
Robert Radtke
Donna J. Roberts
Laura Ruetsche
Brett Gilbert Scharffs
Daniel D. Stid
John K. Tien, Jr.
Hoang Nhu Tran
Jacob Weisberg
Kelly Dean Welch
Michael V. Woodhouse

1988

Karen Avenoso
Peter Bednekoff
Todd R. Breyfogle
Knute C. Buehler
Richard Yoonsik Chin
Sarah Crosby
Michele Denise deCoteau
Alexander E. Dreier
Douglas E. Fraley
Brian Alexander Glasser
Steven B. Harrison
Bryan Hassel
James Andrew Himes
Wen-son Hsieh
Charles E. Jones
Andrew Y. Koh
Modupe Labode
Stace D. Lindsay
Sarah McNamer
Jennifer A. Miller
Caroline Minter
J. Russell Muirhead
John Nagl
Stewart McLellan Patrick
Bobby R. Peck, Jr.
Marilynn J. Richtarik
Ronald C. Ritter
Nicholas S. Souleles
Surachi Supattapone
Melissa Sydeman
Michael Thaddeus
Lisa Van Alstyne

1989

Viva Bartkus
Karl Craig Boatwright
Susan Elaine Bruns
Gerald J. Cardinale
Paul Owen Carrese
Brad R. Carson
John Eugene Crandon III
Jennifer Paine Davis
George M. DeShazo
Douglas Driemeier
Gregory Peter Dubois
Katherine E. Finkelstein

Christopher A. Ford
Stephanie Malia Fullerton
John Michael George
Josephine Greene
Pamela Jane Hill
Blair G. Hoxby
Brad M. Hoylman
Sarah Kass
Mary Ann Lehmkuhle
Nancy A. Levenson
Peter Levine
Tomasz P. Malinowski
Paul S. Markovich
Michael McCullough
Maureen N. McLane
E. Scott Pretorius
Jay C. Rubenstein
Barry J. Uphoff
David Wheeler
Holly Wyatt

1990

Ryan K. Balot
Georgie Holder Boge
Christopher L. Brown
David A. Campbell
Bridget Clarke
Suzanne Lee Corley
Andrew J. Dechet
Christopher Lee Elwell
Carolyn A. Ford
Reza K. Gandjei
Thomas A. Gaziano
S. Kim Grose
Mary E. Hale
Carol E. Harrison
Jennie M. Koch
Janelle B. Larson
Renee B. Lettow
Timothy G. Lyons
Amy Deanne Matthews
Burt Monroe
Robert Bartley Moore
Paul W. Muench, Jr.
Tanya Pollard
Joel L. Shin
Tara Silvestri

Theodore A. Smith
Mark Somerville
Basilios E. Tsingos
Martina Vandenberg
Michael J. Warren
David P. White
David B. Wilson

1991

Sabina Alkire
Lawrence J. Berger
Brad Ronnell Braxton
Stephen P. Brown
Michael Callahan
Marcus A. Christian
David Coleman
Jeffrey A. Dolven
Robert J. Esther
Peter Blair Henry
Christopher B. Howard
Janice Anne Hudgings
Goodwin Liu
Patricia Lopes
Jesse Malkin
Carl D. Marci
Scott Lamont Merriner
Gregory Pyung Won Pak
Edward S. Pallesen
Kristy L. Parker
Todd E. Peterson
Darcy D. Prather
Wesley D. Sand
Jeffrey Shesol
Theresa E. Simmonds
Jonathan E. Skinner
Leonard P. Stark
Micul Thompson
Darreld Turner
Nathaniel N. Urban
Kenji Yoshino
Jason R. Zimba

1992

William David Ball
Douglas A. Beck
Cory A. Booker
Jennifer A. Bradley

Akshay Desai
Benjamin L. Ebert
Jonah Edelman
Noah Feldman
Eric Gregory
Gregory M. Gunn
Nikolas K. Gvosdev
Craig B. Hanson
Jessica Heineman-Pieper
Peter Benjamin Hessler
Piyush Robert Jindal
Molly Ann Kramer
Derek Y. Kunimoto
Marc Lipsitch
Carl Stanley McGee
Laura Ellen McGrane
Todd Millay
Drayton Nabers III
Lisette Nieves
Richard A. Primus
Brian Reed
Stephanie Reents
Peter A. Ruprecht
Jody E. Seim
Catherine M. Sharkey
Robert A. Sternfels
Rebecca Thomas
P. Dmitri Tymoczko

1993

Scott Bear Don't Walk
Peter Beinart
Rujuta M. Bhatt
John A. Cloud
M. Taylor Fravel, Jr.
Eric Garcetti
Ganesh M. Gunasekaran
James A. Hansen
David K. Ismay
Erez Czarnes Kalir
Carrie Lowry LaSeur
Mark E. Lundstrom
Nnenna Jean Lynch
Pamela Dawn McElwee
Mary C. Meaney
Julie M. Mikuta
Alison Morantz
Stephen L. Morgan

Stanley J. Panikowski III
Lisan Peng
Niles Adams Pierce
Gina Raimondo
Faith C. Salie
Jeffrey Seidman
Loredana Soceneantu
Sara L. Toomey
Janice R. Ugaki
John R. Unger II
Amy Wakeland
Andrew P. Wildenberg
Monica Y. Youn

1994

Christine C. Barton
Ritu Sonia Batra
Chaya Bhuvaneswar
Matthew B. Boyle
Eileen L. Brooks
Dana L. Brown
Katharine E. Chubbuck
Sean M. Fahey
Daniel A. Fletcher
Carolyn Frantz
Joanna E. Grant
Alexander John Hartemink
Serena J. Hoy
Ali Husain
Ryan M. Iwasaka
Alexander Johnston
Sarah Levine
Charlotte Morrison
Andre C. Namphy
Leah N. Niederstadt
Eduardo M. Peñalver
Randal D. Pinkett
Munro C. Richardson
J. Adam Rindfleisch
Dacia Meek Sampson Toll
Germaine Trong
Nima A. Warfield
Terri Willard
Trina R. Williams
Geraldine A. Wright
Andrew J. Zawacki
Zachary J. Ziliak

1995

Zayde Gordon Antrim
Jennifer Babik
Jonathan Beere
Rebecca Boggs
Rinku Chandra
Thomas Geiser
Drew D. Hansen
Mallory Ann Hayes
Meiling Hazelton
Robert W. Johnson
Tracy Johnston
Benjamin F. Jones
Maria Kaibel
Drew Dianne Lamonica
John H. Leaman
Sarah E. Light
Rachel Maddow
Lia Pierson
Matthew Polly
Brent Roam
Cristina Maria Rodriguez
Diana M. Sabot
Monica Salamon
Jennifer Santoro
Ryan Sawyer
Jordan I. Schreiber
Rebecca Spies
Heather Ure
James R. Wall, Jr.
Debra L. Walt-Johnson
Michael Wenthe

1996

Priya Aiyar
Ahmad Atwan
Tobias Ayer
David Bonfili
Letitia M. Campbell
Alice Chen
Carolyn Conner
Jeremy Dauber
Juan De Lara
Jennifer DeVoe
Mark Patrick Embree
Angelina Marguerite Foster
Kristen Fountain

Michelle Gavin
Eric Greitens
Rachel Eyre Hall
Laura Nell Hodo
Alvan Ikoku
Tracey Jones
Barnaby Marsh
Abigail Noble
Jennifer Oliva
Adam Russell
Samantha Salvia
Ben R. Sharp
Philip C. Skelding
Robert Matthew Sutherland
Ramin Toloui
Ana L. Unruh
Dayne Walling
Malaika Marie Williams
Mark Wu

1997

John Maxon Ackerly
Hans Christian Ackerman
Adam Kenneth Ake
Edward K. Boyda
Joshua Ian Civin
Ryan David Egeland
Tali Farimah Farhadian
Eugenio Miguel Fernandez
Kerry Elizabeth Francis
Suzanne Goh
Maryana Felib Iskander
Lana Israel
Benjamin Todd Jealous
Daniel Phillip Kim
Jonathan Levine
Shana Marie Lovell
Robert Davis McCallum
Aaron Dean Olver
Charlotte Anne Opal
Stephanie Elizabeth Palmer
Eva Joanna Rzepniewski
Pardis Christin Sabeti
Annette Elizabeth Salmeen
Dean John Sauer
Tess Thompson
Jessika Ebba Trancik

Beth Christine Truesdale
Horacio Ricardo Trujillo
Jeremy Andrew Vetter
Hamed Rahim Wardak
Kweli E. Washington
Olivia Lawrence White

1998

S. Kristine Abrams
Roy E. Bahat
Andrew Castiglione
Gregory Scott Patrick Criste
Douglas M. de Lorenzo
Bryan Shiloh Graham
Blaine Greteman
Scott Adam Hershovitz
Anne Katherine Jones
Narayanan Kasthuri
Leslie Kendrick
David Carlisle Latimer
Julie Haya Levison
Valerie MacMillan
Kirsten Parker
Ebrahim Patel
Laura Provinzino
Adeel Qalbani
Julia Raiskin
Gretchen Rohr
Fiona Rose
Noam Scheiber
Micah J. Schwartzman
Rachel Simmons
Jacob Sullivan
Cullen M. Taniguchi
Laura Tavares
Jonathan Tepper
John Tye
Joy Yu-Ho Wang
Jonathan N. Winkler
Owen Wozniak

SELECT BIBLIOGRAPHY

Alexander, Caroline. "Vital Powers." *The New Yorker,* 30 January 1989. 57-71.

Allen, Carleton Kemp. *Forty Years of the Rhodes Scholarships.* Oxford: Oxford University Press, 1944.

The Alumni Magazine. Published at irregular intervals by the Alumni Association of American Rhodes Scholars, 1907-1913.

The American Oxonian. Published quarterly by the Association of American Rhodes Scholars, 1914 to the present.

Amery. L.S. *My Political Life.* 2 vols. London: Hutchinson, 1953.

Ashby, Stanley Royal. "An American Rhodes's Scholar at Oxford." *MacMillan's Magazine,* n.s. 1 (1906): 181-90.

Atlas, James. *The Great Pretender.* New York: Atheneum, 1986.

Aydelotte, Frank. *The American Rhodes Scholarships: A Review of the First Forty Years.* Princeton: Princeton University Press, 1946.

Aydelotte, Frank. *The Oxford Stamp.* Freeport, NY: Books for Libraries Press, 1967 (orig. ed. 1917).

Aydelotte, Frank. "What the American Rhodes Scholar Gets from Oxford." *Scribner's Magazine,* June 1923, 677-88.

Bamford, Janet. "Rhodes to Glory." *Forbes,* 22 September 1986, 204-6..

Beadle, Muriel. *These Ruins are Inhabited.* Garden City, NJ: Doubleday, 1961.

Beerbohm, Max. *Zuleika Dobson: An Oxford Love Story.* London: Minerva, 1991 (orig. ed. 1911).

Blanshard, Frances Margaret. *Frank Aydelotte of Swarthmore.* Middletown, CT: Wesleyan University Press, 1970.

Blotner, Joseph. *Robert Penn Warren: A Biography.* New York: Random House, 1997.

C-SPAN. "Rhodes Scholars: The Oxford/American Connection." Twelve hours of programming aired in January 1993.

Case, Thomas. "The Influence of Mr. Rhodes' Will on Oxford." *National Review,* 39 (1902): 420-28.

Christianson, Gale E. *Edwin Hubble: Mariner of the Nebulae.* New York: Farrar, Straus & Giroux, 1995.

Clark, G.N. *Cecil Rhodes and His College.* Oxford: Oriel College, 1953.

Corbin, John. *An American at Oxford.* Boston: Houghton Mifflin, 1902.

Crosby, Laurence, and Frank Aydelotte, eds. *Oxford of Today: A Manual for Prospective Rhodes Scholars.* New York: Oxford University Press, 1922.

Currey, Ronald. *Rhodes: A Biographical Footnote.* Private printing, 1946.

Dawkins, Pete. "Pete Dawkins Writes from Oxford." *Cosmopolitan,* 149 (September 1960): 68- 75.

Donovan, Hedley. *Right Places, Right Times: Forty Years in Journalism not Counting My Paper Route.* New York: Henry Holt, 1989.

Ehrenreich, Rosa. *A Garden of Paper Flowers: An American at Oxford.* London: Picador, 1994.

Ellis, Walter. *The Oxbridge Conspiracy: How the Ancient Universities Have Kept Their Stranglehold on the Establishment.* London: Michael Joseph, 1994.

Elton, Lord, ed. *The First Fifty Years of the Rhodes Trust and the Rhodes Scholarships, 1903- 1953.* Oxford: Basil Blackwell, 1955.

Elton, Lord. "An Englishman's Audit of Rhodes Scholars." *Harper's,* May 1964, 98-106.

Fairbank, John King. *Chinabound: A Fifty-Year Memoir.* New York: Harper & Row, 1982.

Feiler, Bruce. *Looking for Class: Seeking Wisdom and Romance at Oxford and Cambridge.* New York: Random House, 1993.

Frey, Herman S. *Oxford: Town, Gown and Rhodes Scholars.* Nashville: Frey Enterprises, [1975].

Gifford, Prosser. *Oxford and the Rhodes Scholarships.* Swarthmore, PA: NP, 1958.

Hale, Robert. "Oxford Again – A Rhodes Scholar Goes Back." *The Outlook,* 11 July 1923, 378- 80.

Hall, Richard. *The Rhodes Scholar Spy.* Sydney: Random House Australia, 1991.

Harrison, Brian, ed. *Corpuscles: A History of Corpus Christi College, Oxford, in the Twentieth Century, Written by Its Members.* Oxford: Corpus Christi College, 1994.

Harrison, Brian, ed. *The History of the University of Oxford.* Vol. 8: *The Twentieth Century.* Oxford: Oxford University Press, 1994.

Harrity, Richard. "63 Years of Yanks at Oxford." *Look,* 4 October 1966, 80-83.

Hibbert, Christopher, ed. *The Encyclopedia of Oxford.* London: Macmillan, 1988.

Hitchens, Christopher. *Blood, Class, and Nostalgia: Anglo-American Ironies.* New York: Farrar, Straus & Giroux, 1990.

Howard, Jeanne G. "The Library of Rhodes House, Oxford." *Library Review,* 39 (1990): 21-27.

Kaiser, Philip M. *Journeying Far and Wide: A Political and Diplomatic Memoir.* New York: Charles Scribner's Sons, 1992.

Keene, Anne. *Oxford: The American Connection.* Oxford: Temple Rock Publications, 1990.

Kenny, Anthony. *A Life in Oxford.* London: John Murray, 1997.

Leacock, Stephen. "The Horrors of Oxford." *Living Age,* 24 June 1922, 779-81.

Leacock, Stephen. "Oxford As I See It." *Harper's,* May 1922, 738-45.

Locke, Alain LeRoy. "Oxford: By a Negro Student." *The Colored American Magazine*, 17 (1909): 184-90.

Lugar, Richard. "Lugar at Oxford." *Denison Alumnus,* June 1955, 3-8.

Mackaye, Milton. "What Happens to Our Rhodes Scholars?" *Scribner's Magazine* (January 1938): 9-15, 84.

Mackaye, Milton. "What Happens to Our Rhodes Scholars?" *Scribner's Magazine,* January 1938, 9-15, 84.

"Man of Eli at Oxford." *Life*, 2 December 1957, 81-82.

Maraniss, David. *First in His Class: A Biography of Bill Clinton.* New York: Simon & Schuster, 1995.

Massie, Robert K. "Many Rhodes to Washington." *New York Times Magazine*, 16 April 1961, 54-56.

Mehta, Ved. *Up at Oxford.* New York: Norton, 1993.

Mitchell, Lynn Boal. *The Rhodes Scholarships.* Albuquerque: University of New Mexico, 1914.

Morris, Jan. *Oxford.* Oxford: Oxford University Press, 1978.

Moran, Michael. "Frank Aydelotte, Oxford University, and the Thought Movement in America." Paper delivered at the annual meting of the Conference on College Composition and Communication." Cincinnati, OH, 19-21, 1992.

Morris, Willie. *Homecomings.* Jackson: University Press of Mississippi, 1989.

Morris, Willie. *My Two Oxfords.* Council Bluffs, IA: Yellow Barn Press, 1989.

Morris, Willie. *New York Days.* Boston: Little, Brown, 1993.

Morris, Willie. *North Toward Home.* Boston: Houghton Mifflin, 1967.

Muscatine, Alison. "Confessions of an Ex-Rhodeo Queen." *Working Woman*, November 1979, 63-64, 66-67.

Osmer-McQuade, Margaret. "The Legacy of Rhodes." *New York Times Magazine*, 20 November 1983, 112, 118-19, 123.

Pagan, John. "Bill Clinton at Oxford." *Postmaster* [Merton College], 1992, 77-81.

Parkin, George R. *The Rhodes Scholarships.* Boston: Houghton Mifflin, 1912.

Pelczynski, Zbigniew. "My Pupil Bill Clinton." *Pembroke College Record* (1992): 40.

Prest, John, ed. *The Illustrated History of Oxford University.* Oxford: Oxford University Press, 1993.

Price, Don K. "A Yank at Oxford: Specializing for Breadth." *American Scholar*, 55 (1986): 195- 207.

Register of Rhodes Scholars, 1903-1981. Oxford: Rhodes Trust, 1981.

Register of Rhodes Scholars, 1903-1995. Edited by Ralph Evans. Oxford: Rhodes Trust, 1996.

Reich, Robert B. *Locked in the Cabinet.* New York: Alfred A. Knopf, 1997.

"Rhodesmen at Swarthmore." *Time*, 5 June 1933, 45-48.

"Rhodes Reunion." *People*, 11 July 1983, 61-68.

The Rhodes Trust and Rhodes House. Oxford: Oxuniprint, 1992.

Roberts, Brian. *Cecil Rhodes: Flawed Colossus.* New York: Norton, 1988.

Roberts, Kenneth. "An American Looks at Oxford." *Saturday Evening Post*, 16 June 1934, 16- 17, 66, 69-70, 72.

Rosenheim, Andrew. *The Tormenting of Lafayette Jackson.* Boston: David R. Godine, 1988.

Rotberg, Robert I. *The Founder: Cecil Rhodes and the Pursuit of Power.* New York: Oxford University Press, 1988.

Rusk, Dean. *As I Saw It.* New York: Norton, 1990.

Scholz, Richard.F., and Stanley K. Hornbeck. *Oxford and the Rhodes Scholarships.* New York: Oxford University Press, 1907.

Saeger, Allan. "The Joys of Sport at Oxford." *Sports Illustrated,* 29 October 1962, 60-69.

Smith, Howard K. *Events Leading up to My Death: The Life of a Twentieth-Century Reporter.* New York: St. Martin's Press, 1996.

Smith, Howard K. *Last Train from Berlin.* New York: Alfred A. Knopf, 1942.

Snow, Peter. *Oxford Observed: Town and Gown.* London: John Murray, 1991.

Stanley, Alessandra. "Most Likely to Succeed." *New York Times Magazine,* 22 November 1992, 26-27, 36-40, 58, 84-85.

Steiner, George, and Ramin Jahanbegloo. *Entretiens.* Paris: Editions du Félin, 1993.

Stewart, Jeffrey C. "A Biography of Alain Locke." Ph.D. dissertation. Yale University, 1979.

Sullivan, Andrew. "All Rhodes Lead Nowhere in Particular." *Spy,* October 1988, 108-14.

Swarthmore College Faculty. *An Adventure in Education: Swarthmore College Under Frank Aydelotte.* New York: Macmillan, 1941.

Symonds, Richard. *Oxford and Empire: The Last Lost Cause?* Oxford: Oxford University Press, 1991.

Thomas, Antony. *Rhodes: The Race for Africa.* London: BBC Books, 1996.

Topping, Graham. "The Best Men for the World's Fight?" *Oxford Today,* Trinity Issue, 1993, 6-9.

Trillin, Calvin. *Remembering Denny.* New York: Farrar, Straus & Giroux, 1993.

Trowbridge, A. Buel. *An Auld Acquaintance Who'll Never Be Forgot: Memories of a Rhodes Scholar at University College, Oxford, 1920-23.* Boston: Branden Press, 1976.

Weisberg, Jacob. "Clinton at Oxford." *GQ,* June 1993, 173-79, 229-31.

Woods, Randall Bennett. *Fulbright: A Biography.* New York: Cambridge University Press, 1995.

Wylie, Francis J. *Cecil Rhodes and His Scholars as Factors in International Conciliation.* New York: American Association for International Conciliation, 1909.

Young, Thomas Daniel. *Gentleman in a Dustcoat: A Biography of John Crowe Ransom.* Baton Rouge: Louisiana State University Press, 1976.

Young, Thomas Daniel, and George Core, eds. *Selected Letters of John Crowe Ransom.* Baton Rouge: Louisiana State University Press, 1985.

INDEX